THE PALAEOGRAPHY OF GOTHIC MANUSCRIPT BOOKS

From the Twelfth to the Early Sixteenth Century

This book is the first to present a detailed survey of all book scripts in use in Western and Central Europe from *c.* 1100 to *c.* 1530 (with the exception of Humanistic script). This period has been poorly served in almost all other palaeographical handbooks. By adopting a largely new classification of scripts based on objective criteria which incorporates many of the terms currently in use, this book aims to end the confusion which has hitherto obscured the study of late medieval handwriting. It is based upon an examination of a very large number of dated specimens, and is thus the first survey to take full advantage of the incomparable palaeographical resource provided by the Catalogues of Dated Manuscripts. The text is illustrated throughout with over 500 drawings of letters and symbols. Actual-size reproductions of 160 manuscripts provide datable specimens of all the scripts discussed, accompanied by partial transcriptions and palaeographical commentary.

ALBERT DEROLEZ is Curator Emeritus of Special Collections in the Universiteitsbibliotheek Gent, Professor Emeritus of Palaeography and Codicology at Vrije Universiteit Brussel and Université Libre de Bruxelles, and holds the presidency of the Comité International de Paléographie Latine. His publications include *The Autograph Manuscript of the Liber Floridus: A Key to the Encyclopaedia of Lambert of Saint-Omer* (1999); *The Library of Raphael de Marcatellis, Abbot of St Bavon's, Ghent, 1437–1508* (1979); *Codicologie des manuscrits en écriture humanistique sur parchemin* (1984); and he is editor in chief of *Corpus Catalogorum Belgii: The Medieval Booklists of the Southern Low Countries*.

Cambridge Studies in Palaeography and Codicology

GENERAL EDITORS

Rosamond McKitterick *Newnham College, University of Cambridge*
Teresa Webber *Trinity College, University of Cambridge*

This series has been established to further the study of manuscripts from the Middle Ages to the Renaissance. It includes books devoted to particular types of manuscripts, their production and circulation, to individual codices of outstanding importance, and to regions, periods and scripts of especial interest to scholars. The series will be of interest not only to scholars and students of medieval literature and history, but also to theologians, art historians and others working with manuscript sources.

ALREADY PUBLISHED

1. Bernhard Bischoff *Manuscripts and Libraries in the Age of Charlemagne*
0 521 38346 3

2. Richard Gameson *The Early Medieval Bible* 0 521 44540 X

3. Nancy Netzer *Cultural Interplay in the Eighth Century: The Trier Gospels and the Making of a Scriptorium at Echternach* 0 521 41255 2

4. William Noel *The Harley Psalter* 0 521 46495 1

5. Charles F. Briggs *Giles of Rome's* De regimine principum: *Reading and Writing Politics at Court and University, c. 1275–c. 1525* 0 521 57053 0

6. Leslie Brubaker *Vision and Meaning in Ninth-Century Byzantium: Image as Exegesis in the Homilies of Gregory of Nazianzus* 0 521 62153 4

7. Francis Newton *The Scriptorium and Library at Monte Cassino, 1058–1105* 0 521 58395 0

8. Lisa Fagin Davis *The Gottschalk Antiphonary: Music and Liturgy in Twelfth-Century Lambach* 0 521 59249 6

FORTHCOMING

Yitzhak Hen and Rob Meens (eds.) *The Bobbio Missal*

Alison I. Beach *Women as Scribes: Book Production and Monastic Reform in Twelfth-Century Bavaria*

THE PALAEOGRAPHY OF GOTHIC MANUSCRIPT BOOKS

From the Twelfth to the Early Sixteenth Century

ALBERT DEROLEZ

CAMBRIDGE UNIVERSITY PRESS
Cambridge, New York, Melbourne, Madrid, Cape Town, Singapore, São Paulo,
Delhi, Dubai, Tokyo

Cambridge University Press
The Edinburgh Building, Cambridge, CB2 8RU, UK

Published in the United States of America by Cambridge University Press, NewYork

www.cambridge.org
Information on this title: www.cambridge.org/9780521686907

First Published 2003
Reprinted 2005
First paperback edition 2006
Third printing 2010

Printed in the United Kingdom at the University Press, Cambridge

A catalogue record for this publication is available from the British Library

Library of Congress Cataloging-in-Publication Data

Derolez, Albert.
The palaeography of Gothic manuscript books: from the twelfth to the early
sixteenth century / Albert Derolez.
p.   cm. – (Cambridge studies in palaeography and codicology; 9)
Includes bibliographical references and index.
ISBN 0 521 80315 2
1. Palaeography – Europe.   2. Manuscripts, Medieval – Europe.   I. Title.   II. Series.
Z106.5.E85 D7   2003   091′.094 – dc21   2002031400

ISBN 978-0-521-80315-1 hardback
ISBN 978-0-521-68690-7 paperback

To the memory of
Gerard Isaac Lieftinck
1902–1994

Contents

Plates

Acknowledgements

The present book grew out of courses in late medieval palaeography I taught in Rare Book School, first in Columbia University, New York, afterwards in the University of Virginia, Charlottesville, and seminars on the same subject that I directed at the University of Princeton and in the Beinecke Library in Yale University. I owe Professor Terry Belanger, Director of Rare Book School, Professor James Marrow (Princeton University) and Dr Robert Babcock (Yale University) sincerest thanks for the unique experience I enjoyed in discussing Gothic book scripts with eager audiences from widely different backgrounds. The distant predecessor of the book, however, was a paper delivered in 1991 at the Hebrew University of Jerusalem at the invitation of Professor Malachi Beit-Arié. But it was the Sandars Lectures, which I was invited to deliver by Cambridge University Library in 1996, that were its real starting-point. My 30-year-long position as a Curator of Manuscripts in Ghent University Library and my almost as long period of teaching at the Vrije Universiteit Brussel and the Université Libre de Bruxelles have offered me ample occasion to study medieval manuscripts and to discuss their problems.

Illustrations for this book have been most generously provided by the Comité International de Paléographie Latine, which, with the consent of the Institut de Recherche et d'Histoire des Textes in Paris, gave me permission to use the photographs of manuscripts in French libraries, made many years ago for the French Catalogue of Dated Manuscripts (these photographs were made by the IRHT and are kept in its Section de Paléographie Latine; thanks to the immense helpfulness of Dr Denis Muzerelle I was able to select as many photographs of dated manuscripts in French libraries as I wished); by Professor J. Peter Gumbert in Leiden, who gave me access to a very large number of photographs from manuscripts in Dutch libraries (made for the Catalogue of Dated Manuscripts in Dutch Libraries); by Professor James Marrow, who had a magnificent set of photographs made from manuscripts in the Fitzwilliam Museum, Cambridge; and by Dr Robert

Babcock, who did the same for a wide selection of manuscripts in the Beinecke Library of Yale University. Professors Monica Hedlund (Uppsala), Edward Potkowski (Warsaw) and Stefano Zamponi (Florence) also liberally provided me with photographs.

This book could not have been printed without almost all libraries involved kindly waiving their reproduction fees. They deserve many thanks.

Research for this book was funded by a grant from the Fonds voor Wetenschappelijk Onderzoek – Vlaanderen, and a grant from the Neil R. Ker Memorial Fund, administered by The British Academy, was used for the same purpose as well as for defraying expenses involved in the illustration. Part of the costs of preparing the book for publication was met by a grant from Cambridge University Library's Dorothea Oschinsky Fund for Medieval Manuscript Studies. I am most grateful to all three institutions.

For the transcriptions of texts in vernacular languages I am thankful for the assistance kindly given by Professor Jesús Alturo (Barcelona), Professor Kurt Gärtner (Trier), Professor Monica Hedlund (Uppsala), Dr Erik Petersen (Copenhagen), Professor Anne-Marie Spanoghe (Ghent), Professor Philippe Verelst (Ghent), Professor Sabine Verhulst (Ghent) and Dr Teresa Webber (Cambridge).

In addition to the persons mentioned above, invaluable help was provided in various ways by Professor Maria José Azevedo Santos (Coimbra), Dr Wouter Bracke (Brussels), Dr Christian Coppens (Louvain), Dr Eef Overgaauw (Berlin), Professor Francisco Gimeno Blay (Valencia), Professor Walter Koch (Munich), Professor Christian Koninckx (Brussels), Professor Aires A. Nascimento (Lisbon), Dr Paul Needham (now Princeton), Mr Gerrit Noordzij (Hattem), Professor Malcolm Parkes (Oxford), Professor Benjamin Victor (Montreal).

The staff of the Royal Library in Brussels and of the university libraries in Brussels, Ghent and Louvain have been extremely helpful.

Mr Michael Gullick (Stevenage) deserves sincerest thanks for the care and craftsmanship with which he made the hundreds of drawings of letters and graphs illustrating this book, as well as for his enlightening observations. The staff of Cambridge University Press, in particular the designer, Peter Ducker, thought nothing too much trouble in meeting the author's wishes; Ms Caroline Bundy was especially helpful and effective during the long preparation of the present work. I thank Professor Rosamond McKitterick most sincerely for the inclusion of my book in the series of which she is one of the General Editors. Her colleague the late Professor Albinia de la Mare years ago played a fundamental role in making this possible. But my most profound gratitude goes to Professor De la Mare's successor as Editor of the series *Cambridge Studies in Palaeography and Codicology*, Dr Teresa Webber. The constant solicitude and endless patience she displayed in the preparation of the book, her painstaking reading and correction of the manuscript, with all its linguistic flaws and offences against the English idiom, and her expertise as a palaeographer have resulted in a text which is not only in infinitely better English, but which also contains fewer incorrect or disputable statements and ideas than it ever could have displayed without her intervention. All remaining deficiencies are of course mine, and responsibility for the contents is entirely my own.

A. D.

Note on the illustrations

It is impossible to provide illustrations covering adequately the entire period and geographical area discussed in this book, as well as all the script types, levels of execution, languages, places of origin etc. included in it. The plates have therefore been selected in such a way as to provide dated or datable examples from all over Europe, in Latin and most vernacular languages, representing the main script types from the entire period and illustrating, as far as possible, various levels of execution, from Currens to Formata. I have avoided using specimens of tiny handwriting wherever it was possible to show the same features in a hand of larger size, as minute details tend to become indiscernible in photographic reproduction.

All reproductions are actual size except where otherwise stated. Each illustration is accompanied by a note giving the current location and shelfmark of the manuscript, an indication of its content, a partial transcription, and a short comment pointing to some distinctive features of the hand shown. In the transcriptions abbreviations have been expanded; word separation, punctuation and the use of capitals follow modern practice. **u** and **v** have been employed for the vowel and the consonant respectively; in vernacular texts both **i** and **j** are used, in Latin texts only **i**.

The hand-drawn figures provide standardized letter forms (not facsimiles) and serve the purpose of illustrating details discussed in the text. Reference to these figures is made by means of a number between parentheses. The reader should note that it has not been possible to illustrate every variant form.

Abbreviated titles

CMDA *Katalog der datierten Handschriften in lateinischer Schrift in Österreich*, Vienna 1969– .

CMDB Masai, F., and Wittek, M. (eds.), *Manuscrits datés conservés en Belgique*, Brussels, Ghent 1968– .

CMDCH *Katalog der datierten Handschriften der Schweiz in lateinischer Schrift vom Anfang des Mittelalters bis 1550*, Zurich 1977– .

CMDD Autenrieth, J. (ed.), *Datierte Handschriften in Bibliotheken der Bundesrepublik Deutschland*, Stuttgart 1984– .

CMDF Samaran, C., and Marichal, R. (eds.), *Catalogue des manuscrits en écriture latine portant des indications de date, de lieu ou de copiste*, Paris 1959– .

CMDF2 Muzerelle, D., Grand, G., Lanoë, G., and Peyrafort-Huin, M. (eds.), *Manuscrits datés des bibliothèques de France*, Paris 2000– .

CMDGBCam Robinson, P. R., *Catalogue of Dated and Datable Manuscripts c. 737–1600 in Cambridge Libraries*, Cambridge 1988.

CMDGBLo Watson, A. G., *Catalogue of Dated and Datable Manuscripts c. 700–1600 in the Department of Manuscripts, The British Library*, London 1979.

CMDGBOx Watson, A. G., *Catalogue of Dated and Datable Manuscripts c. 435–1600 in Oxford Libraries*, Oxford 1984.

CMDIt *Catalogo dei manoscritti in scrittura latina datati o databili per indicazione di anno, di luogo o di copista*, Turin 1971– .

CMDIt2 *Manoscritti datati d'Italia*, Florence 1996– .

CMDNL Lieftinck, G. I., and Gumbert, J. P., *Manuscrits datés conservés dans les Pays-Bas. Catalogue paléographique des manuscrits en écriture latine portant des indications de date*, Amsterdam and Leiden 1964–88.

CMDS   Hedlund, M., *Katalog der datierten Handschriften in lateinischer Schrift vor 1600 in Schweden*, Stockholm 1977–80 (Bibliotheca Ekmaniana, 67–8).

CMDVat   *I codici latini datati della Biblioteca Apostolica Vaticana*, Vatican City 1997– .

Glossary

Ampersand: the **et**-ligature.

Ascender: in minuscule script, the part of a letter which extends above the headline, as in **b** and **l**.

Baseline: the writing line, i.e. the line on which the minims, the ascenders and the majuscules are written.

Biting: *see* Fusion.

Calligraphic script: a script with constructed letters, adopting a complicated ductus with numerous pen-lifts.

Cursive script: a script intended for rapid and fluent writing, which therefore involves a simplified ductus and a reduction in the number of pen-lifts.

Descender: in minuscule script, the part of a letter which extends below the baseline, as in **p** and **q**.

Downstroke: a stroke made with a downward movement of the pen.

Ductus (Italian: **tratteggio**): the number of strokes used for the writing of a single letter or graph, their order and direction.

Final position: the end of a word.

Fusion or **biting**: a coalescence of two successive letters, which end and begin with contrary curves.

Hairline: a thin line, often obtained by using the corner of the nib instead of its full width.

Hand: the personal shape of a scribe's handwriting, whereas **Script** is the model he has in mind.

Headline: the (imaginary) line marking the top of the minims and short letters in minuscule script.

Initial position: the beginning of a word.

Ligature: the linking of two or more letters into one graph, in which the original letter forms have been altered.

Majuscule or **bilinear script**: a script written between two (imaginary) lines, in which the letters are of equal height (in typography: uppercase).

Majuscule: a letter pertaining to such a script.

Medial position: the middle of a word.

Minim: a short vertical stroke running from headline to baseline, as in **i**, **m**, **n**, **u**.

Minuscule or **quadrilinear script**: script written on four (imaginary) lines, comprising short letters (**a**, **c**, **i**, **x**, etc.), and letters with ascenders and descenders (in typography: lowercase).

Serif: a small decorative stroke added to the extremities of a letter, as in Capital **A**.

Shading: the contrast between thick and thin strokes in a given script.

Spur: a pointed projection at the left of an ascender, located at about the headline.

Upstroke: a stroke made with an upward movement of the pen.

Introduction[1]

PALAEOGRAPHY AS AN ART

I cannot teach the art of assigning dates to manuscripts: I am even inclined to think that it cannot be taught. The study of facsimiles to begin with, and, later on, the constant handling of the books themselves – these supply the only safe guidance to that condition of eye and mind which will enable the student to say unhesitatingly 'This is a twelfth century book and this is an early fifteenth; this was written in Italy and this in England'. For myself I have come to depend almost entirely upon general impression in forming an estimate of date. This may seem to the layman a precarious method; and doubtless other workers find that the form of individual letters and similar details stand them in better stead than the general look of the page. Indeed, the study of such minutiae is indispensable in the case of the earlier manuscripts; but for the large majority of those which belong to the later medieval period, from the eleventh century to the fifteenth, the general impression is to my mind a perfectly safe guide. But it is a guide whose aid can only be gained by means of long handling of the books. Viewing practice therefore as the essential, I must entirely abstain from an attempt to help my reader to estimate the date of the manuscript he is to describe.[2]

This quotation from the unpublished notes made by Montague Rhodes James (1862–1936), one of the most experienced specialists in medieval manuscripts yet to have lived, contains a number of fundamental claims and assumptions which, almost a century later, invite comment and constitute an ideal starting-point for the present introduction.

Indeed, one of the most important tasks generally assigned to palaeography is dating and localizing undated manuscripts of unknown origin. This, James says, cannot be taught. For him, it is only through experience that one may gain the 'condition of eye and mind' required to judge the date and origin of a given codex.

---

[1] This introduction is essentially an adaptation of the first two of the Sandars Lectures I was invited to deliver in Cambridge University Library in 1996.

[2] R. W. Pfaff, 'M. R. James on the Cataloguing of Manuscripts: A Draft Essay of 1906', *Scriptorium*, 31 (1977), pp. 103–18 (104).

This belief is not unique to James. Many palaeographers, among them the greatest, believe in the so-called 'palaeographer's eye' and consider palaeography (except for its basic task of deciphering) an art. This was, for example, the opinion of Bernhard Bischoff, the author of the best handbook on the subject yet written, who called palaeography 'eine Kunst des Sehens und der Einfühlung' ('an art of seeing and comprehending').[3] It is also held by Françoise Gasparri, who claims that only 'l'expérience de chacun, expérience que rien ne remplace' ('individual experience, which nothing can replace') will allow the student to ascertain the date of a given manuscript.[4]

Our respect for such authorities as James and Bischoff does not prevent us from placing a question mark over their definition of palaeography as an art gained principally by experience. Indeed, when an extremely experienced palaeographer declares that a given manuscript was written in Northern France in the first half of the thirteenth century, but fails to indicate the criteria on which this statement is based, he may be a perfect connoisseur, but he is not being an effective teacher. What is more, he unconsciously contributes to the present-day crisis of palaeography as a discipline.

THE CRISIS OF PALAEOGRAPHY

There can be no doubt that a crisis now exists in the discipline which started in the seventeenth century with Jean Mabillon (*d.* 1707) and culminated, as many claim, in the twentieth with Jean Mallon (*d.* 1982). The number of handbooks and atlases published today is in marked contrast with the low esteem in which palaeography is currently held as an academic discipline, though one for which Franco Bartoloni still predicted a bright future as late as 1952.[5] Changes in higher education and new trends in historical and literary research have certainly been unfavourable to the study of palaeography. The decline in the study of Latin has been almost fatal for the study of medieval script (vernacular palaeography being a rather narrower field, not fully reflecting general European developments in script). Some modern trends in medieval studies do not look favourably upon the close study of the sources, now often considered time-consuming and irrelevant.

---

[3] Bischoff, *Latin Palaeography*, p. 3; Bischoff's other statement on the same page is as questionable: 'Every manuscript is unique. Our aim should be to recognise that uniqueness, to consider the manuscript as a historical monument and to be sensitive to its beauty, especially when its script and illumination are of a high aesthetic order.' Before Bischoff, Joachim Kirchner had claimed that 'eine Einfühlungsfähigkeit in Schriftformen' is necessary to the student of palaeography: *Germanistische Handschriftenpraxis*, 2nd edn, Munich 1967, pp. 16–17. On dating manuscripts on the basis of their script, see G. Powitz, 'Datieren und Lokalisieren nach der Schrift', *Bibliothek und Wissenschaft*, 10 (1976), pp. 124–37.
[4] Gasparri, *Introduction*, p. 96. [5] Quoted by Armando Petrucci in *Un secolo*, p. 34.

Palaeographers themselves are no doubt not free from blame. In their eagerness to dissociate themselves from the old-fashioned, purely descriptive methods of earlier scholars, many specialists of today search for underlying social developments in the history of script and, in doing so, direct their attention towards matters other than script proper. A vast movement in favour of theory and a tendency to gravitate towards national schools of palaeography are distinctive features of the palaeographical scholarship of the last century. After the 'School of Munich' the 'Nouvelle paléographie française' came to the fore, alongside a sociologically oriented Italian school which attaches major importance to the script of semi-literate people and the history of the teaching of handwriting. Whereas diversity in scholarship is a good thing in itself, exasperated mutual criticism and an overdose of theory weaken the position of palaeography a great deal. The idea has been advanced that the time for palaeography in its traditional conception is over, that the 'history of writing' should take its place. A well-known palaeographer has written that 'nowadays nothing basically new can be done in the field of the palaeography of the fourteenth to sixteenth centuries if we continue to ask the traditional questions proper to the discipline'.[6]

EARLY VS. LATE MIDDLE AGES

This last quotation reinforces James's remark by drawing attention to the difference in treatment between the scripts of the early Middle Ages and those of the late Middle Ages. Whether the turning-point is 800 (as Lowe held) or 1100 (as was, for example, Harrison Thomson's opinion), the number of surviving manuscripts from the two periods is in no way comparable. One can thus understand why manuscripts dating from before 800 enjoy a preferential treatment in handbooks and atlases. This is, nevertheless, a paradoxical situation, as these tools present a great deal of information about those manuscripts which the reader is much less likely to encounter, and ridiculously little about the codices which survive by the thousands.

It is difficult to understand why some palaeographers, from James onwards, draw a distinction between two palaeographies, one of early medieval scripts, where

---

[6] Translated from a passage in B. M. von Scarpatetti, 'Der Katalog der datierten Handschriften als ein bildungsgeschichtliches Instrument für die frühe Neuzeit', in *Studien zum städtischen Bildungswesen des späten Mittelalters und der frühen Neuzeit*, ed. B. Moeller, H. Patze and K. Stackmann, Göttingen 1983, p. 2. Criticism of 'ancien régime' palaeography may be found, for example, in A. Petrucci, 'Au-delà de la paléographie: histoire de l'écriture, histoire de l'écrit, histoire de l'écrire', *Académie Royale de Belgique. Bulletin de la Classe des Lettres et des Sciences Morales et Politiques*, 6th ser., 7 (1996), pp. 123–35. See also Petrucci, *Breve storia*, p. 20; Casamassima, *Tradizione*, p. 15. On the 'crisi', see the discussion between Attilio Bartoli Langeli, 'Ancora su paleografia e storia della scrittura: A proposito di un convegno perugino', *Scrittura e Civiltà*, 2 (1978), pp. 275–94, and Alessandro Pratesi, 'Paleografia in crisi?' *Scrittura e Civiltà*, 3 (1979), pp. 329–37.

'minutiae' count, and one of late medieval handwriting. Gasparri even claims that 'à partir des temps carolingiens l'écriture latine n'a plus d'histoire' ('after the Carolingian period, there is no longer a history of Latin handwriting').[7]

Although the cultural, social and economic conditions that shaped script and writing in the later Middle Ages were very different from those of the early Middle Ages, one suspects that the difference in treatment on the part of the palaeographers has more to do with the immense mass of manuscripts that survive from the period after 1100, which makes it impossible to provide a survey for the whole of Europe. Indeed, most manuals display a strong national bias in their coverage of the later period and tend to concentrate on material from each author's own country. Partial exceptions are the handbooks and surveys by Battelli, Bischoff, Cencetti and some North American scholars.[8]

BOOK SCRIPT VS. DOCUMENTARY SCRIPT

This book deals only with book scripts, which constitutes a serious limitation. As is well known, until the beginning of the twentieth century Latin palaeography comprised the study of documents as well as manuscripts. A scholar like Léopold Delisle (1826–1910) was a specialist who was as much at home in libraries as in archives. The once-popular handbooks of Prou and Reusens discuss, century by century, first manuscripts, then documents. Since Ludwig Traube (1861–1907), however, who was a philologist, there has been a tendency to dissociate the two branches and to pursue the study of book scripts independently from that of documentary scripts. This trend has been reinforced by the great enterprise of the Catalogues of Dated Manuscripts (*CMD*).[9] This invaluable collection should not

[7] Gasparri, *Introduction*, p. 95. This last statement has obviously to be understood in the light of all the scripts which according to Gasparri, following in the footsteps of Mallon, have no history. The same idea of certain scripts being dead ends is found in Casamassima, *Tradizione*, p. 15; Stiennon, *Paléographie*, p. 73. For Paola Supino Martini, too, the study of late medieval scripts is essentially different from the study of early medieval script: 'Paleografia latina: bilanci e prospettivi', in *Bilan et perspectives des études médiévales en Europe. Actes du Premier Congrès européen d'Etudes Médiévales (Spoleto, 1993)*, ed. J. Hamesse, Louvain-la-Neuve 1995 (Fédération Internationale des Instituts d'Etudes Médiévales. Textes et Etudes du Moyen Age, 3), p. 369. Recently Ezio Ornato has demonstrated that the difference between early medieval and late medieval palaeography resides only in the number of available sources, which for the early period he considers in fact insufficient for enabling a reliable reconstruction: E. Ornato, *Apologia dell' apogeo*, Rome 2000 (I Libri di Viella, 22), pp. 7–12.

[8] The latter 'enjoyed freedom from the European preoccupation with national identity, the problem of confounding one's manuscript heritage with one's amour propre' (R. Rouse, 'Latin Paleography and Manuscript Studies in North America', in *Un secolo*, p. 308).

[9] See T. J. Brown, 'Latin Palaeography since Traube', *Transactions of the Cambridge Bibliographical Society*, 3 (1959–63), pp. 361–81; repr. with additional notes in *Codicologica*, 1 (1976), pp. 58–74. Gasparri (*Introduction*, p. 13) thinks that the enterprise of the Catalogue of Dated Manuscripts has had the unhappy result of directing palaeographical research far too exclusively towards book scripts.

blind us to the fact that the separation is an artificial one, even if there are usually intrinsic differences between the two kinds of script. Mallon was in a way correct when, in his characteristically exuberant manner, he fulminated against the division of palaeography into separate branches according to the function, content, form or material of the manuscripts or documents studied.[10]

Such separation between books and documents deprives us of the very basis for understanding the evolution and diversification of scripts. At the risk of simplifying outrageously, the relations between book script and documentary script might be sketched as follows. While book scripts have always involved a minimum degree of formality, the script of many documents tends to be informal. In order to produce documents more rapidly, the standard letter forms were modified and became cursive:[11] they may be marked by such features as roundness, broadness, a reduced number of strokes, by loops and ligatures, fragmentation, etc. Over the course of time, the new letter forms sometimes came to be regarded as the norm and could be stylized and executed in a calligraphic way by augmenting once more the number of strokes and reducing the number of ligatures, thus producing a new canonized book script. Seen in this way, the history of script might be described as an alternation of increasing cursivity, on the one hand, and consolidation and calligraphy, on the other. The field in which the changes take place is the documentary one, the chief domain of the cursive scripts. In their most uncanonized form of 'écriture commune' or 'écriture usuelle', such scripts are (with some exaggeration) said to be 'spontaneous, living scripts, the expression of the real physiology of writing'.[12]

This is the place to mention the strong links that exist between palaeography and diplomatic. In many universities the two disciplines are taught by the same person, and in some handbooks the border between the two is vague. This situation is common to Europe as a whole, but it appears to be especially true of Italy, Spain and Portugal. It goes without saying that a national perspective, never far away in late medieval palaeography, becomes dominant when the scripts of chanceries and their documents are being discussed.

Indeed, the diversification of documentary scripts along national and re-gional lines was infinitely greater than was the case for book scripts. It therefore

---

[10] See, for example, J. Mallon, 'Qu'est-ce que la paléographie?' in *Paläographie 1981*, pp. 47–52. I cannot endorse the statement of F. Gasparri, 'Jean Mallon', *Scrittura e Civiltà*, 8 (1984), p. 271, that after Mallon 'épigraphistes, papyrologues et paléographes n'auront plus le droit de voir dans l'écriture autre chose qu'une activité où toutes les forces de l'homme sont impliquées'.

[11] The term is used here in its technical meaning, i.e. of a script having characteristics proper to allow a rapid execution.

[12] Gasparri, *Introduction*, p. 77. According to this author (p. 61), highly canonized scripts, such as Capital, Uncial, and Gothic book and formal documentary script, are 'autant de chapitres fermés de la paléographie latine'. For a more acceptable position, see Steffens, *Paläographie*, Preface. Criticism of Traube, Lowe and other students of book scripts for neglecting documentary script may be found in Cencetti, *Lineamenti*, p. 12.

may be possible to find a scholar who is competent in all late medieval book scripts used in the various countries of Europe. But it would be impossible to find a palaeographer who is informed on the subject of European documentary handwriting in all its variety from the twelfth to the fifteenth century.[13]

It is indeed the present book's purpose to take a Europe-wide perspective with regard to late medieval handwriting in books, but it cannot take fully into account documentary scripts as well, in spite of the objections raised above. It will therefore be unable to reveal the underlying backgrounds to the genesis and transformation of scripts. But book scripts have the advantage of being a coherent group, notwithstanding the variety of their appearance, in that they must obey two rules, namely the demands of legibility and beauty. Book scripts, to a greater extent than documentary scripts, were intended for a general readership (in so far as one existed) and will generally lack features that impede legibility, such as variant forms for one letter, or ligatures. They also have certain aesthetic qualities, which made them acceptable, even pleasing, to the contemporary reader. The preference for 'constructed' letters, made in several strokes, is one of their basic features. Both elements (but especially beauty) are difficult to define, but we must assume that together they determine the 'formality' of book scripts.[14]

METHOD OF STUDY

Our analysis of scripts will essentially be based on morphology. In the light of all that has hitherto been adduced to argue against focusing on letter forms, this may seem an unfortunate decision. Have we not been told that letter shapes are accidents, and that the ductus is the fundamental factor in handwriting? That it is not the visible forms themselves of the letters, signs and ligatures which are important, but the way they have been traced? That only script 'nel suo farsi' ('as a process') should be studied? Ductus is a much debated and vague concept. For Mallon (whom I follow here), it is the way the letter is constructed by means of a

---

[13] W. Heinemeyer, 'Studien zur Geschichte der gotischen Urkundenschrift', *Archiv für Diplomatik*, 1 (1955), p. 331.

[14] On legibility see R. Bergeron and E. Ornato, 'La lisibilité dans les manuscrits et les imprimés à la fin du Moyen Age. Préliminaires d'une recherche', *Scrittura e Civiltà*, 14 (1990), pp. 151–98 (repr. in E. Ornato, *La face cachée du livre médiéval. L'histoire du livre vue par Ezio Ornato, ses amis et ses collègues*, Rome 1997, pp. 521–54); E. Cottereau, 'Un essai d'évaluation objective de la richesse et de la lisibilité dans les manuscrits médiévaux', *Gazette du Livre Médiéval*, 30 (1997), pp. 8–17. On aesthetics see P. Spunar, 'L'esthétique et l'écriture', in *Actas*, pp. 221–4; G. Costamagna, 'Lineamenti estetici dello sviluppo della scrittura latina', in Costamagna, *Studi di paleografia e di diplomatica*, Rome 1972 (Fonti e Studi del Corpus Membranarum Italicarum, 9), pp. 59–85 (orig. published 1950); and, in general, Fichtenau, *Mensch und Schrift*.

sequence of strokes, what the Italians call 'tratteggio', and Gumbert 'structure'.[15] Ductus in this sense has rarely been studied in the context of late medieval scripts; Gumbert rightly warns us that in calligraphic scripts (such as Textualis Formata) it is often very difficult to distinguish the strokes composing the letters and the order and direction in which they were traced.[16] Gilissen, on the other hand, has become increasingly distrustful of the importance of ductus except for the study of script evolution.[17] As an investigation of ductus is also a very time-consuming affair, it will not be our primary concern. Although the subject of writing technique will not be omitted altogether, we will focus rather on its results, the letter forms.

Neither shall we pay too much attention to general impressions. General impressions are important and, as said at the beginning, are often sufficient for the experienced palaeographer. Their great deficiency, however, lies in the difficulty of putting them into words in an unambiguous way. Also, they are based not only on the script, but also on the appearance of the page as a whole, and consequently take account of codicological and ornamental features.

Since we have deliberately chosen the morphology of the scripts themselves to be the focus for our palaeographical research, one may ask whether morphological features can be described in an objective way. The traditional descriptions of distinctive features as given in innumerable commentaries accompanying plates are mostly unsatisfactory. Many qualifying terms and descriptions are in the last resort the subjective opinion of the author alone. The reader can only guess what is meant by terms such as 'large', 'small', 'clear', 'elegant', 'compressed', 'wide', 'precise', 'workmanlike', 'competent', 'vigorous' etc. Complete descriptions letter by letter, as provided, for example, by Steffens, are off-putting, and descriptions of select letter forms are only useful if the chosen letters are really significant. Which letters are significant depends of course on the type of script being considered, and consequently on the typology of scripts underlying the description. And this leads us inevitably to the problem of the nomenclature of scripts.

How is it possible to proceed in such a way that the description of a specimen of handwriting is as clear and convincing to its reader as it is to its author? An obvious answer is: by replacing qualitative data by quantitative ones, and thus turning palaeography into an 'art of measurement', to quote Bischoff's regretful

---

[15] J. Mallon, *Paléographie romaine*, Madrid 1952 (Scripturae Monumenta et Studia, 3), pp. 22–5; Gilissen, *Expertise*, pp. 40–1; Petrucci, *Breve storia*, pp. 22–3, opposes 'ductus' to 'tratteggio'; similarly Cencetti, *Lineamenti*, p. 52. Other definitions of ductus: Bischoff, *Palaeography*, p. 51, n. 4; Brown, *Guide*, p. 3.

[16] Gumbert, *Kartäuser*, p. 216, n. 7.

[17] See, for example, L. Gilissen, 'Analyse et évolution des formes graphiques', in 'La escritura e su historia', *Anuario de Estudios Medievales*, 21 (1992), pp. 323–46.

words.[18] Indeed there is very much to be said in favour of a quantitative approach to a matter so difficult to treat adequately with other techniques.[19]

Two methods have been tested in this field. The first consists in measuring the letters, calculating their weight, their slant, the pen angle, etc., and then creating a typical alphabet on the basis of numerous examples of each letter that is found in a given script. The method was taken to extremes by Léon Gilissen in his *Expertise*.[20] This work, highly acclaimed at the time of its publication, is simultaneously an unusual enquiry into an extremely difficult problem, and, in its impracticability, a deterrent to all those who might be inclined to follow its example.

The quantitative method which should be applied to palaeography is a statistical one. It consists of counting and measuring significant features of handwriting and charting the results. An attractive and relatively simple example is the method proposed by Anscari Mundó at the Sixth Colloquium of the Comité International de Paléographie in Munich in 1981.[21] It consists of a table in which each of the palaeographical features of a given, undated manuscript is compared with parallel features in a series of dated codices of about the same date.

More sophisticated (and more demanding) are the statistical methods developed by the French team of researchers centred on Carla Bozzolo and Ezio Ornato. In addition to their well-known codicological enquiries, they have also undertaken studies of palaeographical problems.[22] By counting the different types of

---

[18] Cf. n. 3. The full quotation is: 'With the aid of technical advances palaeography, which is an art of seeing and comprehending, is in the process of becoming an art of measurement'. It was used in its original German version as a motto in A. Derolez, *Codicologie des manuscrits en écriture humanistique sur parchemin*, Turnhout 1984 (Bibliologia, 5–6), I, p. 7, before being discussed, at the invitation of Petrucci, by a selection of palaeographers in *Scrittura e Civiltà*, under the title 'Commentare Bischoff'. The participants were: Giorgio Costamagna, *Scrittura e Civiltà*, 19 (1995), pp. 325–34; Françoise Gasparri, *ibid.*, pp. 335–6; Léon Gilissen, *ibid.*, pp. 337–8; Francisco M. Gimeno Blay, *ibid.*, pp. 339–44; Alessandro Pratesi, *ibid.*, pp. 345–8; Armando Petrucci, *Scrittura e Civiltà*, 20 (1996), pp. 401–7. Their reactions, of a very unequal level, are evaluated by J. P. Gumbert, 'Commentare "Commentare Bischoff"', *Scrittura e Civiltà*, 22 (1998), pp. 397–404. The discussion was continued by Pratesi, 'Commentare Bischoff: un secondo intervento', *ibid.*, pp. 405–8 and Costamagna, 'Paleografia: scienza o estetica?', *ibid.*, pp. 409–17.

[19] Armando Petrucci, however, is only the mouthpiece of many colleagues when he writes that quantitative palaeography 'non può semplicemente esistere' (*Scrittura e Civiltà*, 20 [1996], p. 403).

[20] Gilissen, *Expertise*. In addition to much other, often uncritical eulogy, the work was discussed at length in *Scriptorium*, 29 (1975) under the general title 'Paléographie latine: l'expertise des écritures médiévales', by A. d'Haenens, 'Pour une sémiologie paléographique et une histoire de l'écriture' (pp. 175–98); E. Ornato, 'Statistique et paléographie: peut-on utiliser le rapport modulaire dans l'expertise des écritures médiévales?' (pp. 198–234); L. Gilissen, 'Ductus et rapport modulaire. Réponse aux articles de MM. d'Haenens et Ornato' (pp. 235–44). Whereas Ornato's criticism is clear and intelligent, the bearing of d'Haenens's learned comment escapes the writer of the present pages.

[21] A. M. Mundó, 'Méthode comparative-statistique pour la datation des manuscrits non datés', in *Paläographie 1981*, pp. 53–8.

[22] C. Bozzolo, D. Coq, D. Muzerelle and E. Ornato, 'Les abréviations dans les livres liturgiques du XVe siècle: pratique et théorie', in *Actas*, pp. 17–27. See also n. 14. For the general approach of this

abbreviations occurring in Psalm 101 in a large number of manuscripts and printed books, they were able, for example, to identify for the first time some laws that regulated the use of abbreviations, and consequently something of the hidden processes of handwriting. Their results show what can be achieved by well-conducted statistical research on ancient scripts, as long as only measurable and quantifiable data are being considered. By applying statistical methods to palaeography, we will, no doubt, arrive at important new and objective statements.[23] The method applied hitherto in palaeographical handbooks has produced an authoritarian discipline, the pertinence of which depends on the authority of the author and the faith of the reader.

In the absence of sufficient existing quantitative palaeographical research, the morphological method proposed here cannot involve statistics. Instead it will consist in studying principally those graphs which, within a given type of script, display distinctive characteristics, the forms that differ from the 'normal' ones, and other features that are readily identifiable and can be described in an unequivocal manner. This method may be judged crude, inexpert and unrefined. But in the face of the imbroglio into which late medieval palaeography has lapsed, it is hoped that this approach will gain more unanimity than other methods have been able to achieve.

However far we want to go in the search for objective data, our method must always be based on the assumption that script types are historical realities. The starting-point for our research is therefore the classification of scripts and their nomenclature. These two interrelated problems, which have proved a stumbling-block for all students of Gothic palaeography up to the present, will be discussed below (pp. 13–24).

PALAEOGRAPHY VS. CODICOLOGY

James's advice not to look so much at individual letter forms as at the general appearance of the page compels us to reconsider the relationship between palaeography and codicology, between the study of the script and the archaeology of the codex.

---

group of researchers to quantitative codicology and palaeography (and the study of early printing), see the excellent studies collected by E. Ornato in *La face cachée du livre médiéval*, quoted in n. 14.

[23] Constituting a well-sized corpus of convenient manuscripts and assembling the palaeographical data in large numbers as necessitated by statistical enquiry is no small task. But there are features which can easily be described in an objective way. Instead of saying that a script is large or small, one could mention the average distance between the lines in millimetres (Gilissen's 'unité de réglure'), even if this has no strict relationship to the size of the script. Counting the average number of signs on the line would take more time, but in combination with the length of the lines and the distance between them, the numerical result would provide us with a reliable and objective characterization of the density of a given script. See A. Derolez, 'Possibilités et limites d'une paléographie quantitative', in *Mélanges Carl Deroux* (forthcoming).

Despite intensive discussion on this question, the matter is still unresolved.[24] Yet the relation between the two can be expressed in a quite simple way, if we keep to the traditional definition of palaeography: codicology is the study of all the physical aspects of the manuscript book, and palaeography, or the study of script, is a subdiscipline of codicology.

The present book deals with palaeography, not with codicology. But there are many points of connection between script and one of the elements of codicological research: the page. A statement about the size of a given script, for example, only makes sense if the dimensions of the page or of the writing area are also given. The disposition of the text on the page, the techniques, patterns and colour of the ruling, are elements that should also be taken into account by the palaeographer. The presence or absence of a full ruling on the page (by contrast with frame ruling) is of fundamental significance for the student of book scripts.[25]

A survey of the main codicological characteristics of the manuscript in the period discussed here will be given in Chapter 1.

GOTHIC SCRIPT

The term Gothic has many meanings, even within the limited circle of palaeographers. In conformity with widespread practice, it is used here as a generic name for all late medieval scripts that are not Humanistic. This negative definition is fully justified by the immense variety of shapes and aspects exhibited by late medieval scripts: angular or round, vertical or sloping, calligraphic or rapid, bold or thin, compressed or wide, with or without loops, etc.[26] It is in accordance with the distinction between Gothic and Roman type used by the incunabulists. Of course, such a wide definition also embraces scripts that lack all or some of the features that normally are considered 'Gothic'.

This is why some Italian palaeographers consider 'Gothic' to be only one of the script types of the late Middle Ages, alongside Cancelleresca and Mercantesca, for

---

[24] See, for example, F. Masai, 'Paléographie et codicologie', *Scriptorium*, 4 (1950), pp. 279–93; A. Gruijs, 'Paléographie, codicologie et archéologie du livre. Questions de méthodologie et de terminologie', in *La paléographie hébraïque médiévale. Paris, 1972*, Paris 1974 (Colloques Internationaux du Centre National de la Recherche Scientifique, 547), pp. 19–25; *idem*, 'Codicology or the Archaeology of the Book? A False Dilemma', *Quaerendo*, 2 (1972), pp. 87–108. Still of fundamental interest is F. Masai, 'La paléographie gréco-latine, ses tâches, ses méthodes', *Scriptorium*, 10 (1956), pp. 281–302 (reprinted, with a 'Post-scriptum' by A. Derolez, in *Codicologica*, 1 [1976], pp. 34–57).
[25] Most photographs unfortunately do not show the ruling. Remarks on the ability or lack of ability of a scribe, as, for example, liberally provided by Thomson, *Bookhands*, should be tested against the way the page has been prepared for writing.
[26] Why Cencetti, *Compendio*, p. 18 (and elsewhere), reckons the late Middle Ages belong to the period of 'unità scrittoria' begun with the Carolingian age is a kind of mystery.

example.[27] Many palaeographers stick to the term 'Gothic minuscule', although, as far as I know, no books have been written continuously in majuscules other than Capital and Uncial.[28] Some confuse cursive script with documentary script, and contrast minuscule with cursive, as if cursive script was not minuscule.[29]

Of course the above definition of Gothic script as synonymous with non-Humanistic script will require a clear definition of the latter. For this, see Chapter 10.

SOURCES: THE CATALOGUE OF DATED MANUSCRIPTS

We are now infinitely better equipped for the study of late medieval scripts than our predecessors fifty years ago. Thanks to the initiative, the authority and the efforts of the Comité International de Paléographie (Latine) a wonderful tool has been created which earlier specialists lacked. Cencetti, amongst others, had expressed the conviction that palaeography of the Late Middle Ages would only make progress when a large number of reproductions of dated and localized specimens of script had been made available.[30]

The making of a worldwide catalogue of dated manuscripts was decided upon at the historic first colloquium of the Comité in Paris in 1953, together with the compilation of two polyglot lexical works: a vocabulary of codicology, which appeared three decades later in an excellent French version by Denis Muzerelle;[31] and a palaeographical nomenclature, which has not appeared till now.

The first project, the Catalogue of Dated Manuscripts (*CMD*), was embarked upon with enthusiasm, France taking the lead, and most other European countries following suit. Some 45 volumes of the series have been published, providing thousands of full-sized reproductions of medieval book scripts. (The new Italian series *CMDIt2* is the only one that has abandoned the principle of actual-size reproductions in favour of a reproduction of the full page of the manuscripts.)

---

[27] As, for example, Cencetti and Petrucci; similarly Millares Carlo, *Tratado*, I, p. 210.

[28] Maybe 'minuscule' is understood by some in a sense different from the one adopted here: a script written between four imaginary lines, thus comprising short letters, long letters, letters with ascenders, letters with descenders. This definition in Cencetti, *Lineamenti*, p. 51; Strubbe, *Grondbegrippen*, p. 17; Brown, *Guide*, p. 8.

[29] Strubbe, *Grondbegrippen*, pp. 109–11; see also *Handschriftenbeschreibung in Österreich*, ed. O. Mazal, Vienna 1975 (Veröffentlichungen der Kommission für Schrift- und Buchwesen des Mittelalters, II, 1), p. 143: 'Buch- und Kursivschriften'.

[30] Cencetti, *Lineamenti*, p. 210. In contrast at times the strange idea emerges that dated manuscripts are not typical of their age. See, for example, M. B. Parkes on English manuscripts (mentioned in Gumbert, *Kartäuser*, p. 199, n. 3); A. J. Piper in a review of *CMDGBLo*, *Medium Aevum*, 50 (1981), pp. 105–6.

[31] Muzerelle, *Vocabulaire*.

The diversity of approach between the different countries of Europe is readily apparent in the various series of 'Manuscrits datés': although all follow the same overall pattern, no one is made along exactly the same lines as the others. Most series include dated and datable manuscripts; the Belgian and new Italian catalogues are more strict and include only dated ones. The French *CMDF* and the British *CMDGB*, as well as the Vatican series (*CMDVat*), as a rule print more than one reproduction on a page, whilst most other series, dealing with smaller numbers of codices, can afford to reserve full pages for each reproduction (except of course for small-sized manuscripts). The luxurious original Italian series *CMDIt* even went so far as to reproduce full pages of the manuscripts themselves at actual size. It is clear that the larger the amount of text reproduced, the more the catalogue can fulfil the purpose of the series, namely to be a palaeographical tool.[32] The Austrian series (*CMDA*) systematically reproduces pages containing the colophon, while other catalogues often choose pages or passages apparently at random. *CMDF* has changed its format in the new series *CMDF2*. These are just a few of the variations visible in the series as a whole.

The original intention was to make a card index of European scripts by cutting out the plates of the Catalogues of Dated Manuscripts. It very soon proved impracticable. But even without this, we need to consider the impact of this gigantic enterprise upon the study of palaeography, especially that of the late Middle Ages, since manuscripts dating from before 1100 are extremely rare in the series.[33] There is no doubt that codicological studies have profited enormously from the access the catalogues provide to a great mass of critically dated and localized material. But for palaeography one has the impression that the use made hitherto of *CMD* has been limited and that a methodology is sorely needed to make working with them more rewarding and less time-consuming.

Most series present the raw material in a chronological sequence: each item consists of a photograph and a (short) description of the manuscript, containing for example the transcription and interpretation of the colophon or a discussion of the proposed date or date-span and place or area of production. Some also provide conclusions and general observations, either in the introduction or in an appendix. In just two series have the authors thought it necessary to do more in a publication which is of such fundamental palaeographical importance. These are the first Italian series *CMDIt* and the Dutch series *CMDNL*.

---

[32] Especially for large scripts, such catalogues as *CMDF*, *CMDVat* etc., which have two, three or even four illustrations on one page, sometimes offer too little material to be useful.

[33] See the fundamental discussions in *Les manuscrits datés. Premier bilan et perspectives. Die datierten Handschriften. Erster Bilanz und Perspektiven. Neuchâtel/Neuenburg, 1983*, Paris 1985 (Rubricae, 2); Monique-Cécile Garand has calculated that of a total of 11,700 descriptions made at the time, no more than 2,800 belonged to the pre-1400 period, and no more than 909 antedated the year 1200 (p. 3).

The editorial committee of the former rightly believed that the author of a *CMD* would know more about the manuscripts included than the reader, who has access to only one or part of one reproduced page. For this reason, a commentary on the script of each codex was provided in the volumes of text. Any extract from one of these palaeographical notes demonstrates that such a description, even if conscientious and accurate in itself, is not very helpful.[34] The reason for this has already been suggested above: a description of the handwriting in a given manuscript, however precise, is doomed to be of little use if it cannot be related to a recognized system used consistently by the author of the description.

The other catalogue which deviates from the general practice is Lieftinck's *CMDNL*, the first volume of which appeared in 1964. For the manuscripts of the fourteenth and fifteenth centuries, this Dutch palaeographer superimposed another classification upon the purely chronological one, by arranging the plates in three groups according to the nomenclature of Gothic scripts of which he was the author.[35] His system will be discussed in detail in the following pages. Whatever its merits, Lieftinck had taken a logical step, because only in his catalogue does it become possible to compare what is comparable: scripts of the same type – provided that one agrees with his system. For others, the classification of his plates is deemed more of a hindrance than a help.

NOMENCLATURE

The preceding survey of the great undertaking constituted by *CMD* brings us to the nomenclature of Gothic scripts, one of the most debated palaeographical problems of the last century.[36] It is clear that one can only apply names to scripts if there is agreement on classification.[37] So the real issue is not so much nomenclature as classification and the criteria employed to establish it.

A great deal of confusion reigns in the field of the description of late medieval script. In contrast with earlier periods in the history of handwriting, the palaeographical situation in the final centuries of the Middle Ages is extremely

[34] 'Semigotica di unica mano, di modulo medio, dal tratteggio piuttosto pesante e contrastato, discontinua come accuratezza di tracciato, dimensioni e forme delle lettere, . . . sempre scarsamente angolose; abbastanza compatta e con fusione di curve contrarie ma chiara, nitida e con qualche ricercatezza calligrafica specie nelle lettere maiuscole' (*CMDIt*, 1, no. 38). For objections against including palaeographical commentary in *CMD*, see Jan-Olof Tjäder in *Les manuscrits datés* (see n. 33), pp. 71–2.
[35] It was taken over and systematized by his pupil and successor J. Peter Gumbert in vol. II (1988).
[36] A landmark in this field was the already mentioned first Colloque International de Paléographie, Paris 1953, and its proceedings: *Nomenclature*. See a bibliography of reactions to this epoch-making publication in Boyle, *Medieval Latin Palaeography*, no. 1701.
[37] 'Ogni terminologia paleografica è legata ad una particolare visione storica del fenomeno scrittorio' (Petrucci, *Descrizione*, p. 59).

complicated indeed. The causes are well known: the dramatic multiplication of books and written documents; the spread of literacy and the ability to write among people and classes who previously had little or no access to the written word; new schools and learning; the development of private book-ownership, ecclesiastical, princely and civic; the rise of new arrangements for book production, involving both the laity and religious, organized on a commercial basis; the extraordinary increase and diversification in the use of abbreviations; the increasing popularity of vernacular literature, etc.

Above all there were divergent trends in the development of script from the twelfth century onwards – on the one hand a gradual transformation of the Carolingian script into an ever more artificial system of constructed letters and, on the other, the creation of rapid, fluent scripts to suit the purposes of administration, business and scholarship. The inevitable interaction between these two divergent trends created a multitude of intermediate forms, which render the situation even more complicated.

DESCRIPTIONS WITHOUT NOMENCLATURE

It is of some interest to observe how palaeographical handbooks and atlases describe examples of the 'realtà storica molteplice e sfuggente' ('historical reality, multi-faceted and fleeting') they reproduce.[38] Earlier handbooks often seem to avoid all nomenclature in so far as Gothic script is concerned. The *Eléments de paléographie* of Canon Reusens is a good example. He often defines script on the basis of its use.[39] Descriptions by expert palaeographers, which avoid any nomenclature, more than once fail to mention the morphological peculiarities that, to us, seem essential. Edward Maunde Thompson described 'a not uncommon type of the English hand...which has a slightly cursive element in it',[40] but he did not say that, by contrast with the preceding plates, it is (in our terminology) a Cursiva. Hans Foerster, in his well-known atlas, maintains that two specimens of script, both dated 1415, are in the same script, although to us they are quite different.[41] Samuel Harrison

---

[38] Cencetti, *Compendio*, p. 79. The expression is in line with the widespread belief that classification of scripts is inconsistent with historical reality.

[39] His only comment on a plate showing a rapid cursive is as follows: 'Un excellent exemple de l'écriture employée, pendant la seconde moitié du XIVe siècle, pour la transcription des ouvrages philosophiques et théologiques' (Reusens, *Eléments*, pl. 41 and p. 290). Faced with a script which in Lieftinck's terminology would be a Hybrida, he comments simply: 'un spécimen remarquable de belle écriture de bréviaire...; cette écriture, petite mais grasse, est d'une grande netteté' (pl. 40, 2, and p. 284). In the same area and about the same time, Van den Gheyn, *Album belge*, does use a limited but acceptable palaeographical nomenclature.

[40] Thompson, *Introduction*, p. 460 (no. 193).

[41] Foerster, *Mittelalterliche Buch- und Urkundenschriften*, pls. 43–4 and p. 79.

Thomson's atlas is another publication in which the palaeographical comment, although the work of an expert, provokes many questions.[42] One may observe that Thomson, who systematically avoided a palaeographical nomenclature, nevertheless used adjectives that are no less difficult to handle: 'French', 'Spanish', 'school', 'monastic', etc.

RESTRICTED NOMENCLATURE

Most scholars, however, explicitly or implicitly believe that a more precise terminology is necessary, even if the fluidity of the boundaries between one type of script and another, and the impact of individual hands make such a classification necessarily artificial. Some believe that the fewer distinctions that are made, the better. Georges Despy, the most ferocious of the reviewers of Lieftinck's *Nomenclature*, proposed no more than two categories: book script and documentary script.[43] Joachim Kirchner's influential atlas of Gothic book scripts thus distinguishes *textualis* on the one hand, *cursiva*, *notula*, *bastarda* on the other. German scholars have likewise developed a simplified practical terminology with a limited number of distinctions, for the purposes of cataloguing.[44]

COMPOSITE NOMENCLATURE

A better way to characterize script, according to some, may be obtained by mentioning the presence of foreign elements in a given specimen. Armando Petrucci, although convinced of the excellence of Cencetti's terminology, which he calls very 'ricca e articolata' ('full and well structured'), gives the following advice to anyone about to describe a manuscript: when confronted with scripts as difficult to grasp as

---

[42] 'This precise script does not follow Parisian styles' (Thomson, *Bookhands*, pl. 8); 'the script is very distinctively French' (pl. 13); 'this monastic gothic script is much closer to the current hands of the preceding three examples than would at first sight appear' (pl. 47); in fact it is Textualis according to the Lieftinck terminology, like the first of the preceding examples, whilst the two remaining ones are Cursiva Currens.

[43] G. Despy, 'De la terminologie paléographique médiévale', *Revue Belge de Philologie et d'Histoire*, 34 (1956), pp. 174–81.

[44] J. Autenrieth, 'Paläographische Nomenklatur im Rahmen der Handschriftenkatalogisierung', in *Zur Katalogisierung mittelalterlicher und neuerer Handschriften*, Frankfurt am Main 1963 (Zeitschrift für Bibliothekswesen und Bibliographie, Sonderheft), pp. 98–104. O. Mazal (ed.), *Handschriftenbeschreibung in Österreich* (see n. 29), pp. 142–3, on the other hand, distinguishes no fewer than seven categories: 'karolingisch-gotische Mischschrift', 'frühgotische Minuskel', 'textualis formata', 'textualis', 'notula', 'bastarda', 'Spätformen'. More fundamental is E. Overgaauw, 'Die Nomenklatur der gotischen Schriftarten bei der Katalogisierung von spätmittelalterlichen Handschriften', *Codices Manuscripti*, 17 (1994), pp. 100–106.

'semicorsive goticheggianti' or 'gotichette dissociate', he should follow the method of Bartoloni (1955), which produces 'definizioni più sfumate e complesse' ('definitions that are more nuanced and complex').[45] It is, no doubt, an excellent idea to emphasize such features as are not normally to be seen in a given script. But *sfumato* (an over-reliance upon nuance) in palaeography has its drawbacks. It reappears in Françoise Gasparri's book in such questionable terms as 'bâtarde évoluant vers la préhumanistique de chancellerie'.[46]

NOMENCLATURE COMPRISING EXTRA-PALAEOGRAPHICAL ELEMENTS

German palaeographers, more than others, have a tendency to give their terminology greater precision by adding geographical names to the terms they use. Crous and Kirchner's book was a trendsetter in this respect, and Otto Mazal followed their example with such terms as 'Florentiner Bastarda', 'Oberrheinische Bastarda', 'Süddeutsche Buchkursive', 'Kölner Bastarda', etc.[47] In most cases, these geographical specifications are not derived from any special characteristic of the handwriting, but from the place of origin of the manuscript or document. As long as they cannot be demonstrated to indicate the presence of distinctive features different from the script from other areas, such specifications are useless, even deceptive. The terminology proposed by Pavel Spunar, according to which one script type for example is called Gotica Textualis Formata Bohemica, should be dismissed for the same reason, unless the characteristics of a distinctively Bohemian Textualis can be specified.[48]

A similar criticism can be applied to names indicating the religious orders supposed to have developed or favoured a given type of Gothic script. Bischoff had already rejected the term 'Zisterzienserschrift' invented by Kirchner (and still used by Mazal).[49] For the same reason the terms proposed in the thirties by the Dutch palaeographer Bonaventura Kruitwagen are best avoided. Father Kruitwagen studied the books produced by the Dutch Brethren of Common Life and the Augustinian Canons of the Windesheim Congregation, both representatives of the great spiritual movement known as *Devotio moderna*. He became convinced that these orders put their stamp on the system of scripts developed in the Low Countries,

---

[45] Petrucci, *Descrizione*, p. 60. For example: 'corsiva di tipo umanistico, con presenza di elementi semigotici'.

[46] Gasparri, *Introduction*, p. 222.

[47] Crous and Kirchner, *Schriftarten*; Mazal, *Buchkunst der Gotik*.

[48] P. Spunar, 'Sur les questions de la terminologie paléographique des écritures livresques du 9e au 16e siècle', *Eunomia. Ephemeridis Listy Filologické Supplementum*, 1 (1957), pp. 35–40, 95–7.

[49] *Nomenclature*, p. 14.

and consequently called the latter 'Windesheim script' or 'Fratersschrift' ('Script of the Brethren').[50]

The practice of qualifying a term for a script with another referring to its use (as noted above with regard to Reusens's handbook) is another habit so frequently employed that one does not need to dwell on it: 'liturgical hand' is a term familiar to all readers of the Sotheby catalogues, and has its equivalents in 'littera psalterialis' and 'Missalschrift'. More questionable, because largely undefined, are 'monastic hand', 'school hand', 'legal hand', 'notarial hand', 'écriture scolastique', etc.[51]

NATIONAL NOMENCLATURE

No less a source of confusion is the strong element of national bias present in palaeographical studies, already alluded to above. Such national bias in palaeography has much to do with its status as an auxiliary discipline: most publications are destined for university teaching in a given country and focus on their own graphic patrimony as far as the late Middle Ages are concerned.

The classifications and terminologies developed in the various European countries have the advantage of being the work of specialists, scholars expert in the field of ancient handwriting in their own countries. They have the disadvantage of existing almost entirely in a vacuum and being inaccessible to foreigners and unsuitable for international exchange. Some idiosyncratic Italian names have already been mentioned. In the Iberian Peninsula such terms as 'redonda de libros' and 'letra de albalaes' are in common use. The British are now familiar with names such as 'Anglicana' and 'Secretary'. The impression the outsider gains from all this is that an extremely large number of script types once existed and that the use of each was confined within national borders.

ADVERTISEMENT SHEETS AND PRINTING TYPES

It should be the aim of every piece of serious palaeographical research dealing with the late Middle Ages to bring all of these terms into line with each other, so that an exchange of data across national borders (and thus some progress) will become

---

[50] B. Kruitwagen, *Laat-Middeleeuwsche Paleografica, Paleotypica, Liturgica, Kalendalia, Grammaticalia*, The Hague 1942, pp. 23–69 and 81–116 (originally published 1935–6).
[51] The four former names, for example, are given in Thomson, *Bookhands*, pls. 46, 49, 54, 73, 105; the last one in Gasparri, *Introduction*, pp. 198–200, as different from 'écriture universitaire'.

possible. Before going into a little detail on this subject, two important questions need to be addressed: the issues of 'Schreibmeisterblätter' and 'Paläotypie', to use their German names.

The 'Schreibmeisterblätter' or posters of the writing-masters have haunted late medieval palaeography for a long time and lie behind a great deal of nationally focused palaeography.[52] We are concerned here, not so much with the 100 examples of script given by the early sixteenth-century Benedictine monk Leonhard Wagner, which are notorious for their fanciful and inventive character, as with the posters of such German masters as Hermann Strepel (1447) and Johann vom Hagen (early fifteenth century) (pl. 17). These display a limited number of samples of script and a nomenclature which, although not lacking in fanciful and obscure terms, is more rooted in scribal tradition.

Scholarly attitudes towards the terminology of the writing-masters have varied. Françoise Gasparri firmly believes in its validity as a basis for a modern palaeographical nomenclature. The Swiss palaeographer Martin Steinmann investigated the criteria underlying script classification in the leaves of the *Schreibmeister* and argued that they deserve more credit than they have often received. Bonaventura Kruitwagen, mentioned above, based his research essentially on the advertisement sheet of Hermann Strepel.

Nevertheless, Steinmann concedes that the writing-masters' terminology is neither complete nor scientific. Their posters had a commercial purpose. They also had a merely local value and their authors did not feel a need to conform with the terminology in use elsewhere or in earlier times.[53] In general, despite what will be said about Wolfgang Oeser's research into Textualis (below, pp. 75–6), a reliance on the writing-masters' terminology has been more harmful than otherwise in

---

[52] Steinmann, 'Textualis formata', pp. 301–3. For Strepel see Kruitwagen, *Laat-Middeleeuwsche Paleografica* (see n. 50), pp. 1–22; his poster is reproduced in *Nomenclature*, pp. 25–6, and Bischoff, *Palaeography*, pl. 18. For vom Hagen, see our pl. 17. More generally on medieval and early modern writing treatises, models and terminology, see F. Gasparri, 'Lexicographie historique des écritures', in *Vocabulaire du livre et de l'écriture au Moyen Age. Actes de la Table Ronde, Paris, 1987*, ed. O. Weijers, Turnhout 1989 (Etudes sur le Vocabulaire Intellectuel au Moyen Age, 2), pp. 100–10; Gasparri, *Introduction*, pp. 113–35; E. Persoons, 'De namen van de schriftsoorten bij de Moderne Devoten', *Archives et Bibliothèques de Belgique*, 29 (1968), pp. 14–23; E. Persoons, 'De vier soorten boekschrift van de Moderne Devoten', in *Bijdragen over Thomas a Kempis en de Moderne Devotie*, Brussels 1971 (Archives et Bibliothèques de Belgique, Numéro spécial, 4), pp. 90–104. On posters of writing-masters, see especially: S. H. Steinberg, 'Medieval Writing-Masters', *The Library*, 4th ser., 22 (1941–2), pp. 1–24; S. H. Steinberg, 'A Hand-List of Specimens of Medieval Writing-Masters', *The Library*, 4th ser., 23 (1942–3), pp. 192–4, and 5th ser., 2 (1948), p. 203; C. Wehmer, 'Die Schreibmeisterblätter des späten Mittelalters', in *Miscellanea Giovanni Mercati*, VI, Vatican City 1946 (Studi e Testi, 126), pp. 147–61; S. J. P. van Dijk, 'An Advertisement Sheet of an Early Fourteenth-Century Writing Master at Oxford', *Scriptorium*, 10 (1956), pp. 47–64; M. Steinmann, 'Ein mittelalterliches Schriftmusterblatt', *Archiv für Diplomatik*, 21 (1975), pp. 450–8; Spilling, 'Schreibkünste'.
[53] Steinmann, 'Textualis formata', pp. 310–11.

the establishment of a scholarly nomenclature of Gothic scripts. Gumbert's conclusion: 'zuverlässige Grundlagen für die moderne Paläographie sind aus keiner dieser Quellen zu gewinnen' ('one cannot gain a trustworthy basis for modern palaeography from these sources'), is ours also.[54]

The other point of fundamental interest when dealing with the terminology of late medieval – and especially fifteenth-century – script is its relationship with typography ('Paläotypie'). It is general knowledge that the first printers had their typefaces cut in imitation of the book scripts in use in their country. So it is not surprising that at least initially scripts and typefaces conformed with each other in all respects except for the strict regularity produced by the technology of printing. It is then all the more astonishing that there should exist such a gulf between the students of fifteenth-century scripts on the one hand, and those of fifteenth-century printing types on the other.[55] Only a few scholars have ventured on a global study of the two.[56] More recently Ezio Ornato and his colleagues have done excellent work in both fields.[57] A large-scale attempt at bridging the gap was Otto Mazal's *Paläographie und Paläotypie*.[58] Although its author is a recognized authority in both fields, the book has a fundamental weakness: the treatment of script and the analysis of the typefaces as used by hundreds of fifteenth-century printers are divided over two separate sections. The separate treatment of script and type reflects the current state of affairs: a lack of compatibility between the methods of the palaeographer and those of the incunabulist.

It is clear, however, that especially when one is dealing with highly formal scripts such as Textualis Formata, an examination of contemporary so-called 'textura' typefaces would be most profitable, the more so as the morphological niceties of such scripts will appear more clearly in the printed text than in handwriting, which is necessarily always somewhat irregular. It should be observed, on the other hand, that from the last quarter of the fifteenth century onwards in particular, typefaces, which

---

[54] Gumbert, *Kartäuser*, p. 208.

[55] See, for example, D. Coq, 'L'incunable, un bâtard du manuscrit?' *Gazette du Livre Médiéval*, 1 (1982), pp. 10–11.

[56] A. Hessel, 'Von der Schrift zum Druck', *Zeitschrift des deutschen Vereins für Buchwesen und Schrifttum*, 6 (1923), pp. 89–105; Wehmer, 'Namen'; R. Juchhoff, 'Das Fortleben mittelalterlicher Schreibgewohnheiten in den Druckschriften des XV. Jhs.', *Beiträge zur Inkunabelkunde*, n.s., 1, Leipzig 1935, pp. 65–77; B. Kruitwagen (see n. 50); S. Morison, *Selected Essays on the History of Letter-Forms in Manuscript and Print*, ed. D. McKitterick, Cambridge and New York 1981. In Crous and Kirchner, *Schriftarten*, script and typefaces are dealt with separately. A new project is announced by M. C. Vitali, 'Livre manuscrit – livre imprimé aux XVe et XVIe siècles. Projet d'une étude parallèle du point de vue paléographique', in *Probleme der Bearbeitung mittelalterlicher Handschriften*, ed. H. Härtel and W. Milde, *et al.*, Wolfenbüttel 1986 (Wolfenbütteler Forschungen, 30), pp. 47–54.

[57] See n. 22.

[58] See the incisive review of this book by P. Needham in *The Library Quarterly*, 56 (1986), pp. 420–2.

had been based on handwritten models, themselves came to influence handwriting, sometimes removing from the latter what little spontaneity it had retained.

THE LIEFTINCK SYSTEM

The preceding remarks will be sufficient to demonstrate that there is a great need for a clear-cut, objectively defined typology and nomenclature of Gothic script. Such a typology cannot be based, as we have seen, on general impressions or on the observation of the supposed writing technique, ductus or 'tratteggio', but on the letter forms, whatever the shortcomings of the morphological method. Two such systems are now current: one devised by the late Julian Brown and developed and popularized by his pupil Michelle Brown, and one to which the name of the Dutch palaeographer Gerard Isaac Lieftinck is attached. In fact, Brown's system is an adaptation and enlargement of Lieftinck's.[59]

The Lieftinck system is best studied not in the master's own publications, which often lack clarity, but in the descriptions and defence published by his pupil and successor J. Peter Gumbert, who played an essential part in its development.[60] In his more recent publications, however, Gumbert has distanced himself somewhat from the original system by stressing its theoretical character and questioning the historical reality of the Lieftinckian types. A double page in Gumbert's article in the Lieftinck *Festschrift* contains 32 small script samples showing all possible combinations of morphological features, either belonging to Lieftinck's types or to what the latter called 'écritures hors système'. As we shall see, it is possible to reduce the group of 'écritures hors système' to a small, almost negligible minority.

The great novelty of Lieftinck's system, as systematized by Gumbert, is its complete objectivity, at least insofar as its primary distinction of three types is concerned: Textualis, Cursiva and Hybrida (all book scripts, may it be stressed; the full name in Lieftinck's scheme would be 'littera Gothica textualis', etc.). They are not defined on the basis of vague criteria such as general appearance, ductus, speed of execution, roundness or angularity, etc., but on three unmistakable letter forms: the shapes of **a** (in one or in two compartments), of the ascenders (with or without loops), and of **f** and straight **s** (with or without a tail under the line). It was certainly too revolutionary for contemporary palaeographers to accept that handwriting, for

---

[59] Brown, *Guide*, p. 2.
[60] It is to be found at its best in Gumbert, *Kartäuser*, pp. 199–209. It is repeated, with the same exemplary clarity, in his later works: his article 'A Proposal for a Cartesian Nomenclature', in *Essays presented to G. I. Lieftinck*, IV: *Miniatures, Scripts, Collections*, ed. J. P. Gumbert and M. J. M. de Haan, Amsterdam 1976 (Litterae Textuales), pp. 45–52, containing his well-known 'palaeographic cube', and his vol. II of *CMDNL* (1988); J. P. Gumbert, 'Nomenklatur als Gradnetz. Ein Versuch an spätmittelalterlichen Schriftformen', *Codices Manuscripti*, I (1975), pp. 122–5. Lieftinck's own well-known exposition 'Pour une nomenclature de l'écriture livresque de la période dite gothique', in *Nomenclature*, pp. 15–34, lacks clarity and consistency in the terminology.

example, with single-compartment **a**, loops at the ascenders and tails at **f** and **s** would henceforward be called Cursiva, whatever its speed and manner of execution, when for them the term 'cursive' had of old been associated with the idea of rapid, sloping, connected, documentary script. But thanks to his ingenious choice of criteria, Lieftinck was able to create a certain amount of unanimity among the palaeographers of all nations (in so far as they did not reject his proposal altogether).

In the second place, Lieftinck sought for a means by which to distinguish levels of execution within each type – a necessary but evidently hazardous distinction, as it is difficult to find criteria for defining levels of execution and as the numerous, subtle gradations between each level for the most part preclude categorization. He decided to distinguish no more than three levels: Formata for a careful, highly formal, calligraphic execution, Libraria for a medium level of execution and Currens for a rapid, inferior level of writing. Of these terms 'Libraria' is the least appropriate, as all scripts involved are book scripts. Julian Brown suggested replacing it with Media. It is clear that, unless readily observable criteria can be identified, the attribution of labels indicating levels of execution must remain a subjective matter, influenced by the manuscripts with which one is familiar and producing different evaluations from one student to the next.[61] By contrast with the script types, there are no objective criteria for assigning one of the three levels of execution in order to qualify a given script. The letters in Formata will, of course, be markedly 'constructed', in other words made of separate strokes, whereas the number of strokes that form the letters in Currens will have been reduced as a function of speed. Even though there is likely to be general agreement as to whether a given hand should be called Formata, the distinction between Formata and Libraria and between Libraria and Currens will often depend on the observer's own experience and opinion.

Furthermore, a system that distinguishes just three levels of execution may appear too limited for an adequate classification of the various degrees of calligraphy or rapidity of execution. That is why Michelle Brown, following in the footsteps of her teacher, proposed the inclusion of intermediate levels such as Formata/Media, Media/Formata, Media/Currens, etc. The distinction between the first of these two qualifications is perhaps too subtle to be really manageable, but expressions such as 'Libraria fere Formata' ('Libraria/Formata') or 'Currens fere Libraria' ('Currens/Libraria') may be useful if one is in doubt as to which level of execution a given specimen should belong to.

Whatever the inevitable weakness of its second qualificatory tier of distinctions, Lieftinck's system works, not only for manuscripts of the Low Countries, for which

---

[61] Steinmann, 'Textualis formata', p. 306. Some palaeographers, such as M. B. Parkes, use the term Formata in a more precise sense, pointing to a more complicated letter structure (ductus) than in Libraria or Media. For this see below, pp. 137–8.

it was devised, but also for those of large parts of France and Germany. His idea of replacing specific categories of script-type based on the care or rapidity with which the scripts were executed by indications of the level of execution, used to qualify the primary classification, has removed distinctions which were in fact dead ends. It is hard to understand the many negative reactions uttered both at the time of the Paris meeting of 1953, where the system was presented to the scholarly world at large, and afterwards.[62] It is true that the different versions of the system as presented by Lieftinck himself lacked clarity and consistency. He not only first proposed Bastarda (after rejecting Brevitura) for the type he finally would give the non-historical name Hybrida, but he also originally used one term in two different senses: 'textualis' was the name of a type of script, but the term was also used to indicate a level of execution. This resulted in such confusing names as 'cursiva textualis' alongside 'cursiva bastarda'.[63]

These weaknesses were eagerly seized upon by his critics, most of whom seem to have been unable to appreciate the great merits of his system. The numerous reviews of his *Nomenclature* gave voice to feelings of exasperation and a remarkable lack of understanding on the part of some of the world's leading palaeographers. The unreasonable attack by Georges Despy has already been mentioned.[64] In 1956, S. J. P. van Dijk wrote: 'An attempt by M. G. I. Lieftinck…to devise a modern "palaeographical" terminology with the aid of existing terms, must necessarily add to the confusion'.[65] Alessandro Pratesi, too, was extremely critical and tried to demonstrate that traditional terms such as 'gotica francese' (which he thought had to be maintained) cannot be translated into the Lieftinck system.[66] The previous year the famous Belgian codicologist L. M. J. Delaissé was more favourable towards the Dutch palaeographer, but considered his system 'trop analytique et ainsi menacé[e] de subjectivisme' ('too analytical and thus prey to subjectivity').[67] Giorgio Cencetti was also extremely critical of the Lieftinck system.[68] More recently, Armando Petrucci still expressed criticism of Lieftinck's proposals for being 'eccessivamente complicate ed astratte' ('excessively complicated and abstract') and considered his system to be a 'macchinosa classificazione delle scritture di età gotica' ('an overly complicated classification of the handwriting of the Gothic period').[69] This opinion of one of the greatest of living palaeographers testifies to the

---

[62] A survey in Gumbert, *Kartäuser*, pp. 200–204. To these should be added Orlandelli, 'Origine', p. 58. See more thoughtful critical observations in Steinmann, 'Textualis formata', pp. 304–6.

[63] *Nomenclature*, p. 31 and n. 21, p. 32.   [64] Cf. n. 43.

[65] S. J. P. van Dijk, 'An Advertisement Sheet of an Early Fourteenth-Century Writing Master at Oxford', *Scriptorium*, 10 (1956), pp. 47–64; the quotation is on p. 55, n. 1.

[66] *La Bibliofilia*, 58 (1956), pp. 44–7.

[67] L. M. J. Delaissé, 'Le premier colloque international de paléographie à Paris en 1954 [*sic*]. Le problème de la nomenclature des écritures', *Scriptorium*, 9 (1955), pp. 290–3.

[68] Cencetti, *Lineamenti*, p. 479; Cencetti, *Compendio*, p. 79.

[69] Petrucci, *Descrizione*, pp. 58–9.

fundamentally irreconcilable approaches to palaeography that mark the discipline today.

EXPANDING THE LIEFTINCK SYSTEM

Of course Lieftinck's system is not perfect (no classification of scripts could be): it can account only very partially for the extremely rich variety of forms and styles, and it only works well for fourteenth- and fifteenth-century manuscripts from the Low Countries, the greater part of France and, to a more limited extent, Germany. Turning it into a European system, applicable to the main kinds of book script in use in the various countries during the last three centuries of the Middle Ages, requires an expansion in two directions.[70] The basic principles of such an expansion and adaptation of the Lieftinck system may be sketched as follows.

The three categories Textualis, Cursiva and Hybrida are insufficient to classify some widely disseminated script types, such as the very formal script called Bâtarde or Bourguignonne.[71] Scripts such as these often mix Cursiva and Hybrida elements (in other words the ascenders may or may not have loops). For this category, which may be added to the preceding three as a fourth type of script, Gumbert proposed the name Semihybrida.

The two other types which need to be added to make the system complete are scripts which are often – but not exclusively – to be found in books from peripheral areas or in those that date from the early period of Gothic script, that is, from the thirteenth century. One is a Cursiva with two-compartment **a**, the other a Textualis with single-compartment **a**. The former type is very well known in the British Isles, namely Anglicana, to which Malcolm Parkes has devoted an exquisite study;[72] but it is also found on the Continent as the usual form of handwriting in documents of the thirteenth and early fourteenth century. We shall call it Cursiva Antiquior, a term perhaps easier to handle than 'a-cursiva', the term proposed by Gumbert.

The second type, the Textualis with single-compartment **a**, was used mostly in Italy, but was also employed elsewhere. Italian palaeographers appear to use the term 'semigotica' for this type of Textualis, especially when it reveals a tendency towards the characteristics of Humanistic script, as with the so-called 'preumanistica' of

---

[70] A similar expansion, not only in space but also in time, was the aim of Julian Brown's system. See T. J. Brown, 'Names of Scripts: A Plea to all Medievalists', in *A Palaeographer's View: The Selected Writings of Julian Brown*, ed. J. Bately, M. P. Brown and J. Roberts, London and New York 1993, pp. 39–45; and especially M. P. Brown, *Guide*.

[71] Gumbert, *Kartäuser*, p. 210.   [72] Parkes, *Book Hands*.

Petrarch.[73] For obvious reasons, this name cannot be retained within our proposed nomenclature; instead a new term, Semitextualis, will be used.

The overwhelming majority of book scripts used in Europe from the thirteenth to the early sixteenth centuries can be covered by these six names: Textualis, Semitextualis, Cursiva (Recentior), Cursiva Antiquior, Semihybrida and Hybrida, as will be shown in the following pages. These names can be modified by one of the three terms indicating the level of execution, just as in the original Lieftinck system (although the term Libraria can often be omitted). The student should bear in mind the fact that it will never be possible to record objectively every nuance when dealing with something that is, in part, subjective.

The second direction in which the Lieftinck system needs to be amplified in order to make it complete and applicable to all European book scripts, is to bring it into agreement with the existing palaeographical nomenclature and to give all the existing script names a place within it. Where possible, the current, traditional names will often have to be added within parentheses to the two preceding terms to denote a distinctive variety of one or more of the six basic types of script. They will of course have to be defined using objective criteria just like the main categories. What is sometimes called 'Lettre bâtarde', for example, will thus be classified as either Cursiva Formata (Bastarda), Hybrida Formata (Bastarda) or Semihybrida Formata (Bastarda).

A final word should be said about Julian Brown's nomenclature as rationalized and expanded by his pupil Michelle Brown.[74] It was an admirable undertaking to try to extend Lieftinck's system to the whole of the Middle Ages, to create Latin names for all existing types and to bring into line all the different names in use for designating individual script types. It has been stressed above how pressing a problem this is. But because of its completeness and its commendable endeavour to be as precise as possible, this nomenclature has a tendency to become cumbersome, as Michelle Brown herself admits. Also, it is a matter of debate whether the Lieftinck categories can be applied to early medieval scripts.

CHARACTER, QUALITY AND PRACTICE OF HANDWRITING

The question whether script represents anything more than a means of communicating information by means of written signs is an interesting one.[75] The

---

[73] Petrucci, *Breve storia*, pp. 165 ff.; Cencetti, *Lineamenti*, p. 264.

[74] Brown, *Guide*.

[75] I pass over in silence the modern visions of handwriting as a social phenomenon. In addition to members of the Italian school, such as Petrucci and Bartoli Langeli, they are held by such scholars as Francisco Gimeno Blay in Spain and Albert d'Haenens in Belgium. 'Alfabetismo', 'literacy', 'Schriftlichkeit' are concepts beyond the reach of palaeography as studied in the present

fact that one is able to declare, often at first sight: 'this is a German Textualis, and this is a French one', must doubtless be based on different national traditions. These have sometimes been associated with the assumed national characters of the said peoples. In this way Hermann Delitsch in his well-known book alludes to 'völkerpsychologische Momente' as the basis for differences in the appearance of Gothic scripts.[76] This is not the place to pursue or refute the idea of writing as a clue to national psychology. Still less is it possible here to comment on the graphological and esoteric remarks on Gothic script provided by Erich Buchholz in his book *Schriftgeschichte als Kulturgeschichte*.[77] For him the age of Gothic script is marked by the symbols of broken ring and broken staff. Anyone who reads Buchholz's exposition of what he calls the 'graphic drama of the Middle Ages' is likely to become bemused and conclude that there can be no bridge between academic palaeography on the one hand, and hermetic and cosmological interpretation of handwriting on the other.

Returning to a more conventional but not unrelated issue, we must discuss briefly the concept of 'quality'. By this I do not mean the quality of an individual example of script (which Gumbert rightly distinguishes from the Lieftinckian categorization of the level of execution: a Currens can be of good quality, and a Formata of mediocre quality, depending on the scribe's aptitude in relation to his aim).[78] On the contrary, quality is considered here as a grade accorded to a script at a particular point in the history of its use, based (mostly tacitly) on aesthetic appreciation on the part of the modern onlooker and involving the concepts of rise, culmination and decline. The concept is currently found in the older books of palaeography. Reusens and Edward Maunde Thompson are among those authors who considered scripts living beings that are born, grow, attain maturity and then gradually fall into decay.[79] With Samuel Harrison Thomson, this idea developed

---

book. On all the possible meanings of 'script', see Bartoli Langeli, 'Ancora su paleografia' (see n. 6), p. 281.

[76] H. Delitsch, *Geschichte der abendländischen Schreibschriftformen*, Leipzig 1928, p. 142. He sees the 'levity of the French' as the explanation for the French predilection for what he calls 'lettre parisienne' (but what in fact is Bastarda). Delitsch is the prototype of the non-academic, artist palaeographer. His stimulating book, without any subdivision into chapters and illustrated with hundreds of facsimiles in the author's hand, has all the attractiveness and many of the dangers of the unscholarly.

[77] E. Buchholz, *Schriftgeschichte als Kulturgeschichte*, Bellnhausen über Gladenbach/Hessen, 1965, pp. 265 ff., 305. In Gothic script angularity of the curves and fracturing of the minims are explained as symbolic evidence for the victory of the monks over early medieval society; the horizontal aspect of the script stands for the feminine and the cult of the Virgin; the feminine lozenge replaced the masculine circle as the form of **o**; the fracturing of the minims in liturgical manuscripts is reflected in the genuflexion during Mass and stands for the destruction of the free will of the monks, etc.

[78] Gumbert, *Kartäuser*, pp. 218–19.

[79] Reusens, *Eléments*, p. 302, dealing with Gothic book script of the fifteenth century, writes: 'aussi marche-t-elle à grands pas vers la décadence complète'. Thompson, *Introduction*, p. 450, in the same way characterizes the fourteenth and fifteenth centuries as 'a period of gradual decadence from the high standard which had been attained in the twelfth and thirteenth centuries'. Stiennon (*Paléographie*,

into an obsession. From plate to plate, his aim was to show where there is progress, and where there is decline.[80]

More interesting for our purpose are the grounds on which Gothic script of the thirteenth century is considered by some to be of better quality than that of the subsequent centuries. For Maunde Thompson, these grounds comprise its 'exactness and rigidity'. Harrison Thomson, on the other hand, had a preference for the term 'vigour', but he also used the qualifications 'graceful' and 'chaste' for letters of what he called the 'early and middle gothic'.[81] The concept of quality will be used in the following pages, but not in the sense outlined above. In other words, the script of one period will not be considered as being inherently of a higher quality than that of other periods. Quality will, on the contrary, be used in the sense used by Gumbert, namely to refer to the ability of the individual scribe to write a specific type of script at the intended level of execution.

Finally, we should consider the unfortunate gap that exists between palaeography and calligraphy. The last century witnessed an ever-increasing flood of superbly illustrated publications by modern practitioners of handwriting, starting with Edward Johnston. Some of them, such as Alfred Fairbank, were also scholars. The Anglo-American world has, without doubt, taken the lead in this movement.[82] In their directions on how to write (ancient) handwritings today, the authors also discuss examples taken from medieval manuscripts. Their technical comment is often most enlightening (and will be used in the present book), but there are often serious shortcomings in their historical knowledge. To some extent palaeographers are to blame, since they have hitherto not been able to provide interested laymen with adequate answers to their questions about ancient scripts.[83] In a recent new book Michelle Brown has tried to bridge the gap through collaboration with a

---

p. 47) has criticized Thompson's approach. But even modern authors believe in this natural cycle. Battelli, *Lezioni*, p. 10, distinguishes for each script 'la formazione, la perfezione e la decadenza', and gives general features for each phase. Bischoff, *Palaeography*, p. 118, mentions 'a decline of the inner vitality' of later Carolingian script; Viviana Jemolo in *CMDIt*, 1, p. 16, uses the term 'decadenza' in relation to the handwriting of a manuscript dated 1499; Denholm-Young, *Handwriting*, p. 28, uses the term 'decay' in relation to fifteenth-century Textualis.

[80] How tricky this can be may appear from the following. Whereas a Gothic hand dated 1263 is said to be 'in its full vigour' (Thomson, *Bookhands*, pl. 11), another, dated 1277, shows 'the beginning of the decline of the gothic script' (pl. 12); in a German example of 1297, the 'monastic gothic is already showing the rapid decline of calligraphic control' (pl. 41). With reference to a manuscript as late as 1411, however, Thomson observes that 'the monastic gothic here shows its decline' (pl. 23). Obviously in his mind Gothic script had a very short flowering and a very long decline.

[81] Thompson, *Introduction*, pp. 450–6; Thomson, *Bookhands*, pl. 17; see also the preceding note.

[82] E. Johnston, *Writing and Illuminating and Lettering*, rev. edn, London 1939; A. Fairbank, *A Book of Scripts*, London 1952; A. Fairbank, *The Story of Handwriting*, London 1970. Among more recent works may be quoted those by Drogin, Harris and Knight mentioned in the Select Bibliography.

[83] J. P. Gumbert, 'Un calligraphe accuse la paléographie', *Gazette du Livre Médiéval*, 1 (1982), pp. 12–13. See also G. Noordzij, 'Kalligrafie und Paläografie', *Gazette du Livre Médiéval*, 4 (1984), pp. 18–19.

distinguished calligrapher,[84] but the mutual misunderstandings between palaeographers and calligraphers, between historians and practitioners, each with their own distinctive goals, are not likely to be easily removed, despite the growing interest among some palaeographers in the work of calligraphers and vice versa.[85]

---

[84] Brown and Lovett, *Source Book.*
[85] Petrucci, *Breve storia*, p. 14, with reference to Johnston.

I

The manuscript book in the late Middle Ages

CONDITIONS AND CENTRES OF PRODUCTION

In many respects the period from the twelfth century to the end of the fifteenth is different from the preceding centuries.[1] The development of commerce and industry contributed to the growth of urban populations and to the birth of urban culture, in the North replacing the mainly agrarian society of the early Middle Ages. Some of the urban population, and especially its upper ranks, received some form of education and were able to read and write. Urban administration, commerce and trade would have been impossible without these new writers and readers. In general, their education was of a practical nature and often did not include Latin. When requiring reading for business, devotion or pleasure, they consequently wanted books in the vernacular. As a rule, vernacular books usually exhibit a lower level of execution than Latin books and especially Bibles and liturgical books. This general observation is not invalidated by the appearance, from the fourteenth century onwards, of luxuriously made vernacular books commissioned by princes and the nobility.

---

[1] In the absence of good handbooks, this chapter aims only at presenting a brief general survey of this vast subject, largely based on the author's personal experience. From the abundant literature on the medieval manuscript book the following may be quoted: Bischoff, *Palaeography*, pp. 7–34; Stiennon, *Paléographie*, pp. 159–88; C. de Hamel, *A History of Illuminated Manuscripts*, 2nd edn, London 1994; J. Glénisson (ed.), *Le livre au Moyen Age*, Turnhout and Paris 1988; S. Hindman and J. D. Farquhar, *Pen to Press: Illustrated Manuscripts and Printed Books in the First Century of Printing*, College Park 1977; J. Lemaire, *Introduction à la codicologie*, Louvain-la-Neuve 1989 (Université Catholique de Louvain. Publications de l'Institut d'Etudes Médiévales. Textes, Etudes, Congrès, 9); Loeffler, *Einführung*; Mazal, *Buchkunst der Romanik*; Mazal, *Buchkunst der Gotik*; Mazal, *Lehrbuch*; B. A. Shailor, *The Medieval Book: Catalogue of an Exhibition at the Beinecke Rare Book & Manuscript Library, Yale University*, New Haven 1988; Schneider, *Paläographie*, pp. 101–88; A. Derolez, *Codicologie des manuscrits en écriture humanistique sur parchemin*, Turnhout 1984 (Bibliologia, 5–6); P. Busonero, M. A. Casagrande Mazzoli, L. Devoti and E. Ornato, *La fabbrica del codice. Materiali per la storia del libro nel tardo medioevo*, Rome 1999 (I Libri di Viella, 14); E. Ornato, *Apologia dell' apogeo*, Rome 2000 (I Libri di Viella, 22). Wattenbach, *Schriftwesen*, is still not replaced. The best general survey of codicological features, but limited to the early Middle Ages, is J. Vezin, 'La réalisation matérielle des manuscrits latins pendant le haut moyen âge', in *Codicologica*, 2 (1978), pp. 15–51. For the present chapter see especially Derolez, 'Observations on the Aesthetics'. In what follows only very few of the numerous codicological studies published during the last half century can be cited.

In the world of the religious orders, too, the changes were profound. The twelfth century may be called the greatest period of monastic culture and the last when that culture was dominant. It witnessed the production across Europe of huge numbers of well-made, mostly monumental monastic manuscripts. But in the thirteenth and fourteenth centuries the old monastic orders such as the Benedictines, the Cistercians and the Premonstratensians, generally established outside the cities, were in decline by comparison with the new orders of Friars; their place as the leading centres of learning was taken over by the university towns and cities. Monasteries came increasingly to depend upon gifts, bequests and purchases as means of acquiring books, and monastic book production became much more limited. The small order of the Carthusians, however, who claimed that they had never deviated from the old monastic ideals, maintained a greater level of scribal activity throughout the period in certain parts of Europe. They were cited as an example for reformed monastic life by such figures as Jean Gerson, the influential chancellor of the university of Paris (1363–1429), who successfully strove for the enhancement of religious and intellectual life in the Church and especially in the monasteries. The copying of manuscripts, however, which he insisted was a spiritual act, a belief which would be stressed again at the end of the century by the German abbot Johann Trithemius (1462–1516), could not be revived on any large scale. The economic, social and cultural condition of the age was against it, and after the invention of printing all attempts to re-establish and promote monastic scriptoria could not but be in vain. The numerous clerical scribes active in the fifteenth century, regular and secular, should as a rule be considered individual copyists, not members of organized scriptoria.

There were, however, religious houses where handwritten books were produced on a relatively large scale during the fourteenth and fifteenth centuries. The Brethren and Sisters of Common Life, exponents of the *Devotio moderna*, a reform movement in the Catholic Church founded by the Dutch cleric Gerard Groote (1340–1384), considered the writing of devotional books to be at the same time a means to promote Christian faith and an economic activity: the manuscripts produced by them were sold and the income thus raised contributed to the living of the community. In the related convents of Regular Canons of Saint Augustine affiliated to the Windesheim Congregation copying was likewise exercised on a regular basis for export as well as for their own libraries. The leading orders of the time, the Mendicants or Friars, on the contrary used many books for study and preaching purposes, but as a rule did not produce them.

Many books were, then, produced as part of organized lay commercial activity by individuals. Two new kinds of book production centres may be distinguished: those organized by universities and lay commercial enterprises.

The new type of educational institution, the university, needed a system to provide masters and students rapidly with correct and reliable textbooks. The age-old, time-consuming technique consisted usually in copying one manuscript (the *exemplar*) as a whole in order to make a new manuscript and was too slow to meet the new requirements. The revolutionizing technique of the *pecia*, introduced in the thirteenth century, worked as follows:[2] the *exemplar* of each textbook, duly corrected to remove scribal and other errors, was deposited in unbound state in the office of a university employee, called *librarius* or *stationarius*. This official possessed a list of all the *exemplaria* entrusted to his care, in which the number of quires (*peciae*) of each was recorded, as well as the rent to be paid for a *pecia*. A student or a scribe working at the order of a student could rent one *pecia* of a given *exemplar* for a short period, whilst another scribe could copy another quire of the same book during the same period. As the *peciae* normally comprised quires of no more than four folios (*binios*), each *exemplar* consisted of a large number of *peciae* and could consequently be copied simultaneously by a large number of students or scribes. This way copies were not only made much more rapidly than by the traditional technique, but the correctness of the *apopecia* (i.e. the manuscript copied from the *exemplar*) was also guaranteed to a certain extent, as all copies were made from corrected *exemplaria*.

The *pecia* system worked well in the thirteenth and fourteenth centuries in Paris and Bologna. For reasons unknown it was abandoned in the fifteenth.

Manuscripts produced as part of organized lay commercial activity were copied according to traditional methods, but standardized patterns and techniques were introduced in order to save time and produce more economically even the most lavish books. Also in contrast with his predecessor in the early medieval monastic scriptorium, where most activities took place in the same room, the individual in charge, the late medieval *librarius*, was much more an entrepreneur, who took commissions and distributed the work among scribes, rubricators, illuminators and binders, generally working at other locations, often within the family household. At least this was the situation in major cities.

As a rule copying was done on commission, but in the fifteenth century books that were heavily in demand, such as Books of Hours, were probably also sold ready-made or half finished, the illumination to be added subsequently according to the wishes and the purse of the buyer.

Although the production of manuscripts in Europe reached its high point in the third quarter of the fifteenth century,[3] it rapidly faced serious competition

---

[2] Boyle, *Medieval Latin Palaeography*, nos. 1745–61; Destrez, *La pecia*; L. J. Bataillon, B. G. Guyot and R. H. Rouse (eds.), *La production du livre universitaire au Moyen Age. Exemplar et pecia*, Paris 1988 (Centre Régional de Publications de Paris).

[3] See the graphs in C. Bozzolo, D. Coq and E. Ornato, 'La production du livre en quelques pays d'Europe occidentale aux XIVe et XVe siècles', in E. Ornato, *La face cachée du livre médiéval. L'histoire du livre vue par Ezio Ornato, ses amis et ses collègues*, Rome 1997, pp. 197–226 (originally published in 1984); see also Derolez, *Codicologie* (see n. 1), I, p. 14.

from printing during the final decades of the century. By 1500 most commercial organizers of manuscript production had ceased to operate. The new directions in illumination, which can be observed in books of this period and which gave rise to the last flowering of manuscript painting (seen, for example, in the so-called Ghent-Bruges School), should no doubt be interpreted as an endeavour, by the few remaining workshops, to attract the attention of wealthy patrons by offering luxurious manuscripts of totally new conception and alluring splendour, not to be equalled by the printed book. By 1530 even this branch of manuscript production had come to an end.

MATERIALS[4]

Parchment and paper are the basic materials of the late medieval book. Wax-tablets (*tabulae ceratae, tabellae, pugillares*) were in general use for first drafts and school exercises, but are not books properly speaking.[5] Parchment,[6] in use during the entire period, differs on the whole from early medieval parchment in the uniformity of its appearance and quality within each book: its preparation by specialized craftsmen established in the cities resulted in batches of parchment of even quality and the same thickness, stiffness and colour. Calfskin (*carta vitulina*, vellum) was the largest in size and had an even, sturdy surface, its hair side and flesh side having approximately the same white colour. Sheepskin (*carta ovina, froncina*) was sometimes greasy or wrinkly, the hair side mostly yellowish, the flesh side white. The hair side of goatskins (*carta caprina*) is marked by the characteristic 'morocco' grain, often still showing the dark spots of the animal's hair. The extremely thin and white parchment as found in the so-called Parisian Bibles of the thirteenth century is often called uterine vellum (*carta abortiva, virginea*); it is doubtful whether this writing-material, apart from a few exceptions, was really made from the skin of unborn calves or lambs. The widespread use of goatskin in Italy explains why the average size of Italian parchment manuscripts is smaller than that of Northern European books.

Paper came to be used in addition to parchment as a material for books in the thirteenth century, but it was not until the fourteenth and more especially the fifteenth century that paper manuscripts became really numerous. The relatively low cost of the new, mechanically produced material and an element of distrust in it were the cause of its being used primarily for books of a lower class that

[4] See the handbooks mentioned in n. 1 and *Ancient and Medieval Book Materials and Techniques*, ed. M. Maniaci and P. F. Munafò, Vatican City 1993 (Studi e Testi, 357–8).

[5] See *Les tablettes à écrire de l'Antiquité à l'époque moderne*, ed. E. Lalou, Turnhout 1992 (Bibliologia, 12).

[6] See *Pergament. Geschichte, Struktur, Restaurierung, Herstellung*, ed. P. Rück, Sigmaringen 1991 (Historische Hilfswissenschaften, 2).

were not expected to last for a long time. Parchment continued to be used for deluxe manuscripts and for codices exposed to intensive use, such as liturgical and school books. This traditional material was preferred for illuminated manuscripts in particular, as it offered a sturdier base for the application of thick opaque colour layers and gold leaf on gesso ground than the thinner and more flexible paper.[7]

Not surprisingly, vernacular manuscripts made for the use of the ordinary laity and considered lower status than the Latin codices made for clerical use, came to be written more and more on paper. During the fifteenth century even quite luxurious, illuminated books were written on the new material, albeit with the illumination consisting mostly of pen and ink drawings with wash colours. The fact, however, that paper books were deemed cheaper than their parchment counterparts, is generally reflected in their language, content and script.

STRUCTURE

It will remain difficult to make reliable codicological observations about the book in the late Middle Ages until more statistical enquiries have been undertaken and their results published.

Quire structures[8] (a feature that normally does not influence the appearance of the book and remains hidden from the reader) underwent an important change with the introduction of paper. The relative thinness of the new material often induced producers of books to use quires of more than four bifolia, indeed of six or up to twelve and even more bifolia. In mixed codices parchment was routinely used to form the inner and outer bifolia, interspersed with four or more paper bifolia. In their effort to prevent wear after sewing, the makers of this kind of mixed codex used the more resistant material at the most vulnerable places of the quire. In doing this they broke an age-old rule for the making of books: that at every opening within the book the two facing pages should have the same appearance (see below, p. 33). In addition, the natural shrinking of the parchment over time as opposed to the stability of the paper came to create unevenness in the size of the pages. The use of parchment strips in the middle of the innermost paper bifolium was a cheaper as well as more elegant solution to strengthen the spine fold.

It should also be noted that, long before the introduction of paper, the parchment quires, too, had undergone an increase in the number of bifolia. During the thirteenth and fourteenth centuries in particular an impressive proportion of

---

[7] J. J. G. Alexander, *Medieval Illuminators and their Methods of Work*, New Haven and London 1992, p. 35; for the contrary opinion see Lemaire, *Introduction* (see n. 1), p. 13.
[8] P. Busonero, 'La fascicolazione del manoscritto nel basso medioevo', in *La fabbrica del codice* (see n. 1), pp. 31–139.

manuscripts were produced with sexternios (six bifolia, 12 leaves). In the thirteenth century even quires of 12 bifolia (24 leaves) were used in parchment manuscripts, especially in the famous small Parisian Bibles written in so-called 'pearl script' (see below, p. 100) on extremely thin parchment. In the latter case the use of quires consisting of so many bifolia is explicable, but the overwhelming number of sexternios in larger codices made with ordinary parchment remains unexplained. By the fifteenth century, this preference for longer quires had disappeared and, as far as parchment manuscripts are concerned, quaternios (four bifolia, eight leaves) became once more the usual form of quire in Northern Europe.

In Italy, on the contrary, from at least the fourteenth century onwards, one may observe a strong predilection for quinios (quires consisting of five bifolia, ten leaves). No explanation has yet been given for this change. At first sight the quinio has the disadvantage of not being obtainable by simple folding of the sheet or the skin. It would have complicated the making of quires in the quarto (two folds) and in the octavo (three folds) formats. But we may suppose that in a country where commerce was so highly developed, the quires were in that period generally bought ready-made in the shop of the *cartolaio*: in a specialized workshop preparing large quantities of parchment, it cannot have made much difference whether quinios or quaternios were to be produced.

Two rules were strictly observed in assembling parchment quires. The first is the so-called Rule of Gregory, according to which the disposition of the parchment in the codex must be such, that, wherever the book is opened, flesh side faces flesh side and hair side faces hair side.[9] The second rule was invariably followed during the late Middle Ages, and required the outer side of the quires to be the flesh side. In most codices up to the twelfth century, by contrast, the hair side was used for the first and last page of each quire.[10] This change may have resulted from a change in the choice of page for the opening display page of the manuscript. In the late Middle Ages, this display page, often incorporating the major miniature or initial, was in principle folio 1r, whereas prior to the thirteenth century, it was usually folio 1v. There were good reasons no doubt for selecting the better-looking side, namely the flesh side, for that page.

Foliation remained rare till the end of the Middle Ages, but some form or other of quire numbering may generally be found, as long as trimming by successive binders has not entirely removed its remnants. *Quire-marks*, consisting of a Roman numeral (more rarely a Capital letter), written in the lower margin of the first or

[9] Discussed in L. Gilissen, *Prolégomènes à la codicologie. Recherches sur la construction des cahiers et la mise en page des manuscrits médiévaux*, Ghent 1977 (Les Publications de Scriptorium, 7), pp. 14–20.
[10] M. Palma, 'Modifiche di alcuni aspetti materiali della produzione libraria latina nei secoli XII e XIII', *Scrittura e Civiltà*, 12 (1988), pp. 119–33.

more often the last page of the quire, are the norm in the twelfth-century books and are not uncommon in those of the thirteenth. Owing to their large script and their position at a distance from the lower edge, they were rarely trimmed away. We seldom see them in fourteenth- and more especially fifteenth-century books. By that time they had mostly been replaced by *signatures*, a numbering system that ensured the order not only of the quires, but also of the bifolia within each quire. These take various forms, but the most common type consists of a combination of a letter and a numeral, the former marking the quire, the latter the bifolium. They were written on the first half of the quire, the second half being automatically in the right order when the first half is. For example: 'b2' would be written in the lower outer corner of the recto of the second folio of the second quire of a given manuscript, the first quire of which would be marked 'a'.[11] The mostly tiny script and pointed nib used for these signatures, and their position so close to the edges of the leaves, have been the cause of their being easily overlooked and frequently trimmed off.

The introduction of signatures made it easy to take the quires apart and hand them over to various craftsmen such as rubricators and illuminators, often working in places other than where the copying had been done, and then to put them back together once these craftsmen had finished their job.

Catchwords were provided in most manuscripts from the thirteenth century onwards. They appeared in Spain as early as the tenth century,[12] and consist of the first word(s) of a quire's text being repeated in the lower margin of the last page of the preceding quire (like quire-marks, catchwords consequently ensure only the sequence of the quires, not of the individual bifolia). Catchwords were usually written horizontally at the right of the lower margin or close to the fold. In Italian books their normal place is in the middle of the lower margin. In the fifteenth century they may be written vertically, running downwards along the right-hand side of the lower margin, close to the fold or to the inner vertical ruling line(s), a practice which doubtless betrays Italian Humanistic influence.[13]

LAYOUT

The layout and ruling of the Gothic manuscript can take many different forms and involve various techniques.[14] As far as the techniques are concerned, *hard-point ruling*, which had been the normal technique during the early Middle Ages, gave

---

[11] For other systems, see, for example, Loeffler, *Einführung*, p. 67.

[12] J. Vezin, 'Observations sur l'emploi des réclames dans les manuscrits latins', *Bibliothèque de l'Ecole des Chartes*, 125 (1967), pp. 5–33; E. E. Rodríguez Díaz, 'El uso del reclamo en España (reinos occidentales)', *Scriptorium*, 53 (1999), pp. 3–30.

[13] See Derolez, *Codicologie* (see n. 1), 1, pp. 59–63.

[14] H.-J. Martin and J. Vezin (eds.), *Mise en page et mise en texte du livre manuscrit*, [Paris] 1990.

way to *lead ruling* in the course of the twelfth century. In the period considered here it was invariably traced on the hair side of the parchment, so that the ridges appear on the flesh side. In this way hard-point ruling contributed to the harmony of the 'opening' (the two facing pages), by reinforcing the harmony produced by the Rule of Gregory. It had the disadvantage of becoming visible when covered with paint and thus interfering with any pictures. Once the otherwise barely visible relief ruling of the Carolingian codex had finally been replaced by coloured ruling, the ruling assumed a position of importance as an indispensable element within the decoration of the codex, from then on until the end of the Middle Ages. (This explains why incunables and even sixteenth-century printed books were sometimes ruled by hand.) Instead of the grey colour of lead (plummet) ruling, one can often observe brownish lines, obviously produced with a crayon. From the thirteenth century onwards *ink ruling* appears in addition to lead or crayon ruling. Red or pink ink was preferred to black for deluxe codices in particular, except in the Mediterranean area.

As was the case with the earlier hard-point ruling, coloured ruling followed a complete set of *prickings*, mostly in the upper, the lower and the outer margin, one prick corresponding to one horizontal line (1, see p. 46). These prickings were applied to the folded quire, in order to obtain the same pattern on all pages, the rectos being a mirror image of the versos. A row of prickings in the inner margin, parallel to those in the outer margin, seems to be peculiar to thirteenth-century codices (2).[15]

In the vertical row(s) of prickings some prickings may be double, in other words, at certain points in the row, two holes were made next to each other (3). These double prickings would assist the person who had to trace the ruling on the open bi-folium or on the open sheet by indicating where the horizontal ruling was to extend into the margins.[16] The pattern would be apparent from the outset (on patterns see p. 37). The intended pattern might include, for example, two horizontal through lines (i.e. lines extending across the page beyond the vertical rulings) at the top, then a series of short lines stopping at the vertical ruling, two through lines in the middle, and after a second series of short lines, a further two through lines at the bottom. The craftsman would not know where to trace his third and his penulti-mate through lines unless these positions were indicated by a distinct mark: this took the form of the double pricking. In small-sized luxury books, such as Books of Hours, the prickings were mostly placed so as to be trimmed away during binding.

---

[15] Prickings in the inner margin, parallel to prickings in the outer margin, were already a common feature in Insular manuscripts. See Vezin, 'La réalisation matérielle' (see n. 1), pp. 30–1.

[16] There is consequently nothing mysterious about them, as Lemaire, *Introduction* (see n. 1), p. 121, thinks.

We as yet know little about the techniques introduced in the late Middle Ages in order to rule manuscripts in a more economical way. *Frame-ruling*, i.e. tracing only four lines to delimit the text area (six for two-column manuscripts), is seen in many books but was evidently not an adequate solution when a certain degree of formality was required (4, 5). Although some scribes seem to have developed a remarkable skill in making beautiful codices using this simplest of ruling patterns,[17] frame-ruling usually made it difficult to keep the written lines parallel and evenly spaced, and more especially to obtain the same number of lines throughout the codex.

In recent decades attention has been drawn to full rulings (i.e. rulings with at least one horizontal line traced for each line of text), which were *not* based on the traditional full pricking as sketched above. One technique, using a limited number of prickings, has been called *rake ruling*.[18] Here the horizontal lines were not traced one after the other, but in groups of five, six or more lines by means of a ruling instrument featuring five, six or more pens or points. This instrument was moved alongside a ruler, itself following prickings in the outer margins, which had only to be applied at every five, six or more lines (6). This time-saving device was used for the most part in a combination of techniques: the vertical lines were traced in lead in the traditional way, and afterwards the horizontal lines were traced in ink by means of the rake. If a total number of lines was desired which was not a multiple of the number of pens in the rake, additional lines could be traced in the traditional way at the bottom of the page, below the rake-ruled portion, using prickings for each line.

One will note that ruling patterns produced by this technique naturally have no horizontal through lines. When lines extending into the margins are found, they must have been added, in ink or in lead, above and below the rake-ruled portion, or they may have been obtained by extending manually the upper and lower lines to the left and to the right.

It would appear that Italy developed even more sophisticated systems of rake ruling, in which instruments were used to trace in one motion half the number or even the full number of horizontal rulings, in other words some 15 to 30 lines, thereby reducing the number of prickings for the horizontal lines to no more than one or two.[19]

---

[17] There are many examples in *CMDB*, II and III.

[18] J. P. Gumbert, 'Ruling by Rake and Board', in *The Role of the Book in Medieval Culture: Proceedings of the Oxford International Symposium, 1982*, ed. P. Ganz, Turnhout 1986 (Bibliologia, 3), pp. 44–8.

[19] Derolez, *Codicologie* (see n. 1), I, pp. 77–8; A. Derolez, 'Ruling in Quattrocento Manuscripts: Types and Techniques', in *Septuaginta Paulo Spunar oblata*, ed. J. K. Kroupa, Prague 2000, pp. 291–301.

Board ruling, which required no prickings at all, appears in fifteenth-century manuscripts, mostly on paper, but also, at least in Italy, on parchment.[20] This is a relief ruling (like hard-point ruling) obtained by pressing or rubbing the paper or parchment bifolium onto a wooden or cardboard board, onto which strings have been mounted in the mirror-image of the ruling pattern to be obtained. The result is an impression of faint lines, less sharp in their outlines than those obtained by hard point, and never crossing each other (either the vertical, or more often the horizontal lines, are necessarily interrupted at the crossings). In contrast with hard point, too, the distribution of furrows and ridges mostly does not respect the rule that furrows should face furrows and ridges should face ridges. Board ruling doubtless first found favour in Humanistic circles in Italy, where hard-point ruling had been reintroduced by the early Humanists.

Further research will no doubt bring more clarity to our understanding of the use and distribution of the two last-named techniques.

The *ruling patterns* too deserve much more study before satisfactory data can be given about the geographical and chronological scope of their use and distribution.[21] In general, two-column rulings were preferred throughout the period under consideration, but in the fifteenth century a renewed preference among some for layouts with long lines is detectable, probably under Italian Humanistic influence. Gothic books reflect an aesthetic that appreciated the sense of verticality created by the two narrow rectangular text blocks of the two-column layout. The Humanistic manuscript, on the contrary, imitated the typically one-column layout of its Carolingian models and deviated only exceptionally from the broad and square ('Romanesque') form of this type of layout. The use of cursive scripts as book hands may also have contributed to the use of long lines instead of two columns.

As far as the *vertical ruling lines* are concerned, an evolution took place from the twelfth to the fifteenth century, involving the gradual replacement of the double lines at both sides of the written area by single lines (7, 8). Double vertical lines are useful in a layout in which initials and majuscules of sentences opening on a new line are placed in or protrude into the margin, as is generally the case in Carolingian codices. As at that time the ruling technique was hard point, the double lines, only

---

[20] Gumbert, 'Ruling by Rake and Board' (see n. 18); Derolez, *Codicologie* (see n. 1), I, pp. 72–6; Derolez, 'Ruling in Quattrocento Manuscripts' (see n. 19).

[21] J. Leroy, *Les types de réglure des manuscrits grecs*, Paris 1976 (Institut de Recherche et d'Histoire des Textes. Bibliographies, Colloques, Travaux Préparatoires); J. Leroy and J.-H. Sautel, *Répertoire de réglures dans les manuscrits grecs sur parchemin*, Turnhout 1993; M. Dukan, *La réglure des manuscrits hébreux au Moyen Age*, Paris 1988 (Centre Régional de Publication de Paris); Derolez, *Codicologie* (see n. 1), I, pp. 66–70, 85–120. L. Gilissen, 'Codicologie. A propos de publications récentes', *Scrittura e Civiltà*, 10 (1986), pp. 289–302 (p. 296), and Lemaire, *Introduction* (see n. 1), p. 124, underestimate the importance of ruling patterns.

required at the left-hand side of the text area, appeared necessarily at its right-hand side as well. The resulting pattern was originally taken over in the lead and ink rulings of the subsequent period. But this 'open' conception, which also admitted open spaces in the text area, such as at the end of paragraphs, gradually gave way to a typical Gothic 'closed' layout, without open spaces (hence the frequent use of line-fillers) and without any text part protruding beyond the text area. Since initials and majuscules were now placed within the text area, double vertical lines became superfluous.

In manuscripts of the transitional period, namely those of the twelfth and thirteenth centuries, one may often observe that the distance between the vertical lines no longer equals the distance between two horizontal lines, as had been the custom, but has become smaller. In fifteenth-century manuscripts double vertical lines reappear occasionally, again no doubt under Humanistic influence.

The following general observations may be made about the *horizontal through lines*. During the late twelfth and the thirteenth centuries there seems to have been a special predilection for intricate ruling patterns (at least for manuscripts belonging to the higher levels of execution). Double, triple or quadruple through lines may appear at the top, in the middle and at the bottom of the written area, and supplementary lines were added in the margins, thus creating a complicated grid of horizontal and vertical lines, which evokes the buttresses, flying buttresses and pinnacles of Gothic architecture (9). While some of these lines could be used for the writing of running headlines, foliation, marginal notes and catchwords, others, such as the through lines in the middle of the page, had no practical purpose at all. Such practices, as a whole, may be interpreted as playing an important role in the decoration of the page. In those manuscripts of the fourteenth and fifteenth centuries in which the practice of extending lines into the margins was continued, such complicated patterns tend to be absent.[22] Most fourteenth- and fifteenth-century manuscripts reveal a preference for simple patterns of ruling with a limited number of through lines or with no through lines at all.

Special patterns were devised for poetical works and for glossed books. Scribes of the Gothic period had a preference for writing *poetry* in such a way that the first letters of all verses (normally majuscules) were placed in a vertical column at some distance from the remainder of the verse. That is why manuscripts of poetry frequently have an asymmetrical layout, in which double or triple vertical lines are traced at the left of the text column, and not at the right (10), a pattern which cannot be obtained by relief ruling.

As medieval education in general, and that of the schools and universities in particular, was based around commentating upon authoritative texts, *glossed*

---

[22] For a few examples of complicated patterns in the fifteenth century, see: *CMDNL*, II, pls. 578–9; *CMDB*, II, pls. 220–1, 351.

manuscripts, containing text and commentary, played a prominent role.[23] The process of development from the manuscript with free marginal and interlinear glosses up to the integrated school book containing the text and the finished gloss, involved a long series of intermediate stages and various solutions to the problem of arranging text and relevant commentary on the same page. As the commentary was supposed to be written in a smaller handwriting, generally of a lower level of script than the text, the arrangement of both text and commentary on the page necessitated complicated ruling patterns, with narrow horizontal ruling for the commentary, wide ruling for the text. As the amount of commentary in relation to the text constantly changes, a system had to be created to keep the same overall written area, in which the ratio of text surface to gloss could be changed at will. The more sophisticated the conception of the glossed manuscript, the more complicated its ruling pattern had to be and the more calculation required to design each page.

An observation made years ago by Neil Ker about the 'change in scribal practice', which took place in the thirteenth century, remains of foremost importance:[24] the early medieval practice of starting the writing of the page on the top line (a natural procedure), was gradually and definitively replaced by the practice of starting below the top line. In almost all late medieval manuscripts (with the exception of codices in Humanistic script and some glossed books), the text column is thus delimited on all four sides by a straight line, in conformity with the 'Gothic' preference for enclosed areas. Not only was the text block framed, but the line of text was as well, as there was a strong tendency to place the handwriting not *on* the line, but well *above* it. This tendency is best observed in the most formal manuscripts, in Textualis Formata. Manuscripts in one or other variety of cursive script will often reveal it far less clearly, just as they more often display ruling patterns with long lines rather than a two-column format.

DECORATION

The decoration is an essential part of the medieval book and has been given a great deal of attention by scholars, especially insofar as the higher, more artistic forms of illumination are concerned. This means that for the late Middle Ages, a period in which pictures in manuscripts took on an increasingly important role,

---

[23] G. Powitz, 'Textus cum commento', *Codices Manuscripti*, 5 (1979), pp. 80–9; C. F. R. de Hamel, *Glossed Books of the Bible and the Origins of the Paris Booktrade*, Woodbridge and Dover, NH, 1984; J.-H. Sautel, 'Essai de terminologie de la mise en page des manuscrits à commentaire', *Gazette du Livre Médiéval*, 35 (1999), pp. 17–31.

[24] N. R. Ker, 'From "above top line" to "below top line": A Change in Scribal Practice', *Celtica*, 5 (1960), pp. 13–16; Palma, 'Modifiche' (see n. 10), *passim*.

the non-illustrative, decorative elements, which have been studied so intensely for earlier periods, have generally been neglected in art historical research. In this period initials and other elements of decoration in the codex gradually lost their prominent place and became more and more standardized in accordance with the more rapid procedures of commercial production. The place for artistic innovation came to be the pictures (miniatures). In order to make these images as realistic as possible, their size was increased and they became free-standing elements lacking the constraints of the rest of the decorative scheme.

The *highlighting* of the opening letters of sentences was not an innovation of the late Middle Ages (examples can already be found in Insular manuscripts), but it became a standard feature in Gothic manuscripts, from whence it was taken over as part of the finishing of many fifteenth- and early sixteenth-century printed books. The density of the Gothic text column and the absence of open space within it required the provision of additional visual clues to indicate where each sentence began. These took the form of marking the beginning of each sentence by filling up or stroking the majuscule with colour.

In the twelfth century the use of such highlighting was not widespread. When present, the colours may vary (including yellow and green, for example). From the thirteenth century onwards the feature became quite common and the only colour employed was red ('rubrication'). The rubrication of the majuscule that began a sentence was as a rule extended to the majuscule placed immediately after a decorated initial. In the fifteenth century red was often replaced by the softer yellow, most probably under Italian influence.

Paragraph marks in one colour (red) or in alternating colours (red and blue, gold and blue) had the same function as highlighting when placed within the text: that of clarifying the text's structure.

Throughout the Middle Ages the distinctive colour of the headings was red ('rubrics'). In the Romanesque period (the twelfth and early thirteenth centuries), however, headings were often written in lines of alternating colours: red, green, yellow, violet... Whereas the scribes and rubricators of that period normally followed the early medieval tradition of using majuscules (Capitals, Uncials, or mixed Capitals and Uncials) for the headings, those of the Gothic period would usually write them in the same minuscule script as the text. The distorted character of Gothic majuscules generally made them unfit for writing a continuous text (see below, pp. 183–4).

Although retaining their importance in twelfth- and thirteenth-century books, elaborate *initials* rapidly lost their significance when mass production started. The study of the more developed Romanesque and early Gothic initials belongs to art history; here we shall instead confine ourselves to some consideration of the minor initials and to the later Gothic initials as a whole.

Initials not only contribute to the beauty of a book, they also had the essential function of underlining the structure of its text. Even more than in the early Middle Ages, when the decoration of the book was sometimes marked more by an element of fantasy or by considerations of display, a hierarchy of initials came to be employed in the late Middle Ages, in which their type as well as their size (their height is expressed in the number of lines they occupy) played a role.[25] Each level of subdivision of a given text (book, chapter, paragraph) would be indicated by the appropriate kind of initial in the appropriate set size, an exception being made only for the first initial of the text, which was of variable size, although as a rule larger than the others and often of a higher rank in the hierarchy.

In the twelfth century the minor initials were drawn in coloured ink: red, yellow, green, blue, violet... Their decoration was mostly quite simple and consisted, for example, of globular or foliate extensions in the same colour (pl. 6). During the later part of that century, flourishes began to be applied in and around these initials, in the same or in a contrasting colour (pl. 13). The *flourished initial* thus created was to become a standard feature of the Gothic manuscript till the end of the Middle Ages, in addition to the original *plain initials* (pls. 36, 37, 81, 95 etc.). The flourishing, simple and quite crude in the beginning, developed over time into a delicate tracery involving various patterns, some doubtless of a vegetal nature but mostly impossible to define (pls. 18–20, 22, 35, 45, 60, 150 etc.).[26] The standard colours, from the thirteenth century onwards, are as follows: for the initials alternating red and blue, for the penwork the contrasting colours blue and red, mostly, however, in a different shade, such as black and violet. Italian (and Spanish) flourished initials are often distinguished by penwork consisting of parallel rows of vertical lines (pls. 65, 71, 130). In deluxe manuscripts of the fourteenth and fifteenth centuries the red ink of the initials (but not that of the flourishes) was often replaced with gold.

A still higher rank in the hierarchy could be obtained by combining the alternating colours of the flourished initial in the *littera duplex* (pls. 99, 141, 150): here the body of the initial is in red and blue ink, the two colours interlocking but separated by a blank space. Flourishing in the interior of and around the *littera duplex* was as a rule executed in such a way that the 'blue' flourishing faces the red parts of the letter, and the 'red' flourishing faces the blue parts. Another way of enhancing

[25] Hindman and Farquhar, *Pen to Press* (see n. 1), pp. 67–72; Muzerelle, *Vocabulaire*, pp. 171–3; A. Derolez, 'Les fondements typologiques d'une classification et d'une description des initiales dans les manuscrits du bas moyen âge', in *Ornementation typographique et bibliographie historique. Actes du Colloque de Mons, 1987*, ed. M.-Th. Isaac, Mons and Brussels 1988, pp. 17–26; Derolez, 'Observations on the Aesthetics'.
[26] S. Scott-Fleming, *Pen Flourishing in Thirteenth-Century Manuscripts*, Leiden 1989 (Litterae Textuales); P. Stirnemann, 'Fils de la vierge. L'initiale à filigranes parisienne, 1140–1314', *Revue de l'Art*, 90 (1990), pp. 58–73; *Kriezels, aubergines en takkebossen. Randversiering in Noordnederlandse handschriften uit de vijftiende eeuw*, ed. A. S. Korteweg, Zutphen 1992.

the level and the beauty of the flourished initial consisted in colouring part of the background, thus turning the flourishes into a coloured pen and ink drawing.

For the ranks above this series of initials traced in ink, the classic hierarchy employed painted initials, created with paint and gold leaf. A lesser type is the so-called *dentelle initial* comprising a letter in gold on a background mostly alternating red and blue (pls. 139, 158). The more elevated (and more frequently employed) type is the *foliate initial*, in which the letter is red or blue, painted on a gold background and filled with curving tendrils with spiky leaves, the latter generally unnaturalistic in shape and colour (pls. 30, 43, 96). In both types of initial the paint is covered with delicate filigree, mostly in white ink, so that the colours appear as pink and pale blue instead of red and blue.

The *historiated initial* was the highest in rank. It is in most cases a foliate initial in which the tendrils and leaves have been replaced by a picture related to the text (pl. 53). Given the necessarily reduced dimensions of the eye (or counter) of the letter in the narrower proportions of Gothic script (and the fact that such letters as **A**, **B**, **E**, **I**, **M**, etc. do not constitute ideal frames for pictures), one can easily understand why historiated initials during the fourteenth and fifteenth centuries became less frequent.

The hierarchy sketched above should not be taken to imply that all ranks would be represented in one and the same manuscript. This is almost never the case: some of the intermediate levels are often missing. Indeed, most texts do not require more than two or three levels of initials, and the upper ones were only appropriate where luxury was required. One never, however, finds a lesser subdivision of a work beginning with an initial of a higher rank than a main subdivision. For deluxe books, like fifteenth-century Books of Hours, there would be, for example, three grades of initials: foliate, dentelle and flourished. More simple books usually made do with two grades: *litterae duplices* and flourished initials. Luxury Dutch Books of Hours might keep to the lower triad *litterae duplices*, flourished initials, plain initials, etc.

Taken as a whole, the typology sketched above holds true for books from the central area of production of late Gothic manuscripts, i.e. Northern France and the Low Countries, with the exception of the most luxurious manuscripts. The system followed in England was slightly different, it was much more so in Germany, Spain, Portugal and Italy (pls. 58, 86).

In the last decades of the fifteenth century, when the competition of the printed book became obvious, the system was abandoned and new forms of initials, with new colours and new hierarchies, were created.

The general shape of all Gothic initials underwent a remarkable evolution between the twelfth and the fifteenth centuries. In the early period the scribe left an appropriate space free for initials depending upon their shape: half of an isosceles triangle for **A** and **V**, a semi-circle for **O**, irregular shapes for **P** and **Q**, etc. In commercial production, conditioned by the division of labour, such a technique was no doubt considered cumbersome, and from the thirteenth century onwards scribes began to leave a rectangular space free for every initial except **J** (i.e. the lengthened variant of **I**), which could be placed in the margin. As the new initials were at first located half in the margin, half in the text area, this did not result in any severe distortion of the letter bodies: the shafts of **F**, **H** (= **h**), **P** were placed in the margin, so that these letters were taller and looked narrower than the letters without ascenders or descenders, such as **D**, **E**, **M**, **N**, **O**.

The evolution (and the perfection of the 'economic' Gothic page) achieved its zenith when all initials were placed entirely within the text area and occupied the same space, whether **I**, **M** or **P**. The initials were thus reduced to standard sizes and shapes. Their extremely fat, round and compact shapes and exaggerated serifs, emphasizing their 'closed' character, contrast with the narrow and angular forms of Gothic Textualis. Their Northern Italian origin (in German they are called 'Lombarden') is not proven. In fact, their characteristic shape can already be found in Romanesque manuscript decoration. It merely became exaggerated and distorted over the course of time.

Borders or marginal decoration are the most typical form of decoration in the Gothic manuscript. They have their origin in two fundamental characteristics of the Gothic book: the use of vegetal decoration and the preference for enclosed areas. As the 'higher' initials in the Romanesque and Gothic manuscript consist essentially of vegetal elements, it is natural that they should grow shoots in the margin. These shoots developed into tendrils with leaves, covering the margins and tending to surround the text area. In later phases (especially in the fifteenth century) acanthus leaves, flowers and fruit were often added to or replaced the original tendrils and leaves; the link with the initial would generally be severed, so that borders might also be placed around pictures. At the same time the free-flowing border would be framed within straight lines, resulting in decorative rectangles, brackets or full frames covering one, two, three or all four margins.[27]

There is a great deal of variation in border styles and motifs between books from France, Italy, Germany, etc., even more than is the case with their initials. Birds, insects and other animals were often inserted into the margins, which usually display a mixture of realistic and stylized elements. As for the famous grotesques or *drolleries*, humorous or satirical figures and scenes pictured in the margins, especially those of deluxe codices, they are limited to the period of the flowering of pure Gothic book art and were generally abandoned in the fifteenth century.[28]

[27] A useful typology of border forms is given in Hindman and Farquhar, *Pen to Press* (see n. 1), pp. 73–4.

[28] L. M. C. Randall, *Images in the Margins of Gothic Manuscripts*, Berkeley and Los Angeles 1966 (California Studies in the History of Art, 4); M. Camille, *Image on the Edge: The Margins of Medieval Art*, Cambridge, Mass., 1992.

Whilst the initials became more and more standardized and reduced in size, the full development of Gothic decoration is revealed in the borders. Here too the last decades of the fifteenth century mark the beginning of a final new age, with a full reconsideration of the conception, role, motifs and colouring of the borders and their relationship to the initials. In both borders and initials the new principle at the basis of the decoration was illusionism.

BINDING

Most medieval manuscripts have been rebound since the sixteenth century, often more than once. Here only a few observations can be made about ordinary late medieval bookbindings, concentrating more upon their materials and decoration than upon their structure.[29]

The normal binding consists of a series of bands in cord or leather, to which the quires were sewn, and which are attached to two wooden boards. The boards and the spine were covered with a piece of leather in natural colour (brown, white) or stained. Whilst in Romanesque bindings the bands on the spine are mostly inconspicuous, the codex of the fourteenth and fifteenth centuries is generally characterized by raised bands. In contrast with the former, too, which were often cut flush with the leaves, the covers of Gothic bookbindings (like present-day bindings) are somewhat larger. The spine was decorated at each end with headbands often finished with coloured (usually two colours) threads.

The binding was completed by one form or other of fastening, such as clasps or straps. There are normally one or two such devices at the outer edges of the covers; Italian codices often have four, including one at the head and one at the bottom of the covers. Metal corner and side-pieces and bosses on the covers were sometimes added for better protection, and likewise a chain for those books that were to be placed in a chained library (*libri catenati*). A title-label on the front or rear cover, generally protected by a metal frame and window in transparent horn (*fenestra*), helped to identify the books in the typical library room of the fourteenth and fifteenth centuries, in which the books (chained or not) were placed on sloping pulpits for direct consultation.

---

[29] E. Baras, J. Irigoin and J. Vezin, *La reliure médiévale. Trois conférences d'initiation*, Paris 1978; W. K. Gnirrep, J. P. Gumbert and J. A. Szirmai, *Kneep en binding. Een terminologie voor de beschrijving van de constructies van oude boekbanden*, The Hague 1992; O. Mazal, 'Medieval Bookbinding', in *The Book through Five Thousand Years*, ed. H. D. L. Vervliet, London 1972, pp. 314–38; J. A. Szirmai, *The Archaeology of Medieval Bookbinding*, Aldershot 1999. The literature on ancient bookbinding is abundant but very much focused on the decoration and the most exquisite examples. One of the best works is P. Needham, *Twelve Centuries of Bookbinding, 400–1600*, New York and London 1979.

The decoration of the leather is concentrated on the covers and is almost always in relief, without addition of colour or gold. As a rule there is no relation between the imagery of the decoration and the content of the book. One technique, popular in Germany, consisted in carving images or patterns in the leather (*Lederschnitt*). Much more universally applied, however, was *blind-tooling*: the impression, by means of heated brass tools, of lines, patterns or images in the leather. Single, double or triple *fillets* were used to apply a frame onto each cover, and engraved *hand tools* were used to fill up the squares, bands or lozenges thus formed with simplified images of flowers, animals, symbols, etc. The laborious nature of this form of decoration, as well as a desire to introduce more realism to the cover designs, led to the use of *panel stamps*: large rectangular engraved panels, which were of course expensive to acquire, but reduced the labour of tooling considerably. A press was required to impress these panels. One or two panels sufficed for the decoration of an average cover; four panels were needed for decorating bindings of a large size, if no other decoration was added. Panel tooling is essentially a feature of fifteenth- and sixteenth-century bindings, although hand-tooling remained in extensive use. In the sixteenth century hand tools were increasingly replaced by *rolls*, again in order to save time. The Mediterranean countries in general used different patterns of blind-tooling, to which gilding could be added.

In addition to stiff-board bindings with wooden boards (which at the end of this period were sometimes replaced by pasteboards for small sizes), *limp vellum* bindings were used. These could also be made of leather and were thought especially appropriate for archival records. Many Books of Hours and other personal devotional books were covered in fabric.

Ruling Patterns

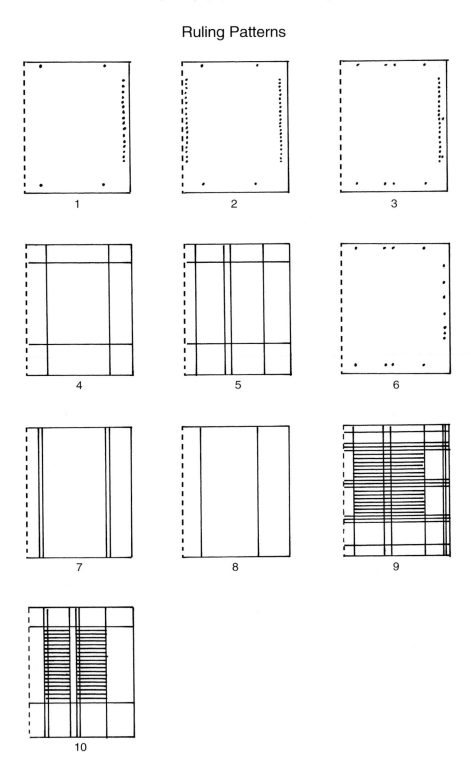

2

The Carolingian heritage
(plates 1–2)

Gothic script was no new creation, but the result of a gradual evolution of late Carolingian script. The latter, which was developed from the so-called Precarolingian scripts during the late eighth century, attained its fully developed form in the later ninth and tenth centuries.[1] It is essentially composed of a selection of forms of various origins, which seem to have been chosen in order to obtain a perfect book script in accordance with the general norms for such a script: legibility, clarity, calligraphy (i.e. the use of 'structured' letters), avoidance of variant letter forms and strict limitation of the number of ligatures. During an initial period of formation, the variant forms which were still in use for a series of letters were abandoned, the ligatures that still remained were reduced to a minimum, and a simple, clear, and exceedingly legible form of handwriting emerged.

Where and how the so-called 'Caroline minuscule' originated is still a matter of debate, but its makers were astonishingly successful. Not only was the script in continual use throughout much of Western and Central Europe for three centuries, but it was also 'rediscovered' about 1400 by the Italian Humanists, imitated and given a new lease of life in the Humanistic script, made into type and used for books, newspapers, advertisements etc. in the entire Western world up to the present day.

---

[1] Bibliography: Battelli, *Lezioni*, pp. 187–98; Bischoff, *Palaeography*, pp. 112–27; the simplified alphabets reproduced by Bischoff are very helpful; Cencetti, *Lineamenti*, pp. 166–205; Cencetti, *Compendio*, pp. 66–71; Gasparri, *Introduction*, pp. 79–88, 95–101; on p. 85, there is a good table of the ductus of the (late) Carolingian alphabet; Petrucci, *Breve storia*, pp. 106–18; Stiennon, *Paléographie*, pp. 110–18, 121–5. More bibliography is provided in Boyle, *Medieval Latin Palaeography*, pp. 140–70. Bischoff's (unfortunately unillustrated) catalogue of ninth-century manuscripts in Carolingian script is being published posthumously: B. Bischoff, *Katalog der festländischen Handschriften des neunten Jahrhunderts (mit Ausnahme der wisigotischen)*, Wiesbaden 1998– . Progressive palaeographers tend to replace the name Carolingian script or Caroline minuscule by 'littera antiqua', which in normal terminology is used for round Humanistic script; they call the latter 'littera antiqua renovata'. Gothic (Textualis) script would then be called 'littera moderna'. See, for example, Casamassima, *Tradizione*, p. 31; Zamponi, 'Scrittura', p. 317; Gasparri, *Introduction*, pp. 217–21. For Precarolingian scripts, see Battelli, *Lezioni*, pp. 119–21 and 156–68; Bischoff, *Palaeography*, pp. 100–108; Stiennon, *Paléographie*, pp. 86–110.

GENERAL FEATURES

Carolingian handwriting in its fully developed form may be considered an almost perfect book script. Although some adjacent letters touch each other at the headline or at the baseline (or both), it is in principle unconnected. The broad and round forms of the letters, the distance between them and between the words on the line (a degree of word separation being systematically aimed at, even if not every word was separate) contribute to the wide and uncompressed character of the script. The use of a pen with a relatively narrow nib, the long ascenders and descenders and, in relation to this, the wide distance between the lines too, give the page a light and aerated appearance that invites reading.

The same characteristics allowed the scribe to copy the text in long lines, even for codices of a large size. Two-column manuscripts do survive from the Carolingian and post-Carolingian period, but the overwhelming majority are in a single column. This may doubtless be related to the special features of Carolingian script discussed here and to the preference for square forms manifested, for example, by Romanesque architecture, just as the round and broad letter shapes correspond with the relatively low church interiors and round arches.

A final feature to be noted concerns the tops of ascenders. In the first century of its existence, Carolingian script was marked by the club shape of the ascenders of the letters **b**, **d**, **h** and **l** (1). This shape was obtained by double penstrokes and was derived from Roman Half-Uncial, in which it was a stylization of the rapid up-and-down movement of the pen visible in Roman Cursive Minuscule (2). The special treatment of ascenders had already been displayed in the triangular serifs and the inflexion of the shafts in Insular script (3), and it would also constitute a distinctive element of various Gothic scripts. In the tenth and eleventh centuries the club shape increasingly gave way to triangular serifs or bifurcation of the top of the ascender, this being an early indication of a new phase in Western script (4, 5).

INDIVIDUAL LETTER FORMS

The variant forms of **a** employed in early Carolingian script, which had their origin in Precarolingian scripts (and consequently in later Roman Cursive – the so-called Cursive Minuscule) (6–8), were gradually abandoned in favour of the Uncial form, derived from Roman Uncial, one of the book scripts that had remained in use after

1   2   3   4   5   6   7   8

the fall of the Roman empire in the West (9).[2] This choice at once eliminated a source of possible confusion between **a** and other letters and letter combinations such as **cc, ci, u**.

As far as **d** is concerned, on the other hand, the form which finally was to prevail was the one with a vertical ascender or the so-called Half-Uncial **d** (10), while the Uncial letter, with shaft sloping to the left (11), which had already been abandoned by most Precarolingian scripts, became of very limited use.[3]

The **e** employed from the beginning in Carolingian script was the rounded Uncial or Half-Uncial form (12); the complicated two-storey or 8-shaped **e**s, which had their origin in later Roman Cursive and had been stylized in several early medieval scripts on the Continent (13), disappeared entirely. The latter forms, however, would continue to flourish for a couple of centuries in the Visigothic and Beneventan scripts, in Muslim-occupied Spain and in Southern Italy respectively, areas situated outside the mainstream of cultural development in Western Europe during that period.[4]

The form of **f** and of the related (straight) **s** did not become completely fixed during most of the period in which Carolingian script was in use: these letters could either stop on the baseline (14), or extend below the line with a mostly short descender (15).[5] In many cases **f** is 'long' (descending below the line), and **s** is 'short' (stopping on the baseline) (pl. 2).[6] Long **s** could sometimes be reserved for the beginning of words, whilst short **s** was used in other positions,[7] or long **s**

9   10   11   12   13   14   15

[2] For later Roman Cursive, see Battelli, *Lezioni*, pp. 88–94; Bischoff, *Palaeography*, pp. 63–6. For Uncial, Battelli, *Lezioni*, pp. 72–80; Bischoff, *Palaeography*, pp. 66–72. See examples of the various forms of **a** in our pls. 1–2; other late examples of **a** in the shape of cc are found in 1028–39 (*CMDNL*, I, pl. 41) and in 1058 (*CMDF*, II, pl. 10). For an example of 'single-compartment' **a** comparable to our handwritten **a**, see *CMDCH*, II, pl. 9 (911).

[3] For Half-Uncial, see Battelli, *Lezioni*, pp. 81–7; Bischoff, *Palaeography*, pp. 75–8. The Uncial **d** was used – for dates only, it seems – in *CMDNL*, I, pl. 1 (816) and *CMDF*, II, pl. 5 (847?); in normal text in *CMDF*, I, pl. 1 (after 862).

[4] On Visigothic script, see Battelli, *Lezioni*, pp. 144–52; Bischoff, *Palaeography*, pp. 96–100; on Beneventan, Battelli, *Lezioni*, pp. 123–38; Bischoff, *Palaeography*, pp. 109–11 and fig. 22.

[5] A few examples in which both letters extend below the baseline: *CMDF*, II, pls. 1 (813–15?), 2 (826), 5 (841–57). It should be observed that **f** and **s** in the alphabet drawn by Gasparri, *Introduction*, p. 85, are untypical of Carolingian script.

[6] Other examples: *CMDCH*, II, pls. 8 and 12–13 (early ninth and late tenth century); *CMDF*, II, pls. 3 (832–3?), 6 (*c.* 844); III, pl. 14 (983–1010, 987–1013); IV, I, pl. 11 (*c.* 1000–11); *CMDNL*, I, pls. 2, 10, 19, 26, 29–33 (all ninth century, except the last example, dated after 929); II, pl. 958 (1113–27).

[7] Bischoff, *Palaeography*, pl. 12 (eighth/ninth century).

could be used in the **st**-ligature only (about which see below).[8] Nevertheless, at the time when the transformation of Carolingian into Gothic began, **f** and straight **s** stopping on the line, without descenders, seem to have been widely adopted, although the practice of extending one or both of these letters somewhat below the line was never entirely abandoned.

The only letter in the Carolingian alphabet for which a definitively Precarolingian form was consciously retained is **g**: in early medieval scripts in general (with the exception of Insular script), and in those of the Frankish kingdom in particular, the custom had been introduced of extending the upper horizontal stroke of the Half-Uncial **g** (which itself was a consolidation of the Roman Cursive Minuscule one) (16) with a bow bending downward towards the left, rejoining the stem and forming a lobe (17).

The minuscule form of **h** was the common form in all scripts used in the early Middle Ages and thus also appears in Carolingian script (18).

As for **i**, early Carolingian hands sometimes still exhibit the short and the long form of the letter (**i** brevis and **i** longa), variant forms which in earlier scripts such as Visigothic and the Precaroline scripts known as Luxeuil minuscule and Corbie 'ab' minuscule, and also Beneventan, were generally used in accordance with certain rules. Thus **i** longa (a majuscule, standing on the baseline) could be written at the beginning of words (except before letters with ascenders), **i** brevis at other places.[9] In Carolingian script, however, the long **i** was soon abandoned and **i** brevis was the only form normally used.[10] In this period **i** longa must be distinguished from long **i** with a descender (looking like our letter **j**). The latter form occurs in ligatures with a preceding consonant such as **l**, **r**, **t** and has its origin in Roman Cursive script (19). Ligatures such as **lj**, **rj** and **tj** are frequent in Beneventan script; in later Visigothic handwriting **tj** was regularly used for the 'tsi' sound ('scientia'), **ti** for the 'ti' sound ('tibi').[11] The **j** form of **i**, already abandoned in most Precarolingian scripts, is extremely rare in Carolingian script, which indeed eliminated almost all ligatures. The form **lj** is sometimes found.[12]

It was natural that the minuscule form of **m** (20), which had its origin in Roman Half-Uncial and had been the sole form used in Precarolingian scripts, continued to be used in Carolingian script. For **n**, however, the situation was more complicated. Neither Roman Uncial nor Half-Uncial had adopted the Cursive, minuscule form

16   17   18

19   20

[8] *CMDVat*, I, pl. 1 (Rome 1097).
[9] Bischoff, *Palaeography*, p. 110.
[10] An example of **i** longa at the beginning of words in Carolingian script: *CMDNL*, I, pls. 20–2 (Reims 854?).
[11] Battelli, *Lezioni*, p. 147; in Beneventan too the two sounds are expressed through different ligatures, but both using **j** (Battelli, *Lezioni*, p. 134).
[12] For example: *CMDNL*, I, pl. 5 (Cologne *c*. 833).

of that letter (21), but had retained the Capital form (22). Insular script, however, although in general comprising Uncial and Half-Uncial forms, had introduced the Cursive form as an alternative for the Capital **n**, at least in the more calligraphic level of the so-called 'Insular Half-Uncial' (it is the normal form in the more rapid 'Insular Minuscule').[13] The Capital form in Insular script, on the other hand, mostly took a distinct shape, with the oblique stroke that connects the two vertical strokes being almost horizontal and placed very low, close to the baseline (23). Some Precarolingian scripts (such as the so-called Luxeuil minuscule), maintained the variant forms of Insular script, others, however, adopted exclusively the Cursive form. Early Carolingian script hesitated for some time between these two or three forms (pl. 2), till the Capital forms were excluded (except as part of an **nt**-ligature) and the Cursive one remained the only type in use.[14] Since that time minuscule **m** and **n** have had a parallel evolution.

The **r** adopted by Carolingian script is a minim, at the top of which a wavy stroke is attached at the right-hand side. Whereas in Half-Uncial and the lower grades of Insular script the latter generally curves down to the baseline (24), Carolingian script follows Precarolingian scripts in adopting an **r** in which the final stroke has a limited extension and ends at the headline (25). Its first, vertical stroke normally ends on the baseline, but quite often, especially in manuscripts of the earliest period, extends below it (26):[15] thus **f, i, r** and straight **s** may have (short) descenders, although they mostly stop on the line. **i** and **r** with descenders would appear again in some Pregothic and Gothic hands.

In addition to the normal Carolingian **r**, a Precarolingian sharp form, making a ligature with the subsequent letter, was sometimes still used (pl. 2).[16]

The straight, Half-Uncial **s** is the only form to be used in Carolingian script (27), the round, Uncial **s** (28) being driven almost entirely into the background for some three centuries.[17]

t has the form of a curved shaft, standing on the line, topped by a horizontal bar extending both to left and right (29). The vertical shaft does not project above the horizontal bar, and **t** is thus a 'short' letter.

21 22 23

24 25 26

27 28 29

[13] On Insular script, see Battelli, *Lezioni*, pp. 171–81; Bischoff, *Palaeography*, pp. 83–95.

[14] An example of capital **N** in Carolingian script: *CMDNL*, I, pl. 5 (*c.* 833).

[15] **r** with descender is still used in the eleventh century: *CMDF*, III, pls. 16 (1030–60), 18 (1031–52).

[16] Another example: Bischoff, *Palaeography*, pl. 12 (eighth/ninth century).

[17] According to Bischoff, *Palaeography*, p. 116, the round form of **s** reappears in the ninth century at the end of words.

u (or **v**: these had the value of a single letter, used for the vowel as well as for the consonant) was usually rendered by the rounded form, well known from the Uncial and Half-Uncial alphabets (30).[18] The reader need not be reminded that **w** did not yet exist. Where the 'w'-sound of Germanic nouns needed to be represented, a scribe would write two **u**s placed one after the other.

x consists of two crossed oblique strokes, the one which goes from bottom left to top right generally extending below the baseline (31). **y** as a rule is topped by a dot (32). **z**, finally, is the only letter in the Carolingian alphabet that admits quite a number of variant forms (33, 34).

LIGATURES

In their general tendency to clarify and simplify book script, the creators of Carolingian script appear to have heavily reduced the number of ligatures and to have standardized the remaining ones. Ligatures constitute by their very nature variant letter forms and in the case of Carolingian script introduce connections in an otherwise fundamentally unconnected book script. Moreover, most ligatures preserved certain Precarolingian letter forms, which Carolingian reform strove so hard to abolish. Carolingian scribes did not go so far as to abandon all those ligatures which Precaroline scripts had taken over and developed from Roman Cursive, but they strictly limited their number and regularized their shapes. The following ligatures are the principal ones to be encountered in early Carolingian script:

(a) **ae**, consisting of Carolingian **e** to which a Cursive **a** in the shape of **u** or **cc** or a simple hook is suspended; the 'cedilla' in this **e** caudata would soon be no longer understood as representing the letter **a** and would take various forms, before disappearing in the course of the twelfth century (35, pl. 1);

(b) **et**, still used and known today as the ampersand (36);

(c) **nt**, in two main forms, one with Capital letters, the other (soon to disappear) with minuscules; both were used especially at the end of words (37, 38; see also pl. 4);

30   31   32   33   34   35   36   37   38

---

[18] The v-shape may be seen in the ninth century 'at the end of a word, and less often at the beginning' (Bischoff, *Palaeography*, p. 116).

(d) **or**, consisting of **o** connected to Capital/Uncial **r** (39), an early example of the phenomenon of 'fusion' or 'biting', a feature that would be so typical of Gothic scripts. In fact, fusions had already occurred in late Roman book scripts at the end of lines, in order to keep within the writing area.[19] From the Carolingian period onwards, the **or**-ligature would have an extraordinary vogue in the **orum**-abbreviation (40);

(e) three ligatures of **t** and a preceding letter, namely **ct, rt, st** (41–3).

Some of these ligatures, most notably the minuscule form of **nt**-ligature, disappeared in the course of the ninth century,[20] others were to have a long history. Those of interest for the development of Gothic script are **e** caudata, **et, or, ct, st**. **rt**, conserving a Precarolingian **r** and too close in appearance to **st**, was among the earliest victims of regularization, although it may still be found in eleventh-century manuscripts, especially those from England.

MAJUSCULES

The minuscule alphabet we have just briefly described was supplemented by a majuscule alphabet, used for titles (pl. 2), incipits, explicits and especially for the first letter of new sentences. This alphabet, which played an important role in the structuring of the text, accompanying the punctuation as an important aid to legibility, was, for the most part, taken over from the Roman Capital script. These Capital letters, however, were quite often intermingled with Uncial forms: in contrast with the Carolingian minuscule script, these majuscules did not acquire uniform fixed shapes. Their forms derive from various alphabets (and would continue to do so till the end of the Middle Ages).

HISTORICAL NOTE

Because of its extraordinary qualities and the active support of ecclesiastical and royal authority, starting with Charlemagne himself,[21] Carolingian script very rapidly spread over Europe, ultimately putting an end to the diversity of scripts

| 39 | 40 | 41 | 42 | 43 |

---

[19] See the alphabets in Bischoff, *Palaeography*, figs. 1 (p. 56) and 7 (p. 67).

[20] A late example of this **nt**-ligature: *CMDF*, II, pl. 10 (1058).

[21] Stiennon, *Paléographie*, p. 116.

that had developed in the preceding centuries and replacing it with a unique and universal type, used for books as well as for documents: there is no such a thing as Carolingian cursive. Some palaeographers, among them the distinguished specialist Bernhard Bischoff, have identified in Carolingian manuscripts a second, smaller variety, used for writing glosses.[22] According to Bischoff, this script is distinguished by long ascenders and descenders and the frequent use of single-compartment (Half-Uncial) **a**, Uncial **d**, etc. As will be observed in a subsequent chapter, the adoption of a very small size of handwriting almost automatically induces the scribe to simplify his letter forms and to emphasize certain features, so that distinguishing a separate type such as 'Glossenschrift' or 'Notula' on the basis of size and function cannot be justified satisfactorily.[23]

This unique script certainly did not remain unchanged during the three or even four centuries of its existence. We have already alluded to changes in the treatment of the tops of ascenders after the ninth century. In the script of the eleventh century more changes become apparent, and in that of the twelfth they have become so striking that in most cases we shall have to use a new name for the script (see below, Chapter 3). Nevertheless, at least until the eleventh century the new features did not depart fundamentally from the features and the general appearance of ninth-century Carolingian script. Local and regional styles, too, are often difficult to determine after about the middle of the ninth century, and 'Caroline minuscule' can consequently be described as a long-lasting creation, admitting neither notable evolution in time nor important geographical differentiation. Characteristically English varieties, however, have been identified from the later tenth and eleventh centuries,[24] and a distinctive 'slanting-oval' style in eleventh-century German manuscripts, especially from the South-East.[25]

The penetration of Carolingian script into areas outside the boundaries of the empire of Charlemagne can be sketched as follows: it began to be adopted by English scribes during the second half of the tenth century and, from the early eleventh century, had replaced the late forms of Insular script, at least for Latin texts; the various Scandinavian countries adopted it mostly under English influence;[26] in Spain the recovery of the country by the Christian Church from the eleventh century onwards provided the context for the replacement of Visigothic by Carolingian script, propagated especially by the Cluniac Order.

---

[22] *Nomenclature*, p. 8; Schneider, *Paläographie*, pp. 26–8.
[23] Stiennon, *Paléographie*, p. 99.
[24] Cf. T. A. M. Bishop, *English Caroline Minuscule*, Oxford 1971; D. N. Dumville, *English Caroline Script and Monastic History: Studies in Benedictinism*, A.D. 950–1030, Woodbridge 1993 (Studies in Anglo-Saxon History, 6); Brown, *Guide*, pl. 24; Brown and Lovett, *Source Book*, pp. 75–86.
[25] Bischoff, *Palaeography*, pp. 120–1, 133; Schneider, *Paläographie*, p. 26.
[26] Bischoff, *Palaeography*, p. 125.

The script that developed in the Carolingian empire, under the impulse of the religious and educational reforms of a gifted ruler, is no doubt one of the greatest achievements of Western culture. It is one of the mysteries of history that this instrument of communication, whose printed form in modern times has conquered the Western world, was replaced from the twelfth century onwards by a fundamentally different script system. The main characteristics of Carolingian script – openness and differentiation of the individual letter form – gave way to the closed forms and uniformity of Gothic script. It was only during the last two centuries of the Middle Ages that the Gothic system of scripts would incorporate additional types that constituted a kind of return to the principles on which Carolingian handwriting was based. At the turn of the fourteenth to the fifteenth century, Italy would succeed in reviving Carolingian script itself in the form of Humanistic script, a rare example of archaizing handwriting being successfully promoted by a group of scholars and, ultimately, enthusiastically adopted by a literate society as a whole.

3

Praegothica
(plates 3–14)

The twelfth century marks a period of transition in the history of the medieval book. It is the last great age of monastic book production. The quantity and quality of manuscripts produced and the spread of centres of production throughout Europe make it the most brilliant period in the history of the monastic book. Monastic scriptoria would continue to flourish into the thirteenth century, but at that time they ceased to predominate and new urban-based centres of book production would take the lead. These emerged towards the end of the twelfth century and in general differed from monastic scriptoria in their commercial character: in contrast with monastic and cathedral scriptoria, they produced books first and foremost with a view to making profit and not for their own personal use.

The transition from the monastic to the mainly secular centres of manuscript production is paralleled by important changes in the format, structure and layout of the manuscript book as sketched above in Chapter 1.

From our point of view the so-called Renaissance of the Twelfth Century was a last flowering, on a European scale, of Carolingian monastic book culture, marked by rich monastic and cathedral libraries that often contained important collections of classical as well as patristic and other religious texts, and comprised mostly stately, well-made volumes, decorated in Romanesque style. At the same time it represented the birth of a new age with new religious, intellectual and aesthetic concerns, which transformed the Carolingian script into various forms of Pregothic, and opened the door to the creation of a multitude of various book types, which would replace the generally rather uniform monastic book.

GENERAL FEATURES

The appearance of Carolingian script certainly changed between the ninth and the eleventh centuries, but these changes were mostly small and unobtrusive. From the eleventh century, by contrast, first in England, Flanders and North-Western France, the changes seem to amount to a new era. Various new features manifest themselves in the traditional body-shape of letter forms and in the general aspect of the page, although not all at the same time and in the same area, and not at first adopted in any consistent way. They are sufficient to compel us to give a distinct name to the script in which they appear. Among the names that have been proposed by specialists are: 'Late Caroline', 'Post-Caroline', 'Early' or 'Primitive Gothic', 'Carolino-Gothica', 'Protogothic', 'Praegothica', 'frühgotische Minuskel', 'caroline gothicisante' (in a further stage: 'caroline gothicisée'), 'minuscola di transizione'.[1] 'Romanesque script' ('Romanische Minuskel') and 'Cistercian script' ('Zisterzienserschrift') have rightly been considered improper terms for the new script.[2] Because of the varying degrees to which the various novelties are present in it, this Pregothic script (littera Praegothica), which will be the term to be used hereafter, is hardly a script type in itself. It is in fact Carolingian script that displays to a greater or lesser extent one or more of the new features. These features would only be present all together in the fully developed Gothic Textualis (discussed in the next chapter). They constitute the basic characteristics of what is often considered Gothic script properly speaking. For the time being, there was no unity in the handwriting as a whole and very diverse forms of script feature under the name of Pregothic.

The new features that appear hesitatingly in Pregothic may be summarized as follows. First, there was a narrowing of the letter bodies. The broad, 'square', round forms of Carolingian script gave way to more narrow, laterally compressed shapes. The almost circular lobe of **o**, for example, tended more and more to become an oval. As all the letters followed this tendency, their concentration gave the written line a compactness which was altogether foreign to Carolingian script.

The lateral compression of the script was enhanced by the introduction of fusions (bitings), in which two adjacent letters are joined together in such a way that part of their strokes are common or overlap. Whereas the system would not reach its full development before the thirteenth century (and thus will be discussed in the next chapter), it appears in many codices of the twelfth century in the compact shapes of **pp** and **bb**, in which the vertical stroke of the second letter coincides with part of the bow of the first (1, pls. 7, 13).[3] Similarly, two successive **ls** would be united

1

[1] Bibliography: Bischoff, *Palaeography*, pp. 127–33; Brown, *Guide*, pp. 72–3; Cencetti, *Lineamenti*, pp. 205–10; Drogin, *Medieval Calligraphy*, pp. 53–7; Gasparri, *Introduction*, pp. 103–6; Petrucci, *Breve storia*, pp. 125–33; Schneider, *Paläographie*, pp. 30–6; Stiennon, *Paléographie*, pp. 125–8; A. Tomiello, 'Dalla *Littera antiqua* alla *Littera textualis*: prime considerazioni', *Gazette du Livre Médiéval*, 29 (1996), pp. 1–6.
[2] Bischoff in *Nomenclature*, pp. 13–14.
[3] None of these fusions is obligatory in Pregothic script. Other examples of **pp**: Thomson, *Bookhands*, pls. 5 (France 1183), 85 (England *c.* 1155).

by a single long serif at their top (2). Other fusions are extremely rare in this period.[4]

At the same time the length of ascenders and descenders became reduced and the body-height was enlarged. Whereas in Carolingian script the normal ratio between minims and letters with ascenders was about 0.4 to 0.5, in twelfth-century script ratios of 0.6 and 0.7 are the norm.[5] It is very noticeable that in many Pregothic hands not all ascenders were treated equally in this respect: l in particular could be much shorter than other ascenders, making the letter almost look like i (pls. 4, 6, 9).

This change in the proportion of the letters had far-reaching implications, as it allowed the reduction of the distance between the lines, and at the same time was a major factor prompting book producers to adopt a two-column layout, as the reading of a horizontally and vertically compressed script disposed in long lines would have been particularly arduous.

The angularity of the nascent Gothic script, generally considered one of its most prominent features, is in fact not easy to define (pls. 6, 11). It is by no means comparable with the strictly rectilinear strokes of one of its progeny, Textualis Formata, since the general aspect of most Pregothic book hands remains round; the angularity is apparent only in some parts of the curves. It is usually most visible at the top and at the bottom of c, e, o, in the limb of h, the headstroke of r, etc. (3, 4).

Pregothic script has without doubt a greater 'weight' than Carolingian script generally has: the shading, i.e. the distinction between the bold strokes and the hairlines, is more pronounced and was obtained by the use of a quill with a broader nib. This, combined with the compactness of the script, resulted in a 'blacker' appearance of the text area, a feature that would remain typical of all the manuscripts emanating directly from the Pregothic tradition.

The most intriguing, and for some the most distinctive, feature in Pregothic (and Gothic) script, however, and one which is a major cause of reduced legibility (at least to the modern reader), is the treatment of the feet of both minims and ascenders. Here a strong equalizing tendency is apparent, whereby these feet all curve to the right, either in rounded or in sharp angles, and may consequently join the next letter (5).[6] This homogenizing tendency is also visible in the tops of ascenders and

2   3

4   5

[4] Two remarkable exceptions towards the end of the century: *CMDGBOx*, pl. 9 (Germany after 1194), and especially Thomson, *Bookhands*, pl. 60 (Italy 1188). Both manuscripts present an extraordinary number of fusions.

[5] N. Daniel, *Handschriften des zehnten Jahrhunderts aus der Freisinger Dombibliothek*, Munich 1973 (Münchener Beiträge zur Mediävistik und Renaissance-Forschung, 11), p. 2.

[6] An example of advanced assimilation of the minims: Steffens, *Paläographie*, pl. 86 (Trier 1191). Brown, *Guide*, p. 73, sees the difference between English and continental examples as being that 'the former [employ] formally applied feet and serifs and the latter [acquire] simple feet to minims which generally consist of an upwards turn of the pen'. See, for example, Thomson, *Bookhands*, pl. 86 (England 1176 [the text only]).

minims: the forking of ascenders (6) has already been mentioned as a characteristic of late Carolingian handwriting; the same technique was applied to the minims too, so that **i**, **p**, **r**, **u** and the first minims of **m** and **n** may have a triangular or forked shape at their top (5). By this 'doppelte Brechung' or 'double breaking' of the minims (as German palaeographers call the phenomenon) the headline acquires an importance approaching that of the baseline. Italian manuscripts often do not display this tendency; their scribes either applied horizontal serifs to the base of ascenders and minims, or let them end straight on the baseline (7, pl. 7).[7] Similarly, the ascenders in these manuscripts often exhibit horizontal serifs instead of forking (8).[8] Spanish codices appear to display a predilection for heavy forking in the form of a short horizontal stroke at the left of the ascender (9).[9]

The deliberate ending of ascenders and minims flat on the baseline or the application of horizontal serifs (what in full Gothic will be called Textus Praescissus) is found already, outside Italy, in some highly luxurious codices (pl. 12).[10]

Descenders often received the same treatment as the feet of ascenders and of minims and either turned over to the right or were given upward-slanting endstrokes (10, 11, pls. 9, 11).

Very early on, the homogenizing tendencies began to make it difficult for readers to distinguish double **i** and **u**, and this was remedied by adding strokes above double **i** (12) and/or by lengthening the second **i** below the line, thus creating the 'new' letter **j**, which for centuries would be merely an alternative form of **i** without any implication in the field of pronunciation (13). The use of **i** as a vowel and **j** as a consonant is essentially post-medieval.

The practice of lengthening and perhaps elaborating the ascenders on the top line and the descenders on the bottom line of the page is rare in Pregothic script (pls. 13, 18).[11] The intrusion of the *litterae elongatae* of documentary script into book script is largely a phenomenon of the thirteenth century.

One is surprised to note that in books produced as early as the twelfth century spiky forms and short hairlines sometimes appear at the headline, aside from the sharp forms of the bifurcations (pls. 6, 13).[12]

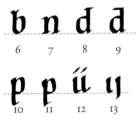

[7] Another example: Thomson, *Bookhands*, pl. 56 (1104).

[8] Thomson, *Bookhands*, pl. 56.

[9] Thomson, *Bookhands*, pl. 109 (1105) and more pronounced Burnam, *Palaeographia*, pl. 33 = Canellas, *Exempla*, II, pl. 42 (1188).

[10] Another example: *CMDGBOx*, pl. 71 (Paris *c.* 1164–70). And see n. 6.

[11] Two English examples: Thomson, *Bookhands*, pl. 84 (*c.* 1132?) and *CMDGBOx*, pl. 87 (1187–1205).

[12] For example, **g** and **q** in Thomson, *Bookhands*, pl. 33 (Germany *c.* 1158).

INDIVIDUAL LETTER FORMS

The individual letter forms in Pregothic are in essence the same as those observed in Carolingian script, but they were submitted to the transformative homogenizing trends sketched above.

The shaft of **a**, which slopes in Carolingian script, became more and more upright, so that finally, in full-grown Textualis, it would usually consist of a minim with a lobe at its left. Its minim-like character was sometimes stressed by the scribe beginning the letter with a horizontal stroke (14).[13] But normally the top of the shaft of the letter turns over to the left (15). In the Iberian Peninsula this form generally alternates (or was replaced) with an **a** with an exceptionally large lobe, similar to or even adopting the form of single-compartment **a** (16, 17, pls. 8, 14).[14] It gave rise to a distinctive **ta**-ligature (18). In Italian manuscripts, by contrast, the tendency to give the letter a very flat lobe signals the arrival of the typical **a** of what is called Rotunda (19, pl. 7).[15]

One very important development involved vertical Carolingian **d** receiving a competitor in the Uncial **d** with sloping ascender (20). The former was given the normal bifurcation or serif at its top, whereas the latter's shaft has either no such feature, or ends in a curve to the right (21). After a long period during which both forms were written interchangeably on a single page, vertical **d** was abandoned in full-grown Northern Textualis. In most codices produced during the twelfth century straight *and* Uncial **d** were used interchangeably. Sometimes, the Uncial form was used only sparingly or only in specific places, such as at the end of a word or of a particle within a word (pl. 14).[16] One can find manuscripts containing only straight **d** until late in the century (pls. 9, 10),[17] but codices of this period with only Uncial **d** appear to be extremely rare. The use of the two forms in immediate succession (22) is perhaps an Iberian and Southern French feature.[18]

[13] *CMDF*, III, pl. 38 (Italy 1188).

[14] See also Thomson, *Bookhands*, pl. III (*c.* 1143); Burnam, *Palaeographia*, pls. 2 (1155), 6 (1160–75), 8 (1183–4), 10 (1189); Canellas, *Exempla*, II, pls. 37 (1160), 39 (1171); Kirchner, *Scriptura Gothica*, pl. 9a (1208).

[15] Thomson, *Bookhands*, pls. 56–7.

[16] A good example is Canellas, *Exempla*, II, pl. 38 (Spain 1162).

[17] See also Thomson, *Bookhands*, pls. 34 (Germany 1186), 86 (England 1176 [the text, not the gloss]).

[18] Burnam, *Palaeographia*, pls. 2 (1155), l. 24: 'redditus', 7 (1183), col. a, l. 21: **dd** = 'David'; Canellas, *Exempla*, II, pl. 36, l. 5 from bottom; *CMDF*, IV, I, pl. 19 (Southern France *c.* 1138–52), l. 2.

A special form of **e** exists in which the first stroke is not a bow, but a minim (23).[19] It may be a survival from a cursive script, in which **e** was linked with a preceding letter, or may represent an unsuccessful early attempt at gothicizing script with the introduction of an additional minim. It may be compared with a similar form of **c** in a late twelfth-century manuscript from Bohemia[20] and with similar forms of **t** in Germany.[21] More fundamental is the change that took place in the direction of the final, straight stroke (or tongue) of **e**. Whereas in typical Carolingian script this stroke is horizontal or almost horizontal, from the eleventh century onwards it tended to slope upwards, and in the twelfth invariably sloped in the direction of the hairlines (24). We still, however, find calligraphic hands in early twelfth-century manuscripts from Italy, that retain the horizontal tongue of **e** as well as the generally broad and rounded letter forms typical of Carolingian script.[22]

f and straight **s** as a rule stand on the line, their shafts receiving the same general treatment at their base as other vertical strokes. The widespread Carolingian tradition of making **f** extend below the baseline (see above, p. 49) survives in some manuscripts from Germany, Italy and Spain (it is typical of Visigothic script).[23] There are also examples from England and Normandy. Another way of differentiating between **f** and **s** is found in manuscripts from Spain; it consisted in adding a loop to the top of **f** (25).[24] A rare variant is the fractured **f** (and **s**), in which the lower and the upper strokes of the letter are not aligned (26).[25]

g, the lower bow of which in the manuscripts of the first half of the twelfth century is often still open as in Carolingian script (pl. 6), gradually adopted a form with two closed lobes, which had become the normal shape by the last decades of the century (27). The development that would lead to the lower lobe gradually

23 24 25

26 27

[19] *CMDF*, III, pls. 22 (Echternach after 1059), 25 (Corbie 1102–23); Millares Carlo, *Tratado*, pl. 181 (León? 1162, mixed with normal **e**); N. Golob, *Codices Sitticenses saeculi XII*, Liubliana 1994, ill. on pp. 40, 74, etc. See on this form N. Ker, *Catalogue of Manuscripts containing Anglo-Saxon*, Oxford 1957, p. xxix.

[20] A. Chroust, *Monumenta Palaeographica. Denkmäler der Schreibkunst des Mittelalters*, Munich and Leipzig 1902–40, III, 15, pl. 6.

[21] See, for example, the so-called Rupertsberg script used in some of the earliest manuscripts of the works of Hildegard of Bingen: M. Schrader and A. Führkötter, *Die Echtheit des Schrifttums der heiligen Hildegard von Bingen*, Cologne and Graz 1956, pl. 4.

[22] Thomson, *Bookhands*, pls. 56–7; Thompson, *Introduction*, pl. 181.

[23] Thomson, *Bookhands*, pls. 29, 56–7, III; J. Alturo, *Studia in codicum fragmenta*, Barcelona 1999, p. 134.

[24] Canellas, *Exempla*, II, pl. 42 (1188).

[25] Thomson, *Bookhands*, pl. III (Spain 1143); New Haven, Beinecke Library, MS 482.40, a Breviary from Germany.

becoming smaller than the upper lobe is already visible, for example, in a few English examples, in which the lower lobe has a triangular shape and the letter looks like a figure 8 (pl. 12).[26] In the later Middle Ages **g** would adopt various forms that are not easy to describe. In the Pregothic script of codices from Italy and the Iberian Peninsula we may already see forms close to those that would be typical of the Southern Textualis or Rotunda (28, pl. 8).[27] The final stroke of **g** is horizontal and normally makes a connection with the following letter when the form of the latter allows this. **g** with an upwards slanting final stroke, or without such a stroke at all, and thus not connected to the next letter, is found in a small minority of hands.[28]

The limb of **h**, originally stopping on the line like its shaft, tended to be made slightly longer towards the end of the century (29). This feature does not appear in Italian manuscripts; here, instead, the limb is very round and at its base almost reaches back to the shaft (30).[29]

The introduction of a stroke above **i** and of the long **i** (**j**) has been mentioned above. In Pregothic script double **i** was either written as **ii** (now generally supplied with diacritical strokes), or **ij**. **j** was rarely used apart from the **ij**-combination and appears to have been typical only of script from the Iberian Peninsula, although examples from the Low Countries, France and Italy are also known. It is found in the sequence **uj** or **ju**; or at the end of the word, or in other combinations (31, 32, pl. 11).[30] More peculiar is the use of **j** linked to the headstroke of preceding **t** in the middle of the word, a ligature already seen in Carolingian script.[31]

The normal form of **m** may be replaced at the end of the line by the Uncial form, a form frequent in documentary script (33, pl. 4).[32]

r is a letter with various forms in Pregothic. The normal, Carolingian shape was used everywhere, and its shaft was subjected to the same homogenizing treatment

28   29   30   31   32   33

[26] See also Thomson, *Bookhands*, pls. 84–6 (1132, 1155, 1176).

[27] See also Thomson, *Bookhands*, pls. 59 (Italy *c.* 1155), 111 (Spain 1143).

[28] With slanting stroke: Kirchner, *Scriptura Gothica*, pl. 2 (Germany 1162); with slanting stroke or no final stroke: Thomson, *Bookhands*, pl. 33 (Germany 1158).

[29] Thomson, *Bookhands*, pl. 57 (1133); Kirchner, *Scriptura Gothica*, pl. 4 (*c.* 1181).

[30] Spanish and Portuguese examples: Burnam, *Palaeographia*, pls. 8 (1183–4), 10 (1189), 49 (*c.* 1174); influence of Visigothic script will have been decisive here. A French example: *CMDF*, v, pl. 18 (Belval 1167). An Italian: L. Light, *The Bible in the Twelfth Century*, Cambridge, Mass., 1988, pl. 6.

[31] Millares Carlo, *Tratado*, pl. 181 (Spain 1162).

[32] See also Thomson, *Bookhands*, pl. 1 (Southern Low Countries 1105); Canellas, *Exempla*, ii, pl. 39 (Spain 1171).

accorded to minims (34). It was rarely, however, the only form used.[33] The constant use of the **or**-ligature, especially in the **orum**-abbreviation, gave birth to the notion that it represented **o** followed by a variant form of **r** in the shape of figure 2 (35). In Pregothic script and its Gothic successors the normal, Carolingian form and the so-called 'round' **r** would be used together, the latter being written after **o**. The hand of the odd scribe betrays some hesitation in using Carolingian and round **r** interchangeably after **o**,[34] but the consistent use of the two forms of **r** became a rule from the middle of the twelfth century onwards.

The lengthened form of **r**, extending below the baseline, may still be found, either as a variant or as the normal form, in books from all countries, but especially in those from Germany and the Iberian Peninsula (36, pl. 10).[35] A curious variant of this form, in which the first stroke is a bow, appears very exceptionally (37).[36] The Capital **R** never disappeared completely from the minuscule alphabet, but it came to play only a marginal role (38). We see it sometimes at the end of a word or of a paragraph, but rarely in the middle of the word.[37] Finally, one is struck by the appearance of decorative hairlines at the top of the usual form of **r** in German manuscripts as early as the twelfth century (39, 40). That way a 'double-horned' **r** may be developed.[38]

In the same way as for **d** and **r**, an alternative form of **s** was introduced in addition to the straight Carolingian **s** (41). This round, 'Uncial' form (42) was only used at the end of the word. Although straight **s** may be observed in final position throughout the twelfth century and indeed is found in many manuscripts of the thirteenth, the basis was laid during the twelfth century for a convention that would last until well into the era of the printed book, whereby the straight or Carolingian form was used at the beginning and in the middle of words, the round or Uncial form at their end. In most twelfth-century codices both forms were used at the end of words, the round **s** being used most often only in short

	r	2	r	r	R	r	r	ſ	s
	34	35	36	37	38	39	40	41	42

[33] For example: Thompson, *Introduction*, pl. 177 (England before 1135); Canellas, *Exempla*, II, pl. 37 (Spain 1160).

[34] For example: Burnam, *Palaeographia*, pl. 9 (Portugal 1185); Thomson, *Bookhands*, pl. 34 (Germany 1186).

[35] Another example from the Iberian Peninsula: Thomson, *Bookhands*, pl. III (1143). From Germany: *CMDGBOx*, pl. 79 (1173–1200). From France: Thomson, *Bookhands*, pl. 5 (1183, exceptionally).

[36] Two German examples: Thomson, *Bookhands*, pl. 29 (1108, used as an alternative form after **o** and **b**), and Chroust, *Monumenta* (see n. 20), I, 4, pl. 10 (1177).

[37] *CMDF*, III, pl. 35 (France 1180/90). At the end of a word or a line: *CMDF*, VII, pl. 209 (France before 1173?); Kirchner, *Scriptura Gothica*, pl. 5 (Portugal 1185).

[38] Steffens, *Paläographie*, pl. 86 (1191); R. G. Babcock, *Reconstructing a Medieval Library*, New Haven 1993, fig. 55.

or abbreviated words ('eas', 'nos'). There are almost no instances of a word written out in full beginning with round **s** (except when this letter is a majuscule); round **s** seems only to have been permitted in initial position when an abbreviation stroke above the line would interfere with the straight **s**, as in the abbreviations for 'sunt' and 'sibi' (43, pl. 12).[39]

Two slightly different forms of **s** may be found that have a common treatment at the baseline. First is the long straight **s**, a counterpart to the long **r**, seen especially in German books (44).[40] When this letter ends in a descender turning to the left, it probably betrays the influence of early documentary script (45). The other, of more long-lasting use, is the narrow, elongated round **s** (46), which has been called trailing **s**.[41] It was used at the end of lines especially where little space was available. It would become an important feature of Mediterranean Gothic script. These two forms of **s** may in fact be related, as is shown by their occasional use in a single manuscript.[42]

In the letter **t** we may observe a tendency for scribes to turn its stem into a minim and to extend its headstroke more to the right than to the left. In some examples from the last decades of the century the headstroke of **t** exhibits a feature which would develop into a very common decorative trait: its end was terminated by a sharp downward stroke (47, pls. 13, 14).[43]

u in its Carolingian, round form was of general use in the twelfth century. The angular Capital form **v** appears very rarely, and its use was usually restricted to the end of a word or of a line, as in the **um**-abbreviation (48); its use in the middle of the word is exceptional.[44] For the sound 'w' two successive **u**s were written, but a new kind of **w** in the form of two successive **v**s was introduced, and became widely used, especially in Germany.[45]

43   44   45   46   47   48

[39] Burnam, *Palaeographia*, pl. 2 (Portugal 1155), l. 19; Kirchner, *Scriptura Gothica*, pl. 7, l. 19 (Switzerland 1197/8). For a remarkably consistent use of round **s** in the middle of the word in a Central European manuscript: Golob, *Codices Sitticenses* (see n. 19), p. 28; see this use also in *CMDNL*, i, pl. 71 (i.e. the manuscript partly reproduced in our pl. 5).

[40] Chroust, *Monumenta* (see n. 20), ii, 21, pl. 2 (Germany 1159); *CMDGBOx*, pl. 79 (Germany 1173–1200); Canellas, *Exempla*, ii, pl. 42 (Spain 1188).

[41] Brown, *Guide*, p. 124.

[42] Burnam, *Palaeographia*, pl. 49 (Portugal *c.* 1174); Canellas, *Exempla*, ii, pl. 42 (Spain 1188). Other examples of trailing **s**, next to other forms: Burnam, *Palaeographia*, pl. 10 (Portugal 1189); Thomson, *Bookhands*, pl. 87 (England; the right date is 1191/2; cf. *CMDGBLo*, no. 878).

[43] *CMDF*, iii, pl. 35 (France 1180–90); *CMDGBOx*, pl. 91 (Germany after 1194).

[44] All our examples are German and late twelfth century: *CMDGBOx*, pls. 84 (*c.* 1178) and 91 (after 1194); Thomson, *Bookhands*, pl. 34 (1186: frequent use of **v**).

[45] Steffens, *Paläographie*, pl. 84 (Austria *c.* 1150). **w** appears in the eleventh century according to Bischoff, *Palaeography*, p. 122.

In the development of **x** various tendencies may be observed. Often the letter was reduced in size so that the two strokes ended on the baseline (49). Sometimes it is clear that the second stroke (the one rising upwards to the right) was divided into two unaligned strokes, a form important for the letter's future development. Instances of an exaggerated version of this feature (50, pl. 8) provide an almost sure clue as to the Iberian origin of the hand.[46]

The common form of **y** is that topped with a dot or a short stroke (51). In some cases the letter is undotted.[47] An alternative ductus is sometimes found, in which the second stroke was traced upwards instead of downwards (52).[48]

z has many different shapes, but these can probably be reduced to three varieties: in France, England and Germany **z** is a 'small' letter written between headline and baseline (53, pl. 12).[49] In Italian script **z** apparently invariably extends above the headline (54, 55),[50] whilst in the handwriting from the Iberian Peninsula it has the form of a figure 3 generally extending below the baseline (56).[51]

LIGATURES

As far as ligatures are concerned there is little difference between Carolingian and Pregothic script. The **ae**-ligature had already replaced the classical spelling of the 'ae' diphthong before the twelfth century. It consists of **e** with a subscript Cursive u- or cc-shaped **a**, the latter taking the form of a cedilla (57). As the diphthong was now pronounced 'e', the actual significance of this **e** caudata became lost, and the ligature was used for 'ae' as well as for 'e', as for example at the beginning of

49   50   51   52   53   54   55   56   57

[46] Thomson, *Bookhands*, pl. 109 (1105); Canellas, *Exempla*, II, pl. 42 (1188); Burnam, *Palaeographia*, pl. 2 (1155).

[47] It may be significant that our examples of undotted **y** come from Germany and Italy: *CMDF*, III, pl. 22 (Germany after 1059); *CMDGBOx*, pl. 84 (Austria *c.* 1178); Kirchner, *Scriptura Gothica*, pl. 4 (Northern Italy *c.* 1181). We will often have occasion to point to parallelisms between German and Italian handwriting of the late Middle Ages.

[48] Two English examples: Thomson, *Bookhands*, pl. 84 (1132); *CMDGBOx*, pl. 69 (*c.* 1161–73). One probably from the Low Countries: Thomson, *Bookhands*, pl. 3 = *CMDB*, I, pls. 27–9 (1156). A strange **y** appears in a French manuscript: *CMDF*, I, pl. 8 (1120–31).

[49] Thomson, *Bookhands*, pls. 5 (France 1183), 32 (Germany 1144); *CMDGBOx*, pl. 75 (England 1167); Thompson, *Introduction*, pl. 178 (England 1176).

[50] Thomson, *Bookhands*, pl. 56 (1104); Kirchner, *Scriptura Gothica*, pl. 4 (*c.* 1181).

[51] Thomson, *Bookhands*, pl. 111 (1143); Burnam, *Palaeographia*, pl. 2 (1155), l. 27; Millares Carlo, *Tratado*, pl. 181 (1162); Canellas, *Exempla*, II, pl. 39 (1171), col. a, l. 14.

the word 'ecclesia'. The cedilla disappeared towards the end of the twelfth century and **e** on its own was employed for both 'e' and 'ae'.[52]

The **st**-ligature was invariably employed, but a new variety of **ct**-ligature was introduced, which would last to the end of the Middle Ages. In many manuscripts the usual Carolingian form is found, in which **c** is connected with **t** by means of a bow above the headline; this bow may adopt various shapes (pls. 10, 11). As a consequence of lateral compression, however, the two letters now often touch each other at the headline and at the baseline (58). The connecting bow, however, tends to be atrophied and becomes either a loop, incurvation or approach-stroke at the left of the ascender of the **t**, unconnected with the **c** (59, pls. 5, 6, 12). The former link may exceptionally be replaced with a pen flourish above **t** or an additional vertical or curving stroke at the top of that letter (60, 61).[53] But even these features may be absent, leaving only a **t** of more than normal height (62).[54] In many books, however, there is no sign of this ligature and **c** is followed by the usual form of **t** (pl. 13).[55]

ABBREVIATIONS[56]

As abbreviations became more numerous from the eleventh century onwards, a few additional forms were introduced. Most noticeable is the tironian or tachygraphic sign for **et** (63), which from the beginning of the twelfth century slowly began to replace the ligature **et** (the ampersand). In the second half of the century both forms were still often used interchangeably (higher levels of calligraphy generally giving preference to the ampersand), but the tironian **et** came to the fore in the last decades of the century. When **et** formed part of a word ('habet') or the abbreviation 'etiam' (64), the ampersand was usually preferred to the tironian note. The ampersand is found in many slightly differing forms (it is, in fact, the graph with the greatest variability in the twelfth century), but its final stroke could be traced with at least two different ductuses: it may have at the headline an approach stroke and would thus have been made in a downward movement from right to left (65), which is

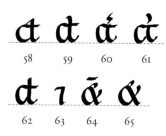

58   59   60   61

62   63   64   65

52 Bischoff, *Palaeography*, p. 122. A late example of the use of **ae** and **e** caudata on the same page is Thomson, *Bookhands*, pl. 29 (Germany 1108), a manuscript with generally strange letter forms.

53 *CMDF*, v, pl. 15 (Clairvaux *c.* 1152–74); Kirchner, *Scriptura Gothica*, pl. 5 (Portugal 1185); a survival of the latter form is shown in Thomson, *Bookhands*, pl. 116 (Portugal 1231).

54 *CMDGBOx*, pl. 91 (Germany after 1194).

55 More examples: Thomson, *Bookhands*, pl. 31 (Germany 1133); *CMDGBOx*, pl. 69 (England *c.* 1161–73); Canellas, *Exempla*, ii, pl. 38 (Spain 1162); Burnam, *Palaeographia*, pl. 10 (Portugal 1189). Ligatured and non-ligatured **ct** may occur in the same hand: see our pl. 5 and Thomson, *Bookhands*, pl. 85 (England 1155).

56 See the note on abbreviations in the Appendix to this book.

the usual case, or it may terminate in an endstroke and would thus have been made upwards from left to right (66, pls. 3, 4, 10). Examples of the latter form, reflecting a simplified ductus, are found especially in German and Spanish books.[57] Another simplified form contains a 3-shaped stroke at the right of the two first strokes (67).[58]

The tironian **et** has approximately the form of a figure 7 and was originally uncrossed. The crossed form appears in English examples of formal book hand from the second half of the century (68).[59] A distinctive form emerged in Italy, Spain, Portugal and Southern France, in which this sign (always uncrossed) consists of a relatively long horizontal bar ending in a minim (69, pls. 7, 14).[60]

Some other abbreviations of Insular origin, likewise based on tironian notes, came to be used, if not very widely. **con** or **com** was replaced by a sign which takes the form of an inverted c or of figure 9, sometimes with an endstroke which makes it resemble a figure 2 (70, 71, pl. 10).[61] Further signs were used for **enim** (72, pl. 4), **est** (73, pl. 10), **id est** (74), etc.

Of the traditional abbreviations, on the other hand, the genitive plural ending **orum** and its derivative, the less frequent feminine **arum**, deserve a special mention. As the letter **a** does not end in a bow, the use of round **r** after it is technically unorthodox and it never attained the general acceptance given to **o** followed by round **r**.[62] Instead of the normal form of **orum** (**arum**), in which round **r** is crossed by a sloping stroke (75), a cursive form, derived from documentary script, was often used. The sloping stroke was connected to the **r** by means of a loop traced with either a normal ductus (76, pl. 11)[63] or more rarely with a reversed one.[64]

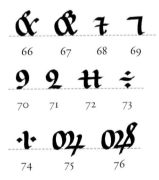

66   67   68   69

70   71   72   73

74   75   76

[57] Thomson, *Bookhands*, pls. 32 (1144), 34 (1186); *CMDGBOx*, pl. 84 (*c.* 1178); still in the thirteenth century: Thomson, *Bookhands*, pl. 35 (1216). A Spanish example: Canellas, *Exempla*, II, pl. 39 (1171).

[58] Steffens, *Paläographie*, pl. 86 (Trier 1191).

[59] Thomson, *Bookhands*, pls. 85 (1155), 87 (1191/2, see n. 42); *CMDGBLo*, pl. 103 (1173/1220?).

[60] Other examples: Thomson, *Bookhands*, pls. 2 (1129), 112 (1173); Burnam, *Palaeographia*, pls. 2 (1155), 7 (1183), 10 (1189, here also used for the **etiam**-abbreviation), 49 (*c.* 1174). An Italian example: *CMDIt*, I, pl. 28 (1193?).

[61] Also Thomson, *Bookhands*, pl. 34 (Germany 1186).

[62] This is testified by the unusual shapes that in the course of the centuries have been given to the **arum**-abbreviation. See, for example, *CMDNL*, I, pl. 27 (816?). The still more uncommon **erum**-abbreviation is seen in a very small Italian hand, dated 1154 (Steffens, *Paläographie*, pl. 83).

[63] *CMDNL*, II, pl. 956 (France *c.* 1106–11); Kirchner, *Scriptura Gothica*, pl. 4 (Italy 1181); Thomson, *Bookhands*, pls. 58–9 (Italy 1145, *c.* 1155).

[64] Thomson, *Bookhands*, pl. 33 (Germany 1158).

In formal script the loop was sometimes applied or completed with a separate stroke.[65]

The **bus**-abbreviation, for the dative and ablative plural, has a form not unrelated to the **que**-abbreviation: in both it consists of the first letter followed by a sign which normally takes the form of a semi-colon (77, pl. 7). In **bus**, especially, the sign came increasingly to be made in one stroke and to assume the form of a figure 3 (78, pl. 12).[66] Italian manuscripts stand apart in displaying a preference for both abbreviations to be written as a single stroke after the letter in the form of a figure 7 or of a narrow letter s or of a curve resembling a comma or an inverted c (79–81).[67] The latter form would remain typical of all later Gothic scripts in Italy.

In Italy, too, **qui** was represented by a distinctive abbreviation, with a horizontal or sloping stroke bisecting the tail of **q** (82).[68]

It may be noted that the horizontal common marks of abbreviation display the general style of Pregothic in their heavy weight and their curved or angular form, at least in Northern European specimens.

CAUSES OF THE TRANSFORMATION OF CAROLINGIAN INTO PREGOTHIC SCRIPT

The causes of the transformation of Carolingian script into Pregothic, or the 'goth-icizing' of Carolingian script, have been debated for a long time and the discussion has virtually come to an end without any one explanation gaining general acceptance.[69]

The early theory proposed by Olga Dobiache-Rojdestvenskaja (1926) claimed to discern the influence of Beneventan script in the genesis of Gothic script and tried to explain the connection between these two systems of script by the contacts that existed between the Normans in Southern Italy and those in Normandy.[70] The relations between the two renowned sanctuaries of St Michael on Monte Gargano and in Mont-Saint-Michel in particular were considered important for this

77 78 79

80 81 82

[65] *CMDF*, I, pl. 8 (France 1120–31); Thompson, *Introduction*, pl. 177 (England before 1135).

[66] For the **que**-abbreviation, see Thomson, *Bookhands*, pl. 5 (France 1183).

[67] Thomson, *Bookhands*, pls. 56–8 (1104, 1133, 1145), etc. The same **que**-abbreviation, however, is already present in a manuscript from Echternach, after 1059 (*CMDF*, III, pl. 22).

[68] Thomson, *Bookhands*, pls. 57–8.

[69] Battelli, *Lezioni*, pp. 224–5; Petrucci, *Breve storia*, pp. 125–7; Stiennon, *Paléographie*, pp. 126–7; Casamassima, *Tradizione*, pp. 153–7.

[70] O. Dobiache-Rojdestvenskaja, 'Quelques considérations sur les orig-ines de l'écriture dite gothique', in *Mélanges Ferdinand Lot*, Paris 1926, pp. 691–721. See an alphabet of formal Beneventan in Bischoff, *Palaeography*, fig. 22 (p. 113).

supposed interchange of graphic influences. The fully developed Beneventan script and the Gothic Textualis do indeed present some extraordinary similarities in their strong shading, angular letter forms, broken minims and the use of fusions. Paul Lehmann, as early as 1925, had been impressed by these similarities.[71] However, Schiaparelli was convinced that the construction of the letters of each script was essentially different and that any similarity between them was fortuitous. His opinion has prevailed.[72]

Jacques Boussard's theory of 1951 has gained wider acceptance than it deserves and is repeated in many a handbook.[73] His observation that for writing early Gothic script the quill was not cut at right angles to the shaft, but had a nib cut obliquely to the shaft (the 'straight pen' of the calligraphers), and that this was done under Insular or Anglo-Saxon influence may perhaps be correct. But that by using such a pen round forms automatically become broken forms, as Boussard asserts, remains unproven. Some authors pass in silence over the technical part of Boussard's theory: there is indeed no proof that, by changing the way in which the nib is cut, one necessarily produces angularity. None of the calligraphic handbooks published in recent decades mentions that possibility. In addition, neither Boussard nor others have any explanation as to why such a new pen came into use, and what the cause of its success was. Boussard's historical conclusions, however, are interesting and will be discussed shortly.

Others have contended that economic constraints account for the introduction of Gothic script.[74] According to them, Carolingian handwriting was unsuited to the needs of economic life and administration that were developing from the twelfth century onwards. But the Gothic Cursive, which took shape in the thirteenth century, would suit such arguments much better. One may question whether the twelfth-century Pregothic was the ideal response to that problem. It is true that

[71] In contrast with Dobiache, he conjectured a direct influence from Beneventan on Italian Gothic: P. Lehmann, 'Zum beneventanischen Schrifttum', *Zentralblatt für Bibliothekswesen*, 42 (1925), p. 608; Foerster, *Abriss*, pp. 200–1.

[72] L. Schiaparelli, 'Influenza della scrittura beneventana sulla gotica?' in L. Schiaparelli, *Note paleografiche (1910–1932)*, ed. G. Cencetti, Turin 1969, pp. 437–62 (originally published in 1929).

[73] J. Boussard, 'Influences insulaires dans la formation de l'écriture gothique', *Scriptorium*, 5 (1951), pp. 238–64. The technical part of this theory was adopted by Cencetti, *Lineamenti*, p. 206 (leaving the possibility open that the nib was not cut obliquely, but that the page on which was written was no longer placed obliquely in front of the scribe, as it was before; his argument is unclear); Petrucci, *Breve storia*, p. 125; Stiennon, *Paléographie*, p. 127; and others. Cencetti has reconsidered this opinion in his *Compendio*, p. 73. It was rejected by Casamassima, *Tradizione*, pp. 103–4. Michael Gullick informs me that he too cannot accept Boussard's technical explanation.

[74] E. Ornato, 'Les conditions de production et de diffusion du livre médiéval (XIIIe–XVe siècles). Quelques considérations générales', in E. Ornato, *La face cachée du livre médiéval. L'histoire du livre vue par Ezio Ornato, ses amis et ses collègues*, Rome 1997, pp. 97–116 (102) (originally published in 1985); Casamassima, *Tradizione*, p. 107, sees the economy of (developed) Gothic Textualis in its use of a limited number of basic elements constituting the various letters.

its compactness and often smaller size allowed scribes to save parchment and to make books smaller and more easily transportable, but it is not easy to see why making the letters angular and more uniform in their construction as described above would have produced a gain in speed of writing.

An interesting idea, defended by many scholars,[75] is that Gothic script was not less, but more legible than Carolingian, because of the stress it laid on the *word* as the basic unit in the text line. The compactness of the letters within the words and especially the Gothic fusions would thus have had a clarifying effect. Instead of the complicating effect that is generally assumed (and is assumed also in this book), Gothic script would have facilitated reading by marking more clearly the successive words and the open spaces between them.

In our opinion the genesis of Gothic script must, at least in part, be understood in the light of a widespread change in artistic taste. The question of whether there are parallels between art (in this case the leading art: architecture) and handwriting has long been debated, with the discussion being dominated by scepticism.[76] We must certainly reject the notion of *influence* from architecture on script, not least because the changes in script predate those in architecture. But the similarities between full-grown Gothic script and Gothic codicological features, on one hand, and Gothic architecture on the other, are too numerous to be fortuitous, and each must be considered an expression of the same aesthetic, of a 'Gothic taste' or 'Gothic mood'. It is expressed in verticality, compactness, angularity, pointedness, closedness and framing, and uniformity. It is a systematic and intellectual approach that sacrificed clarity for style. This point has already been touched upon when dealing with the codicology of the Gothic manuscript book. As for script, the distinction between bold strokes and hairlines is paralleled by the distinction between the load-bearing and decorative parts of a building; the rows of similar minims have a parallel in the tiers and galleries of Gothic cathedrals; the spikiness of the majuscules (see the Appendix, p. 184) corresponds with that of the pinnacles, etc.

The new script originated in the Anglo-Norman kingdom. Boussard was probably right in considering the influence of the British Isles and of Insular or Anglo-Saxon script decisive in the formation of early Gothic. His theory doubtless needs to be clarified by further research. But no evidence has yet been found of any direct link between the use of quires with more than four bifolia (as often encountered in the thirteenth century); the appearance of prickings in the inner as well as in the outer margin; the adoption of uncial **d** and **s**, of the tironian **et** and the other

---

[75] See, for example, Oeser, 'Das *a*', p. 25, after W. Meyer (but Oeser, p. 26, rightly observes that the fusions contribute as well to the compactness of the written area).
[76] Fichtenau, *Mensch und Schrift*, pp. 186 ff.; R. Marichal, 'L'écriture latine et la civilisation occidentale du Ier au XVIe siècle', in *L'écriture et la psychologie des peuples*, Paris 1963, pp. 199–247 (233–44); Mazal, *Buchkunst der Gotik*, pp. 24–6; Stiennon, *Paléographie*, pp. 197–202.

Insular abbreviations mentioned above, and their use in the much earlier Insular tradition.

REGIONAL DIFFERENCES

It is difficult to find characteristics of Pregothic script special to any of the various European countries. Battelli identifies the following features of what he still calls 'scrittura carolina' typical of each part of Europe during the twelfth century:[77]

in Italy the script is large and more beautiful than in other countries;

in Germany it tends to be heavier and more angular;

in England the letters are taller and narrower with finer penstrokes;

script in France is close to English Pregothic, but heavier and rounder, and sometimes angular;

in Spain, finally, the forms are more or less round and similar to those observed in France.

In fact, the heterogeneity of Pregothic script makes it difficult to identify more or less precise national or regional characteristics for the period under discussion. But the differences that from the thirteenth century onwards would lead to a distinction between two branches in Gothic script, both directly derived from Carolingian script and which we will call Northern and Southern Textualis, are already apparent in the twelfth century, as we have seen in a series of graphs distinctive of early manuscripts from Italy, Spain, Portugal and Southern France. The two branches of Textualis will be discussed in the next two chapters.

---

[77] Battelli, *Lezioni*, p. 197.

4

Northern Textualis
(plates 15–46)

Textualis is, without doubt, the most common form of Gothic script, and indeed of all Western medieval scripts. Despite this it has been studied very rarely and by only a few scholars.[1]

Given the gradual nature of the transition from Carolingian to Gothic script, it is impossible to fix even an approximate date from which one may no longer call European handwriting Praegothica or Early or Primitive Gothic, but simply Gothic. In England, France and the Low Countries the full development of Gothic script should probably be dated to the end of the twelfth century, whilst in Italy, the Iberian Peninsula, Germany, Central Europe and Scandinavia it should be placed somewhere in the thirteenth. As it was also from the thirteenth century onwards that cursive forms of Gothic script were developed for documentary use (and soon also for book use), we may conveniently accept the year 1200 as the conventional beginning of the period of fully developed Gothic script, the period to which the Lieftinck classification in its projected expanded form will be applicable. Nevertheless quite a number of hands of the thirteenth century should still be considered representatives of Pregothic script.

Whatever criticism may have been directed at the Lieftinck system,[2] its first category, Textualis, has remained intact. It is generally considered the Gothic script par excellence. Hence the Italian term '(scrittura) gotica' for what is called here Textualis.[3]

---

[1] Bibliography on Northern Textualis: Battelli, *Lezioni*, pp. 223–30; Bischoff, *Palaeography*, pp. 127–36; Brown and Lovett, *Source Book*, pp. 87–94; Cencetti, *Lineamenti*, pp. 205–24; Cencetti, *Compendio*, pp. 71–7; Drogin, *Medieval Calligraphy*, pp. 59–64; A. Kapr, *Fraktur. Form und Geschichte der gebrochenen Schriften*, Mainz 1993; Morison, '"Black-Letter" Text'; Oeser, 'Beobachtungen Textura'; Schneider, *Paläographie*, pp. 36–55; Steinmann, 'Textualis formata'.

[2] For the Lieftinck system, see the Introduction, pp. 20–3.

[3] There is a tendency among present-day Italian palaeographers to use the term 'littera moderna', contrasting with the term 'littera antiqua' applied to Carolingian script. See p. 47, n. 1.

According to Lieftinck Textualis is distinguished by the following letter forms:

(a) two-compartment **a** (1);
(b) ascenders of **b**, **h**, **k**, **l** without loops, their tops being flat or featuring a bifurcation or an approach stroke from the left (2);
(c) **f** and straight **s** standing on the line and having no descender (3).

These are features also typical of Pregothic and later Carolingian script, thus Textualis is no more than a development of the earliest forms of Gothic script. The characteristics of this development will be studied in the pages that follow. It is, however, immediately obvious that it is impossible to deal further with Textualis script as a whole, without taking into account an important distinction between two fundamentally different species, which we shall call Northern Textualis (or simply Textualis) and Southern Textualis, often called Rotunda. The former was in use in England, much of France, the Low Countries, Germany, Central and Eastern Europe and Scandinavia, the latter mainly in the Mediterranean area.

NAMES

Well-executed specimens of the Northern form of this, the highest rank in the hierarchy of Gothic scripts (named after its use in the copying of 'textus', i.e. the Bible), have also been called (if executed with great care) 'textura' (referring to its heavily interwoven appearance), 'littera psalterialis', 'Missalschrift' and 'liturgical hand' (from the categories of books for which it was regularly used), and 'lettre de forme' (drawn from a term used in French late medieval inventories of libraries). We have said above (p. 11) why 'Gothic minuscule' is less suitable. Subtypes within Textualis are discussed at the end of this chapter.

GENERAL FEATURES

In general, Textualis simply accentuates and systematizes the features and forms of the Pregothic scripts discussed in Chapter 3. In its most calligraphic form of Textualis Formata (Textura), especially, it is narrow and vertical, with short ascenders and descenders, composed of generally straight lines and angular curves and marked by heavy shading, in other words a rhythmic alternation of bold strokes and hairlines. The vertical strokes are bold. The hairlines are made in the same plane as that of the constant pen-angle and form an angle with the writing-line of

1   2   3

about 35 degrees. The emphatically constant diagonal direction of the hairlines is one of the basic aesthetic features of Textualis. Whereas the heavy shading is an unchanging feature, there is much variety in the degree of angularity and in the length of ascenders and descenders. Proportions between minims and letters with ascenders of 0.7 or even 0.8 are common.[4] In manuscripts of the fifteenth century in particular, on the other hand, we meet quite a number of hands marked by relatively long ascenders (pls. 41, 42).[5] Rounded letter forms may also be found in books of the same period and earlier, especially in French codices (pls. 41, 43). Extreme angularity, on the other hand, is typical of handwriting from Germany, Central Europe and Scandinavia.

The treatment of the headline and baseline deserves special attention, as this has been the basis on which various categories within Northern Textualis have been distinguished. These distinctions are derived from the rare surviving posters of late medieval writing-masters and a few other sources (see above, p. 18). There is some discussion among palaeographers as to whether these documents reflect a really representative classification of scripts of that period, and whether the terminology they provide is coherent. Although ignoring the more extravagant script names found in these documents, such as 'separatus' and 'argentum extra pennam',[6] modern scholars have admitted the subdivision of Textualis (Formata) into four categories: Textus Quadratus, Textus Praescissus, Textus Semiquadratus and Textus Rotundus.[7] As far as most books in Textualis are concerned, these distinguishing criteria are too subtle to be of much use to manuscript scholars. Only in the most formal and large specimens of Textualis may they be distinguished with ease.

Textus Quadratus (or Textus Fractus; Textus is here a synonym of Textualis) is an extremely angular script mostly used for great Bibles and liturgical books such as missals, psalters, graduals and antiphonaries (pls. 15–16, 26 etc.).[8] It stands at the top of the hierarchy of Gothic scripts. Minims were given a diamond-shaped serif or quadrangle at both the headline and the baseline, made with a separate pen-stroke which required great care (4). When well executed, these applied quadrangles touch each other at their lateral points when several minims occur in sequence, and thus create two highly conspicuous horizontal rows of similar forms, one at the headline, the other at the baseline. In this way the strong sense of a horizontal line

4

4 Zamponi, *Scrittura*, p. 325.

5 See also *CMDGBLo*, pl. 697 (Western Germany 1467); an early example is Kirchner, *Scriptura Gothica*, pl. 10 (England 1250–9).

6 Both terms occur on the poster of Johann vom Hagen (partly reproduced in pl. 17). The reading 'sepatus' = 'saepatus', 'en forme de haie' (Gasparri, *Introduction*, p. 117) would be incorrect given the abbreviation stroke through the descender of the **p**. Comparison with other similar sources, however, seems to indicate that 'sepatus' is the original, correct term. See Spilling, 'Schreibkünste', p. 109.

7 Brown, *Guide*, p. 80; Steinmann, 'Textualis formata', pp. 313–14.

8 Steinmann, 'Textualis formata', pp. 320–5.

is produced, which contrasts with the heavily vertical emphasis characteristic of this type of script, and contributes to the extraordinary dynamism of an otherwise stereotyped script. Some medieval calligraphers created artificial graphic chains by connecting these quadrangles by means of horizontal lines at both the headline and the baseline.[9]

Textus Semiquadratus or Semifractus (pl. 17) is an intermediate form between Quadratus and Rotundus, in other words it combines characteristics of both types and is found in numerous manuscripts. More specifically, according to Bischoff,[10] it has quadrangles only at the headline, not at the baseline. The feet of the minims and ascenders are instead treated in the same way as in Textus Rotundus (5, pl. 29). For a more detailed definition of Semiquadratus, see below, p. 86.

The term Textus Rotundus (pl. 17) is an unfortunate one for two reasons: it applies to a script that may hardly be called rounded, and it may cause confusion with the type of Southern Textualis which has traditionally (and for better reasons) been called Rotunda. Textus Rotundus may be considered the 'normal' Textualis and is in fact closer to the original form of Gothic script, discussed in the preceding chapter, than the three others.[11] As in Pregothic, the base of minims and the shafts of ascenders either turn upwards to the right or have applied feet that slant in the same direction; these feet are hairline strokes and often touch the subsequent letter. If the minims have approach strokes at the headline, a double horizontal chain of connections is created, this time not consisting of quadrangles, but of hairlines (6, pl. 33).

Wolfgang Oeser, in a life devoted to the analysis of Gothic scripts, perceptively went beyond these three traditional distinctions. He discovered more precise rules obeyed by scribes writing the more careful forms of Textualis (with the exception of Textus Praescissus), and was able to refine the existing categories by distinguishing seven variants in addition to pure Textus Quadratus and Textus Rotundus.[12] In addition to the basic difference between the two main categories already mentioned, namely the treatment of the feet of minims and ascenders, he pointed to the form of **a** as a fundamental criterion. We will examine his findings when dealing with that letter below. It is undeniably to Oeser's credit that he was able to reveal sophisticated rules observed by medieval scribes when writing scripts that at first sight are all alike. In practice, however, his system is too refined to be of great use, as it depends on the care with which the feet of minims and ascenders are treated, and on the

5   6

[9] For example the German scribe Wolfgang Spitzweg when writing a large Textualis Formata (1465–7): Fichtenau, *Lehrbücher*, pls. 1, 2, 6, etc.
[10] Bischoff, *Palaeography*, p. 129.
[11] The data advanced by Oeser, 'Das *a*', p. 29, would seem to contradict this opinion. Morison believes that Textus Praescissus is earlier than Textus Quadratus ('"Black-Letter" Text', p. 191).
[12] Oeser, 'Das *a*' (1971) and, in a much more developed form, 'Beobachtungen Textura' (1994).

distinction between two forms of **a**, whilst in fact there are many intermediate forms between these two forms. It can consequently only be applied with success in analysing specimens of Textualis Formata, although the rules seem also to have been known to scribes writing lower levels of Textualis. Many scribes, of course, were never consistent.

The most curious subspecies of Textualis Formata is Textus Praescissus (also called Textus Abscisus, pl. 27), sometimes considered to have been at the top of the hierarchy of Gothic scripts.[13] The variant medieval names 'Praecisus', 'Prescisus' etc., which are recorded in the handbooks, seem to be corruptions of the original term. Like Textus Quadratus, it is a deliberately artificial type of handwriting, but it was used on a much smaller scale. The headline was given the same treatment as in Quadratus, but the minims and the ascenders, or more often a selection of minims and ascenders, end flat on the baseline without any additional stroke, serif or incurvation (7), hence the qualification 'sine pedibus' found in the poster of the German writing-master Johann vom Hagen (pl. 17). It is as if the feet of those vertical elements had been cut off. The etymology 'praescindere', an unclassical form of 'scindere' ('to cut'), is more likely than the meaning 'precise' proposed by some. The artificial square-ended shape of the feet could have been obtained either by twisting the pen at the bottom of the vertical stroke, or by drawing the outline with the corner of the nib and filling in with ink.[14] The use of a 'straight' pen[15] would have been helpful in making the square feet, but would have involved as much twisting in the tracing of the other elements of the script. Textus Praescissus was anyway only considered appropriate for the most formal (usually liturgical) manuscripts.

Examples of hands that display a tendency towards Textus Praescissus may already be seen in Praegothica (pl. 12). The script was used in the thirteenth and fourteenth centuries only sparingly in France, but more often in Germany and especially Austria. It had, however, an extraordinary vogue in England and may in a sense be called an English national type. The letters with straight feet are normally the following: **f**, **h**, **i**, **m**, **n**, **r**, straight **s** and the second minim of **u**; sometimes **a** and tironian **et**. The Textus Praescissus of Johann vom Hagen is extreme in using straight feet even for **c**, **e** and round **r** (pl. 17).[16]

7

13 Brown, *Guide*, p. 80. On Textus Praescissus, see Steinmann, 'Textualis formata', pp. 316–19; Drogin, *Medieval Calligraphy*, pp. 149–52; Harris, *Calligraphy*, pp. 54–7; Knight, *Historical Scripts*, D3.

14 Brown and Lovett, *Source Book*, pp. 107–8; Harris, *Calligraphy*, pp. 55–6.

15 According to Harris (*Calligraphy*, p. 123), a straight pen is 'a pen with the nib cut obliquely to the shaft, facilitating the drawing of an upright stem. When positioned horizontally, it will produce a greater contrast in thick and thin strokes, an effect known as "shading".'

16 A similar observation can be made on the Praescissus of Hermann Strepel (Steinmann, 'Textualis formata', p. 318, n. 43).

In its lack of 'Gothic' feet, Textus Praescissus looks closer in appearance to Carolingian script than the other forms of Gothic handwriting. In this respect it has a certain similarity with the Southern Textualis, in which a selection of 'Praescissus' letter forms are a normal feature.[17]

Textualis script in general, and Northern Textualis in particular, is strongly marked by the so-called rules of Meyer, which regulated its making, although without ever precluding the scribe's own freedom of choice. In an epoch-making paper of 1897 Wilhelm Meyer[18] summarized his observations on Textualis in the following points, quoted here in English from Bischoff's *Latin Palaeography*:[19]

(1) 'When two adjacent letters have bows facing each other (for example **bo**, **oc**, **po**), then they are set so close that the bows partially overlap. But wherever the bows of the textura are changed into straight strokes, there the letters share the vertical parts of the transformed bows' (8).

(2) 'In order to avoid as far as possible the meeting of bow and straight stroke, the "round" **r** from the old ligature "**or**" is also attached to letters with bows: **b**, round [i.e. Uncial] **d**, **h**, **p**, **v**, **y**' (9).

The first rule determines the use of fusions (also called bitings, conjunctions, junctures), already mentioned above (p. 57), the second the use of round **r**. They were by no means considered obligatory and the extent to which they were obeyed varied a lot, not only from country to country, but also from scribe to scribe, and even within the work of a single scribe. Individual scribes chose whether or not to use fusions depending on the space available, especially at the end of the line, just as they would choose between using an abbreviation or writing the word in full in order to end the written line more or less exactly at the end of the ruled line. Northern Textualis rarely involved the use of scribal line-filling devices (about which see the Appendix, p. 186) which are so often found in the Southern group. For this reason, scribes needed freedom in their use of fusions and abbreviations in order to maintain a strictly rectangular text area, a requirement for the most formal manuscripts.

Meyer himself provided a table of the more and less frequently found fusions.[20] Nevertheless it is difficult to attribute a given specimen of script to a particular region solely on the basis of the fusions it contains. In general, French and English manuscripts contain many fusions, whilst German codices as a rule exhibit only a very limited range.[21] German scribes, for example, avoided fusions after the letter **h**, or limited themselves to fusions after **d** or after **d**, **b** and **p**. Two less frequently occurring fusions deserve comment: those ending on **a** and those ending on **s**. In

8   9

[17] Steinmann, 'Textualis formata', pp. 318–19.
[18] Meyer, *Buchstaben-Verbindungen*.
[19] Bischoff, *Palaeography*, p. 130.
[20] Reproduced in Casamassima, *Tradizione corsiva*, p. 123.
[21] Oeser, 'Das *a*', p. 25; Cencetti, *Lineamenti*, pp. 210–11.

Textualis, **a** can be connected with a preceding **b**, **d**, **h**, **p** or **v** if it takes the form of 'box'-**a** (a typical alternative form of Textualis **a** to be discussed below), which opens with a minim stroke, that can be rounded in rapid execution (10, pls. 19, 26, 30). An **aa**-fusion also is found, albeit very rarely.[22] Fusion of the normal, double-bow **a** with a preceding letter is a somewhat fanciful form found in manuscripts from German-speaking countries (11, pl. 16).[23]

Round **s** at the end of the word can be made so rounded that it is as if it opens with a bow, so that it can be fused with preceding **o** (12).[24] This fusion is in fact very rare. The alternative form of 'trailing' **s** lends itself much better to fusions with the preceding letter (13). The same applies to the cursive final **s** (for both last-named forms of **s**, see pp. 64 and 93).

Fusion of **t** with preceding **b** is definitely unorthodox.[25]

Double fusions, in other words fusions of three subsequent letters, seem to be avoided in Northern Textualis. Nevertheless the double fusion **hoc** occurs in France;[26] also **dde**.[27]

The study of fusions becomes extremely complicated as soon as we leave the field of Formata scripts: in more rapid hands, it is often impossible to state whether the scribe did or did not intend to bring two letters together in such a connection.

In an important article, Stefano Zamponi added a third rule to the two discovered (or rediscovered) by Meyer.[28] This is the feature that he calls 'elision'. This feature had already received some attention from Oeser and Gumbert, who referred to it respectively as 'Unterdrückung der Brechung in der Kopfpartie' and '**c**-Konnex'.[29] It had first been described in the sixteenth century by the Italian writing-master Giovanbattista Verini. The rule can be formulated as follows: when the last stroke of a letter ends at the headline and the succeeding letter has an approach stroke also at the headline (as in Textus Rotundus) or a quadrangle (as in Textus Quadratus and Textus Praescissus), the approach stroke or quadrangle is omitted. The same rule governs the use of spurs (on which see below, p. 81): if the succeeding letter has an ascender featuring a pointed projection (or 'spur') at the headline, then the

10   11

12   13

[22] *CMDF*, I, pl. 58 (France 1382), top, col. a, l. 6.

[23] *CMDA*, II, pl. 398 (Austria 1441); *Litterae Medii Aevi. Festschrift für Johanne Autenrieth zu ihrem 65. Geburtstag*, ed. M. Borgolte and H. Spilling, Sigmaringen 1988, fig. 30 (Germany 1512).

[24] Kirchner, *Scriptura Gothica*, pl. 29 (Northern France 1379).

[25] Paris, Bibl. Nat. de France, MS lat. 15874, f. 18r (France 1318–34) (this page is not reproduced in *CMDF*, III, pl. 92).

[26] Same manuscript as in n. 25; *CMDF*, I, pl. 37 (France 1326). This double fusion is avoided in our pl. 26.

[27] *CMDF*, II, pl. 47 (France 1329).

[28] Zamponi, 'Elisione' (1988).

[29] W. Oeser, 'Die Brüder des gemeinsamen Lebens in Münster als Bücherschreiber', *Archiv für Geschichte des Buchwesens*, 5 (1964), cols. 198–398 (col. 254); Gumbert, *Kartäuser*, pp. 222–6.

spur is omitted. The letters that create elision in the succeeding letter are **c**, **e**, **f**, **g**, **r**, **t**, **x**, although in fact only **f**, **g** and **t** end with a horizontal stroke on the headline; the other letters, and most notably **e**, present no real connecting stroke. The letters that undergo elision are **i**, **m**, **n**, **p**, **r**, **t**, **u** and those which have ascenders with spurs (14, 15).

Like the two 'Rules of Meyer', the rule regulating elisions was by no means obligatory and is only clearly discernible in specimens of Textualis Formata (pls. 26, 39, 40, 44). Together, these three rules reveal Textualis as a highly sophisticated script, in which every distinctive feature tends to bring the letters of a single word closer together, to emphasize its 'graphic chain' and to separate the words more clearly from each other, thus supposedly enhancing the legibility of the script.

The treatment of the top of ascenders and the base of descenders may vary a great deal in Textualis. The bifurcation at the top of **b**, **h**, **k**, **l**, obtained by adding a short sloping stroke at the left of the ascenders (very occasionally at the right),[30] as seen in many examples of Praegothica, tends to be a feature of the more rapid forms of Textualis (16). When traced more carefully, the bifurcated ascenders assume either a sloping triangular shape or a more artificial straight one, or they might be reduced to simply a sloped top (17). Heavy triangles on the top of short ascenders appear to be typical of Textualis from Central Europe (18, pls. 34–5, 44). Another, less common shaping of the top of the ascenders is a horizontal or almost horizontal serif extending to both sides of the ascenders or, more frequently, to just its left side (19, pls. 25, 31).[31] Perhaps the most typical form in Textualis Formata (sometimes also in Libraria) from the later fourteenth century onwards is the subtle bifurcation of the shaft, consisting of a sloping top and a sloping (or occasionally vertical[32]) hairline to the left, traced with the corner of the nib (20, pls. 30, 37, 40, 46). This form should be viewed within the context of the habitual practice of multiplying hairlines and other decorative elements common to the late fourteenth and fifteenth centuries, about which see below, p. 82.

Whereas the shaping of the top of the ascenders, where such shaping occurs, would as a rule include an extension to the left, the base of the descenders usually was given an inverse shaping, namely an extension to the right, although true

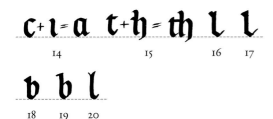

14   15   16 17

18   19   20

[30] Kirchner, *Scriptura Gothica*, pl. 10 (England 1250–9).
[31] Another example: Crous and Kirchner, *Schriftarten*, fig. 21 (Germany 1315).
[32] Vertical hairlines are present in *CMDG-BLo*, pl. 354 (Germany 1419).

bifurcation of the descenders is seldom as conspicuous as it is in the ascenders (21–3, pls. 34, 40).[33]

It seems clear that the general tendency of scribes when writing Textualis was to stress the headline and the baseline, and not to accentuate the lines formed by the top of the ascenders and the bottom of the descenders. This, together with the generally short length of both descenders and ascenders, is why Gothic Textualis, although a minuscule script, tends to give the reader the impression of a majuscule script, written within a two-line scheme.

In manuscripts of the thirteenth and fourteenth centuries (sometimes also the fifteenth), but not in those in Formata script, the ascenders on the first line of the page are often lengthened and even curved to the right (pls. 18, 23). They can form loops or display elaborate calligraphic decoration, pointed extensions etc. (24). These forms were evidently derived from documentary script and seem to be influenced by the *litterae elongatae* on the top line of charters and similar documents. The descenders on the last line of the page may likewise be lengthened, curved and decorated in the same way (25).[34]

These features were in fact already present in twelfth-century codices (see p. 59 and pl. 13) and are related to the earliest forms of Gothic cursive script. It appears that scribes, trained in writing documents in 'documentary' script, took the opportunity when writing books to form 'cursive' ascenders and descenders at those places where space was available on the page, namely on the top and bottom line.

Textualis, and especially Textualis Formata, is a constructed script, obtained by combining a relatively small set of strokes. These strokes, and the way the various letters were constructed from them, are illustrated in the pattern book of Gregorius Bock, a German scribe of the early sixteenth century (pls. 15–16).[35] Most strokes are straight, but in the fourteenth and fifteenth century scribes had a tendency to make some strokes slightly concave, in particular the upper stroke of **a**, **c**, **d**, **e**, **f**, **o** and straight **s** (26, pls. 26, 33, 36, 40, 43). As far as **c** and more especially **e** are concerned, this may perhaps have occurred under influence from Gothic

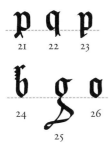

[33] Conspicuous forking of the ascenders is found in Crous and Kirchner, *Schriftarten*, fig. 52 (Low Countries 1456). Sloping serifs at the end of descenders, or descenders ending in an angle to the right are a survival of Praegothic practices as seen in our pls. 3, 6, 9, 11, 13–14. We see them in the thirteenth century, for example, in our pl. 18 and in Thomson, *Bookhands*, pl. 37 (Germany 1240).

[34] Examples: Kirchner, *Scriptura Gothica*, pls. 9 (France 1227), 32b (England 1405); Thomson, *Bookhands*, pls. 12 (France 1277), 36 (Germany 1225), 98 (England 1336).

[35] The strokes composing the Textualis letters are shown in Casamassima, *Tradizione corsiva*, pp. 108–9, figs. 10–11; see also the construction of a few letters in Bischoff, *Palaeography*, p. 113, fig. 25, and the Lucerne writing exercises reproduced in the same book, pl. 19.

cursive script: a simplified ductus with markedly concave upper stroke is normal for these letters in cursive script (see below, p. 145). The use of concave strokes for all the elements of a letter such as **o** is typical of German and Central European manuscripts of the end of the Middle Ages (27, pls. 34–5, 44).

Another characteristic of later Textualis directly linked to the previous one is the addition of decorative forms and ornamental elements, which also took place during the fourteenth and fifteenth centuries. One finds spiky or thorny forms on the one hand, and additional hairlines on the other.

Like Gothic architecture, which is marked amongst other things by its sculptured pinnacles, Gothic script displays a predilection for spiky or thorny projections. These are one of the chief features of the Gothic majuscule script, discussed below in the Appendix, but in the last two centuries of the Middle Ages they come to the fore in minuscule script as well. They are especially conspicuous in the formation of the bodies of letters and the 'spurs' on the ascenders.

Carefully made Textualis has square forms, consisting of bold strokes and hairlines. Where two strokes overlap, as happens at the angles, a spiky angle is created by making one of the strokes slightly too long (pls. 40, 43–6). This can happen by accident, but also became a studied feature; the 'thorn' may even be applied separately. The resulting form is comparable with, and had arisen from, the same stylization as the lozenges or quadrangles that appear on the minims in Textus Quadratus, Praescissus and Semiquadratus. Such thorns are seen at the headline in **a**, **b**, **c**, **e**, **g**, **m**, **n**, **o**, **p**, **q**, etc. (28). They may also be present on the left of the bodies of letters at or close to the baseline, where they reinforce the characteristic appearance of Textus Quadratus (29, pl. 44). Such extensions can exceptionally be seen on a wide range of letters in very early examples of Textualis Formata.[36]

This thorny shaping of the bodies of letters (at least at the headline), which like the concave strokes emphasizes their angularity, normally does not appear before the end of the fourteenth century and is especially typical of German and Central European manuscripts. It became more widespread by the sixteenth century.

When considering the treatment of the ascenders special attention should be paid to 'spurs'. These consist of pointed, triangular extensions attached to the left of ascenders, in principle at the height of the headline, and which were created by tracing a quadrangle to the left of the shaft that had just been traced (pls. 15, 39–41, 44). Spurs, or something resembling spurs, could be considered natural extensions to the left of **f** and straight **s**, whose shafts were traced in two strokes, although such

---

[36] *CMDGBOx*, pl. 110 (England 1254–72).

27   28   29

extensions were not obligatory (30, pls. 26–7, 29, 39, 44). But they are in fact of a different nature from spurs proper. When spurs were added to other ascenders (in Textus Quadratus, Semiquadratus or Praescissus), they testify to a desire to increase the emphasis given to the headline by providing additional quadrangles to the row already formed there by the treatment of the tops of the minims (touching each other at their lateral points), and possibly augmented by the spiky forms of the letter bodies (31).

It is clear that the spurs only have their full aesthetic effect when they are placed exactly on the headline (this is often not the case with **f** and straight **s**, if these letters have 'spurs' at all). A quite striking number of manuscripts contain letters with the spurs placed too low, so that they have much more of a disorganizing effect on the structure of the page than if there had been no spurs at all (pl. 41).[37]

The use of spurs seems to have started in France in the middle of the fourteenth century, and to have been limited at first to the letter **l** in initial position.[38] By the end of the century they were often added to all ascenders in all positions, although their use was sometimes limited either by the rule regulating elisions (see above, p. 78) or for no apparent reason.[39] Their use was by no means restricted to the Formata level, since they may also be found in specimens of lower levels of formality, albeit in the form of short lines instead of triangles.

Gothic Textualis, especially in the last centuries of its use and mainly (but not exclusively) in its highest level, Formata, is distinguished by quite a number of decorative hairlines. The hairlines discussed here are different from the natural sloping hairlines typical of Textualis, which were traced upwards from left to right and the natural counterpart to the heavy down-strokes produced by a broad-nibbed pen (see above, p. 73). By contrast, these hairlines have a purely decorative character and appear as additions to the letters proper. They were mostly traced in various directions with the corner of the nib and have traditionally been considered a sign of decadence and reflection of the Gothic script's loss of vigour.[40] As observed below, it is clear that various parts of single letters in Textualis could also be traced as hairlines using the corner of the nib.

The most frequently occurring ornament of this kind is the vertical pendant hairline at the end of the headstroke of **t**, especially at the end of a word (pls. 26, 33–4, 44). As mentioned before (p. 64), it had its origin in a natural downward movement of the pen when finishing the last stroke of final **t**. This feature came to be applied almost universally, although in the thirteenth century the decorative

30   31

---

[37] Another example: *CMDA*, III, pl. 116 (Southern Low Countries 1456).

[38] *CMDF*, I, pl. 52 (1368); *CMDB*, I, pl. 199 (1385).

[39] The latter seems to be the case in *CMDNL*, II, pl. 609 (Northern Low Countries 1509).

[40] For example, in Thompson, *Introduction*, p. 456, and Thomson, *Bookhands*, pls. 17, 23.

stroke was often still quite bold, and was traced without turning the pen. In more rapid handwriting, the hairline tended to be made very long (32, pl. 32).[41]

The same vertical hairline is sometimes to be seen appended to final **c** (the shape of which can closely resemble that of **t**, pl. 39)[42] and even to final **g** (in German vernacular manuscripts).[43] It is found very rarely in final **r**, where it is probably an alteration of the hairline at the top of the letter **r**.[44]

More significant is the vertical hairline decorating the tironian **et**, where such a line is attached either to the headstroke of the graph, or to the beginning of the cross-stroke, or to its end, or to both (33, 34, pls. 15, 27, 42). The typically German tironian **et** (see p. 98) and similar zigzag abbreviation signs are normally traversed by a long vertical hairline.

A hairline at the top of the final stroke of **r** (in all positions) appeared in Germany at a very early date and is perhaps the oldest evidence of the use of hairlines in Gothic script (35).[45] It was taken over by scribes elsewhere but remained a typically German feature (pls. 28–9, 32, 45–6). It probably had its origin in a Pregothic graph in which **r** was given a 'double-horned' endstroke (36, see above, p. 63).

In some luxury English manuscripts in Textualis Formata of the fourteenth and fifteenth centuries the hairline above the headline may take the form of a flourish, similar to the strokes on **i** in the same manuscripts (37). Some English liturgical codices bear witness to a veritable cult of the flourish; in these it was also used profusely in the forms of punctuation.[46]

Special attention should be drawn to the curved hairline connecting the common form of abbreviation with the letter beneath. It was used in particular with the abbreviation that indicated the omission of **r** + vowel or vowel + **r** (hereafter simply called 'r-abbreviation') and was evidently derived from Gothic cursive script, in which the final part of a letter *and* the mark of abbreviation above it were made in a single stroke as a time-saving device (38). It is noticeable that this use became stylized in Textualis and became a standard form even in Textualis Formata, especially in England (on this level of execution the 'connection' of course no longer

32   33   34   35

36   37   38

[41] *CMDB*, I, pls. 179 (1372) and 180 (1373–4), both from the Southern Low Countries. See, however, also our pl. 44.
[42] Also Thomson, *Bookhands*, pls. 47 (Germany 1384), 106 (England 1442).
[43] Kirchner, *Scriptura Gothica*, pl. 26 (Switzerland 1359).
[44] *CMDS*, II, pl. 76 (Sweden 1460).
[45] Thomson, *Bookhands*, pls. 36 (1225), 37 (1240). See Schneider, *Paläographie*, p. 31.
[46] An obvious example is the 'Luttrell Psalter', with its spiral-shaped flourishes: see L. F. Sandler, *Gothic Manuscripts 1285–1385*, London and Oxford 1986 (A Survey of Manuscripts Illuminated in the British Isles, ed. J. J. G. Alexander, 5), pl. 282. Stanley Morison ('"Black-Letter" Text', p. 192) calls this manuscript an example of 'artificial, not to say decadent, liturgical writing'.

constituted a natural process, but an artificial one, and thus could be traced as a hairline; pls. 27, 39). It was extended to other superscript abbreviations (see pl. 27).

Other commonly occurring hairlines are those terminating the limb of **h**, round **r** and **y**, all three of which extend below the baseline and curve to the right. The hairline extension at the bottom of round **r**, in particular (39, pls. 26, 43), developed into a common feature, typical also of lower-grade manuscripts in which it was exaggerated.[47] In German manuscripts, however, where the usual form of **r** is often topped by a hairline, round **r** does not exhibit this hairline extension at its base.

Finally, hairlines were sometimes added to almost all final letters of words in extremely luxurious manuscripts written in Textualis Formata (pl. 26).

INDIVIDUAL LETTER FORMS

a is a letter which has received much attention from palaeographers seeking different varieties within the otherwise stereotyped forms of Textualis. It has been observed that the top of the shaft of **a** turns over to the left in the thirteenth century, and that the bow thus formed tends to be closed from the fourteenth century onwards (40, 41). But while there are many examples of **a** with closed upper bow in manuscripts of the thirteenth century, especially those produced in France (pl. 19), after 1300 **a** with open upper bow became extremely rare.[48]

A variant form of **a**, known as 'box'-**a** (in German: 'Kasten'-**a**), was made by adopting a new ductus. It consists of two vertical strokes connected with each other at the top and at the bottom, this 'box' being divided by an intermediary horizontal stroke (42). The distinction between the two forms of **a** is often unclear, especially in the early phase of Textualis or in rapid script. We see examples of rounded **a** with closed upper bow approaching the 'box' type about the middle of the thirteenth century,[49] and fully formed box-**a** from the end of the same century.[50] Occasionally the manuscripts reveal how a box-**a** could be made.[51]

The fact that this **a** consists of two strokes resembling minims doubtless gave it a special attraction as conforming to the Gothic aesthetic, in preference to the normal form, which conforms less well to it. Nevertheless, in reality these two strokes were only very rarely treated fully as minims in Textus Quadratus, and were seldom given quadrangles at their base.[52]

39   40

41   42

[47] *CMDF*, I, pl. 44 (France 1343).
[48] For example: *CMDF*, I, pl. 55 (France? 1375).
[49] *CMDF*, I, pls. 14 (*c.* 1245–72), 18 (1282); *CMDGBOx*, pl. 126 (1273–4?); all three examples from France.
[50] *CMDGBOx*, pls. 136 (1290) and 141 (1294), both from France.
[51] *CMDF*, I, pl. 51 (France 1364–73), f. 355v, l. 4. Box-**a** does not occur in Bock's pattern-book (our pl. 15).
[52] As in *CMDA*, III, pl. 379 (Austria 1472).

The use of the two forms of **a** in later medieval manuscripts may sometimes have been random, but more often it seems to have obeyed strict rules. These rules have been studied in detail by Wolfgang Oeser.[53] Here is a summary of his important findings. In Textus Quadratus scribes used exclusively normal, double-bow **a** (in German: 'Köpfchen'-**a**). In Textus Rotundus, on the contrary, they used exclusively box-**a**, which consequently became the 'normal' form at the end of the Middle Ages (pls. 32–3, 42). If **a** was fused with the preceding letter, however, both Quadratus and Rotundus normally used box-**a** (see above, pp. 77–8). Oeser distinguished seven variants between pure Quadratus and pure Rotundus based on various kinds of departures from the above rule, Variants I–IV moving progressively away from the convention of Textus Quadratus, Variants V–VI coming closer to that of Textus Rotundus. For each variant Oeser provides us with numerous examples.

Variant I is a variety very close to pure Textus Quadratus in which box-**a** is consistently used after the seven letters **c**, **e**, **f**, **g**, **r**, **t**, **x**, or after a selection of them. These letters share the same feature of their final stroke ending at the headline. One may observe that these are the same letters that may create elision in the succeeding letter, as noted above (p. 79). Surviving examples of this variant are not very numerous and are mostly confined to books from the area of Ile-de-France and Northern France. The earliest known example according to Oeser is dated 1282.[54]

Variant II is a variety of Textus Quadratus in which the normal, double-bow **a** is used only at the beginning of words, box-**a** in all other positions (pl. 29). It occurs from the end of the thirteenth century till the end of the fifteenth. This variant was used in France and the Low Countries, but there are also English and German examples.

Variant III is Textus Quadratus in which the normal, double-bow **a** has been abandoned altogether in favour of box-**a** (pls. 36, 46). Oeser records numerous examples from England, Northern France, Paris and Belgium. The variant seems to have become less popular in England from the middle of the fifteenth century onwards. It became very popular in the Low Countries, the Lower Rhine area and Westfalia from the second half of the fourteenth century.

Variant IV is typical of English Textualis. It is Textus Quadratus in which box-**a** occurs in all positions, except after the seven letters mentioned under Variant I, or a selection of these, when the normal, double-bow **a** is used instead (pls. 39, 43). The double-bow **a** may also be found at the beginning of words. This variant does not appear before the second half of the fourteenth century. It was used now and then in France during the fourteenth century, but occurs more often in fifteenth-century manuscripts from France and also from the Low Countries, probably under English influence.

[53] See n. 12.   [54] *CMDNL*, I, pl. 131.

Variants v and vi, both based on Textus Rotundus, occur only rarely. According to Oeser they are not variants of Rotundus properly speaking, but represent imitations of Textus Quadratus. Variant v is Textus Rotundus in which the box-**a** is replaced by the normal, double-bow **a** at the beginning of words (it is thus comparable with Variant ii).[55] Variant vi, on the other hand, uses normal, double-bow **a** in initial position and after the seven letters recorded under Variant i and is consequently the Textus Rotundus counterpart of Variant iv. It does not appear before the early fifteenth century and the earliest examples are English.[56]

Variant vii, finally, is a special form of Textualis, to which Oeser applied the name Semiquadratus, following in this the writing-master Johann vom Hagen (pl. 17). It is a Textus Rotundus in which all **a**s are of the double-bow, not of the box, type (pl. 19). It is consequently the reverse of Variant iii. Although not found as frequently as Variants iii and iv, it is very well represented in manuscripts from the second half of the thirteenth century onwards. It is typical of books from South-eastern Europe (Bohemia, Moravia, Austria), and occurs much more rarely in manuscripts from other parts of Europe.

Although palaeographers have not questioned Oeser's findings *per se*, some have considered his system too refined and precise, or too limited to high-status manuscripts, to be of wide application.[57]

There was a great deal of variety in the manner in which **a** was traced in the last centuries of the Middle Ages, especially as far as the normal, double-bow form is concerned. The closing stroke of the upper bow of normal **a** is normally a bold line (41, pl. 25). But in most specimens of Formata one or both of the strokes closing the bows are hairlines made with the corner of the pen (43). Similarly, the dividing line in box-**a** is mostly a hairline in this class of scripts (44). In both forms this transverse stroke, whether bold or a hairline, can either follow the general sloping direction of the hairlines,[58] or, more commonly, be horizontal, or even show an inverse inclination, downward to the right.

In many thirteenth- or fourteenth-century Textuales, especially those of the Libraria or Currens level, **a** rises higher than the other 'small' letters (i.e. those that lack ascenders) and thus deliberately interrupts the four-line scheme (pls. 24–5, 28, 32, 42). This probably resulted from a desire to render more precisely the form of this complicated letter in rapid scripts of relatively small size, a difficult task in a script written with a broad-nibbed pen. We will see (p. 100) that scribes of certain kinds of small handwriting of the same type and level, such as Littera Parisiensis, tended to adopt the single-compartment **a** which, when traced in the same size as

43   44

55 For example: *CMDF*, ii, pl. 56 (France 1357).
56 For example: *CMDNL*, i, pl. 153 (Low Countries 1443), here only as display script (four top lines).
57 Gumbert, *Kartäuser*, p. 232; Schneider, *Paläographie*, p. 50, n. 90.
58 For example: *CMDGBOx*, pl. 216 (Southern Low Countries *c.* 1380–81?).

the other small letters, presents less danger of blurring the letter-image than the Textualis two-compartment **a** had it been made in the same size.[59]

As in Pregothic script, **d** in Textualis may assume two forms, the 'Uncial' one with sloping shaft, and the 'Half-Uncial' one, with vertical shaft (45, 46). The latter, however, was clearly in decline and became extremely rare after the thirteenth century (pl. 27).[60] Until then, both forms could be incorporated within the system of fusions: the sloping **d** for fusions with the succeeding letter (47), the vertical **d** for fusions with the preceding one (48), in conformity with the first rule of Meyer. The disappearance of Half-Uncial **d** explains why, in the later Middle Ages, the fusion **do** is so much more frequent than the fusion **od**. Nevertheless, fusion of Uncial **d** with the preceding letter can be found, and even fusion of two adjacent Uncial **d**s.[61] In practice, Uncial **d** is the only form to be found in Northern Textualis of the fourteenth and fifteenth centuries. When the vertical **d** is found in Northern manuscripts of the fifteenth and sixteenth centuries, it should doubtless be attributed to Italian Humanistic influence.

When writing Textualis at the Currens and Libraria levels, scribes trained within the documentary tradition sometimes took advantage of the space offered by the left-hand margin to extend the shaft of the Uncial **d** at the beginning of the line to the left and might even start it with an upward movement of the pen (49, pl. 22). This phenomenon of the 'falling' **d** (sometimes also observed in the middle of lines, see pl. 18) seems to be limited to manuscripts of the thirteenth and early fourteenth centuries.[62] The feature may be compared with what has been said above about extensions on the upper and lower line (p. 80).

The practice of making the sloping shaft of Uncial **d** so short that the whole letter does not extend beyond the headline is extremely rare.[63] In French and English Textualis Formata dating from the end of the Middle Ages and written under Cursiva influence, the shaft of **d** is often lengthened and convex (50, pl. 43) instead of being straight or concave (which are the more normal forms).[64] The hairline extensions at the top of some **d**s probably also point to cursive influence

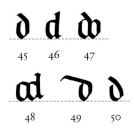

45   46   47

48   49   50

[59] There is probably no reason to suppose, as Karin Schneider does (*CMDD*, IV, pp. xvi–xvii), that this feature has its origin in contemporary cursive script of the type we will call Cursiva Antiquior.

[60] Other English examples: Brown, *Guide*, pl. 28 (c. 1310–20); *CMDG-BCam*, pl. 137 (1320–24).

[61] See n. 27; **dd** is not a fusion in our pl. 39, ll. 5 and 14.

[62] Other examples: Thomson, *Bookhands*, pls. 11 (France 1263), 12 (Southern Low Countries 1277); *CMDF*, I, pl. 28 (a French scribe in Rome, 1299).

[63] *CMDF*, I, pl. 37 (France 1326); in the same manuscript the tail of **q** scarcely extends below the baseline.

[64] French examples: *CMDF*, III, pl. 210 (two manuscripts, 1500); V, pls. 182 (1517), 183 (1522); VIII, pl. 148 (1485). An English example: *CMDG-BCam*, pl. 335 (1490).

on Textualis Formata, which would explain why in French and English manuscripts they mostly extend downward, whereas in German and Central European ones they turn upward (corresponding with the supposed 'counter-clockwise' and 'clockwise' loops observed in the cursive hands of these respective areas, see p. 144) (51, 52, pls. 19, 34). This question needs further investigation. Genuine loops on the ascender of **d** in Textualis point to cursive influence and are extremely rare.[65]

f presents few problems. As in Praegothica, **f** and its sister letter, straight **s**, sometimes have a slight tendency to descend below the baseline in German manuscripts.[66] The later examples may probably be explained by the predominance of cursive script as a book hand in that country. In rare instances, also in German manuscripts, the upper section of both letters, or of **f** alone, is sometimes closed by means of a hairline, which gives the letters an unusual appearance (53, 54).[67] Here too cursive influence may be at work. Finally, double **f** at the beginning of words seems to be a special form of majuscule, as it often occurs at the beginning of a sentence, or as the first letter of a title, proper name, or important word; it should therefore, as a matter of principle, not be transcribed 'ff'. It is found mostly in documentary script. When used in Textualis (which was rare), **ff** was sometimes treated as a ligature with the first **f** being given a shape different from the second.[68]

It has proved difficult to classify the various forms of **g** found in Textualis. The complicated Carolingian **g**, consisting of two lobes connected by a curving stroke, the upper one provided with a final horizontal stroke, was abandoned. The simplified letter that took its place, however, took various forms that are hard to distinguish unless the ductus can be clearly observed with certainty. Palaeographers have distinguished two forms distinguished by their ductus: the 8-shaped **g** (55) and the 'Rücken'-**g** (**g** 'with a back') (56).[69] In the first, the left section of the upper lobe and the right section of the lower lobe were made in a single stroke (pl. 42), in the second the right section of both lobes is formed in a single vertical stroke (pls. 15, 26, 33, 45). After the twelfth century, the lower lobe was normally closed, often by a diagonal hairline. There are also many intermediate forms.

51   52   53

54   55   56

[65] An Austrian example in Textualis Formata: *CMDA*, i, pl. 194 (1383).
[66] Kirchner, *Scriptura Gothica*, pl. 11b (1250–76); Thomson, *Bookhands*, pl. 43 (1323).
[67] Steffens, *Paläographie*, pl. 104 (1339); P. Salmon, *Les manuscrits liturgiques latins de la Bibliothèque Vaticane*, i, Vatican City 1968 (Studi e Testi, 251), no. 251 (c. 1397).
[68] *CMDGBCam*, pl. 362 (England 1523), at the bottom; see also *CMDA*, iii, pl. 379 (Austria 1472), last but one l.
[69] Gumbert, *Kartäuser*, pp. 216–17.

Rare forms are a 'Rücken'-**g** in which the two vertical strokes making the upper lobe cross the upper horizontal stroke (57, pl. 41),[70] and **g** with a looped lower lobe (58).[71] Both betray cursive influence.

Special attention should be drawn to **g** without a final connecting stroke, because it points to a consciously different morphology.[72] This feature is found more often in Southern Textualis. An idiosyncratic form of connecting stroke is observed in certain late deluxe manuscripts of English origin: here the stroke has an angular shape, which seems to be an assimilation with the final stroke of **r** (59).[73]

More important than the preceding distinctions, with a spectrum of intermediate forms between them, is the general evolution one may observe in the relative proportions of the upper and the lower lobe of the letter. Whereas in Pregothic script the lower lobe is generally larger than the upper one, in the succeeding centuries this relationship was gradually reversed and as a rule in the fourteenth and fifteenth centuries the lower lobe was markedly smaller than the upper one. Since it was usual at this time to write a little *above* the ruled line (instead of *on* the line), **g** as a result came to descend very little beneath the ruled line. The final stage in the evolution of this letter form was sometimes reached when scribes abandoned the idea that the upper lobe should stand on the line in the way that the letter **o** does, for example; instead the entire letter was made so short that the lower lobe stood on the line and **g** thus became a 'small' letter. Examples may be found as early as the end of the thirteenth century;[74] the phenomenon is typical of manuscripts from Germany, Austria and Central Europe dating from the late fourteenth and the fifteenth centuries, in which very compact and unusual forms are often found (60, 61, pls. 34–5).[75] This form was doubtless related to the form of **g** in Cursiva Antiquior employed by scribes from these countries in the fourteenth century (see p. 134).

h likewise had undergone a transformation since the time of Carolingian script, but this evolution, already visible in Praegothica (see p. 62), was complete by the thirteenth century. The general Gothic tendency to give identical treatment to the feet of all ascenders and minims, sketched above, had the effect in Textus Rotundus of making the shapes of **h** and **b** more and more similar (2, 62; see pl. 18). In order, no doubt, to avoid confusion between the two letters, scribes extended the limb of

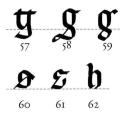

57   58   59

60   61   62

[70] Also *CMDS*, II, pl. 76 (Sweden 1460). An early example: Thomson, *Bookhands*, pl. 39 (Austria 1267).

[71] *CMDB*, I, pl. 50a and b, bottom lines (Southern Low Countries 1265); *CMDGBOx*, pl. 124 (England *c*. 1272?).

[72] *CMDGBOx*, pl. 142 (Germany 1294).

[73] Cambridge, Univ. Libr., MSS DD.I.20 (fourteenth century) and DD.8.18 (fifteenth century).

[74] *CMDF*, I, pl. 25 (France 1296).

[75] *CMDA*, II, pls. 187 (1423), 287 (1433); *CMDGBOx*, pl. 206 (1373).

h below the baseline, which, together with the shortening of its ascender, resulted in the typical Textualis form; in Formata the extension below the line was traced as a hairline (63). In rapid execution the shaft and the limb tended to become dislocated (64, pl. 32).

The practice of marking **i** with a diacritical stroke to distinguish it from the minims of an adjacent **i** or of **u**, **m**, **n**, already observed in Pregothic, grew more common (65). Furthermore these strokes began to be employed in positions where such confusion did not arise. This was taking place already by the middle of the thirteenth century. From about 1300 onwards all **i**s in a given manuscript may have diacritical strokes, although unstroked **i**s were still often being written as late as the fifteenth century. In Textualis Formata the strokes are hairlines or (in some English manuscripts in particular) flourishes (pl. 44). From the middle of the fourteenth century the strokes were sometimes replaced by dots;[76] although far from general, this practice would become a typical feature of German manuscripts in the fifteenth century (66).

j, the variant form of **i**, already introduced in Praegothica, became a distinct feature of Gothic script in general, although quite a number of scribes writing Textualis only employed **i**. In general, however, the Pregothic convention was maintained whereby when two **i**s follow each other, the second would be lengthened into **j**, the latter form usually turning inwards towards its base (67) (in Roman numerals, only the final **i** was normally made as **j**). The **j** form might also be employed after **u**, **m**, **n** to avoid confusion with other letters consisting of minims (pl. 22). The use of **j** in other positions is very rare and was perhaps limited to Germany.

The rare cases in which the combination **ij** is topped by a single stroke, instead of two (68), were probably influenced by the form of **y**.[77] For the use of **y** topped with two dots to represent **ii** (or **ij**), see below, p. 95.

k, of very limited use in Latin, is on the contrary a common letter in German, Dutch, Swedish, English and other Germanic vernaculars. It consists of an **l**, to the right of which a 2-shaped stroke is added.

m and **n** are letters whose shape provides the beginner with a helpful guide for recognizing the various categories of Textualis mentioned above (4–6). 'Cursive' **m** and **n**, i.e. with a lengthened endstroke turning to the left under the baseline,

63   64   65   66   67   68

[76] *CMDF*, I, pl. 47 (Southern Low Countries 1351).
[77] Thomson, *Bookhands*, pl. 12 (Southern Low Countries 1277).

appear sometimes at the end of the line or at the end of a word in more or less rapid writing of the thirteenth century (69).[78]

The practice of replacing **m** in final position by a sign in the shape of figure 3 (70) is probably a stylized form of **m** written vertically in order to save space. Its frequent use at the end of lines points to this. It never became as popular in Northern Textualis as in Italian Rotunda. Examples may be found, however, from the late thirteenth century onwards, first in France, later also elsewhere.[79] German, Austrian, Central European and Scandinavian scribes of the fourteenth and fifteenth centuries routinely transformed it into a kind of vertical zigzag line, often traversed by a vertical hairline (71, pls. 38, 44–5) (like the 3-shaped figure on which it is based, this form of pointed zigzag line was also used as an abbreviation sign and is distinctive of scripts of this area).

The majuscule **r** (**R**) occasionally present in Praegothica is found much more rarely in Textualis, except in a few early English manuscripts.[80] It sometimes replaced the normal minuscule form at the beginning or at the end of a word or at the end of the line, when the available space was too large for a normal **r**.

The two minuscule forms of **r** have been discussed in the chapter on Pregothic script and their use remained a distinctive feature of Gothic Textualis throughout the later Middle Ages. The conventions governing their use were first studied by Meyer (see above, p. 77). According to his second rule, the normal shape was replaced by the 'round' **r** after **o**, but often also after other letters ending on a convex bow to the right: **b**, **d**, **h**, **p**, **v**, **y** (9). It was not, as a rule, used at the end of words. Whereas the writing of round **r** after **o** was almost invariably the rule, admitting few exceptions (pls. 31, 44),[81] its use after other letters obviously depended on individual or local custom. Round **r** after **a** (pl. 32), which is contrary to the rule, is not uncommon in Textualis, probably because the **arum**-abbreviation was widely accepted. Round **r** is sometimes found after other letters such as **e**, **g**, **i**, which likewise do not end in a bow, in manuscripts from Southern Germany and Austria dating from the end of the Middle Ages.[82] Its origin must be sought in Italy, and its use in the North either derived directly from Rotunda, or indirectly *via* Cursiva or Hybrida.

Since round **r** was not considered to be a letter that ended in a bow to the right, when it was followed by another **r** the latter would as a rule have the normal shape. The reverse, however (round **r** after normal **r**), may also be found, although

69   70   71

[78] Our pl. 45, a hand influenced by Fractura, gives a late example of this feature.
[79] A few early examples from France: *CMDF*, I, pl. 25 (1296); II, pls. 43 (1316), 45 (1324).
[80] *CMDGBCam*, pl. 99 (before 1201?).
[81] Another exception: Thomson, *Bookhands*, pl. 35 (Austria 1216).
[82] *CMDA*, III, pl. 379 (1472, Textualis Formata); the feature occurs also elsewhere, in rapid scripts under cursive influence: *CMDGBLo*, pl. 856 (Southern Low Countries 1488).

only very rarely.[83] The case is similar to other uses of round **r** after letters not ending in a bow and should be interpreted as an intrusion of cursive writing habits into Textualis, seen especially in German-speaking countries in the fifteenth and sixteenth centuries.

Like other letters in Textualis, round **r** may be rounded or angular. In English deluxe manuscripts of the late fourteenth and fifteenth centuries it often has an idiosyncratic narrow shape with a shaky bow and an almost vertical stroke (72, pl. 46).[84] One should note that Johann vom Hagen's *textus prescisus* includes a very similar shape (pl. 17), and Gregorius Bock's pattern pages also present this shape in addition to the more normal form of round **r** (pl. 15).

Like **r**, **s** had already developed a binary system before Gothic script had fully emerged (see p. 63). As a rule the Half-Uncial straight **s** was used at the beginning and in the middle of the word, the Uncial round **s** at its end.

Quite a number of manuscripts of the thirteenth and early fourteenth centuries exhibit straight **s** in all positions. This is generally the case in small scripts such as Littera Parisiensis (pl. 24), in which the complicated round **s** would have been difficult to trace between headline and baseline. Numerous manuscripts of the same period use both forms of **s** interchangeably at the end of words (pl. 23), whilst an ever-growing number of codices contain only round **s** in final position. Straight **s** at the end of the word disappears in the first half of the fourteenth century.[85] Like **f**, this form of **s** sometimes extends slightly below the baseline.

Round **s** was sometimes replaced by an alternative, elongated form, called 'trailing' **s** and already encountered in Praegothica (pls. 20, 24).[86] It is much more frequent in Southern Textualis than in Northern (it probably has an Italian origin), but is by no means confined to it. Made in no more than two strokes, it also had the advantage of taking less space than normal round **s**. But it fits less well within the canon of Textualis letter forms, as it either extends beyond the headline, or below the baseline. In deluxe manuscripts it was only used at the end of the line, where there was too little space for round **s**. It is probably to be related to the use of a narrow superscript **s** at the end of lines where space was lacking (pl. 39). Trailing **s** had another advantage over normal round **s**, in that it could more easily be fused with the preceding **o** or another letter ending in a bow.

Round **s** at the beginning or in the middle of words can already sometimes be found in Praegothica (see p. 64), but it is rare in Textualis and appears to be

72

[83] *CMDS*, II, pl. 19 (Low Countries 1400); *CMDA*, III, pl. 228 (1462), *CMDIt2*, I, pl. 71 (1493), both from Austria.
[84] See also *CMDGBOx*, pl. 239 (1398); *CMDGBCam*, pl. 205 (1421–35); Thompson, *Introduction*, pl. 197 (before 1446); *CMDGBLo*, pl. 863 (1489).
[85] Two late examples from France: *CMDF*, I, pls. 36 (1326) and 38 (1328).
[86] Other examples, all from France: Thomson, *Bookhands*, pl. 9 (1239); *CMDF*, I, pls. 24 (1295), 46 (1348). A German example: *CMDF*, V, pl. 139, Colmar, Bibl. mun., MS 450 (1463).

typical of certain English hands.[87] In such cases the influence of the Anglicana cursive script is clear. When used at the beginning of the word, there is always the possibility that it was intended to be a majuscule. But, as observed already with Praegothica, it was common for round **s** to be used beginning a short abbreviated word in which an abbreviation mark was written above **s** ('sibi').

Round **s** comes in a variety of forms, from very round to extremely angular. Austrian and Central European manuscripts present some extreme forms of the angular variety (pl. 44).[88] A sloping hairline closing the two bows is a frequently seen feature in Textualis Formata (73, pls. 27, 33, 40, 43). In rapid, round execution the four-stroke ductus cannot always be discerned and any distinction from cursive **s** may become impossible. The latter has a simplified ductus (74) and in the fourteenth and more frequently in the fifteenth centuries was sometimes used instead of the standard shape: another sign of the intrusion of cursive elements, even in Textualis Formata (pls. 29, 32, 36–7, 42, 46).

From the middle of the thirteenth century, and especially from the fourteenth century onwards, the shaft of **t** normally projects above the headstroke, but the letter was in general still not taller than the other 'short' letters (75). An exception to this may be seen in a number of examples of Textualis Formata from the fifteenth century. Probably under Cursiva influence, the vertical stroke of **t** was lengthened so much as to come close to the height of an ascender (pls. 34, 41). In these cases, its top was sometimes treated in the same way as the other ascenders, by being given a bifurcation or a sloping ending and a hairline to the left (76, pls. 38, 46).

In general, however, with the entire horizontal bar now being placed to the right of the shaft, **t** often resembles **c**. In rapid hands, but sometimes also in carefully executed very angular writing, it can be difficult or impossible to distinguish the two letters apart, the more so as the vertical stroke forming the back of **c** not infrequently projects through its upper horizontal stroke just as in the letter **t**.

Two **ts** following each other were sometimes treated as a ligature: the second **t** was elongated, resulting in a graph closely resembling the ligature **ct** (pl. 36)[89] (on the latter, see below, p. 96). This graph is not limited to Textualis, but occurs in many script types of the Gothic period; it is often incorrectly transcribed as **ct**.

u was the last letter to acquire a variant form. The angular **v**, sometimes seen in Praegothica, was doubtless a remnant of the use of forms from Capital script (in the same way as Capital **R**). In Gothic Textualis, on the contrary, the form was derived

73   74

75   76

[87] Thomson, *Bookhands*, pls. 91 (1247), 102 (1385?); *CMDGBOx*, pl. 124 (*c.* 1272?).
[88] *CMDA*, ii, pl. 287 (1433); *CMDGBLo*, pl. 591 (1459).
[89] Other examples: *CMDNL*, ii, pl. 504 (Northern Low Countries 1390), col. b, l. 3; *CMDGBLo*, pl. 354 (Germany 1419).

from Gothic cursive script and is one of the very rare cursive forms to have gained an official status within a script at the top of the hierarchy. From the thirteenth century onward it was used at the beginning of words and has exactly the same value as **u** (the distinction between **v** as a consonant and **u** as a vowel is essentially post-medieval). It should be observed that the use of **v** at the beginning of words never became the rule and that throughout the period many scribes preferred to write **u** instead of **v** in initial position. Many codices display either form indifferently at that location. The cursive origin of **v** is especially apparent from its frequent use in lower-grade manuscripts and especially in copies of vernacular (English, German, but rather less French) texts. In codices in German it is not rare to find the **v**-shape in the middle of the word as well; this also applies to manuscripts in Dutch.[90]

u may have been preferred in Textualis Formata, because 'cursive' **v**, despite assuming various forms, almost always rises higher than the minims (pls. 29, 31). Its elaborate shapes and unsuitable height were therefore often regularized (this also occurred in Textualis Libraria, pls. 32, 37). In some examples this regularization went so far as to round off the angle at its base and to turn it into a slightly variant form of **u**, scarcely extending above the headline (77, pls. 40, 45). Very tall **vs**, the norm in cursive script, seem to have been unusually popular with certain English scribes (pls. 39, 42).

In Gothic script in general, **u** remained difficult to recognize if it followed or preceded other minims such as unstroked **i**, **m**, **n**. For this reason, in a minority of manuscripts in Textualis a diacritical sign was added above this letter. It takes the form of a circle, a concave stroke, a v or even a double stroke comparable to an umlaut, all mostly traced in hairline, and appears from the fourteenth century in manuscripts from Germany and the Low Countries (pl. 28).[91] This diacritical sign is discussed in the Appendix.

The 'w'-sound, peculiar to Germanic languages, was originally written as two successive **us**. In the twelfth century, however, it was already being written as a ligature of two **vs** in Germany and this form remained in use in German-, Dutch-, Danish- and Swedish-speaking countries till the end of the Middle Ages (78, pls. 28, 31–2, 37). In English manuscripts this ligature generally extends well above the headline, and the notion that it consists of two intertwined **vs** was maintained by the addition of a stroke to the second **v**, which was normally formed with a double curve in its final stroke (79).[92]

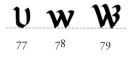

77 78 79

[90] Kirchner, *Scriptura Gothica*, pl. 26a (Switzerland 1359: 'gevarn'); *CMDB*, I, pl. 177a (Southern Low Countries 1372: 'joncvrouwe', 'nu').
[91] Whilst in German texts this sign may have a phonetic significance (umlaut), in Latin ones it is of a purely diacritical nature. See *CMDB*, I, pl. 215 (Southern Low Countries 1396), col. a, bottom l.; *CMDNL*, II, pls. 584 (1477) and 609 (1509), both Northern Low Countries.
[92] *CMDGBOx*, pls. 148 (1305–16), 169 (*c.* 1326), 183 (1340–44).

In Germany, Austria and the Dutch-speaking Low Countries, but also in France (pl. 29), **w** was also used to represent the sound 'vu'.

The alteration of **x** to make it fit into the Gothic aesthetic canon had already begun in Pregothic script. One of the strokes was usually made as a minim, the other one, traced on the diagonal, was often broken into two strokes (80). Various ductuses were employed to obtain the desired shape, though most are difficult to distinguish from one another. In rounded execution the letter may appear to be formed from two curved overlapping strokes with the shapes of inverted c and c (81, pls. 30, 43). **x** was sometimes crossed (82, pls. 25, 39, 40, 42, 45) and sometimes uncrossed. Many later English Textualis **x**s are crossed.

Since Carolingian times **y** was usually marked with a dot or stroke above the letter. Undotted **y**s are, however, not uncommon and are found in manuscripts from France (pl. 29) and the Low Countries, but they are more typical of those from Germany, Austria and Central Europe (pls. 16, 25).[93] The first stroke is normally short (sometimes vertical and made into a minim) and the second, more sloping, goes under the line (83).[94]

In the fifteenth and sixteenth centuries, German scribes often used **y** with two dots as a substitute for **ii** (84), but this feature is rare in Textualis.

z takes essentially three basic forms: the simple form of modern **z** or figure 2, the same form crossed, and the more complicated form of figure 3, going below the baseline (pl. 28). It is not clear whether any one form was preferred above the other two in the various parts of Europe. Crossed **z** traversed by a vertical hairline (85), however, points to Germany or Central Europe.[95] The parallel but more rare **z** with a zigzag shape also points to the same origin.[96]

LIGATURES

Continuing the tendency in Pregothic script, the number of ligatures in Textualis became very much reduced, since the more or less elaborate and curved forms typical of ligatures did not conform to Gothic aesthetic standards. The **et**-ligature or ampersand was almost completely abandoned during the course of the thirteenth

80   81   82

83   84   85

93 An example of the dot being treated as an abbreviation mark and connected with the letter with a curving hairline: Thompson, *Introduction*, pl. 197 (before 1446). It is probably typical of the English predilection for this kind of abbreviation in Textualis.
94 The reverse is seen in Thomson, *Bookhands*, pl. 15 (France 1312); *CMDS*, II, pls. 16 (1391–1406) and 26 (1414), both from Sweden.
95 Mazal, *Buchkunst der Gotik*, pl. 6, col. b, l. 2 (Bohemia 1409).
96 It has its origin in the crossed **z**. See *CMDS*, I, pl. 56 (Sweden 1407); W. M. Voelkle and R. S. Wieck, *The Bernard H. Breslauer Collection of Manuscript Illuminations*, New York 1992, no. 44 (Germany *c.* 1485–9).

century. Examples after 1300 are extremely rare, though they appear in English manuscripts alongside tironian **et**.[97]

The ligature **ct**, already reduced and atrophied in Pregothic script, was treated in various ways during the late Middle Ages but took three main forms: the 'Pregothic' form in which the top of the **t** was lengthened and curved (86, pls. 19, 22), one in which it was lengthened but does not curve (87, pls. 33, 35, 39, 42–5), and a more rare form in which both letters are approximately the same height and where there is no longer a ligature properly speaking (pls. 21, 30). Nevertheless, even when the ligature itself was abandoned, the two letters, like most letters within a single word in Textualis, remained linked at the head- and at the baseline.

The only ligature that was used almost constantly until the end of the period is **st**.[98] Here the lengthened **t** was of course preserved, but the bow that had connected the two letters in Carolingian script was usually flattened or made concave, in accordance with the general treatment of upper closing bows in Textualis (88, pls. 40, 43). The similar-looking **sc**-ligature was only very rarely used in Textualis, and apparently only in England.[99] It was probably derived from cursive script and its form may have been thought far too close to the **st**-ligature to be generally acceptable.

For a discussion of the ligature which can be made when two **t**s were written in succession, see above, p. 93.

ABBREVIATIONS

Although abbreviations are often extremely numerous in thirteenth- and fourteenth-century codices, a full survey of the abbreviation system in Gothic manuscripts would be out of place here. A few general observations on this subject will be found in the Appendix to this book. Here we will discuss only those abbreviations used in Textualis which are of significance from a morphological point of view. Many of the following observations, however, also apply to a large extent to other Gothic scripts.

It is apparent that abbreviation strokes in Northern Textualis, whether written above or behind the letter or traversing its ascender or descender, were treated as if they were parts of letters and thus they display the angularity, boldness and shading characteristic of the script.

86   87   88

[97] *CMDGBOx*, pl. 148 (1305–16); Thompson, *Introduction*, pl. 195 (1400–5).

[98] No **st**-ligature is present in *CMDGBLo*, pl. 827 (Southern Low Countries 1482).

[99] *CMDGBCam*, pls. 178 (1395) and 205 (1421–35).

The abbreviation for **bus**, the ending of the dative and ablative plural in the third declension, was very occasionally formed by means of **b** followed by the usual, 9-shaped **us**-abbreviation. The normal form is **b** followed by two dots resembling a semicolon (89), the latter mostly traced in one stroke and taking the shape of figure 3 (90). In German-speaking and Scandinavian countries in the period between the fourteenth and sixteenth centuries, this form was sometimes replaced by a vertical zigzag line, often decorated with a vertical hairline (91, pl. 38).[100] The typical Southern Textualis form, in which **b** is followed by inverted c, is only found in manuscripts from Southern Germany, Switzerland and Austria (92, pl. 45).[101]

The abbreviation for **con** or **cum** may adopt various shapes: inverted c, figure 9, figure 2, and others (93–5); it may stand on the line or descend beneath it. During the fourteenth and fifteenth centuries, scribes seem to have had a general preference for the 2-shape, except in Germany and Central Europe, partly also in the Low Countries, where from the twelfth century onwards a special form of inverted c in two strokes seems to have been favoured (96, pls. 22, 38).[102]

The Insular **enim**- and **est**-abbreviations went out of use after the thirteenth century, although not entirely. The former consists of n between two dots or a form resembling Capital H (97, 98), the latter of a horizontal stroke with a dot or flourish above and below it (99).[103] The **est**-abbreviation in the shape of a vertical zigzag line possibly traversed by a vertical hairline is a development of the latter form and was still used in the late fifteenth century.[104]

As mentioned above, the ampersand was superseded and eventually replaced by tachygraphic **et** in the form of figure 2 (100). The habit of crossing this tironian sign is seen already in book script towards the end of the twelfth century and became widespread after the thirteenth (101). The double-crossed form seems to be specific to English Textualis Formata (pl. 39, but see also pl. 38). The typical Southern form, uncrossed with long horizontal stroke and vertical shaft (102), is only seen

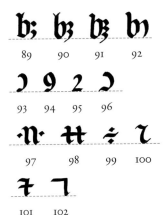

89 90 91 92

93 94 95 96

97 98 99 100

101 102

[100] See also Metz, Bibl. mun., MS 10 (1348; the feature does not occur on the page reproduced in *CMDF*, v, pl. 57 [1348]); *CMDA*, I, pl. 194 (1383); II, pl. 187 (1423); *CMDS*, I, pl. 56 (1407).

[101] See also Kirchner, *Scriptura Gothica*, pl. 25 (1353). For an exceptional French example, see *CMDF*, v, pl. 54, MS 1476 (1346).

[102] Three German examples: *CMDGBOx*, pls. 103 (1238), 142 (1294); Kirchner, *Scriptura Gothica*, pl. 22 (1313).

[103] Relatively late English examples of both: Kirchner, *Scriptura Gothica*, pl. 21 (1296): **enim**, l. 11; *CMDGBCam*, pl. 133 (1304–21): **est**, col. a, last but one l.

[104] Its use was not limited to the Rhineland, as Denholm-Young (*Handwriting*, p. 47) asserts.

in some Austrian manuscripts (compare this with what has been said above about the **bus**-abbreviation).[105] Final **et**, especially after **m**, **n** and **b**, was often treated in the same way as the **bus**-abbreviation and was thus traced as either two dots resembling a semicolon, or a sign in the shape of figure 3, or the 'German' zigzag stroke (pl. 41).

Final **m** written as figure 3 is not an abbreviation properly speaking. It has been discussed above, p. 91.

The preposition **per** was always abbreviated as **p** with a crossed descender. However, the shortness of the descender in Textualis often resulted in the horizontal abbreviation stroke being placed at its base (103, pl. 33). The transverse stroke in Textualis Formata may begin and end with a serif or more often with a dot or quadrangle.[106] A stylized version of this was produced by omitting the stroke and keeping only the two dots or quadrangles at both sides of the descender, a feature typical of English manuscripts from the late fourteenth century onwards (104, pl. 39).[107]

The conjunction **que** had traditionally been written as **q** followed by a mark resembling a semicolon (105). During the later Middle Ages, as in the case of the **bus**-abbreviation, the semicolon was usually written in one stroke as a figure 3 (106, pl. 43), or, in manuscripts from Germany, Central Europe and Scandinavia, as a vertical zigzag line (and especially so from the end of the fourteenth century onwards) (107, pls. 34–5).

The ending of the masculine and neuter genitive plural in the second declension, **orum**, was almost universally abbreviated as **o** followed by round **r**, the final stroke of which was crossed (108). In Pregothic script, it is the variability of this form, together with that of the ampersand, which often provides the only clues to determining individual and regional scribal practices. The looped crossing-stroke, extending from the round **r**, often found either in its original, single-stroke form or a calligraphic variant of it in twelfth-century manuscripts, was used less often in the later Middle Ages (109).[108] By making the 'crossing' stop on the baseline, at

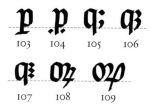

103 104 105 106

107 108 109

[105] Thomson, *Bookhands*, pl. 44 (1337), bottom l.; Kirchner, *Scriptura Gothica*, pl. 25 (1353).
[106] *CMDGBOx*, pl. 122 (Germany 1267–76); *CMDGBCam*, pl. 178 (England 1395). For a Pregothic example, see Thomson, *Bookhands*, pl. 86 (England 1176).
[107] Other examples: *CMDGBOx*, pl. 239 (1398); *CMDGBCam*, pl. 205 (1421–35).
[108] Except in rapid scripts such as *CMDB*, I, pls. 180 (1373) and 206 (1389), both from the Southern Low Countries. It may be observed that this simple loop was rarely found in Praegothica, where a more complicated loop seems to have been preferred (see above, p. 67).

the foot of the round **r**, the graph became a 'short letter' (110, pl. 19).[109] In the fourteenth and fifteenth centuries scribes from Germany, Austria, Central Europe and Scandinavia preferred unusual and square forms, marked by two serifs at the top of the crossing, which afterwards developed into an angular figure 3 or even a vertical zigzag line, and by giving the round **r** the shape of a Capital L (111, pls. 34, 38, 44).

By analogy with **orum** and also continuing Pregothic practice, the feminine genitive ending **arum** was often abbreviated in the same way, although, as mentioned above, **a** is a letter which in principle should not admit round **r** after it. Although quite frequently employed in the thirteenth century, it became more rare in the fourteenth and is seldom found in the generally high-level Textualis script of the fifteenth (pl. 34). An **arum**-abbreviation consisting of **a** followed by crossed majuscule **R** is altogether exceptional.[110]

SUBTYPES

Whereas there is a consensus among palaeographers about what constitutes Textualis Formata, there is no such agreement about the lower levels of execution in Textualis. Some even consider the rapidly executed Currens to constitute a distinct script, which they call Notula.[111] Clearly, here and elsewhere in Gothic palaeography, an element of confusion is involved. Some palaeographers define a script on the basis of its size, and therefore, for example, consider the small so-called Notula to be distinct from larger Textualis. It is, however, obvious that in a small size of script, written with a pen with a relatively broad nib, it is necessarily impossible to execute the distinguishing, often minute characteristics found in larger sizes of the same script (see also above, p. 54). Distinguishing scripts on the basis of size is therefore fundamentally misguided. Script termed Notula may correspond

110   111

[109] Other examples: *CMDF*, 1, pl. 57, f. 27r (France 1379), last but one l.; Kirchner, *Scriptura Gothica*, pl. 33 (France after 1405), top l.

[110] Kirchner, *Scriptura Gothica*, pl. 32 (England 1405).

[111] Lieftinck (in *Nomenclature*, p. 17) believed that the term 'Notula' would be needed whenever in a bookhand we find evident proof that the idea 'book script' has disappeared from the scribe's mind. Gumbert (*Kartäuser*, p. 206) considers Notula a (dispensable) name for a script situated between the lowest levels of Textualis and the earliest forms of Cursiva. The name is used by Petrucci (*Descrizione*, pp. 60–1) for 'fitte corsive più o meno dissociate, a base gotica o semigotica, di modulo piccolo – e usate in ambiente scolastico fra Trecento e Quattrocento'. Notula should be essential for understanding Gothic script according to Orlandelli, 'Origine', pp. 57–8. On Notula, see also Spilling, 'Schreibkünste', pp. 108–10. Brown (*Guide*, p. 80), distinguishes 'littera glossularis' and 'littera notularis' as variants of Textualis.

with our Textualis Currens, but the name has also been applied to varieties of cursive.[112]

'Perlschrift' ('pearl script') is an extremely small size of Textualis, developed by scribes in the thirteenth century especially in order to copy the famous 'Parisian pocket Bibles' (pl. 20).[113] Although it was intended to be a luxurious, high-level script and thus one might expect to call it Textualis Formata, its letter forms, because they are so small, are simplified, often irregular (incorporating, for example, various shapes of **a**) and have few 'Gothic' refinements. Where these do occur, as in the bifurcation at the top of the ascenders, they tend to be exaggerated.

Among the other types that have been distinguished within the family of Northern Textualis, the most important are the 'litterae scholasticae', and foremost among them the Littera Parisiensis (pl. 24).[114] Whereas Cencetti and others have seriously questioned the existence of a specific script proper to the university of Oxford (Littera Oxoniensis), the script developed at the university of Paris, the major centre of learning in Northern Europe during the thirteenth and fourteenth centuries, is generally regarded as a standard type in all handbooks. The name occurs in medieval documents and refers to a 'simplified textura'.[115] The university scripts deserve a closer study, but in the meantime one may classify the Littera Parisiensis as Textualis Libraria or Currens, depending on the level of formality. (It is never found with the refinements proper to Formata.) It is bold and heavily abbreviated, as one would expect in script used for copying scholastic texts, and contains some simplified letter forms. A special feature seems to be the freedom that governed the shape of **a**. Either because of the small size or the rapidity of the writing, the forms vary between Textualis **a** and single-compartment **a** (1, 112). Probably for the same reasons a simple straight **s**, looking somewhat like an elongated **c**, was preferred at the ends of words as well as elsewhere (113). Another typical feature is the short length of the common mark of abbreviation.

The immense mass of Textualis scripts of the end of the Middle Ages, especially of the Formata and Libraria levels, can be subdivided into a Western and an Eastern

112   113

[112] See the poster of Johann vom Hagen, pl. 17.

[113] Bischoff, *Palaeography*, p. 135.

[114] Battelli, *Lezioni*, p. 228; Cencetti, *Lineamenti*, pp. 220–1 (gives characteristics of Littera Parisiensis); Cencetti, *Compendio*, pp. 76–7; Destrez, *La pecia*, pp. 47 ff. The idea that the 'scritture scolastiche' are fundamentally different from general Textualis has in our opinion little justification. It is found, for example, in Orlandelli, 'Origine'; Cencetti (as above); and Gasparri, *Introduction*, pls. 23–4 and 26–32, who distinguishes 'écriture universitaire' from 'écriture scolastique', the latter also used for French verse.

[115] Bischoff, *Palaeography*, p. 135. For a few examples of Littera Parisiensis, see p. 122, n. 88.

group on the basis of a few letter forms. The Western group comprises England, France, the Low Countries and Western Germany; the Eastern group Eastern Germany, Austria, Central Europe and Scandinavia. The latter is distinguished by especially bold and angular forms and the typical vertical zigzag abbreviation, which is entirely absent from the Western group, as noted above.

HISTORICAL NOTE

Textualis is in origin the oldest of Gothic scripts and during the thirteenth century was virtually the only type of book script to be used at all levels of execution, from Currens to Formata. This situation continued during the fourteenth century, although Textualis faced growing competition from scripts of the cursive family for books for which the lower levels of execution were considered appropriate, such as copies of vernacular texts. During the fifteenth century Cursiva and Hybrida acquired such a prominent status as book scripts, not only at the Currens and Libraria levels but also as highly formal calligraphic scripts, that Textualis Currens almost entirely disappeared. Textualis Formata at that time was the most conspicuous form to survive, but with its use strictly limited to copies of the Bible, liturgical and para-liturgical texts, monastic rules, etc.

At the end of the fifteenth and during the early sixteenth centuries, when traditions in manuscript book production were declining under the influence of the triumphant printed book, other texts, considered lower in the textual hierarchy, such as the works of Church Fathers, were sometimes copied in Textualis Formata.[116] When Gutenberg began printing his 42-line Bible around 1455, it was natural that he should model the typeface on Textualis Formata. No other script could ever have been considered appropriate for this elevated purpose.

---

[116] For example: Ghent, Univ. Libr., MS 253, containing the Homilies of Bernard of Clairvaux (Germany c. 1500). Our pls. 34 and 41 prove that this tendency existed already before the introduction of printing.

5

Southern Textualis and Semitextualis
(plates 47–76)

The Mediterranean forms of Textualis can for reasons of convenience be brought together under the generic name of Rotunda, although some of them are not particularly rounded, and may even be quite angular. But in general, the Southern version of Textualis is first and foremost characterized by the roundness of its bows, visible especially in **b**, **c**, **d**, **e**, **h**, **o**, **p**, **q**, round **s**. This does not mean that the Gothic angularity was avoided altogether: it is, on the contrary, quite pronounced in such letters as **a** and **g** and even appears in the 'round' lobes of the letters mentioned above. The boldness and shading of Gothic Textualis is also present; indeed, in the higher levels of execution it was often emphasized. The difference between bold strokes and thin strokes is often so marked that the hairlines become almost invisible, especially in Italian Textualis.

Given the roundness and the width of so many letter forms, the verticality, so typical of Northern Textualis, was replaced by a breadth that makes Rotunda far less typical of the 'Gothic' style than its Northern counterpart. There is thus some conformity between script and Gothic architecture in the Mediterranean area, especially in Italy, where high, narrow spaces were replaced by relatively low and wide ones. The Gothic fusions, on the other hand, which will be discussed in a subsequent paragraph, are extremely numerous and give the script a somewhat compressed aspect.

Roundness and angularity, broadness and compactness are only two of the internal contradictions marking Southern Textualis which clearly distinguish it from Carolingian script, to which it otherwise remained more close than Northern Textualis. Bischoff has rightly drawn our attention to one particular feature that links Carolingian script and Rotunda: the absence of the typical 'Gothic' treatment of the feet of the letters at the baseline.[1] As a result the uniformity to which the minims and the feet of the ascenders had been submitted in Northern Textualis is hardly a feature in Rotunda. Rotunda is, however, formally related to Northern Textus Praescissus, although the specific treatment of the feet typical of that script was only applied to a selection of letters in Rotunda, as we shall see.[2] Nevertheless,

---

[1] In *Nomenclature*, p. 14.　　[2] Steinmann, 'Textualis formata', pp. 318–19.

neither the baseline nor the headline have the marked visual importance in Rotunda that they have in Northern Textualis.

Rotunda is also distinguished from its Northern counterparts by some special letter and abbreviation forms, although these are not always all present in any one specimen of handwriting. It would appear that the purest form of Rotunda is that used in Italy, in which graphic influences from the North are absent or at least not significant. The Italian Textualis may doubtless be considered one of the most eloquent expressions of the Italian conception of Gothic, which was a milder form, apparently more acceptable in the Apennine Peninsula. Rotunda is consequently (and rightly) often considered a specifically Italian script type. Thanks to the fame and influence of the university of Bologna, the script became known all over Europe. The scripts used in the other Mediterranean areas – Spain, Portugal and Southern France – never had the uniform character nor the prestige of Italian Rotunda. Therefore a more detailed description of the latter script is necessary.

Towards the end of this chapter we will deal with an important variant form of Textualis, which differs from other types in the shape of its letter **a**. We shall call it Semitextualis. It has, in general, much closer links with Rotunda than with Northern Textualis.

I TEXTUALIS IN ITALY
(plates 54, 56, 58, 60, 62–3, 65–6, 68–70, 72, 74) [3]

GENERAL FEATURES

The ascenders and descenders may be extremely short, as in the widely used Littera Bononiensis (see below, p. 111). In many hands, however, their height is quite remarkable, and proportions between minims and letters with ascenders of 0.5

---

[3] Given the similarities between Rotunda and Italian Semitextualis, this list includes examples of both scripts, and most characteristics of Rotunda are also valid for Semitextualis. Bibliography of Rotunda: Battelli, *Lezioni*, pp. 227–8; Bischoff, *Palaeography*, p. 131; Cencetti, *Lineamenti*, pp. 213–14, 218–20; Cencetti, *Compendio*, p. 75; G. Orlandelli, 'Ricerche sulla origine della "littera bononiensis": scritture documentarie bolognesi del secolo XII', in G. Orlandelli, *Scritti di paleografia e diplomatica*, ed. R. Ferrara and G. Feo, Bologna 1994, pp. 97–132 (originally published in 1956–7); B. Pagnin, *Le origini della scrittura gotica padovana*, Padua 1933; B. Pagnin, 'La "littera bononiensis"', in *Ricerche Medievali*, 10–12, Pavia 1975–7, pp. 93–168 (originally published in 1934); Petrucci, *Breve storia*, pp. 131–4; P. Supino Martini, 'Orientamenti per la datazione e la localizzazione delle cosidette "litterae textuales" italiane ed iberiche nei secoli XII–XIV', *Scriptorium*, 54 (2000), pp. 20–34 (a paper dating from 1990; partially retracted and replaced by the following work); P. Supino Martini, 'Linee metodologiche per lo studio dei manoscritti in "litterae textuales" prodotti in Italia nei secoli XIII e XIV', *Scrittura e Civiltà*, 17 (1993), pp. 43–101.

or even less are not exceptional (pl. 74).[4] This means that, with the exception of university and other school manuscripts, the distance between the lines is often large compared with other Gothic manuscripts. The top of the ascenders and the base of the descenders are as a rule either undecorated or were treated in an inconspicuous manner. Actual bifurcation or additional vertical or sloping hairlines are uncommon: ascenders and descenders either end flat, or (in Rotunda Formata) are made concave, or have a horizontal serif. One may observe a general tendency towards harmonizing the base of the descenders in accordance with the flat 'Textus Praescissus' feet of certain ascenders and minims.

There is also one striking difference in the treatment of the ascenders in Northern Textualis and Italian Rotunda: artificial spurs do not occur in the latter. (This point does not, however, apply to the 'natural' spurs created by the two-stroke shafts of **f** and straight **s**, which are of a different nature.) The absence of this feature is of course consistent with the general absence in Rotunda of all spiky or thorny extensions at the headline or at the baseline mentioned above.

The following letters and minims are as a rule treated in the same manner as Textus Praescissus (in other words they end flat on the baseline without any incurvation or foot: **f**, the stem of **h**, the first two minims of **m** and the first minim of **n**, the 'straight' **r**,[5] the straight **s** and, in most cases, the tironian sign for **et**, which has a special form in Rotunda (although a form in which the foot is curved to the right also occurs). This feature is easily noticed in Rotunda Formata, although there the final minims of **m** and **n** differ from the other minims of these letters only in having oblique feet (1, pls. 60, 74).[6] In rapid execution, of course, these features of Praescissus were not easy to maintain.

In contrast with Northern Textualis additional decorative hairlines are rare in Italian Rotunda. They are very occasionally seen appended to **r** and final **t**, perhaps under Northern influence (pls. 60, 72).[7]

INDIVIDUAL LETTER FORMS

In contrast with Northern Textualis too, which admits some variety in its letter forms, the shape of the individual letters in Rotunda is mostly strictly fixed. Whereas

1

[4] Earlier examples: Federici, *Scrittura*, pl. 49 (1292); *CMDGBOx*, pl. 162 (c. 1321–4); Mazal, *Buchkunst der Gotik*, pl. 12 (1453).

[5] A rare intrusion of a non-Praescissus form of **r** in Rotunda Libraria is found in *CMDGBLo*, pl. 356 (1419), a manuscript otherwise exceptional for the abundance of decorative hairlines. *CMDGBOx*, pl. 175 (1334), is less conclusive.

[6] **m** and **n** entirely treated as in Textus Praescissus are extremely rare in Italian Rotunda: for an example, see W. M. Voelkle and R. S. Wieck, *The Bernard H. Breslauer Collection of Manuscript Illuminations*, New York 1992, p. 191, fig. 72 (end of the fourteenth century).

[7] See also Thompson, *Introduction*, pl. 194 (1391); *CMDGBLo*, pl. 356 (1419).

in the former the typical style resides in the homogenizing effect produced by the treatment given to the minims, the style of Rotunda is largely determined by the circular and semi-circular shapes of letters, parts of letters and abbreviation signs.

There is only one shape of **a**: the Northern box-**a** is unknown in Rotunda. The letter consists of a minim and a small lobe on the baseline, generally comprising a triangular shape closed by a diagonal hairline (2) – one of the very few spiky forms in Rotunda. The upper lobe is either open, or closed by a hairline traced with the corner of the nib (3). The natural closing of the upper lobe by means of a bold stroke, as often encountered in Northern Textualis Libraria or Currens, is extremely rare in Italy (4).[8] The relative 'openness' of Rotunda is readily apparent in the shape of this letter. In contrast with most of their Northern colleagues, Italian scribes have never felt obliged to close the upper lobe of **a**.

b is marked by the almost circular shape of its lobe (5). So are **c** and **e**, often difficult to distinguish from one another because the final stroke of **e** is a hairline (6, 7).

d is of especial interest in Rotunda. Although the Uncial form is the normal one, the Half-Uncial, straight **d** seems never to have been abandoned, in contrast with Northern Textualis. Throughout the period one can find examples of straight **d** intermingled with the normal Gothic shape, although the latter on its own was used in the large majority of manuscripts. When both forms occur on one page, their use appears generally to have been determined by the Meyer rule regulating the use of Gothic fusions. Thus Uncial **d** would be used before **c**, Half-Uncial **d**, **e**, **o**, **q**; Half-Uncial **d** would be used after Uncial **d**, **o** (8) or where no fusion is involved (see pls. 56, 60, 68, 74).[9] The survival of straight **d** in Rotunda is doubtless to be explained by the longer-lasting influence of Carolingian script in Italy. But as far as the script of the fifteenth and sixteenth centuries is concerned, the obvious and increasing presence of straight **d** (pl. 72) was certainly also the result of the scribes' daily exposure to manuscripts and printed books in Humanistic script or typefaces.

Uncial **d** in Rotunda has an unusual form. Although in some hands the letter has a long sloping shaft (pls. 65, 69),[10] the shaft is normally short and horizontal or almost horizontal (9). This feature, one of the most typical characteristics of Rotunda, can cause confusion with **t** when **d** is fused with subsequent **e** or **o** (pl. 56).[11]

2   3   4   5

6   7   8   9

[8] Examples: *CMDGBOx*, pls. 166 (1325), 179 (1338).
[9] A few other clear examples: *CMDGBOx*, pls. 241 (1399), 250 (1404).
[10] Better examples are: *CMDGBOx*, pl. 162 (Venice *c.* 1321–4); Federici, *Scrittura*, pl. 92 (Rome 1462–75, a documentary text). Influence from Italian Hybrida is in many cases probable.
[11] Another good example is *CMDF*, II, pl. 79, MS lat. 756 (1406).

After a long absence, **e** caudata (**e** with cedilla) occasionally reappears in the fifteenth-century manuscripts, probably under Humanistic influence.[12]

g too usually has a distinctive form. It is a variety of 'Rücken'-**g** (see p. 88), in which the right element is formed in a single curving vertical stroke, while the upper horizontal stroke closes the upper lobe and, where possible, forms a connection with the next letter (10) (the same form can be obtained using a different ductus). A special form of this **g** lacks a connecting stroke; this form is far more frequent in Rotunda than in Northern Textualis (11, pls. 54, 68, 72). Since the lower lobe of **g** was closed with a hairline, it often looks as if it has been left open, as is also the case with the upper bow of **a** and the eye of **e**. In the lower levels of execution and in the earlier phases in particular, this form of **g** alternates with or is replaced by other, more rapid forms corresponding with other ductuses, which mostly take the form of figure 8 (12, pls. 65–6).

h likewise has a distinctive form as a result of the unusual treatment of its limb. In contrast with Northern Textualis, in Rotunda the limb becomes almost circular and does not extend below the baseline. Nevertheless confusion with **b**, which has very much the same form, may usually be avoided, because the ascender of **h** ends straight on the baseline (in Textus Praescissus style), whereas that of **b** does not (13). A curving hairline extension to the limb descending below the baseline is found very exceptionally.[13]

i longa or **j** was only used after short **i**. Exceptions may be found in some manuscripts in the vernacular.[14] In contrast with Northern Textualis, the addition of diacritical strokes to **i** appears to be relatively rare, probably because the minims of **m** and **n** cannot easily be confused with **i**. If present, the stroke supplied to **i** is a hairline and generally barely visible. Dotted **i**s do not occur at all, except in late manuscripts in rapid execution and for private use (pl. 65).

The shapes of **m** and **n** have been discussed above (1). Their distinctive characteristics are, of course, not easily discernible in rapid hands. Final **m** was more often replaced by a sign in the form of figure 3 than in Northern Textualis (the symbol must not be confused with the abbreviation for final **et**) (14, pls. 56, 58, 60, 62, 65, 72). A word ending in **m** could therefore be written in three ways: in full, with the 3-sign, or with the normal horizontal mark of abbreviation. The 3-sign took up less space than **m** in its normal shape. This explains why this form often appears at the ends of lines, as a means of keeping the text within the rectangular ruled

10   11   12

13   14

12 *CMDIt2*, IV, pl. 29 (1439).
13 *CMDGBOx*, pls. 117 (1265), 175 (1334); *CMDF*, III, pl. 83, MS lat. 8073 (1307); *CMDB*, I, pl. 210 (1393). See also Ratdolt's type specimen of 1486 (Updike, *Printing Types*, I, fig. 29).
14 *CMDIt2*, IV, pl. 14 (1395), with **j** at the end of some words.

space. The sign was sometimes made as a short letter, standing on the baseline, or sometimes as a descender with its lower bow extending below the baseline.

Italian Rotunda, like Northern Textualis, permits two forms of **r**: the Carolingian, straight **r** (ending flat on the line as in Textus Praescissus) and the round **r** in the shape of figure 2 (15, 16). Originally the latter form was only written after **o**; but its use was soon extended and it can often be found after **a**, **b**, **d**, **e**, **h**, **p**, even **i**, **u** or straight **r** (pls. 62–3, 70, 72). Although the use of round **r** was only obligatory after **o**, this letter form was used much more liberally in Italy than in the North, even at the beginning of words (pl. 66).[15] The hairline extension of round **r** descending below the baseline, so common in Northern Textualis, is extremely rare in Italian Rotunda, as are all additional hairlines.[16]

As for **s**, up to three forms may be distinguished. The two usual types correspond with those used in Northern Textualis: the straight, Half-Uncial **s** at the beginning and in the middle of words, the round or Uncial **s** at their end. Straight **s** at the end of words still appears in manuscripts at a comparatively late date.[17] As has been noted above, this letter, like **f**, is treated in the same way as in Textus Praescissus. Both **f** and straight **s** mostly have a spur at about the height of the headline (17). The most typical round **s** has a very broad, closed shape and a studied lack of connection between its upper and its lower halves (18). To a much greater extent than in Northern Textualis, round **s** was replaced at the end of words by the so-called trailing **s**, traced in two strokes instead of three or four and occupying less space on the line (19). It usually extends below the baseline and often appears at the end of lines. It also is found far more often in rapid hands than in the more carefully executed ones. In the former it can become the dominant or even the only shape used for final **s**.[18]

In Rotunda **t** very occasionally has a variant form when it is preceded or followed by another **t**. When this occurs, the graph may look like **ct**. It may be difficult to know whether the scribe intended to write **tt** or **ct**, given the Italian tendency to write **ct** instead of **tt** ('mictere').[19] For this practice, see the Appendix. For the **ct**-ligature, see below.

The angular form of **u**, **v**, is not unknown in Italian Rotunda at the beginning of words, but it was not often used, especially in copies of Latin texts (pls. 62, 65,

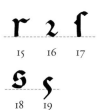

15   16   17

18   19

[15] Even sometimes in Rotunda Libraria/Formata: Federici, *Scrittura*, pl. 49 (1292).

[16] A few examples: Thomson, *Bookhands*, pl. 69 (1308); *CMDGBOx*, pl. 250 (1404); *CMDVat*, I, pl. 30, Arch. S. Pietro, MS B.82 (1423); *CMDF*, II, pl. 156 (1475).

[17] *CMDGBOx*, pl. 166 (1325); Thomson, *Bookhands*, pl. 74 (1366); the case of Federici, *Scrittura*, pl. 92 (Rome 1462–75) will be due to influence from Humanistic script.

[18] *CMDF*, III, pl. 128 (1398).

[19] See *CMDF*, II, pl. 79, MS lat. 756 (1406), col. b, l. 2; *CMDGBLo*, pl. 858 (1489), last but one l.: 'octenuto'.

69, 70). Throughout the later Middle Ages, Italian scribes as a rule wrote round **u** only. **v** may have seemed undesirable given its normal habit of extending above the headline. Furthermore, scribes in general seem to have avoided the intrusion of cursive features in their Textualis (see also below: Abbreviations). **v** may, however, be found much more often in vernacular codices.[20]

It is strange, then, that early printed books in Rotunda types use **v** so frequently at the beginning of words. Perhaps the first German printers in Italy were influenced by the writing habits of their homeland.[21]

x was never crossed in Rotunda. Two different forms occur: one in two strokes, the second stroke going downward (20, pl. 58); and one in two or three strokes, the second or the third stroke going upward (21, pls. 56, 60, 72). In the second structure it is mostly impossible to see from a reproduction which ductus has been applied. Both forms are found in manuscripts from the early thirteenth till the early sixteenth century. The former, however, occurs more often in more rapid scripts; the latter, especially when its right half comes close to the letter **c**, is doubtless the more typical shape in Italian Rotunda, adding another semicircular bow on the baseline to those existing already. Hence another possible ductus for **x** is in three strokes, consisting of two opposed bows (22), the application of which may be supposed in (some) calligraphic manuscripts.[22]

y is undotted. As for **z**, in addition to its normal, 3-shaped form, which does not always fit well on the line,[23] **c** caudata (**c** with cedilla) was often used to represent the same sound (23, pls. 63, 68).

FUSIONS

Gothic fusions were particularly beloved by scribes of Italian Textualis. Given the generally rounded character of the script, these were not genuine fusions, in which two letters share a common stroke, but were only overlapping strokes. Almost all hands, except the most rapid ones, made fusions in every possible place, such as: **bc**, **bd**, **be**, **bo**; **dc**, **de**, **do**, in all of which the Uncial **d** was used. The predominance of the Uncial form of **d** in Rotunda explains why the fusion **dd** is uncommon; when it does occur, either the second, or both **d**s may be of the straight, Half-Uncial

20   21

22   23

[20] An example is the 'codice Poggiali' of Dante (mid-fourteenth century): *Archivio Paleografico Italiano*, x, 69, Rome 1972, pl. 27.

[21] See, for example, the four samples in Erhard Ratdolt's specimen-sheet of 1486, printed in Venice: Updike, *Printing Types*, I, fig. 29.

[22] *CMDGBCam*, pl. 331 (1488); our pl. 74 (the same manuscript) contains only the majuscule form of this **x**; Voelkle and Wieck, *The Bernard H. Breslauer Collection* (see n. 6), p. 160, fig. 7 (late thirteenth century).

[23] Bischoff, *Palaeography*, p. 130.

type.[24] The fusions **he** and **ho**, generally avoided in Northern Textualis, found special favour with Italian scribes, and can be explained by the roundness of the limb of **h**. All possible fusions with **o** as the first letter are found as a rule: **oc**, **od**, **oe**, **og**, **oo**, **oq**, with the exception of **os**, which was not adopted by all scribes (the same applies to **bs** and **ps**), and with some justification since round **s** does not begin with a bow. Trailing **s** lends itself better to such fusions.[25] The fusion **od** occurs as a rule only with Half-Uncial, vertical **d**. **pc**, **pe**, **pg**, **po** are four more almost obligatory fusions; **bb** and **pp** are of Pregothic origin and are a special case (pl. 68). Given the shape of Rotunda **a**, fusions of this letter with a preceding one seldom occur (pl. 60).

One of the most characteristic examples of double fusion in Rotunda is the pronoun **hoc**, a double fusion uncommon in Northern Textualis (pl. 56).[26]

LIGATURES

Among the ligatures only **st** survived in Rotunda (24). The sequence **ct** always seems to have been written without any change in the shape of both letters, in contrast with most Northern Textualis hands.

ABBREVIATIONS

Italian Rotunda is characterized by a set of typical abbreviations and abbreviation marks. The usual horizontal common mark of abbreviation above the letter to indicate the omission of **m** or **n** or other letters is bold and extremely short; in Formata hands it is often no more than a slightly sloping quadrangle, sometimes even appearing as a dot (pl. 74). This stylistic feature contrasts heavily with the horizontal abbreviation signs that cut across the descenders beneath the baseline of the letters **p** (for **per**) and **q** (for **qui**, a specifically Italian abbreviation); these strokes are long and thin, and, in Formata hands, were traced as hairlines which can sometimes be difficult to discern (25, 26, pls. 58, 60, 72).[27]

Two parallel abbreviation marks that are altogether typical of Rotunda are those for **con** and for **us** after **b**. In fact the tendency was to use the same mark for

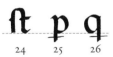

24   25   26

[24] Uncial **d** followed by Half-Uncial **d**: *CMDF*, II, pl. 72 (before 1398), col. a, last but one l.; *CMDVat*, I, pl. 127 (1496), col. b; two Half-Uncial **d**s: Thompson, *Introduction*, pl. 194 (1391). Two successive Uncial **d**s are not made into a fusion, see *CMDGBOx*, pl. 233 (1394?).
[25] Our pl. 60, bottom l., contains both **os** fusions at the end of words.
[26] Another example: *CMDGBLo*, pl. 356 (1419), col. b, l. 2.
[27] Good examples of **per** and **qui** are found in *CMDGBOx*, pl. 162 (*c.* 1321–4); *CMDF*, II, pl. 55 (1356).

both: the inverted c or *antisigma*. **con** represented by an inverted c is also found in Northern Textualis (above, p. 97), but it was universally adopted in Italian Rotunda. In more rapid hands the mark may take on either a more closed or a more extended form (27, 28).[28] The **us**-abbreviation after **b** may assume similar shapes.[29] But the semi-circular inverted c standing on the baseline appears to have been considered the ideal form for both **con** and (**b**)**us**. It is a replica of the bows of **b**, **h**, **p** and an inversion of the bows of **c**, **e**, **q** (29, 30, pls. 60, 72). The semicolon or 3-shaped stroke after **b**, which was the common abbreviation for (**b**)**us** in Northern Textualis, is rare in Rotunda (pls. 58, 62).[30]

This homogenizing tendency was sometimes even extended to the **que**-abbreviation, which in Southern as in Northern Textualis was normally formed with a **q** followed by a stroke in the shape of figure 3 (31, pl. 60). In a number of cases **q** was instead followed by the round antisigma (32), continuing a tradition already visible in some Pregothic scripts of the same area (see above, p. 68).[31]

The form of tironian **et** is another distinctive feature of Southern Textualis. It seems to have totally replaced the ampersand as early as the beginning of the thirteenth century. Its typical shape is already visible in Pregothic manuscripts of this area, but the precise form can vary and especially in lower levels of execution is sometimes hardly typical at all. But in contrast with Northern Textualis the form was invariably uncrossed.[32] It normally has the shape of figure 7 which stands on the baseline; its horizontal headstroke is long, and at its left-hand side curves downwards to a greater or lesser extent. In careful execution the graph is mostly treated as in Textus Praescissus, but in other cases its foot turns slightly to the right (33, 34, pls. 60, 68). One is, however, surprised to note the extent to which in manuscripts of Italian origin **et** is written out in full, especially in those of the fifteenth century.

pro has the standard form of abbreviation, namely **p** with a bow to the left of its descender, but the bow has a distinctive shape (35, pl. 72).

Two remarks should be made about the superscript **r**-abbreviation in Italian Rotunda. Whereas in Northern Textualis this sign normally replaces **r** followed or preceded by a vowel, in Italy it often stands for **r** alone and consequently is not

27   28   29

30   31   32

33   34   35

[28] More closed: our pls. 62 and 70; Federici, *Scrittura*, pl. 59, bottom l. (1334); more stretched: *CMDGBOx*, pl. 233 (1394?).

[29] *CMDGBOx*, pl. 164 (1322).

[30] Other examples: *CMDF*, II, pl. 33 (Naples 1279–82); *CMDGBLo*, pl. 424 (1435).

[31] *CMDF*, II, pls. 55 (1356) and 72 (before 1398).

[32] For an exception in Littera Bononiensis, see Brown, *Guide*, pl. 48.

an abbreviation properly speaking, but a superscript letter. Its form is usually that of a horizontal wavy line, but it may also be vertical, curved or straight. It never, however, contains the 'cursive' stroke connecting it with the letter beneath, as may be seen in many Northern codices, even those written in Textualis Formata.

HISTORICAL NOTE

Italian Rotunda became famous through its use in luxury choir-books of the fifteenth, sixteenth and seventeenth centuries, in which the craftsmen showed off their skill with the perfection of their drawing of its characteristic letter forms even when tracing the largest size (pl. 74). According to Cencetti the script did not attain its full maturity before the fourteenth century.[33] In the course of that century and especially of the fifteenth, the growing popularity of scripts of the cursive family caused Rotunda to be used more and more exclusively for Bibles, liturgical books, statutes, etc.

A special early variety of Italian Rotunda, known as Littera Bononiensis, also became widely known as a script for glossed copies of canon and civil law texts (pl. 56).[34] In both text and gloss, the script is generally extremely compressed both horizontally and vertically. The shortness of its ascenders and descenders creates the impression of an uninterrupted majuscule script. Although it is often considered a script type in its own right, it lacks sufficient distinctive features to distinguish it from Italian Rotunda in general.[35] It was in use at the university of Bologna during the entire thirteenth and fourteenth centuries, but spread also to the university of Padua and other North Italian centres.

II   TEXTUALIS IN SPAIN AND PORTUGAL
(plates 47–9, 57, 61, 64, 71, 73, 75–6)[36]

The study of Gothic book scripts in the Iberian Peninsula suffers from the absence hitherto of catalogues of dated manuscripts, and from the heavy emphasis on

---

[33] Cencetti, *Lineamenti*, p. 214.

[34] On this script see above, n. 3. The so-called Littera Neapolitana is, like Littera Oxoniensis, a university script, studied by Destrez, *La pecia*, pp. 48ff. Both 'scritture scolastiche' are of doubtful reality (Cencetti, *Lineamenti*, p. 218). One author mentions a Littera Assisiensis: C. Cenci, *Bibliotheca manuscripta ad Sacrum Conventum Assisiensem*, Assisi 1981 (Il Miracolo di Assisi, 4), pp. 23–6.

[35] This is also Cencetti's opinion in his later work, *Compendio*, p. 77.

[36] As for Italian Textualis (see n. 3), our plates relating to Textualis in Spain and Portugal include also Semitextualis, namely pl. 71.

documentary scripts in Spanish and Portuguese palaeographic research.[37] It is clear, however, that Textualis in manuscripts from these countries does not present the relatively uniform aspect that it has in Italian books. In addition to round and broad scripts we often encounter narrow, compressed and very angular scripts. Indeed, some of the narrowest of all Gothic scripts are Spanish or Portuguese (pl. 57).[38] Other examples, on the contrary, are close in aspect to Italian Rotunda. French and Italian influences, no doubt, were at work to varying degrees in different parts of the Peninsula at different times, which would explain why, in addition to the indigenous Pregothic elements, the features of such contrasting scripts as Northern Textualis and Italian Rotunda are visible in Iberian Textualis, the cause of its great variety.

GENERAL FEATURES

Iberian Textualis on the whole retains the broadness of Italian Rotunda, but can often be more angular. Spanish sources of the fifteenth century drew a distinction between scribes of 'littera rotunda' and scribes of 'littera formata'.[39] Canellas, in his handbook, distinguishes between 'libraria redonda' and 'libraria fracturada'. Although examples of both variants can easily be found, Canellas's own plates indicate that Spanish Textualis should not be reduced to just these two categories.[40] More

---

[37] Bibliography: Cencetti, *Lineamenti*, pp. 214–16; Cencetti, *Compendio*, pp. 75–6; Thomson, *Bookhands*, pls. 109–32. The most comprehensive works as far as book scripts are concerned are: Alvarez Marquez, 'Escritura'; Burnam, *Palaeographia*; Canellas, *Exempla*, II; D. L. Creasy, *The Development of the Formal Gothic Script in Spain: Toledo, XIIth–XIIIth Centuries*, Cincinnati 1984. The numerous other palaeographical handbooks and atlases focus mainly or entirely on documentary scripts: J. J. Alves Dias, A. M. de Oliveira Marques and T. F. Rodrigues, *Album de paleografia*, Lisbon 1987; A. Cruz, *Paleografía portuguesa. Ensaio de manual*, Porto 1987; Da Costa, *Album*; A. C. Floriano Cumbreño, *Curso general de paleografía y diplomatica españolas*, Oviedo 1946; García Villada, *Paleografía*; T. M. Martínez and J. M. Ruiz Asencio (eds.), *Paleografía y diplomatica*, Madrid 1991 (Universidad Nacional de Educación a Distancia); Millares Carlo, *Tratado*; C. Morterero y Simón, *Apuntes de iniciacion a la paleografía española de los siglos XII a XVII*, Madrid 1963; E. Nunes, *Album de paleografia portuguesa*, vol. I, Lisbon 1969. Numerous, but mostly very reduced, examples of book script can be found in the following two publications: H. Escolar (ed.), *Historia ilustrada del libro español. Los manoscritos*, Madrid 1993 (Biblioteca del Libro, 54); *Inventário dos códices iluminados até 1500*, I. *Distrito de Lisboa*, Lisbon 1994 (Inventário do Património Cultural Móvel).

[38] Two examples are found in J. A. Iglesias, 'Le statut du scripteur en Catalogne (XIVe–XVe siècles): une approche', in *Le statut du scripteur*, pp. 229–66, pls. 46 and 58; see also *CMDF*, I, pl. 56 (1377–96).

[39] See the article by Iglesias mentioned in n. 38, pp. 255–7.

[40] Canellas, *Exempla*, II. His pls. 49–51 are in 'libraria redonda', his pls. 45–8 in 'libraria fracturada'. In our opinion only his pl. 46 should be called 'fracturada', all the others have a pronounced Rotunda character. His pl. 50 is a Semitextualis, as are his pls. 54 ('libraria bastarda') and 79 (our pl. 71, 'bastarda formada'). His pl. 81, the script of which is called 'humanística formada', is also a Rotunda (the same incongruous use of the term Humanistic script is found in García Villada, *Paleografía*; Canellas's pl. 55, which he labels 'libraria bastarda', shows, by contrast, Humanistic script).

recent palaeographers have introduced other classifications, and draw a distinction between 'gótica caligráfica' and 'gótica redonda'.[41]

The dominant characteristic of Iberian Textualis, especially in the early phase, is its boldness. The top of the ascenders and the base of the descenders often exhibit a 'Northern' treatment instead of the 'Italian' flat ending or horizontal serif: in other words they are bifurcated or given a sloping hairline (pls. 48, 57). Spurs, unknown in Italian Rotunda, may be present at the left of the ascenders.[42] Iberian scribes of the fifteenth and sixteenth centuries also often indulged in the use of additional decorative hairlines, so common in Northern Textualis but mostly unknown in Italian Rotunda, appending them, for example, to final **t**, tironian **et** and the inverted c form of abbreviation (36–8, pl. 61).[43]

The treatment of the feet of minims and ascenders, as well as several letter forms, on the other hand, seem to be common to all Southern Textualis scripts. The Textus Praescissus style (the application of flat feet to minims and ascenders) is visible in many Spanish and Portuguese manuscripts, albeit used generally less consistently than in Italian Rotunda. This style is mostly found in the better Libraria or Formata levels, but we may note that minims and ascenders were given flattened feet to varying extents in different examples, while other manuscripts do not display the style at all. A tendency to over-emphasize this style is particularly evident in handwriting of the Formata level and is one of the main features of later Iberian Textualis (pl. 75).[44]

INDIVIDUAL LETTER FORMS

As in Italian Rotunda, box-**a** was not used, except in some rare narrow angular hands.[45] Throughout the period the upper bow of **a**, in so far as there was a bow, was either open or was closed with a hairline. It is notable that this letter, in addition to the 'Italian Rotunda' form (2, 3), is often found in a Pregothic shape with the first stroke making a right angle at the headline and a very large lobe (39, pl. 47).[46] The first stroke can be linked to such preceding letters as **f**, **g**,

36 37

38 39

[41] Martínez and Ruiz Asencio, *Paleografía y diplomatica* (see n. 37), I, pp. 306–9.
[42] R. S. Wieck, *Late Medieval and Renaissance Illuminated Manuscripts 1350–1525 in the Houghton Library*, Cambridge, Mass., 1983, p. 103 (Guadalupe 1506).
[43] Other examples: Canellas, *Exempla*, II, pl. 47 (1476); *CMDGBLo*, pl. 862 (1489); *CMDGBCam*, pl. 358 (1520).
[44] Another example: *CMDGBCam*, pl. 358 (1520). The tendency may already be manifest at an early date: Millares Carlo, *Tratado*, pl. 183 (1246).
[45] Iglesias, 'Le statut du scripteur' (see n. 38), pl. 58.
[46] Other examples: Canellas, *Exempla*, II, pl. 49 (1218); Millares Carlo, *Tratado*, pls. 182 (1222), 267 (1469); *CMDNL*, II, pl. 984 (1576!).

t (40). Even when its angularity is less pronounced, the letter **a** may keep its large lobe. Another typical form of **a** in fifteenth-century Formata exhibits a tendency for the upper bow to be closed with a spiralling hairline (41, pl. 61).[47] Unlike in Italian Rotunda, **a** was sometimes executed with a Praescissus-style minim in Iberian Textualis Formata (pl. 75).

By contrast with Italian Rotunda, too, the Half-Uncial, vertical **d** disappeared in Spain during the course of the thirteenth century, with the Uncial **d** being the only form used. This often has the same almost horizontal shaft as in Italian Rotunda. The reappearance of Half-Uncial **d** at the end of the period studied was due to Humanistic influence. Portuguese manuscripts provide some evidence of the use of Half-Uncial (in addition to Uncial) **d** in the fourteenth and fifteenth centuries (pl. 61).[48]

f and straight **s**, as in Italian Rotunda, were generally formed in the Praescissus manner, but their feet may sometimes turn upwards to the right. The Pregothic practice of lengthening one or both of these letters below the baseline is occasionally found in Iberian Textualis. The presence of long **f** and **s** with shafts consistently descending below the baseline denotes an apparently distinctive Spanish and Portuguese variant between Textualis and Hybrida, which will briefly be discussed in Chapter 9 (p. 175). In the thirteenth century **f** was sometimes given a triangular loop at its top, a feature already encountered in Pregothic script from Spain (pl. 47).[49]

As in Italian Rotunda **g** comes in essentially two forms: the figure 8-form and the typical Rotunda form (10, 12). In the latter one may sometimes observe a slight tendency for 'horns' to appear at the headline by the lengthening of one or both of the vertical strokes across the headstroke, doubtless under cursive influence (42, pls. 57, 71).

The shaft of **h** generally ends flat on the baseline, but in contrast with Italian practice its limb is often angular and descends below the line, bringing it closer in appearance to Northern Textualis (43, pl. 57).

i is another letter which, unlike Italian Rotunda, is often treated as in Textus Praescissus (pl. 75). Its lengthened variant, **j**, was used as elsewhere after **i**, but remnants of the earlier **i** longa tradition are sometimes seen in its appearance in other positions, especially at the end of words.[50]

40   41

42   43

[47] See also *CMDGBLo*, pl. 862 (1489).
[48] Another example: Burnam, *Palaeographia*, pl. 17 (1332).
[49] Another example: Millares Carlo, *Tratado*, pl. 182 (1222).
[50] Thomson, *Bookhands*, pl. 114 (1208); Millares Carlo, *Tratado*, pl. 185 (1280); Canellas, *Exempla*, II, pl. 46 (1354).

All the minims of **m** and **n** tend to have flat feet, a feature extremely rare in Italian Rotunda (44). This fully Textus Praescissus treatment of both letters appears to be one of the most distinguishing characteristics of Iberian Textualis from the thirteenth to the sixteenth centuries, even though a form with a non-Praescissus final minim and the Textus Rotundus form are also found quite often.

Straight **r** is as a rule Praescissus in style in both Italian and Iberian Textualis (15). It is remarkable, then, that some Formata hands in luxury manuscripts of the end of the Middle Ages have flat endings at the baseline in a broad range of letters, but not at that of **r** (pl. 75).[51] **r** longa (i.e. extending below the baseline) disappeared almost entirely.[52] The use of round **r** followed general late medieval practice and it is seldom found at the beginning of words.

The form of round **s** is close to the form in Italian Rotunda (18). Trailing **s** was also used, but in conformity with Northern practice straight **s** in final position appears to have been extremely rare.

The second minim of **u** may be treated in the Praescissus manner, in contrast with Italian usage (pl. 75). **v** in initial position instead of **u** is rarely found. As for **x**, there seems to have been a preference for the two-stroke form (20). In the apparently three-stroke ductus one may often observe a deliberate lack of connection between the two final strokes (45, pl. 61). One should not insist too much on the distinction between the two- and three-stroke forms, as they both may appear in the same hand. The Rotunda form, consisting of two overlapping facing bows, was also used in fifteenth- and sixteenth-century deluxe manuscripts (22).[53]

In contrast with Italian Rotunda **y** is generally dotted. **z** normally takes the 'Iberian' shape of figure 3 standing on the baseline or descending below it and does not extend above the headline (46, pl. 49).[54] It can be replaced by **c** caudata (23, pl. 64).

FUSIONS AND ABBREVIATIONS

Gothic fusions were applied with less consistency than in Italian Rotunda.[55] As for abbreviations, one should note that the ampersand was abandoned at the beginning

44   45   46

---

[51] See also *CMDF*, IV, I, pl. 76, MS esp. 8 (1461).

[52] One example occurs in Burnam, *Palaeographia*, pl. 17 (1332), col. a, l. 17.

[53] Canellas, *Exempla*, II, pl. 79 (1480).

[54] See also Da Costa, *Album*, pl. 142 (first half of sixteenth century); a typical form is present in Thomson, *Bookhands*, pl. 119 (1298).

[55] The more angular character of the script sometimes allowed the scribe to make real fusions, saving a stroke, as in Iglesias, 'Le statut du scripteur', pl. 46 (1423).

of the thirteenth century in favour of the tironian sign, but otherwise Iberian practice represents a free adaptation of that of Italian scribes. In the tironian **et** the typical bow at left of the horizontal stroke is generally absent. Early forms are **et** as an angular figure 7 (47) and, a typically Portuguese trait, the headstroke and upright stem forming a 90 degree angle (48).[56]

con- and (**b**)**us**-abbreviations are indicated by the well-known sign in the shape of figure 9 or by an inverted c (27, 29). The first form, standing for **us**, was frequently used and stands either on the baseline or above the headline. It was also used in diphthongs such as in 'laus'. The Italian abbreviation for **qui** (26) does not occur.

III   TEXTUALIS IN SOUTHERN FRANCE
(plates 50–3, 55)[57]

In the thirteenth and fourteenth centuries, and partly also in the fifteenth, manuscripts copied in such centres as Aix-en-Provence, Albi, Arles, Avignon, Bordeaux, Le Puy, Montpellier, Nîmes, Toulon, Toulouse and others were usually written in a Textualis Rotunda which corresponds quite closely to the Italian standards for that script, and to a greater extent than is the case with Spanish and Portuguese codices. Whereas some Iberian manuscripts were copied in an overtly bold and angular script, angularity and broken curves are only found in books from Southern France at the very end of the period under consideration.[58]

The letter forms, fusions and abbreviations of Gothic Textualis of this region are indeed those of Italian Rotunda. One sometimes finds early examples that still contain the Pregothic form of **a** familiar south of the Pyrenees (39, pl. 51). But, as in Italian practice, straight Half-Uncial **d** was used in addition to Uncial **d** for a rather long period (pl. 51),[59] as was straight **s** at the end of words as an alternative to round **s** (pl. 55).[60] **c** caudata too was used as an alternative for **z**.

One can, nevertheless, detect slight indications of influence from Northern Textualis, some of them also found in the Iberian Peninsula: an angular and lengthened

47   48

[56] An example of each: Thomson, *Bookhands*, pl. 114 (1208); *Inventário dos códices* (see n. 37), no. 249 (thirteenth century).
[57] Pl. 55 is Semitextualis. There is no special literature on the use of Textualis in Southern France.
[58] *CMDF*, III, pl. 209 (1492); VI, pl. 159 (1527).
[59] See also Toulouse, Bibl. mun., MS 93, f. 318v (1331; *CMDF*, VI, pl. 47 reproduces another page in a less typical script); *CMDF*, III, pl. 102 (1333); II, pl. 51 (1343–7).
[60] Another example is Paris, Bibl. nat. de France, MS lat. 13337 (1333; the feature is not visible on the fragment reproduced in *CMDF*, III, pl. 102).

limb of **h**;[61] a lack of precision in the treatment of the feet of **m** and **n**; a hair-line appended to the endstroke of final **t** and to round **r** (pls. 50, 53),[62] and the **con**-abbreviation in the form of figure 9 placed on the baseline.[63] **a** especially may be characterized either by a shape close to the Iberian Pregothic form (as has been said),[64] or more often by its upper bow being closed with a bold line (pl. 55).[65] Lengthened **i** is found in the same manner as in Spain and Portugal.[66] The Praescissus character of Italian Textualis is also often lacking; spurs at the ascenders appear only in the final period.[67]

Instead of being short, the common mark of abbreviation above letters is sometimes quite long. Instances of straight **r** followed by round **r**, perhaps pointing to a lack of experience on the part of individual scribes,[68] are also found in Italian examples.

IV   SOUTHERN TEXTUALIS IN OTHER COUNTRIES

The use of Rotunda or Rotunda-influenced scripts outside the Mediterranean area at the end of the Middle Ages may be attributed to various causes:

(a) The dispersal all over Europe of manuscripts in Littera Bononiensis.

(b) The proximity of and relations with Italy, which may account for the appearance of Rotunda features in Austrian, Bavarian and Swiss manuscripts. We have pointed out a few examples of this when dealing with Northern Textualis.[69]

(c) The spread of books printed with Rotunda types. The rapid dispersal of books printed in Rotunda by German, Italian and Spanish printers[70] soon made this type of script popular in parts of Europe where it had hitherto been unknown or considered unfashionable. This accounts for its use in quite a significant number of Books of Hours and liturgical books written in Bruges, Paris, Rouen, etc. at the end of the fifteenth and during the first decades of the sixteenth century. The presence in Northern Europe of wealthy Italian and Spanish patrons, and the commissions placed by Spanish bibliophiles,

---

[61] *CMDGBOx*, pl. 130 (1283–94).

[62] *CMDF*, VI, pl. 27 (1293: **t**); II, pl. 48 (1333: round **r**).

[63] *CMDF*, VII, pl. 76 (1325).

[64] See also *CMDF*, VI, pl. 180 (beginning of the thirteenth century).

[65] See also *CMDF*, II, pls. 58 (1364: only some **a**s), 88, MS lat. 967 (1423, same remark). Even box-**a** is found: see our pl. 52.

[66] *CMDF*, II, pl. 88, MS lat. 967 (1423).

[67] See n. 58.

[68] *CMDF*, II, pl. 88, MS lat. 967 (1423).

[69] An example of real Rotunda written in Sion, Switzerland: *CMDCH*, III, pl. 25 (1319).

[70] Mazal, *Buchkunst der Gotik*, pp. 149–50.

would have acted as an incentive to the making of deluxe codices in this script, just at the moment when the industry of manuscript production was coming to its close.[71]

Although Northern scribes mostly managed to imitate Italian Rotunda quite well, they generally betray their origin by a certain hesitation in the tracing of the letters, by an overtly marked angularity, by the application of spurs, etc. The presence of Humanistic elements in these manuscripts, such as Half-Uncial **d** and Roman Capitals, is not surprising given the period when they were produced.

V SEMITEXTUALIS

This variant of Textualis is barely mentioned in palaeographical handbooks.[72] It is distinguished by single-compartment **a**, all other features being those of Textualis (49–51). Starting with Cencetti, some Italian palaeographers call this script 'semi-gotica', a logical name for those by whom only Textualis is regarded as Gothic, but which we cannot retain for obvious reasons. Instead we shall use the new, parent name Semitextualis, since this script, though occurring most frequently in Italy, was not limited to the Apennine Peninsula.

In rapid execution the upper bow of early Textualis **a** is sometimes so reduced that it is impossible to decide which form the scribe intended to write. There are also many university manuscripts of the thirteenth and fourteenth centuries in which the combination of small size, a pen with a relatively broad nib and rapid execution induced the scribe to write one-compartment **a**, or a letter in which the upper section is so little developed as to bring it close to one-compartment **a** (above, p. 100). But when single-compartment **a** appears on a regular basis in handwriting of the Libraria or Formata level, there is no doubt that the scribe was deliberately writing a script that differed from Textualis. It would be interesting to trace the descent of this script, but such an enquiry is difficult without a thorough knowledge of the documentary scripts that lie behind it. Certainly Insular and especially Anglo-Saxon script, as well as occasionally early forms of Caroline, provide examples of highly calligraphic scripts with single-compartment Half-Uncial **a**.[73] Although in Carolingian script this shape was soon abandoned in favour of the Uncial **a**, there are quite a number of eleventh- and twelfth-century codices in which only the

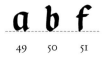

49 50 51

71 For examples of late medieval manuscripts copied in Rotunda in Northern European workshops for Southern commissioners, see, for example, M. Smeyers and J. Van der Stock (eds.), *Flemish Illuminated Manuscripts 1475–1550*, Ghent 1996, no. 1; T. Kren (ed.), *Renaissance Painting in Manuscripts: Treasures from the British Library*, New York 1983, nos. 5 and 7.

72 Crous and Kirchner, *Schriftarten*, p. 18; Cencetti, *Lineamenti*, p. 264.

73 Brown, *Guide*, pls. 16–18, 20–1.

Half-Uncial **a** is found, even in highly formal specimens.[74] The feature appears in informal handwriting in England, but its use in formal handwriting is confined to Anglo-Saxon 'square minuscule' and to the Anglo-Saxon script used for vernacular texts.[75]

VI SEMITEXTUALIS IN ITALY
(plates 58, 63, 65–6, 68–70)

Semitextualis as a canonized book script is first and foremost an Italian phenomenon of the thirteenth, fourteenth and fifteenth centuries.[76] It was used for both Latin and vernacular texts, but not for liturgical books. It is in essence a Rotunda with all the characteristics of this script as sketched above, except for the use of round single-compartment **a**. This simplified form of a letter with an otherwise complicated ductus seems to have been favoured all the more, as it allowed the scribe to make even more fusions than was normal in Rotunda, namely a fusion with the preceding letter if it terminated in a bow (52).

As the script clearly occupied a lower rank in the hierarchy of scripts in comparison with Rotunda, and was often used for the copying of vernacular texts, it normally exhibits more frequently the forms that we have called typical of the lower levels of Rotunda: the preponderant or exclusive use of round **r**, even at the beginning of words, and the widespread adoption of trailing **s** in final position. The ductus of both letters is simpler than that of straight **r** and round **s**.[77]

The name of Petrarch (1304–1374) is traditionally associated with this type of script (pl. 58). His autographs, in hands often described as Gothico-Antiqua or (better) Praehumanistica, are indeed mostly examples of Semitextualis, although they reveal a tendency for **f** and straight **s** to extend somewhat below the baseline, as in Hybrida. Petrarch is known as the eloquent spokesman for criticism of Gothic (i.e. Textualis) script in Italy. In his words, it was 'a diffuse ["vaga"] and exuberant ["luxurians"] letter written by the scribes (or more accurately the painters) of our time, charming the eye from a distance, but nearby disturbing and fatiguing it, as

52

[74] *CMDNL*, I, pl. 82 (1153–4).

[75] I thank Dr Teresa Webber for this information. See, for example, Brown, *Guide*, pl. 21 (end of the tenth century).

[76] Petrucci, *Breve storia*, pp. 165–9. Supino Martini, 'Per la storia' is an erudite but questionable approach. The existing atlases do not provide us with a satisfactory survey of Italian Semitextualis. See, for example, Thomson, *Bookhands*, pls. 62 (1226), 66 (1285), 67 (1289), 68 (1301), 79 (1441); Kirchner, *Scriptura Gothica*, pl. 17a (1285), 27 (1370, Petrarch); Ehrle and Liebaert, *Specimina*, pl. 43 (1353, 'Littera Bononiensis').

[77] On the basis of this combination of forms Julian Brown called this script 'as-Textualis' or 'as-glossing script', because it is often used for the copying of glosses to a text written in Textualis Rotunda (Brown, *Guide*, p. 117). There are, however, numerous non-glossed manuscripts in which the text is written in Semitextualis.

if it were devised for something other than to be read'. Instead, good handwriting should be 'neat ["castigata"], clear and easy to read ["se ultro oculis ingerens"]'. As Petrarch's own handwriting was also admired by his like-minded contemporaries, it has been considered worthy of intensive study by modern palaeographers. The general belief is that the Humanist Petrarch consciously purified his Gothic script to make it more suitable for conveying the ideas of Roman Antiquity and of its contemporary admirers. It has been suggested that, although the script in the manuscripts entirely or partly copied by himself is fundamentally Gothic, it was written under the influence of Carolingian models. His script, in its various forms, has been praised for its precision, clarity and studied separation of letters.[78]

However, if one compares samples of his hand with other book scripts of the same time in Italy, the difference is not so striking: his script is basically in line with his contemporaries' treatment of Italian Gothic script. He may perhaps have used a slightly wider distance between the lines (which could easily be measured), and he certainly favoured Capital script for some majuscule letters (**A, N, R** ...). As Kirchner observed, his hand displays a striking and, for his time, exceptional preference for straight **r** in certain positions.[79] Another detail which does not seem to have been noted before is his occasional use of straight instead of round or trailing **s** at the end of words.[80]

Whether this is sufficient to deem Petrarch's scribal activity a 'graphic reform' and to make him a precursor of Humanistic script is a matter of opinion. Whilst Paul Lehmann was convinced of the purely Gothic character of his handwriting,[81] others, such as Kirchner, Hessel and, more recently, Billanovich, Cencetti and Petrucci have considered him a pioneer reformer, whose work was of lasting influence and led directly to the creation of Humanistic script by Salutati, Poggio and others.[82] One cannot help having the impression that Petrarch's literary fame and his extraordinary statements about handwriting have led modern scholars unconsciously

---

[78] The problem of Petrarch's supposed role as a reformer of script and a forerunner of Humanistic script cannot be discussed here. Among the most enthusiastic supporters of this theory are Cencetti (*Lineamenti*, pp. 260–6) and A. Petrucci (*La scrittura di Francesco Petrarca*, Vatican City 1967); the latter work contains a complete bibliography up to 1966, a *status quaestionis* and numerous illustrations. Supino Martini ('Per la storia') is another champion of Petrarch's innovative activity. De la Mare, *Handwriting*, I, I, pp. 1–16, provides an excellent and well-illustrated survey but does not take a position in the debate.

[79] Crous and Kirchner, *Schriftarten*, p. 15.

[80] *CMDF*, II, pl. 58 (1374).

[81] P. Lehmann, 'Aufgaben und Anregungen der lateinischen Philologie des Mittelalters', in Lehmann, *Erforschung des Mittelalters*, I, Stuttgart 1959, pp. 1–46 (13–14) (originally published 1918).

[82] See n. 78. Both Hessel, 'Die Entstehung der Renaissanceschriften', *Archiv für Urkundenforschung*, 13 (1933), pp. 1–14, and Kirchner called Petrarch's bookhand 'goticoantiqua'. Ehrle and Liebaert, *Specimina*, pl. 45, used the term 'fere humanistica'.

to see in his handwriting many more revolutionary features than are actually there.[83]

Although of frequent use in Italy, even for luxury manuscripts,[84] Semitextualis never seems to have attained the stability of Rotunda. It could be used for the gloss of manuscripts in which the text was written in Rotunda.[85] In the fourteenth and fifteenth centuries frequent departures from the Rotunda elements came about under the influence of two competing scripts. The first of these was Italian Hybrida, which is probably the origin of Uncial **d** with long sloping shaft (53) which we observe repeatedly in Semitextualis.[86] The second was Humanistic script or Antiqua. The influence of the latter is visible in the broad character of so many fifteenth-century hands, in which horizontal and vertical compression and most fusions are absent, ascenders and descenders are long, and Half-Uncial straight **d** reappears.

In fact, the transition from Semitextualis to Antiqua (more precisely to the latter's variant form with single-compartment **a**) was so fluent, and there are so many intermediate forms, that it is often difficult to decide whether a given fifteenth-century specimen is to be placed in one or in the other of these two categories. In the face of the triumph of Humanistic script and the authority of Rotunda, on the one hand, and Italian Cursiva and Hybrida, on the other, Gothic Semitextualis was reduced to playing finally a role of minor importance, such as for the copying of Italian devotional texts.

VII   SEMITEXTUALIS IN OTHER COUNTRIES

Semitextualis was a minor script type in Spain, Portugal and Southern France, used from the end of the thirteenth century till the end of the Middle Ages (pls. 55, 71).

53

[83] Fundamental criticism is made in E. Casamassima, 'L'autografo Riccardiano della seconda lettera del Petrarca a Urbano V (Senile IX, I)', in *Quaderni Petrarcheschi*, 3 (1985–6), pp. 17–34.
[84] A splendid example is the St Petersburg Petrarch: T. Voronova and A. Sterligov, *Western European Illuminated Manuscripts of the 8th to the 16th Centuries in the National Library of Russia, St Petersburg*, Bournemouth and St Petersburg 1996, pp. 252–4. Other examples of careful Italian Semitextualis: our pls. 63, 68; *CMDF*, II, pls. 62 (1379), 77 (1402–3); III, pl. 141 (1419); *CMDGBOx*, pls. 134 (1288), 167 (1325), 244 (1400); *CMDIt2*, III, pls. 2–3 (1281), 25 (1418), 47 (1448); IV, pls. 7 (1293), 40 (1451); *CMDNL*, II, pl. 980a (1512); *CMDVat*, I, pl. 22, MS Ott. lat. 2837 (1406); Thomson, *Bookhands*, pl. 68 (1301).
[85] *CMDIt*, II, pl. 97 (1453).
[86] Examples: *CMDF*, VI, pls. 96, MS 490 (1445) and 98, same MS (1446).

In manuscripts from the Iberian Peninsula it can have a general aspect close to the Hybrida typical of this area.[87]

Elsewhere (pls. 59, 67) we need to distinguish between its use during the fifteenth century on the one hand, and that of the thirteenth and fourteenth centuries on the other. In the earlier period numerous university and other manuscripts, especially in France, were written in Semitextualis or contain both two-compartment and one-compartment **a**.[88] A more conscious and deliberate use of Semitextualis is revealed by a small number of mostly carefully executed fifteenth- and sixteenth-century codices made in France, the Low Countries and Germany, among them liturgical books and Books of Hours.[89]

Whatever the interest of these examples, Northern Semitextualis remains a marginal phenomenon in books produced at the end of the Middle Ages. Its use may be explained by Italian influence, as in the case of the parent Rotunda, and by the desire either to simplify Textualis somewhat, or to elevate Hybrida to a slightly higher rank.

---

[87] Other examples from Spain: Canellas, *Exempla*, II, pl. 50 (1348); *CMDF*, IV, I, pl. 76, MS esp. 5 (1461); Millares Carlo, *Tratado*, pl. 268 (fifteenth century); from Southern France: *CMDF*, III, pl. 78 (1299).

[88] Their script generally belongs to the category that is called Littera Parisiensis and they are particularly numerous. A few examples: *CMDF*, I, pl. 39 (1330); III, pls. 59, MS lat. 15349 (1271–88), 66 (*c.* 1280–1306), 78 (1298), 85 (1310–11), 89, MS lat. 12590 (1316); *CMDGBOx*, pls. 119 (1265–77), 151 (1309). A late example: *CMDF*, III, pl. 180, MS lat. 15856 (1467). English examples are rare: *CMDGBOx*, pls. 138 (*c.* 1292), 150 (1308).

[89] *CMDF*, II, pl. 164, MS lat. 4219 (1484).

6

Cursive scripts in general

From the thirteenth century a series of new types of book script were developed, which would soon take their place alongside Textualis and during the two following centuries would supersede it for many types of book. They were born of the desire to produce books more rapidly – and consequently more cheaply – and were based on the rapid scripts which had been created to fulfil the fast-growing needs of business and administration, and which we call cursive.

DEFINITION

No term has given rise to so much debate in palaeography in general, and in late medieval palaeography in particular, as cursive. Much unfruitful discussion could have been avoided if the protagonists had taken the trouble to define in advance the exact sense in which they were using the term. The persistent confusion of *cursive script* and *documentary script* has contributed to clouding the issue. The term cursive is used in two senses. It has in the first instance a technical meaning and is applied to scripts in which rapidity of execution is the primary, if not the only, intention of the writer. It is consequently an informal script and is synonymous with the term 'current'.[1] The opposite of cursive script in this sense is calligraphic script. In its second meaning, the term is applied to a series of script types deriving from this 'technical' cursive (what Muzerelle calls 'cursive opératoire'[2]), but in which the features of rapid handwriting have been reduced in order to obtain a more formal script, suitable either for documentary purposes or for books. Both cursive book hands and most documentary and especially charter hands are consequently not (or at least not entirely) cursive in the first, technical sense of the term. Roman cursive in its two forms (Capital and Minuscule Cursive or 'nouvelle écriture commune'), Merovingian Cursive, Papal Cursive ('Kurialkursive'), Humanistic Cursive, etc. are just a few of such 'cursive' scripts in the second

---

[1] This term should not be identified with the Lieftinckian term Currens.
[2] D. Muzerelle, in a forthcoming essay on Latin palaeography, the text of which he kindly put at my disposal.

sense of the term. It is clear that they cannot be reduced to a single category, as some of them are indeed rapid scripts, while others on the contrary are quite formal and far removed from the informal cursive models on which they were based.

In the discussion that follows we will reserve the term 'cursive' for informal, rapid Gothic handwriting and its characteristic features, and apply the names Cursiva, Bastarda, Hybrida, etc. to the script types derived from it and adapted for use as book scripts. In fact the latter, being more or less canonized scripts, are much better documented than the cursive scripts from which they were developed. The calligraphic treatment which they underwent in order to make them fit for use in books was in some cases minimal, in which case they are very close in appearance to their informal antecedent. In other cases the calligraphic process has been carried out so thoroughly that almost nothing remains of the original rapid and informal character of the script, except for some letter forms and an element of the personal and fanciful character typical of cursive script.

Many palaeographers, convinced that cursive script is only to be found in archival documents, use the term 'bastard script' (bâtarde, Bastarda, etc.) whenever cursive is found in books.[3] German scholars may even distinguish between 'Buchkursive' and 'Bastarda', depending on the degree of formality of the various cursive book scripts.[4] In the present book the term Bastarda will be used for one canonized form of book script, and will be avoided as a generic term for more or less formal book script derived from cursive.

The cursive book scripts discussed in the following pages should be viewed as intermediate types between Textualis and cursive script, and as a response to the widespread need for a book script that combined the rapidity (i.e. the lower cost) of cursive with the formality of Textualis. There are innumerable ways of combining features of both scripts to form new types, as we will see. But for some scholars there were essentially two ways of obtaining such an intermediate script: a scribe either started with cursive and applied to it a more or less calligraphic technique; or his starting point was Textualis, which was then written with a more or less cursive (i.e. current) technique.[5] They accordingly distinguish two types of Gothic cursive book script, which Strubbe calls respectively 'cursive bastarda' and 'minuscule [i.e. Textualis] bastarda'. It seems, however, much more likely that cursive book scripts

[3] See the definition of 'bastard script' by Casamassima, *Tradizione corsiva*, p. 98: 'national documentary and especially chancery scripts, which through a refined process of stylization become regular book scripts used for texts in the vernacular'.
[4] See, for example, Mazal, *Buchkunst der Gotik*, figs. 20–2 and 23–37; Schneider, *Paläographie*, pp. 59–65 and 65–78.
[5] Strubbe, *Grondbegrippen*, pp. 115–16; J. John in *Dictionary of the Middle Ages*, ed. J. R. Strayer, IX, New York 1987, p. 348; Obbema, 'De opkomst van een nieuw schrifttype', p. 70.

were created using cursive script as a base and applying Textualis elements, rather than the opposite, as will be explained in the following pages.

GENERAL FEATURES OF CURSIVE SCRIPT

Gothic cursive is a development of existing script (Textualis or Praegothica), which was thoroughly modified by rapid execution. Its features are the result of the 'current' execution and can be summarized as follows.[6]

(a) An emphasis upon the horizontal axis of the handwriting, instead of a (more time-consuming) focus upon the vertical axis. As a result, the script tends to be broader and to lack the lateral compression proper to Textualis.

(b) Extension of the ascenders and descenders, which in rapid writing tend to be exaggerated in length. The extension of the letters **f** and straight **s** below the baseline is particularly noteworthy. The height of the bodies of letters in relation to the height of the ascenders is consequently smaller than in Textualis. This feature by itself induced the producers of manuscripts to adopt wider distances between the lines, so that the vertical compression characteristic of Textualis too became generally far less obvious in Gothic cursive.

Both characteristics give the effect of largely eliminating the compactness of the 'Gothic' (i.e. Textualis) written area. The more 'open' character of cursive script consequently permitted the adoption of a layout in long lines instead of the two-column layout preferred by the scribes of Textualis. The precedent provided by charters which were always written in long lines (lines which are frequently of considerable length) may well have exercised some influence upon the layout of manuscript books written in a cursive book script.

(c) The rapid execution often (if not generally) tended to make the script slope to the right (or, conversely, to the left in many early and lower-level book scripts derived from cursive). This tendency is contrary to the general Gothic predilection for vertical strokes. In the more formal cursive book scripts, this feature is less apparent and may be reduced to a few graphs, as in Bastarda (see p. 158). The letter forms in many Gothic cursive book scripts do not slope at all.

(d) The introduction of loops has generally been considered a determining characteristic of cursive script. In many twelfth- and early thirteenth-century documentary hands the tops of the ascenders turn to the right, and the bottoms of the

[6] The following observations are only very partially based on the available literature: Battelli, *Lezioni*, p. 230; Bischoff, *Palaeography*, pp. 136–7; Casamassima, *Tradizione corsiva* (the most fundamental discussion of cursive script); Gasparri, *Introduction*, pp. 108–10; Kisseleva, *Goticheskij kursiv*; A. Mastruzzo, 'Ductus, corsività, storia della scrittura: alcune considerazioni', *Scrittura e Civiltà*, 19 (1995), pp. 403–64; Petrucci, *Breve storia*, pp. 143–5; Schneider, *Paläographie*, pp. 55–7; Stiennon, *Paléographie*, pp. 129–30.

descenders turn to the left, but the utility of these 'loops' is not always apparent (pl. 87).[7] They do not, for example, serve to link subsequent letters to each other. In fact, the hands were already somewhat stylized versions perfected in chanceries and other offices and do not appear to reflect the original cursive features to their full extent. The loops should then be understood in the light of the new ductus, which is the basic feature of cursive. They will be examined in the next paragraph. One may note that the looping tendencies in book scripts would soon be limited to the ascenders, including that of **d**, and their appearance on descenders would be reduced considerably: **f**, **p**, **q** and straight **s** rarely show any loops at the bottom (some exceptions may be seen in English manuscripts); only **g** may display quite extensive elaboration below the line.

(e) The simplified ductus is the essential feature of cursive script. In order to write rapidly, the number of strokes required to execute given graphs should be reduced as far as possible, in other words the pen must be lifted from the writing surface as rarely as possible. Instead of lifting the pen when moving it from one point to another between two strokes, the 'aerial strokes' are actually traced and become visible as loops, thus changing considerably the original letter form. The new ductus thus on the one hand produces new complicated letter forms, on the other it simplifies existing letter forms such as **m** (1), **n**, **u**, all of them traced in a single stroke (without lifting the pen). Because of the rapidity of the handwriting, graphs still traced in two strokes may be disjointed, the second stroke being traced too far to the right and thus unconnected with the first stroke, as is often the case with cursive **e** (2).

(f) The extraordinary development of ligatures in cursive should be interpreted in the same way. Two, three or more succeeding letters or parts of letters may be traced in one stroke, which of course results in new forms and considerable distortion of the original ones (3, 4).[8] It is clear that the latter feature conflicts with the general rule that book scripts should avoid ligatures. Consequently these ligatures were only admitted in the lowest levels of cursive book script (pls. 97–8, 106). Ligatures generate various forms of the same letter, according to its position within the graph: linked with the preceding letter, with the succeeding letter, or with both or neither. These variant letter forms likewise conflict with a general rule for book script, but are nevertheless present in many cursive book scripts.

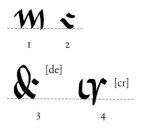

1   2

[de]

[cr]

3   4

[7] See also, for example, Foerster, *Buch- und Urkundenschriften*, pls. 23, 28, 31–3; Steffens, *Paläographie*, pls. 78 (1159), 81 (1138), 87 (1203), 93 (1249). On the utility of loops, see Steinmann, 'Vom *D*', p. 295; according to Casamassima, *Tradizione corsiva*, p. 26, the loops and ligatures, at least originally, were primarily a means to stress the type of organization proper to a given type of cursive script.
[8] The Table in Casamassima, *Tradizione corsiva*, pp. 160–1, gives an impressive survey of all possible ligatures found in cursive handwriting of the second half of the thirteenth century.

(g) The cursive ductus as sketched above assumes that the pen can be moved in all directions, and not only in the 'natural' directions of downwards and left to right, as in the various forms of Textualis discussed above. The technical problem of moving the pen against these directions, of 'pushing' the pen upwards and from right to left, especially on rough parchment, has hitherto not received the attention it deserves. The general opinion among calligraphers is that this technique cannot be applied if the pen has a broad nib (as was employed for Textualis). A narrow-nibbed pen, however, that produces a threadlike script, is able to move in all directions and can trace a circle, for example, in one stroke without blotting.[9] One is very much inclined to accept this view, given that many early cursive book scripts do not display the natural shading proper to Textualis.

(h) This does not mean that Gothic cursive lacks any bold strokes. On the contrary, thirteenth-century examples, in particular, exhibit some exceptionally heavy strokes, a feature found in many documentary and some book hands. These bold strokes, however, were not produced by using a broad-nibbed pen, but by exerting pressure on the nib, causing its split edge to open and the ink to flow liberally. This is proved by the swelling and diminishing width of such strokes and by their direction, which is diagonal from top left to bottom right or horizontal left to right, such as in **d**, **v**, the loop of **g** or the horizontal abbreviation stroke (5–7).[10] It would be impossible to exert pressure on a pen moving against these natural directions. How later cursives could achieve natural shading without always adopting 'constructed' letters is a problem that has yet to be investigated.

(i) The special treatment of the minims at the baseline and the headline, as seen in Textualis, is, of course, not found in a script in which rapidity was the primary goal. Minims in initial and final position, however, were often supplied with extensions, termed approach strokes and endstrokes, which may descend beneath the baseline. The former are often present in words beginning with **i**, **m**, **n**, **r**, tironian **et** (8–9), and the latter in words ending in **m** and **n** in particular (10–11). They are no doubt related to the tendency, natural to rapid writing (see above, p. 48), to begin strokes at an earlier point than they are supposed to begin, and to end them beyond their proper ending. They contribute by their position to the legibility of the script by stressing the words as units within the line of script.

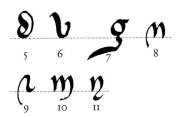

5   6   7   8

9   10   11

[9] See Noordzij, *The Stroke of the Pen*. Michael Gullick has confirmed this view.

[10] A few examples in documentary script: Brown, *Guide*, pl. 34; Denholm-Young, *Handwriting*, pl. 14; a striking example is also found in *CMDGBOx*, pl. 140.

(j) Perhaps related to this is a curious phenomenon in cursive script, which has received little attention hitherto: the increasing tendency to begin words with a majuscule or at least a special letter form (*littera notabilior*). In many cases it is obvious that a majuscule was actually intended, because the word in question is a proper name or one that may be considered as such. This practice is not unknown in Praegothica and in Textualis: in the former the name 'Maria', for example, is very often written with a majuscule **M**.[11] Given that in cursive scripts **r** is the letter most often written in majuscule form when in initial position, one may probably conclude that this practice has its origin in charter hands, and especially in royal charters, where the word 'Rex' usually follows the King's name and was, like the name itself, written with a majuscule out of deference.[12] The use of 'majuscule' or special forms at the beginning of words in cursive script may, however, also have a technical basis, as it would make no sense to use letter forms in that position which would permit a ligature to be made with the preceding letter when other forms were available. At any rate, the practice was taken over in the execution of many book scripts that had their origin in cursive script, and it must be considered the origin of the modern use of majuscules for writing all proper names or even, as in German, all substantives.

MAKING CURSIVE INTO BOOK SCRIPT

The various ways of introducing greater formality in an informal cursive script, or to 'textualize' a cursive,[13] may be summarized as follows.

(a) A reduction in the number of ligatures, or even eliminating them entirely. Although they were sometimes retained in large numbers in schoolbooks, manuals, private books in the vernacular, etc., these complicated forms were avoided for the more formal levels of execution, and the letters that originally were linked were separated from each other (although they would often still touch each other). The important thing to note is that despite this they retained the form they had in the ligature, thus creating double, triple or even multiple forms of the same letter. In contrast with Textualis, in which variant forms were used only for **a** (though not in Rotunda), **r** and **s**, these variant forms are a standard feature of those Gothic book scripts that were derived from cursive.

(b) During the later fourteenth and fifteenth centuries the ensuing lack of connection between the letters within the word was counterbalanced in the higher levels of execution by the introduction of fusions (pls. 109, 112, 114). This means

---

[11] For example: Thomson, *Bookhands*, pl. 85 (England 1155), col. b, l. 13.
[12] Examples: Foerster, *Buch- und Urkundenschriften*, pls. 31–3.
[13] The expression 'Textualismen' is used by Gumbert, *Kartäuser*, pp. 247, 260, etc.

of connecting letters when two curves face each other is at odds with the essential feature of cursive script – its rapidity – and is a clear indication of the impact of Textualis on cursive book script. The uncompressed character of cursive is thus combined with the opposite tendency towards compactness, a feature which may be more or less marked.[14]

(c) Many cursive book hands, especially of the earlier period and of the lower levels, retain to a greater or lesser extent the simplified ductus and the narrow-nibbed pen proper to cursive. More often, however, the scribes of cursive book scripts appear to have adopted the broad-nibbed pen and complicated ductus of Textualis. The cursive letter forms, traced originally in one stroke, were now often 'constructed' in the same way as Textualis letters, with the additional complication that the loops, which in cursive were produced by the natural movement of the pen, often had to be added by means of separate strokes. In compensation the natural shading produced by the broad pen gave the letters a 'body', which they lacked in the original cursive, and which at all times has been considered an essential feature of good book scripts or good typography. The heavy bold strokes, typical of early cursive and obtained through pressure upon the nib, were generally abandoned in the process. (In Textualis too, shading by applying pressure to the nib never seems to have played a conspicuous role[15].) None the less, they survived in a sense in the unusually fat and, at their base, pointed shapes of **f** and straight **s**, typical of so many cursive book scripts, which like the bold strokes in early cursive were not obtained by the natural antithesis of thick and thin strokes produced by a broad-nibbed pen (12).

It is often difficult to discern the ductus employed in formal cursive book scripts. Furthermore there is a wide range of intermediate types between purely cursive scripts on the one hand and purely calligraphic cursive book scripts on the other. These matters require much further study.

(d) Cursive forms may sometimes have been replaced by Textualis forms deliberately.

(e) 'Textualizing' did not only happen as a result of scribes eliminating ligatures, focusing on horizontal compression and adopting more elaborate ductuses and Textualis letter forms. It could also be obtained by reducing the length of ascenders and descenders and consequently the distance between the lines. On the whole, however, scribes came to aim less at producing such vertical compression, and compact text blocks comparable to those in Textualis are to be found only in some cursive book scripts, such as Netherlandish Hybrida.

12

14 Examples of very compressed cursive handwriting: *CMDS*, I, pl. 31 (1377); Thompson, *Introduction*, pl. 196.
15 See a discussion of the 'weight' of a handwriting in Gilissen, *Expertise*, pp. 33–9.

(f) Finally, another feature of Textualis was introduced in Northern cursive book scripts of the later fourteenth and the fifteenth centuries, or at least those of the Libraria and Formata levels, namely angularity. This feature, which is at odds with the nature of cursive script, in combination with the shading obtained by the use of a pen with a relatively broad nib, contributed strongly to the unique aspect of late medieval cursive book scripts. Angularity creates unusual square, pointed or spiky forms in an otherwise naturally rounded script. Spurs even sometimes appear at the left of the looped ascenders **b**, **h**, **k**, **l**, and quadrangles, typical of Textus Quadratus, may also be visible at the headline or at the baseline in late cursive book scripts of the higher levels.

MAIN SUBDIVISIONS OF GOTHIC CURSIVE BOOK SCRIPT

According to Lieftinck, Gothic Cursiva, that is, the most widespread variety of cursive book script, can be defined by no more than three basic letter forms or groups of forms: single-compartment **a**; **b**, **h**, **k** and **l** with loops at the right of their ascenders; and **f** and straight **s** descending below the baseline. His system does not take into account another, minor variety, which has the same characteristics except for **a**, which features the two-compartment, Textualis form. Since this latter variety is the earliest to appear, we shall call it Cursiva Antiquior, in contrast with the main form, which we shall call Cursiva Recentior or simply Cursiva.[16] Some palaeographers add to the Lieftinck criteria two more: looped **d** and **g** with a 'simplified' form. Although both may be typical of cursive book scripts, the former criterion has no absolute validity, and the latter deserves a more precise definition.

In what follows the three distinctive criteria first mentioned above, whether appearing in rapid and ligatured script, or in highly calligraphic handwriting, will be considered sufficient to call a given script Cursiva or Cursiva Antiquior. In the first case we will use the term Cursiva (Antiquior) Currens, in the second the term Cursiva (Antiquior) Formata. As in Textualis, intermediate levels of execution will be labelled Cursiva (Antiquior) Libraria or simply Cursiva (Antiquior).

A difficult problem of classification is raised by book scripts apparently based on cursive but having no loops at the ascenders of **b**, **h**, **k** and **l**. Prior to Lieftinck few palaeographers had paid attention to the difference between these scripts and looped cursive book scripts. By reserving to them the name Bastarda (later

---

[16] Schneider, *Paläographie*, pp. 59–62, distinguishes 'ältere' and 'jüngere gotische Kursive'; Gumbert, *Kartäuser*, p. 204, n. 30, proposed the term 'a-Cursiva' for what is called Cursiva Antiquior here.

happily replaced by the non-historical term Hybrida), the Dutch palaeographer gave rise to a debate which is still going on. His opinion – now generally shared – was that Hybrida is a fifteenth-century phenomenon limited to the Netherlands, Belgium and the Rhineland, of which the earliest examples date from the second decade of the fifteenth century.[17] The term would therefore not be applicable to scripts having the same basic features (i.e. cursive **a**, **f** and straight **s**, and Textualis **b**, **h**, **k** and **l**) but originating from other European countries. Indeed, these have generally been considered to have nothing in common with Lieftinck's Hybrida.[18] We are here confronted with a basic problem of palaeography: what constitutes a script type, a problem which, unfortunately, cannot be considered here.[19] We will deal with the special case of the 'schleifenlose Bastarden' (as the German palaeographers call them) in a separate chapter, but some discussion is required in order to make clear our position within the wider debate. Whether the absence of loops is a criterion important enough on its own to define a single family of scripts depends on the consistency with which medieval scribes in various parts of Europe employed this feature and on the extent to which the overall appearance of the script was affected. In countries like Germany the same hand may, on the same page, write ascenders with and without loops (following Gumbert we will call such a script Semihybrida[20]). In some deluxe scripts, like Burgundian Bastarda, some scribes wrote loops, others used Textualis ascenders, and still others employed a mixture of both forms. Here too, this feature seems to have had little impact on the character of the script, and the three variants must be treated as constituting the same script. In many other cases, however, the loopless ascenders appear to be a noteworthy feature of the highest importance for defining a distinct type of script within the family of cursive book scripts.

In the light of what has been said above about the techniques applied to transform cursive script into a book script, the absence of loops in a 'cursive' script may have had a definite significance: omitting them would have been one of the means – even one of the most radical means – to remove the unwanted cursive character of a given script. In that case it can only be interpreted as a deliberate choice made by the scribes involved in the creation of the script. Viewed this way, Hybrida would be a cursive book script like the other ones, but one in which an essential feature of cursive script has been given up. While this interpretation is no doubt true for

---

[17] See, for example, Obbema, 'De opkomst van een nieuw schrifttype'.
[18] J. P. Gumbert, 'A Proposal for a Cartesian Nomenclature', in *Essays presented to G. I. Lieftinck*, IV: *Miniatures, Scripts, Collections*, Amsterdam 1976 (Litterae Textuales), pp. 45–52 (49).
[19] See D. Ganz, 'Traube on "Schrifttypen"', *Scriptorium*, 36 (1982), pp. 293–303.
[20] Gumbert, *Kartäuser*, p. 210.

'Northern' Hybrida, its validity for Southern European Hybridae, which appear earlier than their Northern counterparts, remains to be seen.

In the next pages three families of cursive book script will therefore be studied, including the intermediate forms between them: Cursiva Antiquior, Cursiva (Recentior) and Hybrida.

7

Cursiva Antiquior
(plates 77–86)

This script, which contains an astonishing variety of forms and shapes, is defined by the following three letter forms or groups of forms: two-compartment **a**, loops at the right of the ascenders of **b**, **h**, **k** and **l**, **f** and straight **s** descending below the baseline (1–3). These forms seem to have been normal features of thirteenth-century documentary scripts,[1] and they are characteristic of the earliest cursive book scripts in large parts of Europe: from the thirteenth century onwards in England, in the fourteenth century in Germany, Central Europe, Scandinavia. In France, the Low Countries and Italy the early cursive with two-compartment **a** had generally already developed into cursive with single-compartment **a** by the fourteenth century, when it was adapted for use as a book script. The Iberian Peninsula seems to present a similar situation. The use of Cursiva Antiquior as a book script was extremely limited in all of these countries. The Spanish examples which at first sight would be classified under this category are in fact 'hors système' scripts, variants of Iberian Hybrida (see below, p. 175).

Whereas this form of Cursiva does not seem to have developed into a canonized book script with its own special character in continental Europe and had given way to Cursiva before the fifteenth century, in England its use was both extremely precocious and long lasting, and led to the creation of a highly idiosyncratic script. Cursive book script in this country will therefore be discussed in a separate section.

I CURSIVA ANTIQUIOR IN THE GERMAN-SPEAKING COUNTRIES, CENTRAL EUROPE AND SCANDINAVIA
(plates 78, 83)

Karin Schneider attributes the appearance of the 'ältere gotische Kursive' as a book script in Germany to the second and third quarters of the fourteenth century. These are the characteristics she lists for this script:[2]

1   2   3

[1] Examples: Steffens, *Paläographie*, pls. 87 (1203), 96 (1275), 99 (1291; **a** often single-compartment); Foerster, *Buch- und Urkundenschriften*, pls. 31, 33–6; Millares Carlo, *Tratado*, pl. 195.
[2] Schneider, *Paläographie*, pp. 59–62.

(a) A two-compartment **a** which extends far above the headline and can be as tall as the ascenders (1). We have seen the same phenomenon in Northern Textualis of a small size, and we will meet it again in English cursive book script.

(b) A short **g** in the shape of figure 8, its lower lobe often standing on the baseline (4).

(c) The final curve of the following letters extending below the baseline and turning to the right: **h**, **y**, **z**, and often also **m** and **n** (5).

(d) In the higher levels of execution only: a very bold dagger-like form of the shaft of **f** and straight **s**, both letters descending below the baseline and narrowing to a point (6). The origin of this feature, typical of so many cursive book scripts, will be discussed when dealing with Cursiva (p. 145). Boldness may also appear in the loops at the ascenders, which often have a triangular shape.

To these characteristics may be added looped **d**, a form used in all fourteenth-century and in many fifteenth-century cursive book scripts (7).

Book scripts of this type are always of a rather low level (Currens or Libraria) and in their lack of uniformity are typical of the earliest phase in the use of business scripts as book scripts. They are seen in manuscripts from Austria, Bohemia and Scandinavia as well as from Germany and (sometimes) the Low Countries. They do not occur before the second quarter of the fourteenth century and only a few survived after the beginning of the fifteenth; many late examples reveal a transition towards Cursiva, in that they alternate two-compartment with single-compartment **a**.[3]

II CURSIVA ANTIQUIOR IN ENGLAND: ANGLICANA
(plates 77, 80–1, 84–6)

Only in England did Cursiva Antiquior develop into a canonical book script with its own definitive character. It had developed its set of distinctive characteristics as early as the middle of the thirteenth century and was soon adopted for use in books

[3] A few more examples of Cursiva Antiquior in this area: Kirchner, *Scriptura Gothica*, pl. 40 (Switzerland 1359, 'notula'); Thomson, *Bookhands*, pl. 46 (Germany 1367); *CMDB*, I, pl. 217 (Low Countries 1400); *CMDNL*, II, pls. 628 (1397), 630 (1401), 634 (1405), 637 (1411), all from the Northern Low Countries, the last two with alternating use of the two forms of **a**; *CMDS*, I, pl. 16 (Sweden 1336).

and continued to be used till well into the sixteenth century. This extraordinary and long-lasting script is well-documented thanks to the British series of Catalogues of Dated Manuscripts and several atlases, and its features, peculiarities and types have been studied in an exemplary way by Malcolm Parkes in a monograph which has been a classic ever since it was published in 1969.[4] Although we are not able to adopt all of its subdivisions and nomenclature, the clarifying effect of this work has been considerable.

GENERAL FEATURES

It would appear that the script of the royal chanceries and other agencies had a long and lasting influence on cursive book script in England and that it was not until the fifteenth century that the European Cursiva Recentior began slowly to replace the peculiar forms that had hitherto marked English script.

English Cursiva Antiquior, to which Parkes gave the historical name Anglicana, is indeed a most striking testimony to England's geographical position and its reduced political involvement on the Continent between the loss of Normandy in the early thirteenth century and the outbreak of the Hundred Years' War over a century later. In earlier examples, in particular, it retains from documentary handwriting the heavy emphasis upon certain downward diagonal strokes, such as in **d** and other letters (8, pls. 77, 80), and in the cursive **r**-abbreviation (9). This preference for extremely bold strokes is especially apparent in the top lines of some manuscripts, where, following the documentary tradition, the ascenders are not only lengthened, but also thickened, with decorative highlighting sometimes augmenting the heaviness of these strokes (pl. 81).[5] As noted above, these bold strokes cannot be due to the holding or cutting of the pen at an extremely oblique angle, as has been thought,[6] but must have been obtained by exerting pressure on the nib.[7]

In general, Anglicana is not a sloping script and, except in fifteenth-century examples written under the influence of Bastarda, even **f** and straight **s** are mostly vertical. Thirteenth- and early fourteenth-century hands display a tendency to slope to the left (pl. 77).

The rarity of approach and endstrokes is distinctive: in contrast with most continental Cursivae, final **m** and **n** are mostly not different from the same letters

8   9

[4] Parkes, *Book Hands*. Two other atlases are Denholm-Young, *Handwriting*; Wright, *Vernacular Hands*. See on this script also Cencetti, *Lineamenti*, pp. 238–42.
[5] Parkes, *Book Hands*, pls. 5 ii (*c.* 1394–7), 7 i (mid-fourteenth century), 23 ii (1412?).
[6] Parkes, *Book Hands*, p. xv, comment to pl. 1, etc.
[7] As Cencetti, *Lineamenti*, p. 239, also asserts.

in other positions. As for the approach strokes, those of initial **u** (in the angular form of **v**) and tironian **et** (pl. 84) may be extremely prominent.[8]

The most peculiar feature of early Anglicana especially, however, is the treatment of the ascenders of **b**, **h**, **k** and **l** (pl. 77). These, which are very heavy at the top, display the normal cursive loop at their right side, which can be traced as a hairline, but their shaft has a marked bold bifurcation, as if Textualis and cursive elements were combined in the same letter (10).[9] What we see is in fact the result of an originally single-stroke ductus, still visible in some early examples (11),[10] which has been replaced by the execution of the same shape in two strokes. It is no doubt to the latter ductus that Parkes alludes when he mentions that the loop is an approach stroke to the right:[11] this can scarcely have been the original ductus. When two such looped and bifurcated letters follow each other, the second one normally loses the forking.[12]

In parallel with this, hands of the thirteenth and early fourteenth centuries often show a singular treatment of the top of **f** and straight **s**: above the normal, bold curve towards the right a second, hairline curve in the same direction has been traced (pl. 77). Here too one must assume that an originally single-stroke ductus lies behind these unique forms (12, 13).[13] Two successive **fs** or straight **ss** of this kind may display a different treatment corresponding with that given to pairs of looped ascenders.[14] More normal looped **f** and straight **s** are also found (14).[15]

Looped descenders are sometimes seen in long **i**, **p** and **q**.[16]

INDIVIDUAL LETTER FORMS

The following are the most noteworthy individual letter forms. The two-compartment **a** is noticeably higher than the other small letters, but this feature is

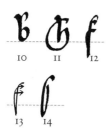

10   11   12

13   14

[8] Other examples: *CMDGBOx*, pls. 160 (*c.* 1320), 171 (after 1327), 196 (*c.* 1353); Parkes, *Book Hands*, pl. 3 i (mid-fifteenth century).

[9] Good examples are Parkes, *Book Hands*, pls. 1 i (end of thirteenth century), 4 i (1291). This feature is also known in continental documentary scripts: Steffens, *Paläographie*, pl. 96, 2 (1275). It disappears in Anglicana at the beginning of the fourteenth century. A late example is *CMDGBOx*, pl. 160 (*c.* 1320). A remnant of it may perhaps be seen in the spurs appearing at the left of the looped ascenders in Kirchner, *Scriptura Gothica*, pl. 34b (1446).

[10] See, for example, Parkes, *Book Hands*, pl. 4 i (1291).

[11] See his comment to pls. 1 i and 4 i.

[12] For example, Parkes, *Book Hands*, pl. 1 i, l. 1 ('nullas').

[13] This ductus is easily visible in Brown, *Guide*, pl. 36 (beginning of the fourteenth century).

[14] An example: Thomson, *Bookhands*, pl. 95, l. 10 (1291: 'passionem').

[15] Brown, *Guide*, pl. 35 (*c.* 1300); Kirchner, *Scriptura Gothica*, pl. 37b (1310–15); Parkes, *Book Hands*, pl. 7 i (mid-fourteenth century).

[16] Parkes, *Book Hands*, pl. 1 ii (*c.* 1340–50: **p**).

by no means distinctive of Anglicana (1). Its top comes close to the headline only in the fifteenth century. The upper lobe is closed, except in some of the earliest examples, where it is open in the same manner as in early Textualis.[17] Its curve is generally bold in fourteenth- and fifteenth-century manuscripts, betraying the use of a rather wide-nibbed pen at that time.[18] Single-compartment **a** may occur in addition to the normal form, even at an early date (pls. 77, 85), but remained rare until the fifteenth century, when under Cursiva influence it was frequently used interchangeably with the two-compartment form.

Anglicana **d** almost always has the normal, counter-clockwise loop and is generally distinguished (as mentioned above) by its more or less bold, curved and shortened diagonal final section, which turns it into an essentially unconnected letter (8). It can be almost circular in shape. With the introduction of greater angularity in the fifteenth century (under the influence of Cursiva according to Parkes[19]), **d** often has a pointed curve at left at the baseline as it does in that script (pl. 86).

Loopless **d** (15, pl. 85) appears exceptionally in addition to looped ones in manuscripts from the end of the fourteenth century onwards. This form is the only one used in some fifteenth-century codices as part of a practice of incorporating elements from Textualis.[20]

e has two forms: the normal two-stroke form (16) and a distinctive circular form made in one stroke and obtained using the same ductus but not lifting the pen from the writing surface (17). It is notable that the latter form (which is not unknown on the Continent) does not occur before the middle of the fourteenth century and was generally used together with the normal form (pl. 85). Although typical of Anglicana till the end of the Middle Ages, it was not adopted by every scribe: many hands do not display it, perhaps because it could lead to confusion with **d**, unless the latter letter had a conspicuous height. The simpler **e** consisting of two parallel curves and typical of continental Cursiva (18) was not particularly favoured by English scribes.

The Anglicana **g**, like that of continental Cursiva Antiquior, has the form of figure 8 and extends very little below the baseline, or even stands on it (4).

m and **n** may be traced in one stroke (in which case the minims generally slope to the left) (19),[21] or they may be 'constructed' and made in several strokes (20).

15 16 17

18 19 20

[17] A late example is *CMDGBOx*, pl. 160 (*c.* 1320).
[18] One has the impression that the same form is typical of English Textualis of the same period.
[19] Parkes, *Book Hands*, p. xxii.
[20] Thomson, *Bookhands*, pl. 103 (1396?); Kirchner, *Scriptura Gothica*, pls. 48 (1406; the script is not Anglicana properly speaking), 34b (1446, same remark); *CMDGBCam*, pl. 256 (1450); also in the 'Bastard Anglicana', Parkes, *Book Hands*, pls. 8 i and ii.
[21] See Parkes, *Book Hands*, pls. 1–3.

For Parkes this was one of the criteria used to distinguish two types: Anglicana and Anglicana Formata. This objective criterion is relatively easy to employ and would be perfectly acceptable, if it did not conflict with Lieftinck's concept of Formata, which assumes careful execution of the script. Whereas several of Parkes's Anglicana Formata hands perfectly qualify for this name, others look too rapid to fit the Lieftinckian category of Littera Formata.[22]

With its tail descending beneath the baseline, **r** is without doubt the most distinctive letter in Anglicana. It can be linked to the preceding and to the subsequent letter. In the early period, up to the middle of the fourteenth century, it could be made in two strokes, resembling a Textualis **r** (21, pl. 77). But more normal is the sharp v-shaped **r**, which at first was formed with a shoulder at the right making a link with the subsequent letter at the headline (22);[23] in the course of the fourteenth century that shoulder became diminished and finally disappeared; the link with the subsequent letter was then made at the baseline (23, pls. 80, 85–6). This is the common form in manuscripts of the fifteenth century.

In the fourteenth and early fifteenth centuries scribes sometimes used the short form of **r** (pls. 81, 84).[24]

From the beginning round **r** was usually written after **o** and other letters ending in a bow. It is noticeable that this letter often has a prominent hairline extending below the line, which is sometimes extremely long (24, pl. 84). The frequent writing of majuscule **R** in the initial position is a feature common to almost all Gothic cursive scripts (pl. 86).

Anglicana is most idiosyncratic in its use of the two forms of **s**. Straight **s**, originally found in all positions, including at the end of words, was soon replaced, as in Textualis, by round **s** in the final position. As has been mentioned already, it sometimes retained a curved descender typical of documentary script and a remnant of the original one-stroke looped **s** (25–6).[25]

In Anglicana the upper lobe of round **s** is left open, thus acquiring the form of figure 6 (27). It was traced in a simple one-stroke clockwise ductus, and may often be observed in the lower levels of execution.[26] More typical and sophisticated is the form giving **s** the same style as **d** and **e** which was obtained through a different

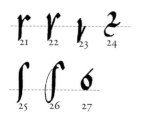

[22] According to this definition all our plates would show Anglicana Formata, which seems unacceptable regarding pl. 77. Similarly, Parkes's pl. 5 i can hardly be called Anglicana Formata.

[23] For example, *CMDGBOx*, pl. 123 (*c.* 1272); Brown, *Guide*, pls. 35 (*c.* 1300), 36 (beginning of fourteenth century).

[24] This happened under the influence of university book hands (i.e. less elaborate forms of Textualis) according to Parkes, *Book Hands*, p. xvii.

[25] For example, Parkes, *Book Hands*, pls. 4 ii (*c.* 1315–52), 8 i (second half of fifteenth century).

[26] An example: Parkes, *Book Hands*, pl. 1 ii (*c.* 1340–50).

ductus (28, pl. 85).[27] This form, also found in certain documentary scripts, is in fact not far removed from the looped straight **s** (26), especially if the round letter was made taller than the other short letters.[28] This could explain a most noteworthy feature of Anglicana: the use of round **s** at the beginning of words. With the exception of a few German hands, this feature occurs only in Anglicana and gives this script a unique place among late medieval book scripts. Although round **s** in initial position may alternate with straight **s**, and tended to disappear in the course of the fifteenth century under Cursiva influence, the feature remains a remarkable characteristic of Anglicana. Straight **s** was always used in the middle of words.

Untypical of Anglicana are the 8-shaped Textualis **s**, observed in many manuscripts of the fourteenth and fifteenth centuries and close in form to Anglicana **g** (29, pls. 80, 85, 86), and the B-shaped Cursiva form of the same letter, seen in some fifteenth-century books (30, pls. 84–6). Both appear only in final position.

For a quite long period, and well into the fourteenth century, **t** was made in the old-fashioned way, in which the stem did not cross or barely crossed the headstroke, thus bringing **t** close in appearance to **c** (31).

Initial **u** sometimes took the round form, but as a rule was written as **v**, and in such a way that the letter might begin with a long approach stroke (32).[29] **v** with its first element curved inward (33, pl. 80), no doubt under the influence of French examples, was used far less frequently, especially in the period before the last decades of the fourteenth century.

w, a letter frequently used in copies of Middle English texts, has many and often complicated forms, depending on the ductus involved. There are basically two types, each with several variants. In the first, used throughout the whole period under consideration, the two interlocking **v**s were traced in several strokes and can easily be recognized. Normally the second **v** has a 3-shaped final stroke (34, pl. 84), a feature we have also observed in English Textualis. In the fifteenth century this form was sometimes replaced by a simpler one under continental influence (35).[30]

The second type is circular and made in a single stroke, in the manner of **d** and **e**, which renders the letter almost unrecognizable and resulted in various idiosyncratic

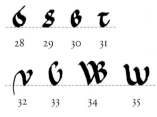

28   29   30   31

32   33   34   35

[27] Another example: Parkes, *Book Hands*, pl. 4 ii (*c.* 1315–52).
[28] See Hector, *Handwriting*, pl. 8 (1317); Kirchner, *Scriptura Gothica*, pl. 38 (1314–25).
[29] Most conspicuous in Parkes, *Book Hands*, pl. 3 i (mid-fifteenth century). v used in the middle of the word is not exceptional in vernacular texts: see Wright, *Vernacular Hands*, pl. 19 (1445).
[30] Kirchner, *Scriptura Gothica*, pl. 55 (1433).

forms (36). It is typical of manuscripts of the fourteenth century, but is also found in later books.[31]

Apart from a few exceptions, found in some fifteenth-century manuscripts, **x** was always made in two strokes and in a distinctive manner (37, pls. 81, 85, 86). The letter **y** was, as a rule, dotted, not in order to distinguish it from Anglo-Saxon thorn (which may have the same form but is undotted, see below, p. 189), but according to general medieval practice.

SUBTYPES

Parkes's Anglicana Formata has already been mentioned. According to him the earliest datable example of this type was produced in 1291.[32] A manuscript datable *c*. 1264 seems, however, already to display the criteria required for that category.[33]

More important is the category 'Bastard Anglicana', which Parkes defines as follows: 'This Bastard hand is larger than those of Anglicana Formata, better spaced, and with greater emphasis placed upon its calligraphic execution. It is composed of elements and features proper to two scripts', namely Anglicana and Textualis. Textualis elements in this script may be box-**a**, loopless **d**, fusions, angularity, spikiness, etc. Bastard Anglicana appears in the middle of the fourteenth century. The constituent elements were not well integrated in its early phase, and it is only later in the century that 'the details of both scripts have been fully assimilated' (Parkes). Through its use for luxury manuscripts, it became a serious competitor to and often supplanted Textualis (except for the most formal books) at the end of the fourteenth and in the fifteenth century.[34]

Whether Bastard Anglicana is a script type in its own right depends on personal opinion. The introduction of Textualis elements in cursive scripts when these were adapted for calligraphic use is a universal phenomenon in the later fourteenth and fifteenth centuries. As long as the new mixture did not result in a script written in a heavily uniform manner and with characteristics which may be objectively defined, one might hesitate to give it a special name.

A distinct minor variant of Anglicana is marked by the absence of loops on ascenders and was used sporadically in the fourteenth and fifteenth centuries. By analogy with Lieftinck's Hybrida we could perhaps call it Hybrida Anglicana.

36   37

[31] For example, *CMDGBOx*, pl. 123 (*c.* 1272); Parkes, *Book Hands*, pls. 1 ii (*c.* 1340–50), 6 ii (1475).
[32] Parkes, *Book Hands*, p. xvi (his pl. 4 i).
[33] *CMDGBOx*, pl. 116.
[34] Parkes, *Book Hands*, p. xviii. He gives examples of Bastard Anglicana in pls. 7–8.

Parkes calls a late example reproduced by him 'fere-textura'.[35] In it, as may often be observed, loopless ascenders alternate with looped ones, so that it comes close to Semihybrida.[36] This specific type of script was sometimes also used to distinguish the first verse of each strophe of poetry, written in Anglicana.[37]

[35] Parkes, *Book Hands*, pl. 8 ii (*c.* 1500).
[36] A few more examples: *CMDGBOx*, pls. 159 (*c.* 1318), 188 (*c.* 1345–6); Wright, *Vernacular Hands*, pls. 12 (1340), 14 (end of fourteenth century), 19 (1445).
[37] Wright, *Vernacular Hands*, pl. 18 (1433). This use is evidently related to the writing of elongated ascenders on the top line of the page.

8

Cursiva
(plates 87–117)

Cursiva (the name henceforward to be used in place of Cursiva Recentior) was by far the most widely used type of script in the fourteenth and fifteenth centuries.[1] It is found in thousands of manuscripts all over Europe, from the most informal ones (these are the majority) to the various calligraphic versions which developed in different countries, and to the large group of codices in Cursiva Libraria.

Its distinctive letter forms are:

(a) single-compartment **a** (1);
(b) **b**, **h**, **k**, **l** with ascenders with loops at the right-hand side (2);
(c) **f** and straight **s** extending below the baseline (3).

In spite of the apparently confusing variety of scripts conforming to these criteria defined by Lieftinck, it is difficult to subdivide the group into geographical entities or chronological sections. Even the Mediterranean Cursiva is not as easy to distinguish from its Northern counterparts as Rotunda was from Northern Textualis. In contrast with the more geographically restricted use of Cursiva Antiquior, it was essentially a universal European script. Differences are much more pronounced between the levels of execution than between the practices of scribes from different countries or periods.

The letter forms are those of Textualis, transformed through the use of a cursive ductus, but taking various different aspects when the cursive ductus was partly or even entirely given up by scribes adapting the script for use in books. The impact made by the individual scribe upon the appearance of the script is usually strong. It is evident, for example, in the choice of forms to be used for those letters, which, in the creation of the cursive script, developed double or even multiple forms.

The less obvious features of Cursiva, which are on the whole difficult to define in an objective way, have till now not been well studied; the following observations can only be tentative. It should be stressed that although the examination of the ductus is essential for understanding the origin of letter forms in Cursiva, the way

1   2   3

---

[1] The literature on Cursiva as a book script as conceived here is scant. See above, p. 125, n. 6, to which should be added Federici, *Scrittura*, and Poulle, *Paléographie*; Gumbert, *Kartäuser*, pp. 242–63.

the letters are actually traced in the individual Cursiva book hands cannot be fully discussed here.

The loops at the ascenders take various forms. In addition to the rapid rounded form, scribes appear to have favoured a triangular shaping, as it accorded with the general preference for angularity (4, pls. 101, 107). Over the passage of time, they tended to make the loops smaller or open instead of closed. The latter tendency no doubt has its origin in the closing of the loop with a hairline.

Quadrangles were sometimes applied at the base of the ascenders and the minims or angularity was introduced into the curves (5, 6, pls. 104, 116). Quadrangles are even sometimes found at the headline (pl. 111). It is interesting to note that angularity (a feature in itself contrary to the nature of cursive script) was frequently applied only to the first letter of the word, which emphasized the importance of the word as a unit.

In books produced outside Italy during the fifteenth century, one sometimes may even observe a spur at the left of the ascenders, which may be the accidental consequence of the loop or the lobe (in the case of **b**, for example) simply crossing the ascender, but which may also have been applied intentionally in order to raise the level of execution of the script (7, pls. 116–17). Similar spiky extensions may sometimes be observed at **f** and straight **s** (8, pl. 98).

The pointed descenders of **f**, **p**, **q** and straight **s** are another almost constant feature in Cursiva (9), which, however, sometimes disappeared in rapid execution, where the script often is linear and unshaded. These pointed forms were sometimes abandoned during the fifteenth century under Textualis or Hybrida influence (pls. 107, 115).

It would be difficult to indicate further general features. Cursiva as a book script is in essence a stylized cursive script. This process of stylizing went in two contrasting directions: one already mentioned consisted in bringing the script closer to Textualis by introducing Textualis letter forms into a cursive context. The other involved an emphasis upon and application of a calligraphic technique to specific cursive letter forms. We see examples of both in books of the fifteenth century, and they contribute greatly to the confusing variety of the hands here studied as variants of a single script.

INDIVIDUAL LETTER FORMS

The single-stroke **a** lies at the root of this letter's development (1). Other than in the Mediterranean area[2] and in the most rapid levels of execution, the second side of the letter generally shifted slightly to the right as it approached the headline, following the writing direction, a feature that will be seen in other Cursiva letters too (10). This produced the typical shape of Cursiva **a**, traced in one or two strokes and presenting a slightly concave, spiky form at the top (11). Many other hands, on the contrary, gave **a** a somewhat triangular form with a pointed top (12). A two-stroke ductus is often clearly visible in such cases (13).

The original rapid tracing of **c** in two strokes gave this letter an angular form at the headline, which makes it resemble **e** as well as **t** (14). This is especially so when the first stroke was lengthened beyond the headline, as happened frequently in rapid execution (pls. 99, 106, 110, 113). The headstroke is horizontal, which allowed the letter to be linked to the next one.

Cursiva **d** is by definition looped. In its original rapid form, traced in one stroke, it has the normal, counter-clockwise loop (15), which allows connection with the subsequent letter. If connected to the preceding letter, **d** takes a slightly different, open shape, which is, however, rather rare in books (a similar observation can be made about **e**) (16, pl. 106).[3]

In Germany and especially Austria, but also in Central Europe and Scandinavia, this 'normal' form of **d** was usually narrow and upright, with a straight or even concave back (17, pls. 95, 101, 103). This form is not far removed from the typical Italian cursiva **d**, which often gives the curious impression of having a clockwise loop (18, pls. 89, 92, 94).[4] (In many cases, however, the distinction between **d** with normal loop and **d** with apparently inversed loop is not clear.[5]) This and the variants of **d** discussed next did not lend themselves to forming links with the subsequent letter.

This 'inversed' loop, like the loops on ascenders, tends to be closed with a hairline (pls. 95, 112). This may have been why some scribes left the loop open, resulting in a curious form of **d** which no doubt required a complicated three-stroke

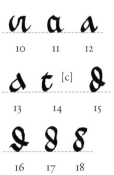

10   11   12

13   14   15

16   17   18

[2] *CMDF*, II, pl. 73, MS lat. 6069 H (1397) is perhaps an exception.
[3] **d** ligatured with preceding letter: *CMDF*, V, pl. 105, Troyes, MS 681 (France 1445); *CMDNL*, I, pl. 178 (Southern Low Countries 1458).
[4] See also Federici, *Scrittura*, pl. 58 (1334–6); *CMDF*, I, pl. 43 (1339–49).
[5] One scribe may write the two forms. See, for example, Thomson, *Bookhands*, pl. 22 (Southern Low Countries 1404).

ductus (19, pls. 112, 117).[6] This indicates how laborious the writing of Cursiva could become when the letters were 'constructed'.

Much more frequent than this stylish form is the loopless **d**, which in the course of the fifteenth century in most countries replaced the looped one (20), a highly remarkable departure from the earlier practice (pls. 96, 104, 109, 111, 113–14, 116–17). It was both relatively simple to trace (being made in two strokes) and conformed with the more fashionable book script of the time: Hybrida.

The normal looped **d** – by far the most common form – is generally rounded. Nevertheless, in initial position in particular, it often has a larger size and an angle at the baseline, which bring it close in appearance to majuscule **D** (21, pls. 90, 93, 100, 108). This feature became so fashionable, that during the fifteenth century there was sometimes a tendency to use the 'majuscule' looped **d** consistently at the beginning of words, while loopless **d** was written in all other positions.[7]

As with other letters in Cursiva, the diagonal hairline in 'majuscule' **d** was sometimes dropped. In so doing, some scribes of luxury manuscripts of the fifteenth century re-created in stylized form the original 'open' **d** mentioned above (16).[8]

The typical form of Cursiva **e** is the one in two curved strokes traced in the same direction, which can cause confusion with **c** (22, 23). It could be connected with the subsequent letter (pls. 97, 106) and, like **d**, also with the preceding one by changing its first stroke (24, pls. 97–8), but the latter connection was mostly avoided.

Although the scribes of some highly luxurious manuscripts of the later fifteenth century in France, the Southern Low Countries and (under the latter's influence) Germany maintained this original form in their sophisticated scripts, most scribes who wrote Cursiva actually preferred the Textualis shape of **e**, likewise traced in two strokes but much more familiar to the reader not well acquainted with documentary scripts (25). The two forms may occur on the same page, according to whether they are or are not connected to the subsequent letter.[9]

As always in Gothic script **f** and straight **s** need to be studied together. These letters generally came to have a remarkably fat and pointed form, which has its origin in the cursive ductus, consisting of a downward and upward movement of the pen. In many specimens of more rapid handwriting this ductus is still visible (26, pl. 97), but in general the space between the two lines was filled up

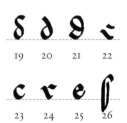

19   20   21   22

23   24   25   26

[6] An early example is *CMDF*, ii, pl. 85, ms lat. 1063 (France 1417).

[7] See n. 6. Other examples: *CMDF*, ii, pl. 156 (France 1476); Parkes, *Book Hands*, pl. 12 ii (England *c.* 1470).

[8] *CMDNL*, i, pl. 277 (Southern Low Countries after 1473).

[9] *CMDF*, i, pl. 68 (France 1394); Kirchner, *Scriptura Gothica*, pl. 49 (France 1406).

with ink. In the Libraria and Formata levels of execution the bodies of these highly characteristic letters could be stylized in various ways (27, 28). In many cases a two-stroke ductus for **s** (three strokes for **f**) is visible in the specific form adopted by these letters; here the upstroke does not start at the bottom, but close to the top of the letter (29, pl. 98). **f** may have a loop at its top, betraying a simplified ductus (30, pl. 102). Both letters are generally sloping, sometimes very much so, and this is all the more conspicuous as the other letters are often made upright (pls. 96–7, 100). This feature is typical of French and Southern Netherlandish Cursiva, whilst in books from the other parts of Europe it is far less obvious. In manuscripts from Italy and the Iberian Peninsula the position of these letters is strictly vertical or even backward sloping (pls. 89, 92, 94, 99).

Double **ff**, used at the beginning of words, should be considered a majuscule. It conforms to the widespread practice in cursive scripts to multiply such forms in the initial position. It is rare in book script except in England[10] and Spain (pls. 93, 99).

The specific form of Cursiva **g** is based on an original one-stroke ductus, in which the tail of the letter curves to the left and is continued up to the headline and turns to the right closing the u-shaped body and forming the headstroke (pl. 108).[11] This ductus accounts for the 'horns' at the headline, a persistent stylistic feature of Northern Cursiva, even when the original ductus had been replaced by a more complicated one (31, 32, pls. 103, 109, 111). The second horn is generally longer than the first one (pl. 104), and the first one often disappears entirely, leaving **g** one-horned (33, pls. 98–9, 101, 114). The latter form, and still more, **g** without horns at all is quite understandably typical of Italian manuscripts, given the general aversion of Italian scribes to spiky forms.

While the original looped form is seen in some rapid hands, most **g**s in Cursiva appear to have been made in two, three or four strokes. Three main variants may be distinguished on the basis of the form of the tail, although there are many intermediate forms. In addition to the common form with a curving tail to the left (32, 33) or, a more sophisticated variant, an undulating tail (34, pl. 114), there is the typically French **g** with its tail curving to the right, thus abandoning the notion of

10 According to Denholm-Young, *Handwriting*, p. 33, this feature occurs in documentary script from the second quarter of the thirteenth century onwards. More examples: Wright, *Vernacular Hands*, pl. 24 (England, before 1469); in Germany: *CMDF*, v, pl. 76 middle picture (1403); in France: Thomson, *Bookhands*, pl. 21 (1391).
11 Other examples: Thomson, *Bookhands*, pls. 26 (France 1452), 55 (Germany 1478).

the original single-stroke ductus (35).[12] Italian scribes had a preference for a looped tail, from which any reminder of the single-stroke ductus is equally absent (36, pl. 89). Other forms, such as **g** with a looped tail entirely traced in hairline (37, pl. 97), are rare, but point to a stylistic feature proper to many later French and Burgundian Cursivae of the highest level, namely the reduction in prominence of all descenders and strokes below the baseline.[13]

Cursiva **h** can be traced in one or in several strokes and accordingly can take one of two basic forms (38, 39). In the single-stroke ductus (pls. 97–8, 100, 105) we sometimes may observe at the baseline the same shift towards the right between the downward and the upward pen movement as already mentioned when dealing with the letter **a** (40).[14] Here it produces increased angularity at the bottom of the shaft. As in Textualis the limb of **h** generally descends below the baseline and sometimes ends in a curved hairline in the documentary tradition, especially in the Mediterranean area (pls. 94, 99). In some fifteenth-century books, however, one may observe a tendency for both shaft and limb to stop at the baseline, probably under Humanistic influence (pls. 109, 114).

The letter **i** was normally treated as a minim and may be difficult to distinguish from the minims composing **m** and **n**, unless a diacritical stroke or dot has been placed above it. Dotted **i**s appear exceptionally in books from other countries (pl. 98),[15] but they are a feature typical of Germany and Central Europe (this should be compared with what has been said above about this feature in the discussion of Textualis). In many Cursiva hands **i** has no diacritical sign and may (though should not) be lengthened to aid legibility. **i** longa or **j** is thus found after short **i**, as in Textualis, and in a minority of manuscripts in initial and in final position, preferably before (or after) a letter consisting of minims: **m, n, u**. **i** longa is, however, often found in initial position in French Cursiva and in its derivative, Bastarda (pls. 97, 98, 104). The use of **i** longa at the end and especially in the middle of words points with great probability to Southern France or Spain (pl. 99).[16]

35 36 37

38 39 40

[12] Our plate 97 shows, however, that this shape of **g** is the remnant of an original single-stroke ductus, in which the tail makes a counter-clockwise loop. Other examples of this form of **g**: *CMDF*, I, pls. 64 (France 1390), 64 (France before 1392); *CMDNL*, I, pl. 266 (France 1403).

[13] Other examples: *CMDF*, I, pl. 109 (1451–82); *CMDNL*, I, pl. 252 (1428); Brown, *Guide*, pl. 41 (middle of fifteenth century).

[14] See, for example, *CMDF*, II, pls. 63 (France 1380), 63 (Southern France 1381); Thomson, *Bookhands*, pl. 24 (Southern France 1429); Kirchner, *Scriptura Gothica*, pl. 66 (Germany 1478).

[15] Also *CMDF*, II, pl. 174, MS lat. 6202 (Lyons? 1503–5).

[16] Other examples: Thomson, *Bookhands*, pls. 24 (Toulouse 1429), 127 (Perpignan 1408); Kirchner, *Scriptura Gothica*, pl. 44 (Barcelona 1392).

The modern use of Capital **I** for the pronoun of the first-person singular in English texts goes back to the end of the fourteenth century. It is a standard feature in English cursive of the fifteenth century.[17]

The letter **k**, frequently used in the writing of Germanic languages, consists of an **l** to the shaft of which a figure 2-like stroke has been added (41, pls. 91, 103, 105, 115).

Like most Cursiva letters **m** and **n** may have a simple or a more complicated ductus (the difference is not always clearly visible). The original cursive form has single-stroke ductus (42). The use of two or three strokes can produce various forms closer to Textualis (43). That way a 'Textus Rotundus' form of **m** and **n** can be produced (a form seldom seen) (44),[18] and even a 'Textus Quadratus' form was sometimes introduced in Cursiva Formata (pls. 111, 116). The final minim of both letters usually received a different treatment: it may be curved or hooked (45). Typical of Northern Cursiva in general, and the Formata level in particular, is a form in which the final minim is given an angular and concave shape at the headline, a stylistic feature also seen in the letter **a** (46, pl. 111).[19]

As in Textualis, **m** in final position was sometimes replaced by a sign in the shape of figure 3 (47, pls. 94–6, 98, 100, 116), but this feature is very rare in manuscripts outside Germany, Central Europe and Italy.

Two different single-stroke ductuses, both starting at the headline, lie behind the development of Cursiva **p**. One is similar to the ductus of **f** and straight **s** and is formed in a clockwise loop, ending at the baseline (48, pl. 94).[20] The other comprises a counter-clockwise loop and ends in the tail (49, pls. 97, 100, 106, 110–11).[21] Outside Italy, in particular, the latter form of **p** was generally given a more sophisticated, somewhat spiky shape (50). The fat, pointed shape of the descender, resembling the tail of **f** and straight **s**, which is seen in so many manuscripts, can in principle only be obtained using the first type of ductus. The hairline treatment of the descender as observed in luxurious codices of the fifteenth century, on the other hand, is obviously a calligraphic elaboration of the second type (pls. 111, 114).

41 42 43 44

45 46 47

48 49 50

[17] See Wright, *Vernacular Hands*, pls. 15–17, 20–4. Scribes of earlier English manuscripts used minuscule **i**: Wright, pls. 5 and 14.
[18] Kirchner, *Scriptura Gothica*, pl. 46 (Germany 1396).
[19] A few examples from the Southern Low Countries: *CMDNL*, I, pls. 277 (after 1473), 278 (after 1505), 283 (end of fifteenth century; the manuscript is undated).
[20] For better examples of this single-stroke ductus, see *CMDB*, I, pl. 153 (Low Countries? 1358); *CMDF*, II, pl. 57 (Italy 1370).
[21] A single-stroke ductus is obvious only in pls. 97, 106 and 110.

As has already been said regarding **g** with a hairline tail, this form, together with **q** with hairline descender and the shortening of the tails of **f** and straight **s**, points to a tendency observable in later, especially French and Southern Netherlandish, Cursiva for the appearance of all descenders to be diminished.

The two variants of **p** are generally difficult to distinguish in carefully executed handwriting, especially when the original ductus was changed. In many cases, however, it is obvious that a decidedly different, third type of ductus involving two or three strokes lies behind Cursiva **p**, in which one stroke forms the descender, the other one or two the lobe, which in rapid execution is often left open at the headline (51, 52, pl. 109).[22] As far as can be ascertained, there seems to have been some preference for this ductus in Germany, Central Europe, Scandinavia and Italy.

p has generally (but not always) the same inclination as **f** and straight **s**, in other words vertical in Italy, more sloping in the other European countries, especially in France.

The same observations apply to **q**, which generally has a pointed, straight or slightly curved descender. Like **a, m, n** it has often a somewhat angular form at the headline, except in Italy (53).

r is altogether the letter with the greatest variability in Cursiva. The most common form (which was also often the only form to be used) is the single-stroke, v-shaped **r**, which allows links to be made with the preceding as well as the subsequent letters (54). This is basically the same form as used in Cursiva Antiquior (especially in Anglicana), but there as a rule it extends below the baseline. In addition to this, a more traditional form frequently is found which, at least originally, was made in one counter-clockwise stroke, permitting linkage only with the preceding letter (55). It was given a spiky shape at the baseline in Northern Cursiva Formata, in conformity with the general trend towards angularity (56). It is in fact a variant of Textualis (two-stroke) **r** (likewise used in Cursiva) (57), from which it is sometimes not easily distinguished, especially where the two strokes of the Textualis form are linked by a hairline (58). A hairline connecting the foot of the minim with the left of the headstroke can, on the contrary, give Textualis **r** an appearance close to the v-shaped variant (59). In general, however, Textualis **r** when used in Cursiva has a remarkably backwards-sloping and rounded shape. The 'round' **r** shaped as figure 2, also known from Textualis (60), may be used after **o**

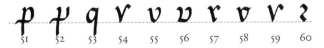

22 A more obvious example of **p** with open lobe: Brown, *Guide*, pl. 39 (Germany 1390).

and other letters ending in a bow, just as in Textualis, or in all positions. There is only one form whose use was limited to the beginning of words: majuscule **R**. There was a marked predilection for using **R** in this position, except among scribes from Germany and Italy (61, pls. 90, 97, 104, 112–13).

Whereas many codices contain three, four (pl. 112) or even five forms of **r**,[23] many others display just one (pl. 102) or two. The greatest variety in individual manuscripts appears to be characteristic of France, the smallest is found in books from Germany, where there was a predilection for Textualis **r** only or Textualis and round **r**.

Like other letters, Textualis **r** may be given an applied foot at the baseline (62). A curious form, similar to this, which looks Textualis but is probably in fact a stylized version of v-shaped **r**, comes to the fore in fifteenth-century manuscripts, first in Italy, later especially in Germany, and would be typical of the early modern development of Gothic script. It has a serif at the baseline, which is doubtless based on an original one-stroke ductus (63); it would lead to an x-shaped **r** (pls. 94, 103, 112).[24]

r, v-shaped or Textualis, is sometimes decorated with a vertical hairline or flourish, as in Textualis (64, 65, pls. 108, 115). French, English and Mediterranean examples of this feature are extremely rare. The hairline extension of round **r** below the baseline, which is frequent in Textualis, even at the lower levels (and also in Anglicana), does not occur in Cursiva, except for a few examples from France[25] and – quite understandably – from England (66).

As there does not seem to be any general rule for the use of the various forms of **r** in Cursiva (with the exception of the majuscule), it is not surprising to find two successive **r**s written in almost all possible combinations, according to the scribe's whim.

The letter **s** in Cursiva, in contrast, conforms entirely to late medieval practice. Thus straight **s**, discussed above together with **f**, was used consistently in initial position and in the middle of words, and round **s** in final position. The latter form was also used in abbreviated words involving an initial **s** alone, as in 'supra', 'sibi', etc. Straight **s** in final position does not occur, or at least is definitely exceptional.

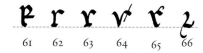

61   62   63   64   65   66

[23] Thomson, *Bookhands*, pl. 22 (Southern Low Countries 1404).
[24] See also *CMDGBLo*, pl. 836 (Austria 1484).
[25] *CMDGBOx*, pl. 194 (Southern France *c.* 1350).

Cursiva round **s** was originally traced in one clockwise stroke (and remained so in rapid handwriting). If the upper lobe is closed the letter resembles capital B; if it is left open, it looks like figure 6. Hence the two basic forms of Cursiva round **s** (67, 68). When both were employed by a single scribe, there was a tendency to use the open form at the end of the line, where more space is available, the closed one in other positions (pl. 100). The somewhat complicated form of the more common closed **s** explains why this letter in small hands extends above the headline (pl. 108). In Cursiva Libraria and Formata, closed round **s** appears mostly to have been traced in two strokes: a curved or straight vertical first stroke and a 3-shaped second stroke (69). In Northern Cursiva this second stroke was made in an increasingly angular and even spiky manner (70, pls. 104, 109–10, 112, 114, 116).

The trailing **s**, as seen especially in Rotunda and Semitextualis, plays a markedly minor role in Cursiva compared with round **s** (71, pls. 96, 112).[26] It is not surprising that Textualis round **s** (72), with its complicated ductus (although the letter could also be traced in a more simple way), was extremely rarely used in Cursiva (pl. 111).[27] Yet more forms of final round **s**, based on originally different ductuses, can be found very occasionally (73, pl. 111).

Cursiva **t**, made in two strokes, was originally a short letter, but from the end of the fourteenth century it began to project conspicuously above the headline, so that in manuscripts from the end of the fifteenth century and those of the sixteenth, its headstroke often is at the middle of its shaft. In Cursiva Formata the top of the shaft is pointed or traced in hairline. The shaft itself can be either rounded or entirely straight (74, 75, pls. 106, 108, 110, 117).

Final **t**, like **r**, was sometimes decorated with a vertical hairline appended from its headstroke (76). This feature did not occur in Italy, was very rare in France, somewhat more frequent in the Southern Low Countries (pl. 104) and especially in Germany.[28]

The two forms, round **u** and angular **v**, encountered in many Textuales, derive from a basic distinction made by scribes when writing in Cursiva. Here too either form could be used both for the vowel and for the consonant. **u** was written in all positions, but **v**, which is in fact a cursive **u** with an approach stroke or a loop, was, as a rule, only used in initial position. Nevertheless, in vernacular manuscripts in

67   68   69   70   71   72   73   74   75   76

[26] It is consistently used in Kirchner, *Scriptura Gothica*, pl. 43 (Germany 1385); Thomson, *Bookhands*, pl. 76 (Italy 1395).
[27] See also the manuscript mentioned in n. 25.
[28] Crous and Kirchner, *Schriftarten*, fig. 32 (c. 1430); Steffens, *Paläographie*, pl. 113 (1455).

particular, this rule was sometimes infringed and we may find **v** in the middle of the word (pl. 101).[29]

The looped form of **v** can lead to confusion with **b**, unless it is made sloping to the left or stylized in some other way (77, 78). This was the only form used in France up to the beginning of the fifteenth century. From then onwards, and especially from the middle of the century, the open form (79) came into vogue, either as the only form to be used or as a variant. In Cursiva Formata of the second half of the century in particular, one finds an intermediate form (80, pl. 117). Scribes from Germany, Central Europe and Scandinavia appear, from the beginning, to have had a marked preference for the open form as first letter of the word, often in alternation with **u**. The **u**-form is also found in books from Southern France and Italy, alternating with one or other form of **v**. The looped form naturally extends above the headline, the open **v** may or may not do so. The tall, open **v** is characteristic not only of rapid scripts but also, it would seem, of Cursiva from France, the Southern Low Countries, and, to a lesser extent, Spain and Italy. The two forms are seen in England. Short open **v**, which extends between the baseline and the headline and is closer in appearance to **u**, was more common elsewhere (81).

The two forms of **v** cannot have been far apart in the eyes of contemporaries to judge from the number of scribes who used both forms interchangeably (pls. 100, 107).

Since so many vernacular texts were copied in Cursiva, the letter **w** has an importance it lacks in Textualis. In English, German, Dutch and the Scandinavian written languages it is found frequently; in the countries where these languages were spoken it was also used in Latin texts, either for proper names or as a variant for **vu** or even **u** (see the Appendix, p. 189). Since it is a ligature of two **v**s, two basic variants can be found, depending on the form of its components – looped **v**s (82, pls. 93, 115) or 'open' **v**s (83, pls. 91, 105, 113). The combination of both forms in a single letter is very exceptional.

Most Cursivae contain an **x** which is, in essence, made in one stroke and often extends in a curve below the baseline (84). This is, however, apparently not the original form, as all early examples of Cursiva display a two-stroke Textualis **x** (as

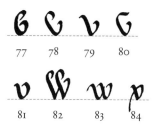

77   78   79   80

81   82   83   84

[29] Our pl. 101 is a Latin manuscript. An example in the vernacular: *CMDNL*, I, pl. 182 (Southern Low Countries 1470).

also did Cursiva Antiquior) (85, pls. 88–9). In the last decades of the fourteenth century this type was generally replaced with the single-stroke form. The original form survived in a small proportion of books produced in England, the Northern Low Countries and Germany, and in Italy (pls. 94, 100, 102). In the fifteenth century, and especially in its second half, the two-stroke **x**, now mostly rounded and in a different ductus (86), had a remarkable revival, especially in Cursiva Formata, doubtless under Textualis influence (pls. 116–17).

Cursiva **y** is almost always undotted. Its peculiar shape is explained by its originally single-stroke ductus (87, pl. 105). Even dotted **y** could be made in a single stroke (pl. 106). **z** took the shape of figure 3 and extended generally below the baseline (88).

<h3 style="text-align:center">LIGATURES AND ABBREVIATIONS</h3>

As a rapid script for practical use, Cursiva was originally marked by an almost limitless number of ligatures and abbreviations, which can make it extremely difficult to read, especially in copies of texts of an academic nature such as those on theology, philosophy, law or medicine. These ligatures and abbreviations are too numerous and too diverse to be discussed here. But, as has already been said, most book scripts moved away from this originally cursive character and the number of ligatures was strictly limited. Many scribes even formed the letters without any connecting link at all. As in Textualis, the only important ligature that remained obligatory was **st**, or perhaps other ligatures beginning with **s**. The straight **s** and high **t** were linked by a concave or even looped stroke at the top to form a highly conspicuous **st**-ligature (89, pls. 104, 110–11, 114). Unlike Textualis, the same linking stroke was employed in Cursiva also for **so** (90), **sa**, **si**, **sp**, etc. and even **sc**, thus creating a ligature almost undistinguishable from **st** (pls. 97–8).

Among the other remaining ligatures **ct** and **tt** very often took the same form of a **c** linked with a **t**, making it impossible for the reader to determine which letters were meant by the scribe (91, pl. 96). The same phenomenon has been observed in Textualis and poses special problems for reading and transcribing texts in Romance languages.

Outside the circle of the schools, on the other hand, the number of abbreviations employed in Cursiva lessened rapidly during the fourteenth and fifteenth

$$x \quad x \quad y \quad 3 \quad \text{ſt} \quad \text{ſo} \quad \text{ct}$$
85   86   87   88   89   90   91

centuries. Toward the end of the Middle Ages, manuscripts written almost without abbreviations are not uncommon.[30] The widening circle of readers inexperienced or lacking instruction in the complicated world of the scholastic forms of abbreviation is the main reason; but the conspicuous presence of vernacular texts in books written in Cursiva should also be taken into account, since these languages did not lend themselves to extended use of abbreviations. Furthermore, from a technical viewpoint, the introduction of paper provided a relatively cheap form of writing material, and the need to save space became less important. Scribes may have taken the view that they might as well copy texts in Cursiva in full, rather than in abbreviated form, since many abbreviation strokes required a supplementary pen-lift.

Abbreviation strokes in cursive script are in general long and often curved, in accordance with the tendency towards a horizontal emphasis natural to such scripts. Where possible, and if the scribe so desired, they were made in one stroke as a continuation of the letter (or part of the letter) to which they refer, as in **per** (92). The best-known example of this is the **r**-abbreviation written above the line, which was represented by a curved stroke connected to the letter beneath (93, pl. 100). This form of abbreviation exerted a remarkable influence on the writing of Northern Textualis, since it was adopted by many scribes even when writing the highest grades of that script. In Cursivae of lower levels, the same technique of an abbreviation stroke issuing from the letter beneath was extended to other abbreviations, such as **in**, **an**, **um** (pls. 93, 97, 107, 108, 113).[31] In Cursiva Libraria and Formata, what had originally been the connecting stroke generally lost its function and became stylized as a flourish. In Germany especially the mark was reduced to a semicircular curve above the written line (94, pls. 95, 113). In Italy the **r**-abbreviation was often used to represent **r** alone, not **r** + vowel or vowel + **r**. In this country the abbreviation mark was not connected to the text beneath, but took the shape of a wavy line (pl. 94).

The **orum**- and **arum**-abbreviation also had a characteristic form in Cursiva, comprising a simple or sometimes a more complicated loop, reminiscent of similar forms in Praegothica and early Textualis (95, 96, pls. 92, 100, 110). Many later Cursivae abandoned this feature and instead used the unlooped form well known from Textualis (pls. 102, 107–8).

92   93   94

95   96

[30] An example: *CMDNL*, 1, pl. 271 (Southern Low Countries c. 1454). The same observation can be made about Textualis.
[31] According to Prou, *Manuel*, 2nd edn, p. 132, this technique of abbreviation was rare in thirteenth-century documents, was frequently used in the fourteenth, and became the rule in the fifteenth century.

SUBTYPES

Cursiva took many forms in Germany, often halfway between Cursiva and Hybrida; Formata, however, was exceptional there before the last quarter of the fifteenth century.[32] In Italy, many informal scripts (especially Mercantesca, but not Cancelleresca) are marked by the greasy aspect of the pages: they are written on poor quality paper with the result that the ink spreads and shows through on the back (pls. 92, 118, 133). Few examples of Cursiva book script are encountered in Spanish and Portuguese manuscripts (pl. 99):[33] here Hybrida seems to have been the preferred late medieval book script in addition to Textualis.

Within the diffuse mass of Cursiva scripts used all over Europe, one may discern several special styles developed by scribes in certain countries or regions. Their intention was mostly to create a high-quality book script that was better suited to the vernacular than Textualis and appropriate for use in luxury manuscripts for wealthy patrons. These scripts were therefore relatively late creations and display a high degree of artificiality. We will see the same tendencies at work in Hybrida, the script type derived from Cursiva. The script upon which such special styles were developed was generally a formal chancery script held in high esteem in the particular country in which they originated. The particular features developed by chancery scribes in order to distinguish the documents issued by their chancery from those issued by other agencies accounts for the regional or national character of the subtypes discussed below, as well as their artificial character. As a matter of course they generally belong to the Cursiva Formata class, the only level of Cursiva that would allow subtle stylistic features to be executed. It is curious to note, however, that such scripts in Italy as well as in France and the Southern Low Countries also exhibit an intrusion of Hybrida elements. It was no doubt the exceptionally favourable economic and cultural circumstances that contributed to the extraordinary success of these scripts in Italy in the fourteenth century and in the Burgundian Low Countries in the fifteenth.

Elsewhere, and more specifically in England, where scribes had continued to write a variety of Cursiva Antiquior, the practice in the late fourteenth and fifteenth centuries was to modernize the native cursive script by bringing it in line with the standard of European cursive. The resulting script is called Secretary. In Italy too, but at an earlier time, a rapid script of relatively low level had developed, which will be discussed in our chapter on Hybrida: Mercantesca.

---

[32] The number of manuscripts in Cursiva or Semihybrida in the hitherto published volumes of *CMDD* is simply overwhelming.

[33] Examples: Canellas, *Exempla*, ii, pls. 60 (1404), 63 (1391), 65 (1454). The 'cortesana' was a cursive documentary script and was rarely used in books: Cencetti, *Lineamenti*, pp. 313–14.

I CANCELLERESCA
(plates 89, 94) [34]

Since Italy was without doubt the cradle of Cursiva, it is no wonder that it was the first country to develop a luxury book script based upon Italian cursive chancery script. The so-called 'minuscola cancelleresca italiana' was used on a large scale from the end of the thirteenth till the end of the fourteenth century especially for the making of vernacular literary manuscripts of high quality, although it was used for Latin texts as well. Kirchner called it 'Florentiner Bastarda'.[35] Numerous copies of Dante's *Commedia* in particular were copied in this luxurious script.[36] It has all the characteristics of Italian Cursiva Formata, but its style is particularly marked by its long looped ascenders and long pointed descenders, both strictly vertical, and its small size of the letter bodies in comparison with the ascenders and descenders. The uncompressed character of the script is also counterbalanced by numerous fusions.

The generally triangular and highly conspicuous loops on ascenders consist of a bold diagonal downstroke and a closing hairline which is often invisible (if traced at all) (97, 98). In some manuscripts looped and unlooped ascenders alternate (although unlooped ascenders are always in the minority, pl. 89); these unlooped ascenders, which in fact turn the script into a Semihybrida, are either bifurcated, or more often have a bold horizontal approach stroke from the left, which gives the script a highly idiosyncratic aspect (99). Two adjacent ascenders were often treated as a ligature: either the first one was given an incomplete loop (100), or the second one was traced with a smaller shaft (101), or both were formed without loops and linked with a long horizontal serif (102).[37]

The letter **d** generally has either the normal or the apparently clockwise loop discussed above (18), which sometimes runs more or less parallel with the loops on the ascenders, especially when both have a triangular shape.[38]

g may have various forms, but never has the 'horns' present in Northern Cursiva. Scribes had a particular liking for **g** with a looped tail (36).

Approach strokes and endstrokes are very rare (in part because final **m** and **n** are rare in Italian); the limb of **h** (and the final minim of **m**), however, usually extends

97   98   99

100   101   102

[34] Battelli, *Lezioni*, p. 232; Cencetti, *Lineamenti*, pp. 228–9; Petrucci, *Breve storia*, pp. 151–6. The use of the name 'Cancelleresca' for a kind of Humanistic cursive script (Brown, *Guide*, pp. 126–7 and pl. 52), although historically based, should best be avoided.

[35] Crous and Kirchner, *Schriftarten*, pp. 14–15, fig. 16; cf. Mazal, *Buchkunst der Gotik*, p. 44.

[36] Good reproductions in *Archivio Paleografico Italiano*, x, 69 (*Codici danteschi*), Rome 1972; Crous and Kirchner, *Schriftarten*, fig. 16.

[37] The first ligature is seen in *Codici danteschi*, pl. 21, the last ones in *Codici danteschi*, pl. 16.

[38] See, for example, Federici, *Scrittura*, pl. 58 (1334).

below the baseline, making a generous curve to the left like **g**, and may end with a reversed hairline curve (103).

The letters **p** and **q** have straight, pointed descenders just like **f** and straight **s**. The straight **s** usually has a spur on the left, a feature otherwise uncommon in Cursiva, especially in the fourteenth century (104). The rarity of **s** in final position in Italian texts prevents us from determining which shape of round **s** was preferred in Cancelleresca. In Latin texts it is Cursiva **s** (pl. 94).

Two forms of **r** were normally employed interchangeably: Textualis **r**, generally with a serif at the baseline (62), and round **r** (60), although the latter was often omitted entirely.[39] The v-shaped **r** is found in addition to the two other forms in some manuscripts (pl. 89).

u in initial position was either written as **u** or as open **v**, extending well above the headline (79).

As might be expected in fourteenth-century Cursiva, **x** took the Textualis, two-stroke form (85). **z** was often replaced by **c** caudata (**c** with a cedilla, **ç**) (105). The typical Southern tironian **et** sign, unidentifiable in normal Italian Cursiva, was used in Cancelleresca (106).

Abbreviation strokes are long, and are mostly straight and thin.

With the introduction of Humanistic script in Italy, the days of Cancelleresca seem to have been numbered. From the first decades of the fifteenth century Italian texts would be copied either in Humanistic Antiqua or Humanistic cursive, or in a more or less informal Cursiva or Hybrida, in addition, of course, to the formal Rotunda which had never ceased to be used for vernacular texts on the Apennine Peninsula. Mercantesca, which belongs to this category, will be discussed below.

II BASTARDA
(plates 104, 109, 110, 114; see also plates 131, 137, 139, 149)[40]

This famous deluxe script, commonly called 'bâtarde' or 'lettre bourguignonne', achieved its most glorious expression in the illuminated manuscripts commissioned by Philip the Good (1419–67) and his son Charles the Bold (1467–77), dukes of Burgundy. Like the script they favoured, the dukes of Burgundy had their origin in

103 104

105 106

[39] *Codici danteschi*, pls. 11, 19, 29.

[40] Battelli, *Lezioni*, pp. 229, 233; Bischoff, *Palaeography*, p. 143; Brown and Lovett, *Source Book*, pp. 95–102; Drogin, *Medieval Calligraphy*, pp. 153–64; Harris, *Calligraphy*, pp. 70–3. More specifically: E. Bruinsma, 'The lettre bourguignonne in Cambridge University Library Nn.3.2 and other Flemish Manuscripts: A Method of Identification', *Transactions of the Cambridge Bibliographical Society*, 10, 2 (1992), pp. 156–64. Interesting personal ideas of a calligrapher are given in G. Noordzij, *Letterletter*, 13, 'The Burgundian Issue', Zaltbommel n.d.

France, being the descendants of a brother of King Charles V (1380–1422). The script was not limited to codices produced for the court and its entourage in the Southern Netherlands, but was used in France as well, and was exported from the Low Countries to England in the second half of the fifteenth century. Although Latin, Dutch and English texts were copied in Bastarda, the script was used first and foremost for French texts. Abbreviations are thus rare in this script, and even when Latin texts were copied in it they played a very limited role.

The script is in fact a calligraphic version of the Cursiva book script used in France in the second half of the fourteenth and in the fifteenth century, and it brought to the world of the deluxe book characteristics of French royal chancery script. It has no special letter forms, but comprises the forms discussed above in the section on Cursiva scripts in general. The earliest examples are French and may probably date from the last quarter of the fourteenth century (pl. 90). This, and the high level of execution (the script is Formata or at least Libraria), explains why it retains nothing of the original rapid Cursiva, other than the letter forms themselves. In this respect one might often question whether a given hand of the Libraria level should be called Bastarda or simply Cursiva. As far as specimens in Formata hands are concerned this distinction is usually easier to draw because of the care taken by their scribes to produce all the refinements proper to Bastarda.[41]

Of all Cursivae, Bastarda is, first and foremost, marked by its bold character. Shading is extremely apparent, with very thick strokes alternating with very thin hairlines. Additional hairlines (i.e. those that do not form part of the essential elements of the letters), however, are rare in French, but not Burgundian Bastarda (pl. 104). The bold, pointed **f** and straight **s**, a common characteristic of cursive book scripts, is the most distinguishing feature here. These fat, sloping (and sometimes extremely sloping) letters, which were artificially made much bolder than any other letters, contrast with the overall somewhat vertical character of the script. Their emphatic appearance on the page creates, at first sight, a confusing and restless impression, which is special to this type of Cursiva.

Another internal contrast in Bastarda consists in the combination of roundness and angularity. It is close to its cursive models in maintaining essentially round letter forms, but it is full of angular and spiky details, most of them already discussed

[41] The study of Bastarda has been neglected in favour of the study of the illuminations contained in the manuscripts written in that script. The following observations are based on the examination of a large number of specimens but cannot be related to individual manuscripts within the scope of this book. Dated examples can easily be found in the Catalogues of Dated Manuscripts. See, for example, *CMDB*, II, pls. 361–5 (1435); III, pls. 565, 566–7, 568–71, 572–3 (all 1451), 674–5 (1459), 678–80 (1460); *CMDGBLo*, pls. 606 (1460), 742 (1470), 771 (1473), 772 (1473), 774 (c. 1473–4), 784 (1475), 813 (1479), 814 (1479), 815 (1479), 816 (1479), 823 (1480), 832 (1482), 853 (1487), 890 (1498); *CMDNL*, I, pls. 266 (1403), 269 (1451), 270 (1453), 271 (c. 1454), 276 (1463), 277 (after 1473), 278 (after 1505), 279 (1511), 282 (1552), 283 (apparently dated 1498). An English example: *CMDGBLo*, pl. 882 (1496).

above in the section on Cursiva in general, but in Bastarda taken to extremes. We see projecting points at the headline in **a**, **c**, **e**, **m**, **n**, **q**, round **s** (11, 46, 53, 107–9); one or two horns at the headline in **g** (32, 33), one horn at **t** (110); thin spurs on the ascenders of **b**, **h**, **k**, **l** (7); projecting points at the baseline at the lower left angle of **b**, **d**, **r** and other letters (6, 21, 56). In very calligraphic execution quadrangles were sometimes added at the headline and the baseline, which bring this script even closer to Textualis, although its fundamentally different letter forms prevent it from being confused with Textualis.

A final and parallel distinctive feature in Bastarda as compared with other Cursivae is the relative shortness of the ascenders and descenders, giving the script a large height of the letter bodies unusual in Cursiva. Even the typically long **f** and straight **s** were sometimes made so short that they hardly cross the baseline. Associated with this trend is the very limited exploitation of loops at the top of the ascenders. While these are very visible or even emphasized in other Cursivae, such as Cancelleresca, in Bastarda they are often very small, not closed at all, or reduced to a slight incurvation of the ascender to the right (111, 112). So it is no wonder that a variant of Bastarda was developed later in the fifteenth century, which in all other respects is identical to the main type, but which has no loops at all at its ascenders, or exhibits looped and unlooped ascenders on the same page. In the first case the script is, properly speaking, a Hybrida (pls. 131, 137, 139), in the second a Semihybrida (pl. 149). The treatment of the ascenders in this Semihybrida can be haphazard, or conform to given rules: some Burgundian scribes, for example, traced loops on all ascenders, except when two succeeding letters had ascenders, in which case they made them without loops and occasionally joined them by means of a hairline serif at their top.[42]

In this Burgundian 'Hybrida' the contrast in the direction of the shafts can be even more striking than in its more normal 'Cursiva' counterpart: the ascenders of **b**, **h**, **k**, **l** are strictly vertical, in marked contrast with the sloping shafts of **f**, straight **s**, and often **p** and **q**. One should note that these ascenders are often unadorned (113).

Little can be added about specific letter forms in Bastarda, as in general it contains the wide array of forms for the same letter that is typical of French Cursiva. All forms of looped **d** were used that were then employed in French Cursiva (15, 16), including the 'majuscule' **d** written in initial position (21); but more studied forms were preferred, such as **d** with reversed loop (18) and **d** with open loop terminating

107   108   109   110   111   112   113

[42] See, for example, *CMDGBLo*, pl. 742 (1470).

in a horizontal stroke (19), and lastly loopless **d** (20). An intermediate form with a fancy little loop was also created by means of the addition of a hairline at the top of loopless **d** (114, pls. 112, 139).

p and **q** are pointed and slope in the same direction as **f** and straight **s**, but the tails of both letters were sometimes treated as hairlines, thereby giving full weight to the body of the letter. When this was done the descender of **p** tends to be more sloping than **f** and **s** (115, pl. 114). A typical feature is the presence of three or four different forms of **r** in the same manuscript, although many scribes still kept to two – Textualis and round **r**. The stylized 'single-stroke' **r** (56) was favoured in Bastarda, since the v-shaped cursive **r** (54) was no doubt considered too humble to be used in so cultivated a script. In common with French Cursiva in general, Bastarda rarely included the vertical hairline appended to final **t**, whilst the addition of a similar decoration to **r**, in the middle or at the end of a word, is altogether exceptional (64–5). **v** has the tall open form (79), which, however, often terminates in a horizontal stroke to the right (80); in this way **v** and **d** sometimes have parallel shapes. **x**, finally, always takes the cursive 'single-stroke' form (84) which was given the peculiar Bastarda style by scribes emphasizing the angularity of the body and forming the endstroke as a hairline (116). It should be noted that a similar form reappears in one variant of **p** and a variant of **r**.

The impact of the individual scribes on the appearance of the script was quite strong, and, whilst the main characteristics remain the same, the visual impression produced by different pages of Bastarda script can be very varied. More than once in the manuscripts produced for the dukes of Burgundy, the size of the script is so large, that the scribes, however well trained, appear to have had difficulty in tracing it according to the usual standards for this script.

The importance of Bastarda for the development of German Fractura cannot be overrated. This type of script will be discussed in the next chapter.

III SECRETARY
(plates 93, 102)[43]

The English form of Cursiva as described here is commonly called Secretary, and represents less of a special category than the two Formata varieties of Cursiva just discussed above. For two centuries English scribes had adhered to Anglicana, a book

114 115 116

[43] Parkes, *Book Hands*, pp. xix–xxii, pls. 11–15; Bischoff, *Palaeography*, p. 142; Cencetti, *Lineamenti*, pp. 250–1. There does not seem to be a good reason to use the term Secretary for continental cursive scripts. A few more examples: Thomson, *Bookhands*, pls. 104 (1411), 105 (1429); Kirchner, *Scriptura Gothica*, pl. 59 (1451?).

script belonging to the family of Cursiva Antiquior. But during the course of the fifteenth century this script gradually gave way to the continental cursive under the influence of prolonged (if generally unfriendly) contacts with France during the second half of the fourteenth and the first half of the fifteenth century. Some scribes began to abandon the more complicated and, by continental standards, old-fashioned forms of Anglicana (which, however, till the sixteenth century continued to betray their origin in early documentary script), and adopted to a greater or lesser extent the simplified forms of French documentary and book cursive, which were easier to trace and (perhaps) to read.

In essence, therefore, Secretary is the same script as has been described above as Cursiva and presents the same peculiarities and diversity – often multiplicity – of letter forms. Like Cursiva it may display a more or less strong influence from Textualis, such as the way **m** and **n** were traced or the treatment of the base of minims. Instead of the typical, backward-sloping minims of single-stroke **m** and **n**, these letters can be 'constructed' and made in several strokes, and the minims can be provided with feet at the baseline. These transformations led Malcolm Parkes to create a special name for this more formal Secretary: 'Bastard Secretary': 'large, well-spaced, calligraphic hands containing the typical "Bastard" combination: cursive forms and features (this time derived from Secretary) with the proportions and stylistic features of Textura [i.e. Textualis] superimposed upon them'.[44] We would not hesitate to use the term Cursiva Formata for the hands reproduced in his examples. Some 'Bastard Secretaries' are very close to the French or Burgundian Bastarda and indicate just how strong French and especially Flemish influence upon England was during the second half of the fifteenth century.[45] These display the partially round, partially angular and spiky forms special to Bastarda. This European context makes it difficult to retain the term Secretary as a name for a specific type. It could easily be replaced by Cursiva, unless it proves possible to distinguish distinctive features peculiar to the English variant.

English Cursiva has many different aspects, often being bold and marked by a strong tendency towards angularity and spikiness, so that in some more carefully executed specimens the lobes are shaped as lozenges and short letters have extremely well-developed horns and projecting points.[46] Sometimes, on the contrary, the script is very light. In addition, the script is often marked by the survival of one or more Anglicana characteristics and forms. Anglicana influence especially in vernacular manuscripts may be evident in the strong shading, the very bold strokes being reminiscent of the earliest forms of documentary cursive.

[44] Parkes, *Book Hands*, p. xxi.   [45] Parkes, *Book Hands*, pls. 15 i and ii.
[46] As in Parkes, *Book Hands*, pls. 11 ii, 14 i and ii, 15 ii.

The influence of Anglicana is especially noticeable in the presence of typical Anglicana letters, either as the sole form or as variants for Cursiva forms (pl. 93). Forms that were frequently used include the round Anglicana **e**, the long, forked **r**, the round **s** in a form resembling figure 6 (especially when used at the beginning of words), the 8-shaped Anglicana **g**, etc. Some examples seem, in fact, to be no more than Anglicana in which the two-compartment **a** has been replaced by a single-compartment one.

9

Hybrida and Semihybrida
(plates 118–56)

Hybrida, the most debated of Lieftinck's categories, has already been touched upon in Chapter 6, a discussion of Gothic cursive script in general (pp. 130–2).[1] In the present chapter we will take a closer look at this script, or more exactly, at those scripts which have the following basic characteristics: single-compartment **a**, **f** and straight **s** extending below the baseline, and loopless ascenders (1–3). Hybrida is thus the most deliberate of combinations of Cursiva and Textualis forms. The omission of loops on the ascenders of **b**, **h**, **k**, **l** is widely considered to have been a matter of choice on the part of individual scribes. But the history of the origin of this 'loopless cursive', which is essentially a phenomenon of the fifteenth century, may well be more complicated, as Oeser has rightly pointed out. It may go back to the fourteenth and, in Italy, perhaps even to the thirteenth century.[2]

Many scribes were hesitant in their treatment of the ascenders in this kind of script and appear to have been indifferent in their tracing of looped or unlooped ascenders, either because they relapsed time and again into writing the customary Cursiva, or because the distinction held no significance for them. For other scribes, on the contrary, the writing of looped and loopless ascenders adheres to a strict rule. To all of these cases, whether conforming to a strict rule or not, we will apply the term Semihybrida as a classification of this intermediate type between Cursiva and Hybrida.[3]

Hybrida and Semihybrida, like Cursiva, but starting at a later date, were used in an enormous number of manuscripts all over continental Europe. It is very striking that both types were extremely rare in England, whilst in France and the Southern Low Countries, the two countries which exercised influence upon English script in the fifteenth century, Hybrida was well known, if not as popular as in the other

[1] On Hybrida from a European viewpoint, as considered here, there is one fundamental study: Oeser, 'Beobachtungen Bastarden'. See also J. P. Gumbert, 'Italienische Schrift – humanistische Schrift – Humanistenschrift', in *Renaissance-und Humanistenhandschriften*, pp. 63–70 (63–5).
[2] Oeser, 'Beobachtungen Bastarden', p. 245.
[3] The term was first used by Gumbert, *Kartäuser*, p. 210. 'Semicursiva' would have been more justified, being comparable to our Semitextualis, but Semicursiva has already been used in palaeography for entirely different notions.

European countries. The loopless Cursiva Antiquior (see pp. 140–1), sometimes used in England in the fourteenth and fifteenth centuries, does not appear to have been sufficiently widespread there to account for the notable absence of Hybrida.

GENERAL FEATURES

Hybrida, or at least the Northern group of Hybridae, is essentially a variant form of Cursiva and, except for the treatment of its ascenders, maintains the letter forms characteristic of the latter script. It is significant in this respect that almost all Hybridae and Semihybridae outside Italy maintained, in addition to Cursiva **a, f** and straight **s**, the round cursive **s** in final position (4). Therefore most of what has been said about Cursiva and the various ways cursive script became formalized into a book script applies also to Hybrida. This also explains why the general aspect of a page written in Hybrida can vary so widely, from a script which at first sight would be called Cursiva (even Cursiva Currens), to scripts that are extremely close to Textualis or even Textualis Formata. It is therefore difficult to isolate the general characteristics of Hybrida other than the treatment of ascenders.

INDIVIDUAL LETTER FORMS

In conformity to the underlying trend towards a more 'Textualis' appearance, Hybrida greatly reduced the elaboration and multiplicity of letter forms character-istic of Cursiva. The various forms of **r** observed in so many Cursiva hands generally gave way to the traditional late medieval dual use of Textualis **r** and round **r** (5, 6).

In this 'loopless Cursiva' **d** is almost always devoid of a loop (7). Exceptions are quite naturally to be found in rapid script of the Currens level, and especially in script in which looped and loopless ascenders alternate (Semihybrida).

The distinctive feature of Hybrida as a script type in its own right is the treatment of the top of the ascenders, which represents a break with age-old practice. Three solutions can be distinguished.

(a) The ascender has an upwards sloping approach stroke from the left (8, pl. 127). This frequently observed feature may be simply an extrapolation of the general cursive practice, which consists in adding an approach stroke to minims at the beginning of words (see above, p. 127). It thus represents an adaptation for ascenders of what had already been applied to initial **i, m, n, v,**

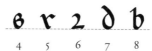

4   5   6   7   8

etc. But it can also be interpreted as the residue of a loopless connection with the preceding letter. This cursive ligature can often be seen in documentary scripts and was also taken over in some book scripts (9).[4]

(b) The top of the ascender lacks any approach stroke or other decoration (10). This is probably the most common form, and is the one that gives Hybrida its most distinctive aspect.

(c) The top of the ascender is bifurcated and/or decorated with a vertical or downwards sloping hairline to the left (11–12). This ultimate assimilation with Textualis occurs not only in the most calligraphic versions of Northern Hybrida, but also in simple Hybrida Libraria and even Currens (pl. 123).

The three forms occur together in our pl. 120. Closely associated with this is the tendency for Hybrida to be adorned with all the forms of hairline decoration and spurs already mentioned in the discussion of Textualis.

SUBTYPES

Within the confusing mass of Hybridae and Semihybridae encountered in late medieval manuscripts, which reflect so many different influences, it is not easy to distinguish groups with their own distinctive features. Among the Northern specimens, however, two more or less canonized types, both centred in the Low Countries, may immediately be recognized: loopless Bastarda and 'Netherlandish' Hybrida. Scribes in other countries also developed Hybrida scripts which have their own more or less pronounced character.

I   LOOPLESS BASTARDA

(plates 131, 137, 139, 149)

In the discussion of Bastarda, a subtype of Cursiva, it was observed that part of the manuscripts apparently written in this script are in fact written in Semihybrida or Hybrida (above, p. 159). Other than their often strikingly vertical ascenders (or some of their ascenders in Semihybrida), they have all the features of Bastarda: they often exhibit as many as three or four different **r**s, have sloping **f**s and straight **s**s, **v**s

ʠ [ol] b b b

9   10   11   12

[4] See examples in documentary script: Poulle, *Paléographie*, pls. 4 (1485), 6 (1505). In *CMDNL*, II, pl. 835a (Low Countries 1458), these ligatures appear to be apparent.

rising high above the headline, etc., as well as the generally decorative character and the combination of round and angular forms typical of this script. The ascenders are either unadorned, or have the sloping approach stroke mentioned above (8, 10). Like the more normal variant of Bastarda, their use was limited to France and the Southern Low Countries. It is important to note that in general this script may be associated with the circles of the court and nobility and with lay manufacture. It did not, as a rule, play much of a role in the revival of scribal activity in the monasteries.[5]

II NETHERLANDISH HYBRIDA
(plates 122, 127, 142, 151)[6]

The Netherlandish Hybrida, on the contrary, constitutes a new script and is a pure Hybrida, in other words, looped ascenders were as a rule not permitted (our pl. 151 does not, strictly speaking, belong to this category). It inhabited the world of monasteries much more than that of the courtly circles. Its name points to the area where this subtype developed during the fifteenth century and it became very much a national script. Lieftinck and after him other Dutch palaeographers call it simply Hybrida. Kruitwagen, in view of its frequent use in the houses of the Brethren of Common Life and of the Augustinian Canons affiliated to the Windesheim Congregation, considered Netherlandish Hybrida to be specially associated with these followers of the Devotio Moderna, and called it 'Friars' Script'.[7] 'Devotenbastarda' is another name given to it in the palaeographical literature.[8] As a result of its use by the Windesheim Congregation it became disseminated all over the North-western part of Germany and even to some houses in Southern Germany. The Friars and the Regular Canons, together with, it should be noted, the Crutched Friars, without doubt contributed greatly to the dissemination of the script; but the role of other religious orders should not be underestimated.

---

[5] Exceptions are, for example, certain Flemish abbeys, such as St Bavo in Ghent, where the works of prior Oliver de Langhe (d. 1461) were copied in Bastarda; see Ghent, Univ. Libr., MS 82.

[6] J. P. Gumbert in CMDNL, II, pp. 24, 26; Gumbert, 'Iets over laatmiddeleeuwse schrifttypen', pp. 279–82; J. P. Gumbert, *The Dutch and their Books in the Manuscript Age*, London 1990 (The Panizzi Lectures, 1989), p. 29; Obbema, 'De opkomst van een nieuw schrifttype'; E. A. Overgaauw, 'Les hésitations des copistes devant la *littera gothica hybrida* pendant le deuxième quart du XVe siècle', in *Scribi e colofoni. Le sottoscrizioni di copisti dalle origini all'avento della stampa*, ed. E. Condello and G. di Gregorio, Spoleto 1995, pp. 347–57.

[7] B. Kruitwagen, 'De drie soorten van Fratersschrift: Fractura, Rotunda, Bastarda', in Kruitwagen, *Laat-Middeleeuwsche Paleografica, Paleotypica, Liturgica, Kalendalia, Grammaticalia*, The Hague 1942, pp. 23–78.

[8] Oeser, 'Beobachtungen Bastarden', p. 243, n. 11; Schneider, *Paläographie*, p. 71.

The script functioned as a less formal counterpart to Textualis and stands just a short (sometimes very short) distance from that more old-fashioned script. A vertical, bold script, used for copies of Latin as well as Dutch and German texts, generally executed at the Libraria level, sometimes even at the Formata level, it may be considered one of the major graphic innovations of the later Middle Ages. It was used from the second quarter of the fifteenth century onwards, and may constitute a Northern response to Italian Humanistic script, arising from a desire to create a script suited to the spiritual, literary and cultural aspirations of a new age. It is more than likely that the exchanges between Northern and Southern participants in the Council of Constance (1414–18, see pl. 120) lie behind if not the creation, then at least the spread and the success of this formal Hybrida (despite the fact that Netherlandish Hybrida was an imitation of Italian Hybrida much more than of Italian Antiqua).[9] What prompts such thinking is the kind of texts for which this script was used. There are of course innumerable devotional manuscripts in Dutch, German or Latin written in Hybrida, but the most striking genres written in Latin in the new script are the same as those for which Littera Antiqua was used in Quattrocento Italy: the Church Fathers, the Classics, Humanistic texts, history.[10] The revival of monastic libraries in the regions in question (especially in Flanders) was above all marked by the acquisition of books written in Hybrida with these very same contents, together with the works of the leading authors of the twelfth century such as Bernard of Clairvaux and Hugh of Saint-Victor. In returning to a book culture reminiscent of the 'Renaissance of the Twelfth Century', the promoters of the Renaissance of the Fifteenth Century outside Italy seem to have preferred Hybrida – a book script that, in its relatively simplified shapes, was a departure from the overly formal Textualis as well as from the overly fanciful Cursiva, and which, in this way, had some points of resemblance with Humanistic script.

Netherlandish Hybrida is generally easily distinguishable from Bastarda, but less so from other Hybridae. Its main features are: the avoidance of fantasy, verticality, angularity, and the abandonment of round forms; a large height of the letter bodies as compared with the ascenders and descenders, bifurcation and/or a hairline at the top of the ascenders (in more careful execution) (11–12); the absence of approach and endstrokes; unlooped **d** (7) and no use of 'majuscule' **d** except where convention dictated the use of a majuscule; **f** and straight **s** with vertical shafts, not bolder than the other letters and not ending in a point (3), barely extending below the baseline; **g** without horns; frequent use of 3-shaped **m** in final position (in the Italian-German

---

[9] See the article by Gumbert mentioned in n. 1.

[10] This statement, which needs further investigation, is especially based on the book production in Hybrida in the Southern Low Countries. Gumbert's analysis of the contents of fifteenth-century manuscripts in the Northern Netherlands (*CMDNL*, II, pp. 303–5) is somewhat less conclusive.

tradition); the descenders of **p** and **q** not pointed; only two forms of **r**: Textualis **r** and round **r** (5, 6; one form only in our pl. 127); **t** with short ascender; **v** not extending above the headline (our pl. 151, which is Semihybrida, is an exception[11]). A common feature is the hairline decoration of **r** and of the headstroke of final **t** (13, 14); spurs on the ascenders may also be part of the decorative treatment.[12] This script can come deceptively close to Textualis: when executed carefully only **a**, **f** and straight **s** and round final **s** (4) distinguish it from Textualis.

The mutual influence of Bastarda and Hybrida explains why Bastarda features, such as pointed descenders, may appear in Netherlandish Hybrida (pl. 151, Semihybrida). Towards the end of the fifteenth and during the sixteenth century especially, a general intrusion of foreign elements took place in almost all cursive scripts just as in Textualis.

III HYBRIDA AND SEMIHYBRIDA IN GERMANY AND OTHER NORTHERN EUROPEAN COUNTRIES
(plates 123, 125, 129, 138, 140, 143–5, 154)

In Germany and Central Europe Hybridae and especially Semihybridae were widespread and took many forms. Various local or regional subtypes have been identified by Joachim Kirchner, and, following him, Otto Mazal.[13] In the following list of regional styles identified within what German palaeography calls 'Bastarda' the equivalent names in our system have been supplied between parentheses:

Upper Rhine (Cursiva)

Swabia (Cursivae of various aspects)

Transitional type (Semihybrida, our pl. 125)

Bavaria and Austria (Cursiva, later examples Hybrida, our pl. 138)

Franconia (Cursiva or Semihybrida)

Cologne (Hybrida, resembling our Netherlandish Hybrida)

Lower Germany (Cursiva or Hybrida, the latter style close to Scandinavian examples; see below)

Lower Rhine (sixteenth century, Hybrida)

To these regional styles Mazal added a Nürnberg type (Hybrida) and a Bohemian type (Cursiva). Apart from a few exceptions, all these styles are difficult to define, based as they are more on impressions than on distinct features. Kirchner was aware of the tentative character of his classifications. It is typical of his

13   14

[11] It also has occasionally looped **d**; Gumbert classifies it under the Cursivae.
[12] *CMDNL*, II, pls. 765b (1471), 819a (1532).
[13] Crous and Kirchner, *Schriftarten*, pp. 19–22 and figs. 31–51. Mazal, *Buchkunst der Gotik*, pp. 42–3 and figs. 25–36; Mazal, *Paläographie und Paläotypie*, pp. 20–2.

caution that he abandoned them in his more recent *Scriptura Gothica Libraria*. Modern scholars, too, have distanced themselves from these supposed subdivisions of German Hybrida.[14] An expert eye may be able to distinguish different varieties, but the mobility of lay scribes and the individual characteristics of the hands of their monastic colleagues make it very difficult to link them to specific areas in the fifteenth century. They generally all share a preference for the conventions of Semihybrida.

It seems that almost all these German, Central European (and Scandinavian) examples may be classified as belonging to the Currens or Libraria levels. Bohemian manuscripts, whether written in Cursiva, Hybrida or Semihybrida, seem commonly to display bold script tightly written on lines close to each other.[15] The Scandinavian Hybrida, on the other hand, comprises simplified, angular, large and extremely bold forms (pl. 154; see also pl. 115).[16]

IV FRACTURA
(plates III, 116, 148, 150, 156)[17]

If it is difficult to generalize about continental Hybrida of the middling class, it is also not easy to provide an adequate description of the calligraphic 'German' script which goes under the name of Fractura (Fraktur). It is very difficult to find specimens of Hybrida Formata in German manuscripts dating from before the 1460s.[18] Although Fractura is generally considered a type font, not a type of book script, its appearance in manuscript books of the later fifteenth century cannot be ignored.[19] Bischoff, referring to Fractura's origin in the German imperial chancery under Frederick III (1452–93), characterized Fractura as follows: 'an oblong chancery script with slightly flamed rectangles, spindle-shaped **s** and **f**, and majuscules that have the "elephant trunk" as a special ornament'. He provided the qualification, 'Prefraktur', for the famous example of a similar script (minus the 'Elefantenrüssel') in a schoolbook made for the young Maximilian of Austria, Frederick's son and future successor, and copied by Wolfgang Spitzweg in the years 1466–7 (pl. III). This manuscript has been considered by some to represent the origin of 'German

---

[14] Schneider, *Paläographie*, p. 78.

[15] Examples: *CMDA*, II, pls. 301 (1434), 427 (1443); III, pls. 453 (1478), 495 (1482).

[16] See also Bröndum-Nielsen, *Palaeografi*, A, figs. 33, 61.

[17] Bischoff, *Palaeography*, p. 140; Cencetti, *Lineamenti*, pp. 330–1; Mazal, *Buchkunst der Gotik*, pp. 44–5, fig. 38. Fundamental is Fichtenau, *Lehrbücher*. See also Harris, *Calligraphy*, pp. 76–7.

[18] Two early examples: *CMDF*, V, pl. 127 (Trier 1458–9); *CMDGBCam*, pl. 285 (Lüchtenhof 1462).

[19] Updike, *Printing Types*, I, pp. 139–41; Crous and Kirchner, *Schriftarten*, p. 36.

Renaissance handwriting'.[20] The extravagant printing types that were developed for a few luxury editions commissioned by Maximilian when emperor, and the letter forms in later printed Fraktur should help us to define this script type in a more objective way.

In its combination of rounded and angular forms, its fanciful character, the large height of its letter bodies, its bold strokes and its pointed **f**, straight **s**, **p** and **q**, Fractura is very close to Bastarda. The studied and spiky character of the letter forms typical of Bastarda was taken to extreme lengths in Fractura: all short letters have spikes at the headline, and many letters have them at the baseline as well. On the other hand hairline extensions and flourishes abound, and the script, unlike Bastarda, is strictly vertical and generally quite horizontally compressed.

The treatment of the tops of the ascenders is a special characteristic of the script. These were originally apparently looped, but with the loops being often very small or traced in hairline (another Bastarda feature, pls. III, 116). These loops were, for the most part, subsequently reduced to a slight incurvation of the top of the ascender towards the right (pls. 150, 156).[21] One can often find straight ascenders with hairline decoration (pls. 116, 148, 156). It is therefore often impossible to decide whether the script should be classified under Cursiva, Semihybrida or Hybrida. Its level of execution, at any rate, was always Formata. The minims were provided with quadrangles as in Textus Quadratus.

The letter forms are essentially the Bastarda ones, but they exhibit a marked preference for somewhat tortuous shapes. The following are conspicuous: **o** in the form of a 'flame' or pointed oval (15), a form also visible in **d** (16). **o** and **a** may have alternative and more fanciful forms (17, 18, pl. 156).

Fractura, as a purely luxury book script, was used on only a quite small scale in Germany, Austria, Bohemia and Poland during the last decades of the fifteenth century and the first decades of the sixteenth. Although influenced by one or more varieties of German Hybrida (visible in its verticality, short **v**, avoidance of multiple forms of **d** and **r**), there is no doubt that it is based on Southern Netherlandish Bastarda. The marriage of Archduke Maximilian with the heiress of the Burgundian state, Mary of Burgundy (1477), important in so many respects, would have provided the impetus for the dissemination of a basically French style

15   16

17   18

20 Kapr, *The Art of Lettering*, p. 92.

21 It may be noted that several German type-fonts of the late fifteenth and early sixteenth centuries are equally Semihybridae: see Crous and Kirchner, *Schriftarten*, figs. 119 ('Gebetbuchschrift', 1513), 120 ('Teuerdankschrift', 1517); others are pure Hybrida: figs. 117 ('Schwabacher', 1485), 118 ('Wittenberger Schrift', 1520); or pure Cursiva: fig. 116 ('Oberrheinische Type', 1486).

of writing in Germany, where, during the next century, it would develop into what became regarded as a national script.

V ITALIAN HYBRIDA AND SEMIHYBRIDA; MERCANTESCA
(plates 118–19, 124, 133, 135)

Italian Hybrida, like Italian Cursiva, is not easy to define, unless executed in a very careful manner. We have noted that in Cancelleresca (a canonized style of Cursiva) the ascenders sometimes have no loops; in which case such specimens should be classified under Semihybrida (see p. 156). Italian Hybrida usually resembles Italian Cursiva in the verticality of its ascenders and descenders, including those of **f** and straight **s**, the long, pointed shape of these same letters and also **p** and **q**, the preference for Textualis **r** in one of two variants: rounded and sloping (5) or with a foot at the baseline (19) (in addition to round **r**), and a preference for **x** traced in two strokes. **d**, as one would expect, is unlooped, but has a long sloping shaft, which distinguishes the script immediately from Rotunda (20). Final **s** is either Cursiva, Textualis or the typically Italian trailing **s**.

Among the Italian Semihybridae and Cursivae in the lower levels of execution a special subtype has been distinguished, called Mercantesca (pls. 118, 133).[22] It was the handwriting used by the merchants and other business people for their affairs, first in Florence in the first decades of the fourteenth century, and later also in the other cities of Northern and Central Italy. As a documentary script it has a very cursive ductus, no shading, and displays numerous complicated ligatures. When used for the copying of books (mostly by private persons for their own use, on paper, and for vernacular texts), the script became more calligraphic and upright, the distorted letter forms made place for more normal ones, and more shading is visible. Apart from the looped **d**, the long curved endstrokes on the limb of **h**, the frequent use of long **i** in final position and the rapid, personal character of the script, little can be said about this widespread type, which as a book script never became very important, but remained in use until the middle of the sixteenth century.

In general, however, and especially in Latin manuscripts, in the course of the fifteenth century the influence of Humanistic script on Hybrida became so strong that it tended to disappear as a script in its own right and its role was taken over by mixed scripts.

---

19   20

[22] Orlandelli, 'Osservazioni'; Petrucci, *Breve storia*, pp. 157–64 (examples on pp. 162 and 164).

VI SPANISH AND PORTUGUESE HYBRIDA AND SEMIHYBRIDA
(plates 121, 126, 128, 130)[23]

The situation in the Iberian Peninsula was totally different. Here a distinctive style of writing was developed for the production of well-made manuscripts, especially those in the vernacular, which takes its place alongside Textualis. It has until now not been incorporated within the Lieftinckian system, although it generally displays the same basic characteristics as Hybrida. The script is bold, with club-shaped ascenders that are vertical or slope to the left. It does not exhibit horizontal compression, but contains numerous Gothic fusions, at least when traced with some care (pl. 128).

Although sometimes Bastarda influence is visible, and an exceptionally pure Bastarda in the Semihybrida form was sometimes used, the descenders of **f** and straight **s** are as a rule not pointed (and, as has already been said, these letters do not slope to the right).

The letter **d** is mostly marked by a rather long, bold and club-shaped shaft traced on the diagonal (21). This shaft may be paralleled by the first stroke of **v**, a feature that is found especially in Spanish hands. Looped **d** is found not only in more rapid hands. But the three letters that give Iberian Hybrida its typical appearance are **g**, **i** and **r**. **g** has an almost horizontal tailstroke, located rather high and stretching far to the left, either with a clockwise or counter-clockwise loop or simply a bold stroke (the bold variant is based on an originally looped ductus) (22–4).[24] This idiosyncratic form, however, was often replaced by a more traditional **g** somewhat in the shape of figure 8 (pl. 128), or with its tail reduced in length.

The preference for **i** longa or **j** was already a well-established tradition in the Iberian Peninsula, and it is often the only clue to the Spanish or Portuguese origin of a hand. This does not mean that it was constantly used (short **i** is in fact the more common form), but there was a strong tendency to write **j** in specific positions: after or before **m**, **n**, **u**, after **l**, or at the opening of words. In the latter case it generally extends above the headline and is one of those 'majuscule' forms favoured by most Gothic cursive scripts in initial position. This form may, however, also appear in the middle of words, where it may have the value of a consonant, and thus constitute

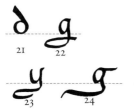

21 22
23 24

[23] Bischoff, *Palaeography*, p. 142; Cencetti, *Lineamenti*, pp. 242–6; Millares Carlo, *Tratado*, I, pp. 193–4. A few more Spanish examples: Canellas, *Exempla*, II, pls. 62 (1496), 76 (1432); Kirchner, *Scriptura Gothica*, pl. 53 (1425); Millares Carlo, *Tratado*, pls. 269 (1455), 273 (1389), 276 (1429); Thomson, *Bookhands*, pls. 121 (1328), 123 (1355), 125 (1388). For Portuguese examples, see n. 32.

[24] This feature does not appear in our plates.

an exception to the rule that in late medieval scripts **i** and **j** were used indifferently as vowels and as consonants.[25]

   r extending below the baseline is likewise a feature found in earlier Spanish and Portuguese Textualis hands. The letter was frequently reduced to a hook (25). There was no fixed rule for the use of long **r**, as existed for the use of **j**, and short **r** (in addition to the round **r**) is a quite common form. Nevertheless long **r** was used on a regular basis especially in Portuguese Hybrida, of which it is extremely typical.

   Iberian Hybrida is also marked by the form of **c** caudata (**ç**, which was used as an alternative to **z**): the cedilla was placed well below the baseline and is unconnected with the **c** (26). **f**, **r** and **s** were sometimes doubled when occurring at the beginning of words (pl. 126). In such cases, and elsewhere when the same letter occurs twice in succession, the pair of letters was often treated as a ligature and the second letter was given a shape different from the first (27, 28).[26] Majuscule **r** was sometimes used in initial position instead of **rr**, as in Northern (especially French) Cursiva or Hybrida.

   The generally heavy shading of the horizontal strokes, according to Cencetti, was due to the use of a pen whose nib had been cut obliquely, the *pes superior* being longer than the *pes inferior*.[27]

In Spanish Hybrida or Semihybrida final **s** is either of the Cursiva or the Textualis form (in Cursiva the figure 6-shape is most prevalent (29)), but even straight **s** may be found in final position.[28] The latter feature is probably a survival of an early practice which was never entirely abandoned. Round **s** in initial and medial position (as seen in Anglicana) is encountered in some rapid hands (pl. 121). **z** has a curious shape resembling a flattened **s** placed on the baseline (or slightly lower) and provided with a long horizontal top stroke (30, pl. 126). The long, bold horizontal abbreviation strokes are generally very noticeable.[29]

   The chancery script which lies behind this script is called 'Letra de albalaes'.[30] The scripts discussed here can take on many different aspects and are therefore

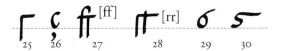

25 26 27 28 29 30

---

[25] This seems especially to be the case in Portuguese manuscripts: see Burnam, *Palaeographia*, pl. 37 (1445) and *CMDF*, IV, I, pl. 70 (1453).

[26] Millares Carlo, *Tratado*, pl. 269 (1455), col. b, l. 10; see also Canellas, *Exempla*, II, pl. 76 (1432).

[27] Cencetti, *Lineamenti*, p. 244.

[28] Thomson, *Bookhands*, pl. 121 (1328); Millares Carlo, *Tratado*, pl. 269 (1455).

[29] This feature does not appear in our plates.

[30] Millares Carlo, *Tratado*, pls. 186–9, gives a survey of the letter forms in 'gótica cursiva castellana denominada "de albalaes"'. The multiplicity of forms shown and the absence of the baseline in the drawings make these charts of little interest for the student of book scripts.

called by Canellas variously 'Cursiva formada', 'Cursiva textual', 'Bastarda corriente' and 'Bastarda textual'. One difference is that his 'Cursiva' (which corresponds to our Cursiva or Hybrida) has looped **d**s (pls. 121, 126), whereas his 'Bastarda' has unlooped ones (pl. 130). 'Redonda de libros' is another name given to this kind of script. It had its origin in a Spanish charter hand called 'Letra de privilegios'.[31]

Portuguese Hybrida (pl. 128) developed a proper canonized form in the fifteenth century, best known from the luxury manuscripts of *Leitura nova* and royal chronicles of the late fifteenth and early sixteenth centuries.[32] It is especially marked by final **s**, which has a very idiosyncratic shape. It consists of a closed counter-clockwise curve, ending in a bold horizontal stroke on the baseline, which itself terminates in a sharp angle formed with a sloping hairline (31).[33] **z** has for the most part the normal shape, that of figure 3 extending below the baseline, but may also stand on the baseline in the Iberian tradition (pl. 128). **d** has the normal Uncial form, but Half-Uncial **d** may be found now and then.[34]

In addition to the normal bold abbreviation stroke, a thin stroke with a dot in its middle is typical of Portuguese manuscripts (32); it sometimes also appears in manuscripts from Spain and Southern France.[35]

In Formata execution, especially in the later fifteenth century, the script may be quite angular, as is visible, for example, in the shape of **a**, comparable with the same letter in Northern Hybrida or Cursiva (33).[36] In addition, various decorative hairlines were employed, especially appended to tironian **et** (34). The ascenders lost their club shape and were treated very much as in Northern Textualis, being provided with a serif or bifurcated at their top. A tendency towards assimilation with Rotunda is clear from the shortening of the abbreviation strokes and the adoption of **d** with short, horizontal shaft.[37]

31   32   33   34

[31] See Cencetti, *Lineamenti*, pp. 253–4; Bischoff, *Palaeography*, p. 142.

[32] Numerous other examples of Portuguese Hybrida are provided by the following publications: Burnam, *Palaeographia*, pls. 37 (1445), 51 (fourteenth century according to Burnam), 59, 60; Da Costa, *Album*, pls. 139 (1431–46), 140–1, 143 (1510), 147 (1521); *Inventário dos códices iluminados até 1500*, 1. *Distrito de Lisboa*, Lisbon 1994, pls. 64, 69 (1434), 143 (1475), 263 (1444), 264 (1442–3), 312, 313 (1431–46), 345, 359, 440 (mostly small). Excellent reproductions of manuscripts containing the *Leitura nova* and similar manuscripts are to be found in the review *Oceanos*, 26 (April–June 1996), *passim*.

[33] The same **s** is found already in Iberian Textualis in the thirteenth century: see Thomson, *Bookhands*, pl. 117 (1253).

[34] See an example in a variant form of Portuguese Hybrida: Burnam, *Palaeographia*, pl. 19 (*c.* 1430).

[35] Thomson, *Bookhands*, pl. 24 (Toulouse 1429); Canellas, *Exempla*, II, pl. 65 (Huete 1454).

[36] Burnam, *Palaeographia*, pl. 59.   [37] See, for example, *Oceanos* (see n. 32), p. 95.

The lack of sufficient available published material (especially of a Catalogue of Dated Manuscripts) does not allow us to provide any details about the history of Iberian Hybrida. Its use as a book script is attested in Spain as early as the second half of the thirteenth century; examples from the fourteenth and fifteenth centuries are numerous. The Portuguese variant is typical of the fifteenth century.

An important variant of Iberian Hybrida, however, which combines Hybrida ascenders and **f** and straight **s** with two-compartment **a**, should be mentioned briefly here (pl. 157).[38] From the end of the fourteenth century onwards this intermediate form between Textualis (Rotunda) and Hybrida was frequently employed in Spanish and Portuguese manuscripts, and mostly those containing texts in the vernacular. This is the only canonized and widely used script we have encountered that does not fit into our expanded Lieftinck system. In all other respects it is comparable to the Hybrida used in the same area.

---

[38] More examples: Burnam, *Palaeographia*, pls. 19 (*c.* 1430), 20 (1439–40), 36 (1399), 52, 54 (1434, 1461–75), 55 (1439); Millares Carlo, *Tratado*, pl. 274 (1398); Thomson, *Bookhands*, pl. 126 (1396).

IO

Gothico-Antiqua and other 'hors système' scripts

I GOTHICO-ANTIQUA IN ITALY
(plates 158–9)

Some confusion surrounds the scripts which, in the palaeographical literature, have been called variously Gothico-Antiqua, Gothico-Humanistica, Fere Humanistica, etc.[1] Humanistic script itself was only created in Florence about 1400 by scholars such as Salutati (1331–1406) and Poggio (1380–1459), imitating earlier, especially late Carolingian, models (hence the term 'littera antiqua renovata', now preferred by some palaeographers). Therefore the names mentioned above cannot be applied to scripts dating from the fourteenth century. Even if it were true that Petrarch not only criticized Gothic Textualis in his writings but also contributed to a change by 'purifying' his own script under the influence of earlier models, the results he achieved could only be termed Praehumanistica, not Gothico-Antiqua (pl. 58). We have therefore discussed his script in the section devoted to Gothic Semitextualis (see above, pp. 119–20).

Humanistic script or, to be more precise, Antiqua (also called Humanistic Minuscule, as opposed to Humanistic Cursive), constitutes in essence a conscious return to Carolingian script.[2] It is clear, however, that the changes in society, economy and culture that had occurred between the last flowering of monastic culture

---

[1] Battelli, in *Nomenclature*, pp. 35–44 (38); Cencetti, *Compendio*, pp. 84–5; Crous and Kirchner, *Schriftarten*, figs. 15, 17, 26 (see also fig. 24); Gasparri, *Introduction*, pp. 119–25; A. Hessel, 'Die Entstehung der Renaissanceschriften', *Archiv für Urkundenforschung*, 13 (1933), pp. 1–14; Mazal, *Buchkunst der Gotik*, p. 39; B. L. Ullman, *The Origin and Development of Humanistic Script*, Rome 1960. Petrucci (*Breve storia*, pp. 170–3) uses the name 'pre-antiqua' for the type of handwriting employed by Coluccio Salutati and his circle. In the captions to her plates, Gasparri, *Introduction*, distinguishes 'gothico-humanistique', 'fere-humanistica' and 'préhumanistique', and occasionally adds to these and to other terms the adjective 'italianisante'. For a sounder approach to the script of the early Humanists, see the fundamental work by Albinia de la Mare, *Handwriting*.

[2] Basic works are those by Battelli and Ullman mentioned in n. 1. All handbooks contain a chapter on Humanistic script, for example, Battelli, *Lezioni*, pp. 245–9; Bischoff, *Palaeography*, pp. 145–9; Brown and Lovett, *Source Book*, pp. 111–25; Cencetti, *Lineamenti*, pp. 266–99; Cencetti, *Compendio*, pp. 81–4; Harris, *Calligraphy*, pp. 90–101; Stiennon, *Paléographie*, pp. 143–4.

in the twelfth century and the Italian Renaissance in the fourteenth and fifteenth would contribute to make the new script quite different from that produced by scribes in monastic and other scriptoria three or four centuries earlier. It is not surprising that when scribes used this anachronistic type of script in the numerous codices produced for a wealthy and educated commercial society their hands would inevitably deviate from the original models: these differences may be explained by the dominant Gothic aesthetic (even in Italy) and Gothic writing practices, commercial production, and the individuality of the scribes themselves. The latter introduced foreign elements into their script, either as a result of their own antiquarian research (which lay behind the introduction of monumental Capitals, for example), or for reasons of publicity: by entering one or more fanciful features, it was possible to create an individual hand of high aesthetic quality, capable of attracting the attention of the customers.[3]

But the main cause of the deviation of Humanistic script from pure Carolingian practice is to be sought in contamination with contemporary Gothic script, which in the last resort was itself no more than a development of Carolingian script. This contamination is as a rule so unobtrusive in Humanistic script as to enable one immediately to recognize the Humanistic script as something totally different, a striking novelty. That it could be accepted so rapidly, within a few decades, by a whole society, and ultimately by the whole world as the preferred script for the Latin alphabet, remains a fact of the utmost importance and testifies to the superior intrinsic qualities of the script.

Its features may be summarized as follows.[4] Like Carolingian script, Humanistic script is round with relatively long ascenders and descenders, and consequently a comparatively wide distance between the lines: the 'airy' quality of the Humanistic page is one of the most striking differences from the general appearance of Gothic script. Remnants of Gothic angularity are, however, often perceptible. The script is wide and does not exhibit lateral compression, despite the fact that Gothic fusions were often retained. There is relatively little shading. Unlike Carolingian script, the descenders of **p** and **q** end in a sloping serif, and **f**, **m**, **n** and straight **s** have horizontal serifs at the baseline. There was a strong tendency to add Gothic feet to

---

[3] It is to be noticed that the hands of some celebrated later fifteenth- and sixteenth-century scribes of Humanistic script, such as Tophio, Pierantonio Sallando and Bartolomeo Sanvito, display letter forms, ligatures and other features that depart from all tradition and are to be considered personal innovations. See, for example, J. Wardrop, *The Script of Humanism: Some Aspects of Humanistic Script 1460–1560*, Oxford 1963, pls. 4, 5, 34, 35.

[4] See, in addition to the literature mentioned in nn. 1 and 2, J. J. G. Alexander and A. C. de la Mare, *The Italian Manuscripts in the Library of Major J. R. Abbey*, London 1969, pp. xxii–xxxiii, and especially A. C. de la Mare, 'Humanistic Script: the First Ten Years', in *Das Verhältnis der Humanisten zum Buch*, ed. F. Krafft and D. Wuttke, Boppard 1977 (Kommission für Humanismusforschung. Mitteilung 4), pp. 89–108 (91).

the base of ascenders and minims. 'Carolingian' letter forms (see Chapter 2) were used, of course, especially the following:

(a) vertical, Half-Uncial **d**;

(b) two-lobe **g**, as in modern Roman type;

(c) **h** not extending below the baseline;

(d) **i** without stroke or dot: in fact, the use of these diacritical marks had become so common by the fifteenth century, that the great majority of the scribes retained them in their script; **i** longa or **j**, on the contrary, was almost wholly abandoned;

(e) **r** only in the Carolingian form; round **r** was rejected, except in the **orum**-abbreviation;

(f) straight **s** in all positions (ideally). Its use was prescribed by Poggio[5] but it was adopted by only a minority of scribes, and then mostly in the beginning of the fifteenth century. In fact, the use of straight and round **s** according to Gothic convention (in other words the straight form at the beginning and in the middle of words and the round one in final position) was adopted by most scribes of Humanistic script;

(g) **u** only in the round form, not as **v**;

(h) Roman capitals instead of the fanciful Gothic majuscules;

(i) **et** is always rendered by the ampersand (&), never by the tironian symbol;

(j) in addition to the **st**-ligature, which never went out of use, the ancient **ct**-ligature was revived;

(k) abbreviations were used only sparingly;

(l) the reintroduction of the spelling **ae** instead of simple **e** for the diphthong; this is an orthographical, rather than, strictly speaking, a palaeographical novelty. It was quite often wrongly applied (for example 'aecclesia'), classical orthography being generally not well known to the scribes in Italy as elsewhere. Many scribes continued to write **e**, or even reintroduced **e** caudata following in the footsteps of Poggio.

It seems reasonable to consider scripts that do not correspond with the totality of the criteria mentioned above not as Humanistic Antiqua, but (in so far as they should not be labelled Textualis or more precisely Rotunda) to refer to them by the term Gothico-Antiqua.[6] Thus conceived Gothico-Antiqua is a script that combines Antiqua features (including the 'Gothic' features which normally seem to have been admitted in Antiqua) with one or more features of Gothic Textualis. It is distinguished, for example, by a marked angularity and shading, or by one or

---

[5] It is a distinct feature of his formal hand.

[6] Examples are abundant: see, for example, Thomson, *Bookhands*, pl. 77 (1408); *CMDIt2*, II, pls. 32 (1447), 117, 139; III, pls. 38 (1444), 66 (1465).

more Gothic letter forms. The most frequent of these are: Uncial **d**, round **r** after **o** and other letters ending in a bow, and tironian **et**.

It is clear that Gothico-Antiqua, thus defined, is not a single script but stands for a wide range of handwriting with many different aspects. The term has been applied to some printing types for referring to less perfect forms of Roman (i.e. round Humanistic) type letters.[7]

The minor variant of Antiqua proper in which single-compartment **a** was used instead of the two-compartment one is related to the Italian Semitextualis. This script, originating in the fourteenth century and often associated with Petrarch, has been discussed above. The idea that Semitextualis as such was the result of the same efforts that later on would lead to the creation of Humanistic script should perhaps not be rejected entirely. But the examples we know of Antiqua with all of the distinctive characteristics recorded above, except for the inclusion of single-compartment **a**, are certainly not the earliest form of Humanistic script, which consistently exhibits two-compartment **a**.[8]

One may probably suppose that Gothico-Antiqua was normally the result of the inability of a scribe to write full Antiqua: the latter constituted such an archaism that many scribes could not succeed in freeing themselves entirely from Gothic features or shapes. In Northern Italy, where Gothic traditions were particularly strong and Humanistic models few, writing Antiqua would have presented a particularly difficult challenge to scribes. No wonder then that Gothico-Antiqua is a common phenomenon in books from this area.[9] But, on the other hand, throughout Italy, it is clear that all book scripts, except formal Rotunda, became subject to the influence of Antiqua during the fifteenth century.

In a book devoted to Gothic script Humanistic Cursive, or Italic, does not need to be discussed at length, in spite of the Gothic influences that were at work in it. Its creation has often been attributed to Niccoló Niccoli (*c.* 1364/5–1437), and dated about 1420;[10] it was to play an immensely important role as the handwriting of educated people first in Italy, afterwards all over Europe (with the exception of Germany). But it was of limited use as a book script. It was not introduced into printing before the beginning of the sixteenth century, when Aldus Manutius had the first successful font cut for his octavo books.[11] It was based on Antiqua and Italian chancery script, and is a narrow, slanting script almost without shading, with long

---

[7] Mazal, *Paläographie und Paläotypie*, pp. 181–97.
[8] Examples of this variant of Antiqua are: Alexander and de la Mare, *The Italian Manuscripts* (see n. 4), pls. 27 (*c.* 1480–90), 50–1 (*c.* 1450–65), 67a (1456); *CMDIt2*, II, pl. 158; III, pl. 65 (1464).
[9] J. P. Gumbert, 'Italienische Schrift – humanistische Schrift – Humanistenschrift', in *Renaissance- und Humanistenhandschriften*, pp. 63–70 (66; n. 9 provides a short list of such manuscripts).
[10] On the handwriting of Niccoli, see de la Mare, *Handwriting*, pp. 44–61.
[11] Updike, *Printing Types*, I, pp. 125–32.

ascenders and descenders not unlike Gothic Cursiva. It has single-compartment **a**, long **f** and straight **s** curving to the left below the baseline, and ascenders with no loops or loops reduced to a slight incurvation or dot at the top; **d** is always Half-Uncial. As is to be expected in a Cursive script, fanciful forms are much more prominent than in Antiqua, especially when the scribe was an artist calligrapher.[12]

II THE DIFFUSION OF GOTHICO-ANTIQUA
OUTSIDE ITALY
(plate 160)[13]

As people from many European countries studied in Italy or worked there as scribes or in other capacities, and since Italian scribes were more than once invited to practise their skills abroad, Humanistic script, with its distinctly different aspect, soon became known outside the Peninsula. The Councils of Constance (1414–18) and Basel (1431–49) were the first large-scale occasions to bring together Italian and Northern European scholars. We have already suggested that the Council of Constance probably was important for the dissemination of a new script, Hybrida, in Northern Europe, which was obviously an imitation of Italian Hybrida. But from the 1470s the printing press was rapidly to familiarize the whole of Europe with the forms of Antiqua. Few manuscripts, however, were written in the new script before the end of the century outside Italy,[14] but the influence of Antiqua is often perceptible in the areas or circles most exposed to Italian influence. It may appear in the occasional use of Roman capitals, of Half-Uncial **d**, of Antiqua **g**, in a diminished shading or wider spacing of the script, etc. Such features are visible in the circles of Humanists or 'Prehumanists' in France (in the handwriting of Jean de Montreuil, Pierre d'Ailly, Jean Gerson, Nicolas de Clamanges)[15] and

[12] See Wardrop, *The Script of Humanism* (see n. 3), pls. 16, 17, 18, etc., all by Bartolomeo Sanvito; A. J. Fairbank and B. Wolpe, *Renaissance Handwriting: An Anthology of Italic Scripts*, London 1960, pls. 8, 9 (both by Sanvito), 10, 11, etc.

[13] Bischoff, *Palaeography*, pp. 148–9. Some basic studies on this subject have been assembled in *Renaissance- und Humanistenhandschriften*, especially: Gumbert, 'Italienische Schrift' (see n. 9); M. Steinmann, 'Von der Übernahme fremder Schriften im 15. Jahrhundert' (pp. 51–62). See also, by the same author, 'Die lateinische Schrift zwischen Mittelalter und Humanismus', in *Paläographie 1981*, pp. 193–9; M. B. Parkes, 'Archaizing Hands in English Manuscripts', in *Books and Collectors 1200–1700: Essays Presented to Andrew Watson*, ed. J. P. Carley and C. G. C. Tite, London 1997, pp. 101–41.

[14] In England Duke Humphrey of Gloucester (1390–1447) commissioned manuscripts in Humanistic script. Given the intense political contacts between Aragon and Naples, it is no wonder that manuscripts in Humanistic script were occasionally copied in Spain during the fifteenth century. See, for example, Thomson, *Bookhands*, pls. 130 (1452), 132 (1478).

[15] See Gasparri, *Introduction*, p. 125 and pls. 54–65, and especially the studies by G. Ouy on this subject, for example 'Jean de Montreuil et l'introduction de l'écriture humanistique en France au début du XVe siècle', in *Essays presented to G.I. Lieftinck, 4: Miniatures, Scripts, Collections*, ed. J. P. Gumbert

Southern Germany (in that of Hartmann Schedel, Hieronymus Rotenpeck and others). Basel and Augsburg especially seem to have been important in this respect.[16] Humanistic features also appear in areas where the commercial contacts with Italy were intense, especially in Flanders. Here Antiqua elements or full imitations are sometimes seen in manuscripts commissioned by wealthy prelates.[17] In some cases it was not Antiqua itself that was adopted, but the very idea of reviving an ancient script. Gumbert has tentatively proposed the name of 'Neoromanesque' for such imitations of earlier scripts from one's own country or region, as encountered in the work of some scribes in Germany, Flanders, England and France.[18] The whole question of the revival of earlier scripts in the fifteenth century, a fascinating subject of interest to the history of learning as well as palaeography, deserves further study.

III OTHER SCRIPTS OUTSIDE THE EXPANDED LIEFTINCK SYSTEM
(plate 157)

It would be an illusion to believe that our expanded Lieftinck classification (or indeed any classification) could encompass the whole range of script forms encountered in books from the various European countries during the last four centuries of the Middle Ages. In this period the freedom of the scribes to choose the details of their handwriting was much greater than it had been before, and the impact of the individual or occasional scribe upon the appearance of a book's script would have been quite important, within the constraints provided by the general type and level of script required by the text (or the customer). Gumbert's well-known two plates featuring 32 samples, showing all possible combinations of Lieftinck's three distinctive letter forms, speak volumes.[19] Nevertheless, it appears that the 'hors système' scripts are for the most part only to be found in the Currens level, in scripts of small size, in documentary scripts and in scripts outside the mainstream of book production. A well-known example of a highly luxurious manuscript in

---

and M. J. M. de Haan, Amsterdam 1976 (Litterae Textuales), pp. 53–61; 'Nicolas de Clamanges (ca. 1360–1437), philologue et calligraphe. Imitation de l'Italie et réaction anti-italienne dans l'écriture d'un humaniste français au début du XVe siècle', in *Renaissance- und Humanistenhandschriften*, pp. 31–50.

[16] M. Steinmann, 'Die humanistische Schrift und die Anfänge des Humanismus in Basel', *Archiv für Diplomatik*, 22 (1976), pp. 376–437; H. Spilling, 'Handschriften des Augsburger Humanistenkreises', in *Renaissance- und Humanistenhandschriften*, pp. 71–84.

[17] See *Vlaamse kunst op perkament* [exhibition catalogue], Bruges 1981, pls. 74–6; A. Derolez, *The Library of Raphael de Marcatellis*, Ghent 1979, pls. 8–10, 14.

[18] Gumbert, 'Italienische Schrift' (see n. 9), especially pp. 67–70.

[19] J. P. Gumbert, 'A Proposal for a Cartesian Nomenclature', in *Essays presented to G.I. Lieftinck*, 4: *Miniatures, Scripts, Collections* (see n. 15), pp. 50–1.

Textualis Formata (Textus Praescissus no less) with looped ascenders is a copy of the rite for the coronation of the English king Edward II, dated 1308.[20]

In general, however, only one form seems to have acquired a more than marginal status: Hybrida with two-compartment **a**. In England this script appears to have been a variant of Anglicana, and was of limited use (see above, p. 140). In the Iberian Peninsula, however, there are quite a large number of manuscripts written in a canonized form of this script, which is clearly a variant of Iberian Hybrida, as noted above (p. 175) (pl. 157).

[20] Thompson, *Introduction*, pl. 189.

Appendix
Observations on majuscules, punctuation, abbreviations, special signs and orthography

MAJUSCULES

At least since Carolingian times the practice had become widespread of marking the beginning of a new sentence by a taller letter from a majuscule alphabet; such letters are commonly called *litterae notabiliores*.[1] This usage of course greatly facilitated reading. The alphabet originally used was (as it is today) the Capital alphabet, but very soon Uncial majuscules were also used, often mixed with Capitals. This would remain the case by and large for the rest of the Middle Ages, but during the twelfth century a new development took place which would result in the highly fanciful and elaborate majuscules so well known in early printing, in which the original form often can hardly be recognized.

Majuscules (also called versals) should not be confused with initials, which form part of the decoration of the codex: the latter were made in colour, or in colour and gold, and were not 'written', but drawn and painted (hence the special term 'lettering'). Majuscules, on the contrary, are part of the script proper, written at the same time, with the same pen and in the same ink as the minuscule script of the text. As a rule, however, their execution involved a larger number of strokes than the corresponding minuscules.

A lack of preliminary research prevents us in what follows from providing more than a few general observations on the majuscules in Gothic book script.[2] Their form and degree of complexity depend to a large extent on the date of the manuscript and its origin, and on the level and the type of the minuscule script with which they are combined. In other words, majuscules will be different according to their use, whether found, for example, in Praegothica, Textualis Formata, Rotunda Libraria or Cursiva Currens. The impact of the individual scribe was also important. Nevertheless, a few general observations may be formulated.

---

[1] This term has the advantage over 'majuscule' in that it covers also letters not keeping to the bilinear scheme proper to the latter.

[2] Literature on majuscules in Gothic manuscripts is almost non-existent, and the examples shown in calligraphic handbooks have to be handled with circumspection. See Battelli, *Lezioni*, p. 227; Brown and Lovett, *Source Book*, pp. 92, 100, 107; Derolez, 'Observations', pp. 7–8; Drogin, *Medieval Calligraphy*, pp. 70, 134, 142–4, 158–9; Harris, *Calligraphy*, pp. 58–61, 78–9, 88–9. Note: the study of majuscules in black and white photographs is often hampered by the red or yellow highlighting applied to them. The latter covers, or cannot be distinguished from, the strokes composing the majuscule.

(a) The main characteristic of Gothic majuscules is their fancifulness; many scribes used various forms for the same letter on the same page.

(b) As they are written with the same pen, held in the same manner, the distribution between bold lines and hairlines (i.e. the shading) will be the same as in the accompanying minuscule script.[3]

(c) The typical Gothic initial, with its extremely bold, round, broad and exaggerated forms (see above, p. 43) seems to have been a model for the Gothic majuscules, at least from the thirteenth century onwards.

(d) The tendency for Gothic majuscules to take on exaggerated forms is extremely conspicuous. An increased width and the combining of curved and angular strokes are especially noticeable features (1, 2).

(e) The problem of how to give the majuscules more body, and thus bring them closer in shape to initials and make them more visible on the page, was resolved by duplicating the vertical or sloping strokes. This was accompanied by taking the letter elements apart (3–5). The deconstruction of the letter is one of the most fundamental characteristics of Gothic majuscules. The idea of writing double **f** at the beginning of words no doubt had its origin in this feature.

(f) In more careful execution, and especially in handwriting of the fourteenth and fifteenth centuries, these strokes were sometimes traced as double or triple hairlines with the corner of the pen, or were traced either horizontally or obliquely (6–8).

(g) Dotting the lobe of letters such as **D, O, P, Q** was another means of giving them more prominence (9).

(h) Except in Italy, a series of thorny projections comparable to spurs were sometimes added at the left of the vertical opening stroke of the majuscules (10). This 'elephant trunk' decoration is not limited to the majuscules of Fractura script, but had also occurred much earlier, especially in German manuscripts (pl. 39).[4]

(i) In general, legibility was sacrificed for display. Lines of text written entirely in Gothic majuscules are generally difficult to decipher and were usually avoided (pl. 146 'AMEN').[5] In spite of this they are sometimes found in codices from certain areas and periods in the form of text incipits immediately following an initial. A much more common practice in Gothic manuscripts was the use of a script of a higher hierarchical level than the script of the text for purposes of display (pls. 96, 99, 105, 119). The use of a majuscule as the first text letter after an initial, in contrast, was a common practice in Gothic manuscripts. Humanistic script would reintroduce the use of rubrics and other text lines written entirely in majuscules, and replaced the elaborate Gothic majuscules with antique Capitals (pls. 69, 71, 134, 160).

[N]   [E]   [S]   [H]

1   2   3   4   5   6   7   8   9   10

[3] There are exceptions to this rule.

[4] See the following German examples: Kirchner, *Scriptura Gothica*, pl. 22b (1313); Thomson, *Bookhands*, pls. 39 (1267), 41 (1297).

[5] Other examples: *CMDNL*, 11, pl. 772 (Northern Netherlands 1475); Thomson, *Bookhands*, pl. 68 (Italy 1301).

PUNCTUATION

Punctuation is a complicated and much debated matter, connected as it is with such different subjects as grammar, prosody, rhetoric, liturgical practice and music, and because it is immediately concerned with the sense of the text.[6] Only its most elementary features can be dealt with here. Modern punctuation is of a syntactical nature, that is, it indicates the grammatical structure of the text. Medieval punctuation had partly the same function, but was to a great extent rhetorical, in other words it underscored the structure of the text (its rhetorical units) as it was read aloud. It not only marked the pauses the reader had to observe while pronouncing the written text and their length, but also the pitch. This is clearly visible in the question-mark (*punctus interrogativus*), of general use in the period studied in the present book, which has its origin in a neume or sign of musical notation, which indicated that the voice had to rise at the end of the sentence (11).

Ancient punctuation theory distinguished three signs for three different pauses: *comma*, for the short pause; *colon*, for the medial pause; and *periodus* for the final pause (which can be replaced by the question-mark). In the so-called Cistercian punctuation system a second sign for a medial pause was added, the *punctus flexus*, which has approximately the shape of figure 7 (12) and was used mainly in Bibles and liturgical books by the scribes of that order, by the Carthusians, Dominicans and the Augustinian Canons of the Windesheim Congregation (pls. 33, 45, 57, 95).

In the late Middle Ages the set of three (or four) punctuation signs recommended by the grammatical treatises is rarely found in Latin manuscripts. Most scribes kept to one or two signs in addition to the question-mark. The point on the baseline, or slightly above it (*punctus*), was frequently used as a sign for all pauses. More sophisticated punctuation normally provided two pauses: *punctus*, which was used for the final pause (where it is followed by a majuscule) and for a short pause; and the 'tick-and-point' (inverted semi-colon) or *punctus elevatus* (13), which likewise indicated a short pause. The final point often took the shape of a semicolon (*punctus versus*). In the fourteenth and fifteenth centuries the points were often replaced by slanting hairline strokes (*virgulae suspensivae* (pls. 68, 71, 139)). The exclamation-mark (*punctus exclamativus*) appeared in the second half of the fourteenth century but was of extremely limited use.[7]

One finds in general a great deal of freedom and inconsistency in the punctuation of later medieval manuscripts especially. Although its importance for understanding the sense of a given text should not be underestimated, the reproduction of medieval punctuation in a modern transcription can render the reading of the text cumbersome and we would generally not

11 12 13

---

[6] Bischoff, *Palaeography*, pp. 169–71; more bibliography is given in Boyle, *Medieval Latin Palaeography*, pp. 265–6; P. Rafti, 'L'interpunzione nel libro manoscritto. Mezzo secolo di studi', *Scrittura e Civiltà*, 12 (1988), pp. 239–98. See also *Grafia e interpunzione del latino nel Medioevo. Seminario internazionale, Roma, 1984*, ed. A. Maierù, Rome 1987 (Lessico Intellettuale Europeo, 41) and especially the fundamental work by M. B. Parkes, *Pause and Effect: An Introduction to the History of Punctuation in the West*, Cambridge 1992.

[7] See examples in Parkes, *Pause and Effect* (see n. 6), pls. 30–9.

recommend it.[8] The same applies to the rendering of the majuscules of the original manuscript, with the additional complication that it is often difficult for the transcriber to know whether the scribe actually intended to write a majuscule or not.

Sloping hairline strokes were used as *hyphens* throughout the period under consideration when words were split at the end of the line. Double hyphens are found from the fourteenth century onwards and are typical of the fifteenth and sixteenth century, especially in Germany, Austria, Scandinavia and the Low Countries (pls. 38, 101, 108, 115, 129, 139). Unusual splittings of words at the end of lines, i.e. splittings falling within a syllable, occurred mostly in Italy (pls. 118, 159). The Portuguese splitting 'se-nhor' is normal.[9]

Parentheses are said to have been introduced by Coluccio Salutati in 1399.[10] They are seen in no more than a few fifteenth-century Gothic manuscripts (pl. 144).

Line-fillers are small signs which the scribe could place in blank spaces at the ends of lines in order to fill them out to the full width.[11] They should not be confused with the decorative line-fillers, which were made by the rubricator or the illuminator to fill up open spaces at the end of incomplete lines, as in psalms, litanies, tables of contents, etc. Many, even luxury manuscripts, do not seem to display much concern to preserve a straight right edge; this is especially so for codices written in a script of the cursive family. But as far as well-made prose manuscripts in Textualis, Rotunda or Semitextualis are concerned, a regular text area seems to have been an ideal which the scribes normally sought to attain. They could make lines of approximately the same length by a judicious use of abbreviations and fusions. In broad scripts with fewer abbreviations this would have been more difficult. That may be the reason why line-fillers were rarely used in Northern Europe, but more frequently in the Mediterranean area, especially in Italian Rotunda, even if there the choice between two forms of final **m** and final **s** allowed some latitude.

In Northern and Southern France, in England, rarely in Germany, a line-filler in a form resembling expunged **i** (14) was sometimes used in the thirteenth and fourteenth centuries (pl. 50).[12] It was not unknown in the Iberian Peninsula.[13] The typical Spanish and Portuguese line-filler in this early period, however, takes the shape of figure 3 (15, pl. 49),[14] later sometimes of figure 2 (pl. 61). In the late fifteenth and in the sixteenth centuries, it would develop into a vertical zigzag line, a duplication of simpler forms typical of that period (16, pl. 76).[15] Many

14   15   16

[8] Most palaeographers are of the contrary opinion; but see G. I. Lieftinck in his review of Kirchner, *Scriptura Gothica* in *Scriptorium*, 22 (1968), pp. 66–71; Strubbe, *Grondbegrippen*, pp. 25–9; Denholm-Young, *Handwriting*, p. 84. Strictly 'diplomatic' transcriptions as provided by Wright, *Vernacular Hands*, are almost illegible for somebody without palaeographical schooling.

[9] See, for example, Burnam, *Palaeographia*, pl. 56 (1442–3), col. a, ll. 3–4.

[10] Parkes, *Pause and Effect* (see n. 6), p. 84.   [11] Bischoff, *Palaeography*, p. 171.

[12] Other French examples: *CMDF*, 11, pls. 32 (1273), 55 (1357); English examples: Thomson, *Bookhands*, pl. 91 (1247?); *CMDGBOx*, pl. 170 (1326–7); an Austrian example: Thomson, *Bookhands*, pl. 44 (1337).

[13] Thomson, *Bookhands*, pl. 119 (1298).   [14] Another example: *CMDF*, 1, pl. 56 (1377–96).

[15] Another example: Burnam, *Palaeographia*, pl. 59.

Spanish and Southern French scribes, on the other hand, adopted the 'Italian' form of line-filler which is a crossed **i** (17, pls. 52, 64), and very occasionally a crossed **o**.[16] Line-fillers seem to have been virtually unknown in the rest of Europe throughout the period, and in Northern France and England after the fourteenth century.

ABBREVIATIONS

All handbooks of palaeography give a full survey of the abbreviations used in medieval manuscripts, discuss the principles on which the various systems are based and provide a classification of the diverse abbreviation techniques.[17] In several chapters of the present book forms of abbreviation typical of specific scripts and regions have briefly been dealt with (pp. 66–8, 96–9, 109–11, 153–4), but a fresh discussion of abbreviations as such would be no more than a duplication of what can easily be found elsewhere. There follow here, therefore, no more than a few especially important observations regarding the practice.

Scholastic manuscripts and those of the thirteenth and fourteenth centuries in general contain without doubt the largest number of abbreviations (mostly specific to the subject concerned: theology, philosophy, law, natural science, medicine...), but the degree of abbreviation is far less in liturgical and literary manuscripts. Since the abbreviation system was developed for Latin texts and exploits features of the spelling and word-formation of that language, it is not surprising that vernacular manuscripts contain only a small quantity of abbreviations. The fifteenth century saw a marked general diminution in the employment of abbreviations and a return to the more moderate use typical of the twelfth century.

Attention should be drawn to two minor variants of the common mark of abbreviation. One is the double horizontal abbreviation stroke (18), the other the curved or semicircular stroke with a dot in its centre (19). The first occurs sometimes in German and Central European manuscripts in Cursiva or Hybrida and perhaps had the value of a 'double abbreviation' (pls. 98, 123, 129, 136). The second is typical of English manuscripts of the fifteenth century, also of the cursive family, but has no special significance.[18] Dotted horizontal marks of abbreviation have been mentioned above (p. 174).

One feature in English vernacular manuscripts can easily be misinterpreted as an abbreviation mark: the so-called 'otiose stroke'. Whereas an extension at the right of the final (or medial) letter of a word, or a stroke added to it, should normally be considered an abbreviation mark, in English vernacular manuscripts, especially those written in cursive scripts, such strokes or extensions

17   18   19

[16]   A few Italian examples: *CMDGBOx*, pls. 164 (1322), 165 (1323), 220 (1384).

[17]   Good surveys (although often focusing on the early Middle Ages) are to be found in Dekker, Baetens and Maarschalkerweerd-Dechamps, *Album palaeographicum*, pp. xxviii–xli; Battelli, *Lezioni*, pp. 101–14; Bischoff, *Palaeography*, pp. 150–68; Cencetti, *Lineamenti*, pp. 353–475; Cencetti, *Compendio*, pp. 89–94; Hector, *Handwriting*, pp. 29–39; Stiennon, *Paléographie*, pp. 145–9. The best general dictionary of abbreviations is still Cappelli, *Lexicon abbreviaturarum*.

[18]   Examples: Parkes, *Book Hands*, pls. 3 i and 8 i. See Denholm-Young, *Handwriting*, p. 83.

often occur without having any grammatical value and pose a serious problem to the transcriber (pl. 105).[19]

Regional variation in the use of abbreviations is difficult to trace in the Gothic period: in the late Middle Ages the system seems to have acquired a large degree of uniformity all over Europe. It is only in the Pregothic script of the Iberian Peninsula that we find multiple remnants of the 'Hebraicized' or consonantal abbreviations typical of Visigothic, such as **apstls** for 'apostolus', **dbli** for 'diaboli', **dcpls** for 'discipulus', **ihnne** for 'Iohanne' (pl. 14), **isrhlita** for 'Israhelita', **mm** for 'meum', **pccm** for 'peccatum', etc. (each identified as an abbreviation by the common mark of abbreviation).

SPECIAL SIGNS AND LETTERS

Except for **e** caudata (in fact a form of **ae**-ligature) and **c** caudata (ç), Latin manuscripts do not normally use any other letter signs than those of the modern Latin alphabet. Some letters may have an accent upon them for reasons of legibility, such as the acute accent on monosyllables, which for a long time were not separated from the ensuing word with a space ('ábeato'; pls. 3, 7, 12).[20] Certain texts were accented throughout for the purposes of reading aloud (pls. 7, 47, 61).

Medieval French texts contain neither accents nor apostrophes nor even **c** caudata (except in Southern France where ç was used). Scribes writing German texts originally used various ways to indicate diphthongs and the umlaut, until from the fourteenth century onwards, superscript **o** over **u** came to be reserved for the diphthong **uo** and superscript **e** for the umlaut, as in **ä**, **ö**, **ü** (pls. 28, 83, 145). The increasing tendency of scribes to write cursively soon meant that superscript **e** was written as two strokes and finally two dots, thus resulting in the modern shape of German umlaut (20).[21] In Latin manuscripts of the fifteenth century, in Germany and especially in the Northern Netherlands, the practice was introduced of marking **u** with a superscript concave curve in order to distinguish it from an adjacent **m** or **n**. This practice has its origin in Cursiva but was adopted by scribes for other scripts. The mark may take the shape of superscript **o** or **v** instead of a curve.[22] It did not change the sound of the letter underneath (21–3).

In late medieval Danish and Swedish manuscripts the diphthong **ae** was represented by the **ae**-ligature, and **o** umlaut by crossed **o**. Both signs may take various shapes (24–7, pls. 37, 91, 115, 154). Scandinavian handwriting retained a special letter for the 'th' sound, which we also find in English manuscripts, where it is called 'thorn'. Even the parallel special letter which

20	21	22	23

24	25	26	27

[19] Parkes, *Book Hands*, pp. xxix–xxx; Hector, *Handwriting*, p. 38.
[20] Bischoff, *Palaeography*, p. 171.
[21] Bischoff, *Palaeography*, pp. 122, 135; Schneider, *Paläographie*, p. 92.
[22] Examples in Textualis: *CMDNL*, 11, pls. 584 (1477), col. b, l. 6, 602 (1496), 608–9 (1509), 618 (1539), all from the Northern Low Countries.

is called 'eth' in Anglo-Saxon palaeography is found in the earliest Swedish manuscripts.[23] English influence on Scandinavian handwriting seems to have been strong.

Two or three special Anglo-Saxon letter forms survived in late medieval English handwriting.[24] 'Wyn', used for the sound 'w', resembling somewhat the letter p (28), tended to disappear during the course of the thirteenth century. It was more and more replaced by **w**, i.e. double **v**. 'Thorn', representing the English 'th' sound, had originally, as in Scandinavia, a form resembling a p with the shaft ascending above the lobe as well as descending below it (29, pl. 9). From the early fourteenth century onwards, the ascender became shorter and the letter generally became indistinguishable from an undotted y (pl. 84). The false modern reading 'ye' instead of 'the' for the definite article has arisen from this, and should be considered a pseudo-archaism. The same sound was expressed in Pregothic manuscripts by the letter 'eth', resembling a Uncial **d** with a cross-stroke through the shaft (30, pl. 9). 'Yogh', a modified form of Insular **g** in the shape of figure 3, was employed for various sounds. Only thorn, however, would play a prominent role right until the end of the Middle Ages.

ORTHOGRAPHY[25]

Orthography does not strictly belong to the domain of palaeography, but the student of that discipline should know that regional differences in Latin orthography are an important help in localizing manuscripts or the area where their scribes were trained. In Germany, for example, **w** was often written where standard spelling requires **ui**, **uu**, or **u**: 'sangwis', 'wlnus' 'conswetudo'; **y** too was frequently written in place of **ii** or **i** ('hys', 'peyor'). Spanish and Portuguese scribes tended to write **b** instead of **p** ('scribtus'; pls. 8, 14), to duplicate consonants ('occulos') or to write single consonants where double ones are required ('flama'). They were also uncertain in their use of **h** ('peribente', 'hodium'; pl. 8). Italian copyists had the same tendency to intrude an **h** or to use single and double consonants inappropriately ('hedificare', 'occassio', 'aparet'; pl. 62). They often betray their origin by their generally poor spelling of Latin (which they no doubt had difficulty in distinguishing from their own language), writing, for example, **g** or **di** for consonantal **i** ('magestas', 'Madius'), and **x** for **s** ('anno milleximo ducenteximo', 'ecclexia'). Such apparently wrong spellings as 'actendere' in Latin, 'tucto' in Italian, 'mectre' in French need not necessarily be judged as such, since what may appear to be successive **c** and **t** (i.e. the **ct**-ligature) could equally represent **tt** (pl. 36): this is obvious in texts in Germanic languages, where there is no doubt that what appears as 'ricter' (in German) and 'dactu' (in Dutch) should

28   29   30

[23] Bischoff, *Palaeography*, p. 125. 'Thorn' in Kirchner, *Scriptura Gothica*, pl. 15 (1281–90); Bröndum-Nielsen, *Palaeografi*, A, figs. 42 (*c.* 1250), 46 (*c.* 1285), 47, 48, etc. 'Eth' in Bröndum-Nielsen, *Palaeografi*, A, fig. 42 (*c.* 1250).

[24] Wright, *Vernacular Hands*, pp. xiv–xv; Denholm-Young, *Handwriting*, pp. 17–19.

[25] See, for example, *Grafia e interpunzione del latino nel Medioevo* (see n. 6). Thomson, *Bookhands*, frequently provides comment on the orthography of the reproduced pages. For the orthography of Italian texts, see F. Ageno, 'Particolarità grafiche di manoscritti volgari', *Italia Medioevale e Umanistica*, 4 (1961), pp. 175–80.

be read 'ritter' and 'dattu' respectively. The supposed **ct** spellings of French and Italian scribes cited above (found also in copies of Latin texts) can, as a matter of course, also be considered 'hypercorrect' spellings, as Gumbert suggests.[26] The same form of ligature was also used for **cc**, giving birth to such apparent (and certainly incorrectly interpreted) spellings as 'pectatrix' in Latin and 'suctession' in French (pl. 136).

[26] On **ct** and **tt**, see Gumbert, *Kartäuser*, pp. 244–5.

Select bibliography

Handbooks are marked by *, atlases by †.

Actas del VIII Coloquio del Comité Internacional de Paleografía Latina, Madrid-Toledo, 1987, Madrid 1990 (Estudios y Ensayos, 6).

Alvarez Marquez, M. C., 'Escritura latina en la plena y baja Edad Media: la llamada "Gotica libraria" en España', *Historia, Instituciones y Documentos,* 12 (1985), pp. 377–410.

Anderson, D. M., *The Art of Written Forms: The Theory and Practice of Calligraphy,* New York 1969.

Aris, R., and von Arx Anderson, D., *Explicatio formarum litterarum: The Unfolding of Letterforms from the First Century to the Fifteenth,* St Paul, Minnesota, 1990.

* Battelli, G., *Lezioni di paleografia,* 3rd edn, Vatican City 1949; 4th edn, Vatican City 1999. References are to the 3rd edn.

* Bischoff, B., *Latin Palaeography: Antiquity and the Middle Ages,* trans. D. Ó Cróinín and D. Ganz, Cambridge 1990 [original title: *Paläographie des römischen Altertums und des abendländischen Mittelalters,* Berlin 1979, no plates; French trans. J. Vezin and H. Atsma: *Paléographie de l'Antiquité romaine et du Moyen Age occidental,* Paris 1985; Italian trans. G. P. Mantovani and S. Zamponi: *Paleografia latina. Antichità e Medioevo,* Padua 1992 (Medioevo e Umanesimo)].

Boyle, L. E., *Medieval Latin Palaeography: A Bibliographical Introduction,* Toronto, Buffalo and London 1984 (Toronto Medieval Bibliographies, 8) [updated Italian trans. M. E. Bertoldi: *Paleografia Latina medievale. Introduzione bibliografica con supplemento 1982–1998,* Rome 1999].

* Bröndum-Nielsen, J. (ed.), *Palaeografi.* A. *Danmark og Sverige,* Stockholm, Oslo and Copenhagen 1944; B. *Norge og Island,* by D. A. Seip, Stockholm, Oslo and Copenhagen 1954.

† Brown, M. P., *A Guide to Western Historical Scripts from Antiquity to 1600,* London and Toronto 1990.

Brown, M. P., and Lovett, P., *The Historical Source Book for Scribes,* London 1999.

† Burnam, J. M., *Palaeographia Iberica. Fac-similés de manuscrits espagnols et portugais (IXe-XVe siècles),* Paris 1912–25.

† Canellas, A., *Exempla scripturarum Latinarum in usum scholarum,* 2 vols., 3rd edn of vol. I, 2nd edn of vol. II, Saragossa 1967–74 [vol. II deals with Spanish manuscripts].

Cappelli, A., *Lexicon abbreviaturarum. Dizionario di abbreviature latine ed italiane,* 3rd edn, Milan 1929 [many repr. since].

Casamassima, E., *Tradizione corsiva e tradizione libraria nella scrittura latina del Medioevo*, Rome 1999 [1st edn 1988].

* Cencetti, G., *Compendio di paleografia latina per le scuole universitarie e archivistiche*, Naples 1968 [repr. with new illustrations and updated bibliography by P. Supino Martini, Rome 1978 (Guide allo Studio della Civiltà Romana, 10,3)]. References are to the original edn.

 * *Lineamenti di storia della scrittura latina*, Bologna 1954 (Paleografia e Diplomatica) [new edn by G. Guerini Ferri, Bologna 1997]. References are to the first edn.

Codicologica: A. Gruijs, M. J. M. de Haan and J. P. Gumbert (eds.), *Codicologica: Towards a Science of Handwritten Books. Vers une science du manuscrit*, Leiden 1976– (Litterae Textuales).

Creasy, D. L., *The Development of the Formal Gothic Script in Spain: Toledo, XIIth–XIIIth Centuries*, Cincinnati 1984.

† Crous, E., and Kirchner, J., *Die gotischen Schriftarten*, Leipzig 1928 [repr. Brunswick 1970].

* Cruz, A., *Paleografia Portuguesa. Ensaio de manual*, Porto 1987.

† Da Costa, A. de Jesus, *Album de paleografia e diplomatica portuguesas*, 4th edn, Coimbra 1983.

† Dekker, C., Baetens, R., and Maarschalkerweerd-Dechamps, S., *Album palaeographicum XVII Provinciarum. Paleografisch album van Nederland, België, Luxemburg en Noord-Frankrijk. Album de paléographie des Pays-Bas, de Belgique, du Luxembourg et du Nord de la France*, Turnhout 1992.

De la Mare, A. C., *The Handwriting of Italian Humanists*, I, 1, Oxford 1973.

† Denholm-Young, N., *Handwriting in England and Wales*, 2nd edn, Cardiff 1964.

Derolez, A., 'Observations on the Aesthetics of the Gothic Manuscript', *Scriptorium*, 50 (1996), pp. 3–12, pls. 1–5, 13–17.

Destrez, J., *La pecia dans les manuscrits universitaires du XIIIe et du XIVe siècle*, Paris 1935.

Drogin, M., *Medieval Calligraphy: Its History and Technique*, Montclair and London 1980.

† Ehrle, F., and Liebaert, P., *Specimina codicum latinorum Vaticanorum*, 2nd edn, Berlin and Leipzig 1932 (Tabulae in Usum Scholarum, 3).

Engelhart, B., and Klein, J. W., *50 eeuwen schrift. Een inleiding tot de geschiedenis van het schrift*, Amsterdam 1986.

La escritura e su historia. III Curso de Benassal: Paleografía. Benassal, Castellón, 1986, Barcelona 1992 [offprint of *Anuario de Estudios Medievales*, 21 (1991)].

† Federici, V., *La scrittura delle cancellerie italiane dal secolo XII al XVII. Fac-simili per le Scuole di Paleografia degli Archivi di Stato*, Rome 1934.

Fichtenau, H., *Die Lehrbücher Maximilians I. und die Anfänge der Frakturschrift*, Hamburg 1961.

 Mensch und Schrift im Mittelalter, Vienna 1946 (Veröffentlichungen des Instituts für Österreichische Geschichtsforschung, 5).

* Foerster, H., *Abriss der lateinischen Paläographie*, 2nd edn, Stuttgart 1963.

 †*Mittelalterliche Buch- und Urkundenschriften*, Bern 1946.

Frenz, T., 'Gotische Gebrauchsschriften des 15. Jahrhunderts. Untersuchungen zur Schrift lateinisch-deutscher Glossare am Beispiel des "Vocabularius ex quo"', *Codices Manuscripti*, 7 (1981), pp. 14–30.

* García Villada, Z., *Paleografía española, precedida de una introducción sobre la paleografía latina*, Madrid 1923 [repr. Barcelona 1974].

* Gasparri, F., *Introduction à l'histoire de l'écriture*, Louvain-la-Neuve 1994 (Reference Works for the Study of Mediaeval Civilisation).

Gilissen, L., *L'expertise des écritures médiévales. Recherche d'une méthode avec application à un manuscrit du XIe siècle: le Lectionnaire de Lobbes, codex Bruxellensis 18018*, Ghent 1973 (Les Publications de Scriptorium, 6).

Gumbert, J. P., 'Iets over laatmiddeleeuwse schrifttypen, over hun onderscheidingen en benamingen', *Archives et Musées de Belgique*, 46 (1975), pp. 275–82.

Die Utrechter Kartäuser und ihre Bücher im frühen fünfzehnten Jahrhundert, Leiden 1974.

Harris, D., *The Art of Calligraphy*, London, New York and Stuttgart 1995.

† Hector, L. C., *The Handwriting of English Documents*, 2nd edn, London 1966.

John, J. J., 'Latin Paleography', in J. M. Powell (ed.), *Medieval Studies: An Introduction*, Syracuse, NY, 1976, pp. 1–68 [2nd edn, 1992, pp. 3–81].

Kapr, A., *The Art of Lettering: The History, Anatomy, and Aesthetics of the Roman Letter Forms*, trans. I. Kimber, Munich 1983 [original German edn, Dresden 1971].

† Katterbach, B., Pelzer, A., and Silva-Tarouca, C., *Codices latini saeculi XIII*, Rome 1929 (Exempla Scripturarum, I).

† Kirchner, J., *Scriptura Gothica libraria a saeculo XII usque ad finem Medii Aevi*, Munich and Vienna 1966.

†*Scriptura Latina libraria a saeculo primo usque ad finem Medii Aevi*, LXXVII *imaginibus illustrata*, 2nd edn, Munich 1970.

Kisseleva, L. I., *Goticeskij kursiv XIII–XV vekov* [Gothic cursive, thirteenth–fifteenth centuries], Leningrad 1974 [Summary: *Scriptorium*, 30 (1976), p. 182].

Knight, S., *Historical Scripts from Classical Times to the Renaissance*, 2nd edn, New Castle, Delaware, 1998.

Loeffler, K., *Einführung in die Handschriftenkunde*, new edn by W. Milde, Stuttgart 1997 (Bibliothek des Buchwesens, 11) [original edn Leipzig 1929].

Mazal, O., 'Beobachtungen zu österreichischen Buchschriften des 14. Jahrhunderts', *Codices Manuscripti*, 16 (1992), 9, pp. 1–26; also *Scriptorium*, 54 (2000), pp. 40–63.

Buchkunst der Gotik, Graz 1975 (Buchkunst im Wandel der Zeiten, 1).

Buchkunst der Romanik, Graz 1978 (Buchkunst im Wandel der Zeiten, 2).

Lehrbuch der Handschriftenkunde, Wiesbaden 1986 (Elemente des Buch- und Bibliothekswesens, 10).

Paläographie und Paläotypie. Zur Geschichte der Schrift im Zeitalter der Inkunabeln, Stuttgart 1984 (Bibliothek des Buchwesens, 8).

Meyer, W., *Die Buchstaben-Verbindungen der sogenannten gothischen Schrift*, Berlin 1897 (Abhandlungen der königlichen Gesellschaft der Wissenschaften zu Göttingen, Philologisch-historische Klasse, N.S., 1, 6).

* Millares Carlo, A., *Tratado de paleografía española*, 3rd edn by J. M. Ruiz Asencio, Madrid 1983.

Morison, S., '"Black-Letter" Text', in S. Morison, *Selected Essays on the History of Letter-Forms in Manuscript and Print*, ed. D. McKitterick, Cambridge and New York 1981, pp. 177–205 [first published 1942].

Muzerelle, D., *Vocabulaire codicologique. Répertoire méthodique des termes français relatifs aux manuscrits*, Paris 1985 (Rubricae, 1) [Italian version: M. Maniaci, *Terminologia del libro manoscritto*, Rome 1996; Spanish version: P. Ostos, M. L. Pardo and E. E. Rodríguez, *Vocabulario de codicología*, Madrid 1997].

Nomenclature des écritures livresques du IXe au XVIe siècle, by B. Bischoff, G. I. Lieftinck and G. Battelli, Paris 1954 (Colloques Internationaux du C.N.R.S., Sciences Humaines, 4).

Noordzij, G., *The Stroke of the Pen: Fundamental Aspects of Western Writing*, The Hague 1982.

Obbema, P. F. J., 'De opkomst van een nieuw schrifttype: de littera hybrida', in P. Obbema, *De middeleeuwen in handen. Over de boekcultuur in de late middeleeuwen*, Hilversum 1996, pp. 69–76 [this is the final version of 'A Comparison of Dated Latin and Middle-Dutch Manuscripts', in *Miscellanea Martin Wittek*, ed. A. Raman and E. Manning, Louvain and Paris 1993, pp. 285–93].

Oeser, W., 'Das *a* als Grundlage für Schriftvarianten in der gotischen Buchschrift', *Scriptorium*, 25 (1971), pp. 25–45.

'Beobachtungen zur Entstehung und Verbreitung schleifenloser Bastarden', *Archiv für Diplomatik*, 38 (1992), pp. 235–343.

'Beobachtungen zur Strukturierung und Variantenbildung der Textura. Ein Beitrag zur Paläographie des Hoch- und Spätmittelalters', *Archiv für Diplomatik*, 40 (1994), pp. 359–439.

Orlandelli, G., 'Origine del gotico e scritture scolastiche', in G. Orlandelli, *Scritti di paleografia e diplomatica*, ed. R. Ferrara and G. Feo, Bologna 1994, pp. 247–54 [originally published 1981].

'Osservazioni sulla scrittura mercantesca nei secoli XIV e XV', in *Studi in onore di Riccardo Filangieri*, 1, Naples 1959, pp. 445–60.

Paläographie 1981. Colloquium des Comité International de Paléographie, München, 1981. Referate, ed. G. Silagi, Munich 1982 (Münchener Beiträge zur Mediävistik und Renaissance-Forschung, 32).

† Parkes, M. B., *English Cursive Book Hands 1250–1500*, Oxford 1969.

Persoons, E., 'De vier soorten boekschrift van de Moderne Devoten', in *Bijdragen over Thomas a Kempis en de Moderne Devotie*, Brussels 1971 (Archives et Bibliothèques de Belgique, No. spécial, 4), pp. 90–102.

Petrucci, A., *La descrizione del manoscritto. Storia, problemi, modelli*, Rome 1984.

Breve storia della scrittura latina, Rome 1989.

† Petzet, E., and Glauning, O., *Deutsche Schrifttafeln des IX. bis XVI. Jahrhunderts aus Handschriften der Bayerischen Staatsbibliothek München*, Munich and Leipzig 1910–30 [repr. in one vol., Hildesheim and New York 1975].

Poulle, E., 'L'écriture latine au Moyen Age', in *L'écriture: le cerveau, l'oeil et la main*, ed. C. Sirat, J. Irigoin and E. Poulle, Turnhout 1990 (Bibliologia, 10), pp. 335–48.

†*Paléographie des écritures cursives en France du XVe au XVIIe siècle. Recueil de fac-similés de documents parisiens*, Geneva 1966.

* Prou, M., *Manuel de paléographie latine et française du VIe au XVIIe siècle*, 4th edn, with the collaboration of A. de Boüard, Paris 1924 [1st edn Paris 1889].

Renaissance- und Humanistenhandschriften, ed. J. Autenrieth, Munich 1988 (Schriften des Historischen Kollegs. Kolloquien, 13).

* Reusens, E., *Eléments de paléographie*, Louvain 1899.

Romanova, V. L., *Rukopisnaya kniga i goticheskoe pis'mo vo Francii v XIII–XIV vv.* [The manuscript book in Gothic script in France during the thirteenth and fourteenth centuries], Moscow 1975.

* Schneider, K., *Paläographie und Handschriftenkunde für Germanisten. Eine Einführung*, Tübingen 1999 (Sammlung kurzer Grammatiken germanischer Dialekte. Ergänzungsreihe, 8).

†*Gotische Schriften in deutscher Sprache*, Wiesbaden 1987– .

Un secolo di paleografia e diplomatica (1887–1986). Per il centenario dell' Istituto di Paleografia dell' Università di Roma, ed. A. Petrucci and A. Pratesi, Rome 1988.

Spilling, H., 'Schreibkünste des Mittelalters', *Codices Manuscripti*, 4 (1978), pp. 97–119.

Spunar, P., 'Zum Aufkommen der gotischen Kursive in Mitteleuropa', *Scriptorium*, 54 (2000), pp. 14–19 [paper dating from 1990].

'L'évolution et la fonction de la bâtarde en Bohème et en Pologne', *Studia Źródłoznawcze*, 6 (1961), pp. 1–19.

Le statut du scripteur. Actes du XIIe Colloque scientifique du Comité International de Paléographie Latine (Cluny 1998), ed. M.-C. Hubert, E. Poulle and M. Smith, Paris 2000 (Matériaux pour l'Histoire, 2).

† Steffens, F., *Lateinische Paläographie*, 2nd edn, Berlin and Leipzig 1929.

Steinmann, M., 'Vom *D*', in *Litterae Medii Aevi. Festschrift für Johanne Autenrieth zu ihrem 65. Geburtstag*, ed. M. Borgolte and H. Spilling, Sigmaringen 1988, pp. 293–300.

'Textualis formata', *Archiv für Diplomatik*, 25 (1979), pp. 301–27.

* Stiennon, J., *Paléographie du Moyen Age*, 3rd edn, Paris 1999 [1st edn 1973].

* Strubbe, E., *Grondbegrippen van de paleografie der Middeleeuwen*, 2nd edn, Ghent 1961.

Supino Martini, P., 'Per la storia della "semigotica"', *Scrittura e Civiltà*, 22 (1998), pp. 249–64.

* Thompson, E. M., *An Introduction to Greek and Latin Palaeography*, Oxford 1912.

† Thomson, S. H., *Latin Bookhands of the Later Middle Ages, 1100–1500*, Cambridge 1969.

Updike, D. B., *Printing Types. Their History, Forms and Use: A Study in Survivals*, Cambridge, Mass., and London 1962.

† Van den Gheyn, J., *Album belge de paléographie. Recueil de spécimens d'écritures d'auteurs et de manuscrits belges (VIIe–XVIe siècles)*, Brussels 1908.

Wattenbach, W., *Das Schriftwesen im Mittelalter*, 3rd edn, Leipzig 1896.

Wehmer, C., 'Die Namen der gotischen Buchschriften', *Zentralblatt für Bibliothekswesen*, 49 (1932), pp. 11–34, 169–76, 222–34.

† Wright, C. E., *English Vernacular Hands from the Twelfth to the Fifteenth Centuries*, Oxford 1960.

Zamponi, S., 'Elisione e sovrapposizione nella *littera textualis*', *Scrittura e Civiltà*, 12 (1988), pp. 135–76.

'La scrittura del libro nel Duecento', in *Civiltà comunale: Libro, scrittura, documento. Atti del Convegno, Genova, 1988*, Genoa 1989, pp. 317–54.

Acknowledgements for illustrations

The author and the publisher wish to thank the following for their kind permission to re-produce the plates: Universiteitsbibliotheek Amsterdam (UvA) (pl. 129), Staatsbibliothek zu Berlin Preussischer Kulturbesitz (pls. 17, 58, 68, 103, 125, 138); Koninklijke Bibliotheek Albert I/Bibliothèque Royale Albert Ier, Brussels (pls. 22, 31, 104, 120, 123, 139); the Master and Fellows of Corpus Christi College, Cambridge (pls. 27, 102); The Fitzwilliam Museum, Cambridge (pls. 12, 21, 25–6, 30, 39, 46, 51, 62, 74, 76); the Syndics of Cambridge University Library (pls. 4, 42, 67, 73, 77, 81, 84–6, 93, 105); Det Kongelige Bibliotek, Copenhagen (pl. 115); The Metropolitan Chapter, Cracow (pl. 116); Stadsarchief en Athenaeumbibliotheek, Deventer (pl. 101); Biblioteca Medicea Laurenziana, Florence, by permission of the Ministero per i Beni e le Attività Culturali; any further reproduction, by whatever means, is forbidden (pl. 89); Biblioteca Riccardiana, Florence; any further reproduction, by whatever means, is forbidden (pl. 54); Universiteitsbibliotheek, Ghent (pl. 24); Bibliotheek der Rijksuniversiteit, Groningen (pl. 143); Koninklijke Bibliotheek, The Hague (pls. 11, 32, 100, 107); Museum Meermanno-Westreenianum, The Hague (pl. 5); Universiteitsbibliotheek Leiden (pls. 10, 122, 140–1); Biblioteca Nacional, Lisbon (pls. 14, 61, 128); Universitetsbiblioteket, Lund (pl. 37); Biblioteca Nacional, Madrid (pls. 8, 47, 49, 64, 71, 75, 121, 126, 130); The Beinecke Rare Book and Manuscript Library, Yale University Library, New Haven (pls. 15–16, 18, 65, 69, 124, 149, 159); Biblioteca Pública Municipal, Porto (pls. 48, 57); Stedelijk Museum Roermond (pl. 56); Kungliga Biblioteket, Stockholm (pls. 38, 91, 145, 154); Universiteitsbibliotheek Utrecht (pls. 33, 40, 82, 127, 142, 151); Biblioteca Apostolica Vaticana, Vatican City (pls. 92, 118–19, 133); Österreichische Nationalbibliothek, Vienna (pls. 28, 34–5, 44, 78, 95, 111); Biblioteka Narodowa, Warsaw (pl. 156). For the remainder of the plates permission has been granted by the Comité International de Paléographie Latine to reproduce the photographs made for the *Catalogue des manuscrits en écriture latine portant des indications de date, de lieu ou de copiste*.

Index of the manuscripts reproduced in the plates

General index

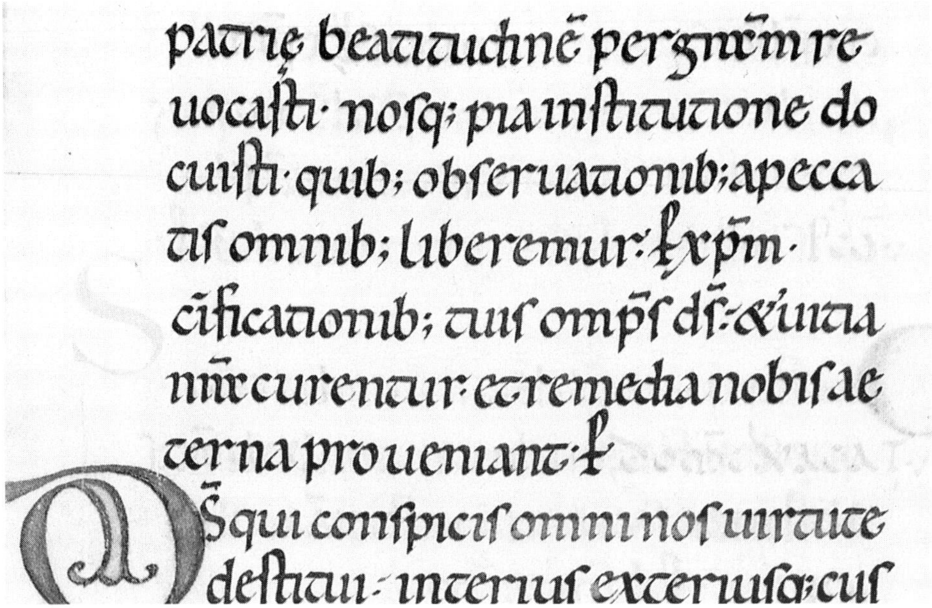

Pl. 1. *Sacramentarium*, copied in the abbey of Saint-Wandrille (diocese of Rouen) between 1033 and 1053. Rouen, Bibl. mun., MS 272, f. 16r (another page: *CMDF*, VII, pl. 14): patriẹ beatitudinem per gratiam re/vocasti nosque pia institutione do/cuisti quibus observationibus a pecca/tis

A large round late Carolingian script, still using cursive **a** in addition to the normal Carolingian one, **ae** in addition to **ẹ**. Note the abbreviations for **bus** and **que**.

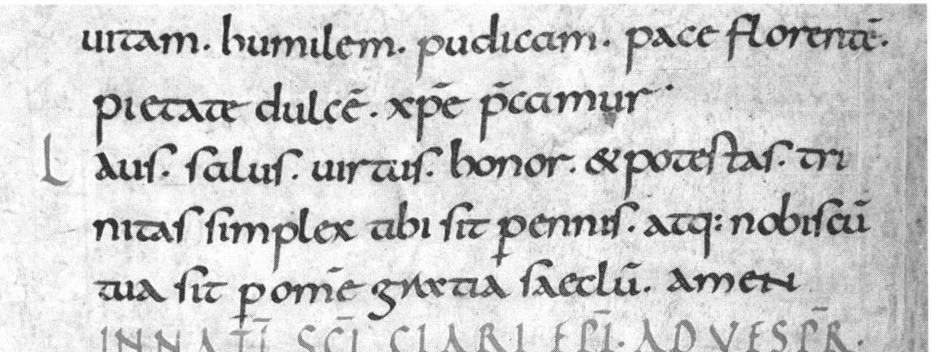

Pl. 2. *Psalterium-Hymnarium*, copied in the abbey of Saint-Aubin in Angers in the second half of the eleventh century. Angers, Bibl. mun., MS 19, f. 106v (*CMDF*, VII, pl. 182): vitam humilem, pudicam, pace florentem, / pietate dulcem, Christe, precamur

A late example of Carolingian script with a quite early general aspect and several early features: three forms of **a**, two forms of **n** and **r**, **f** extending below the baseline. The treatment of the shaft of **h** on the baseline is the only element pointing to Pregothic script. Rubric in Rustic Capitals. The punctuation consists of *distinctiones* and, elsewhere in the manuscript, *punctus*, *punctus elevatus* and *punctus flexus*.

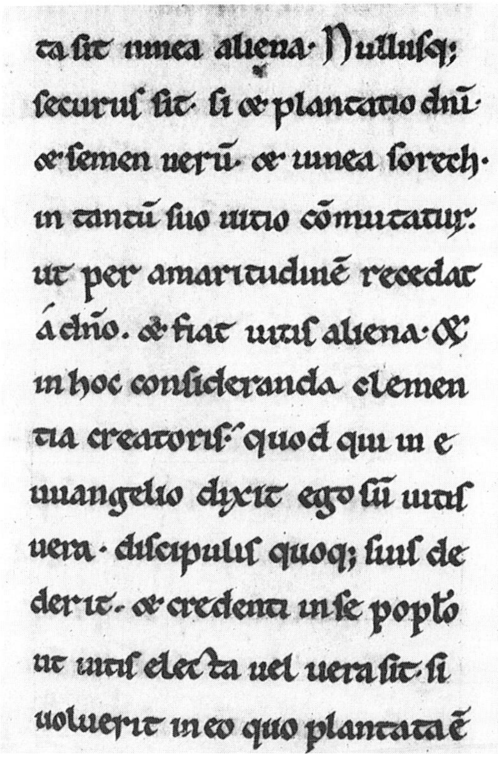

Pl. 3. Hieronymus, *Commentum in Ieremiam*, copied in the abbey of St Vaast in Arras, *c.* 1125. Dijon, Bibl. mun., MS 130, f. 11ra (another page: *CMDF*, VI, pl. 11): [fac]ta sit vinea aliena. Nullusque / securus sit, si et plantatio Domini / et semen verum et vinea sorech / in tantum suo vitio commutatur, / ut per amaritudinem recedat / a Domino

Praegothica, close to Carolingian script in its lack of horizontal and vertical compression and its letter forms. Its boldness, the treatment of the feet of minims and ascenders and the short ascenders and descenders, however, point to an advanced degree of gothicizing. Note **a** with extremely small upper section, Half-Uncial **d**, straight **s** in final position, the wide **ct**-ligature and the pointed and lengthened **r** on the bottom line. The punctuation consists of *punctus* and *punctus elevatus*. The accent on **á** (l. 6) marks the monosyllable.

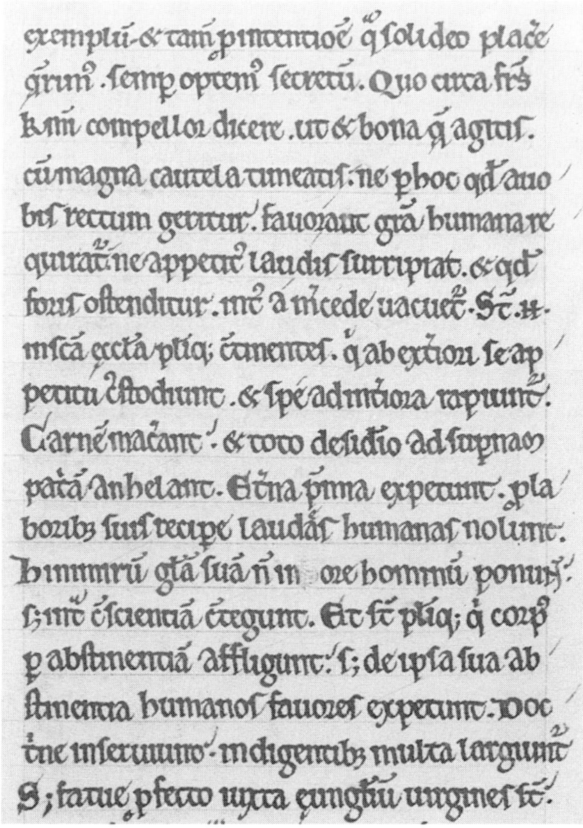

Pl. 4. Guillelmus Malmesberiensis, *Deflorationes Gregorii*, copied in the abbey of Malmesbury, before 1137. Cambridge, Univ. Libr., MS ii.3.20, f. 74rb (*CMDGBCam*, pl. 59): exemplum et tamen pro intentione qua soli Deo placere / quęrimus, semper optemus secretum. Quocirca, fratres / karissimi, compellor dicere ut et bona quę agitis

Praegothica. Note the exclusive use of straight **d** and the ampersand and the almost exclusive use of straight **s** in final position (an exception: 'fratres', l. 2). Uncial **m** is found in final position at the end of lines (l. 10); also in final position the **nt**-ligature (l. 13 'ponunt'); **ct** is not treated as a ligature (l. 5 'rectum'). The cedilla is appended to **q** for abbreviated 'quę'. Among the numerous abbreviations is also Insular **enim** (l. 7).

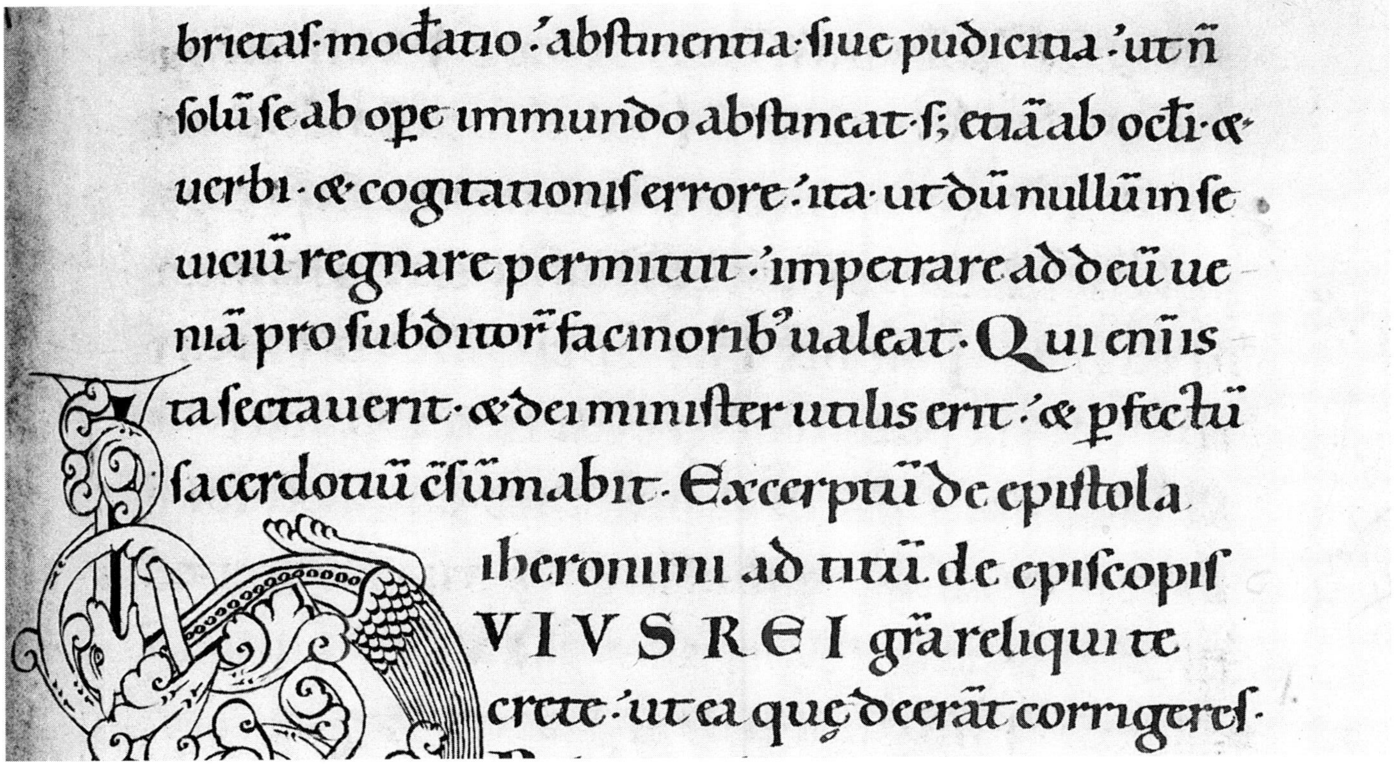

Pl. 5. *Regulae canonicae*, Utrecht, after 1138. The Hague, Mus. Meermanno-Westreenianum, MS 10 B 17, f. 73r (*CMDNL*, 1, pl. 71): [so]/brietas, moderatio, abstinentia sive pudicitia, ut non / solum se ab opere immundo abstineat, sed etiam ab oculi et / verbi et cogitationis errore, ita ut, dum nullum in se / vicium regnare permittit, impetrare ad Deum

A round and broad Praegothica showing few Pregothic features. Two forms of **d** (Uncial **d** has a conspicuous serif at the top of its shaft); round or straight **s** in final position; no round **r**; **ct** is either a ligature or no ligature ('sectaverit', 'perfectum', l. 6).

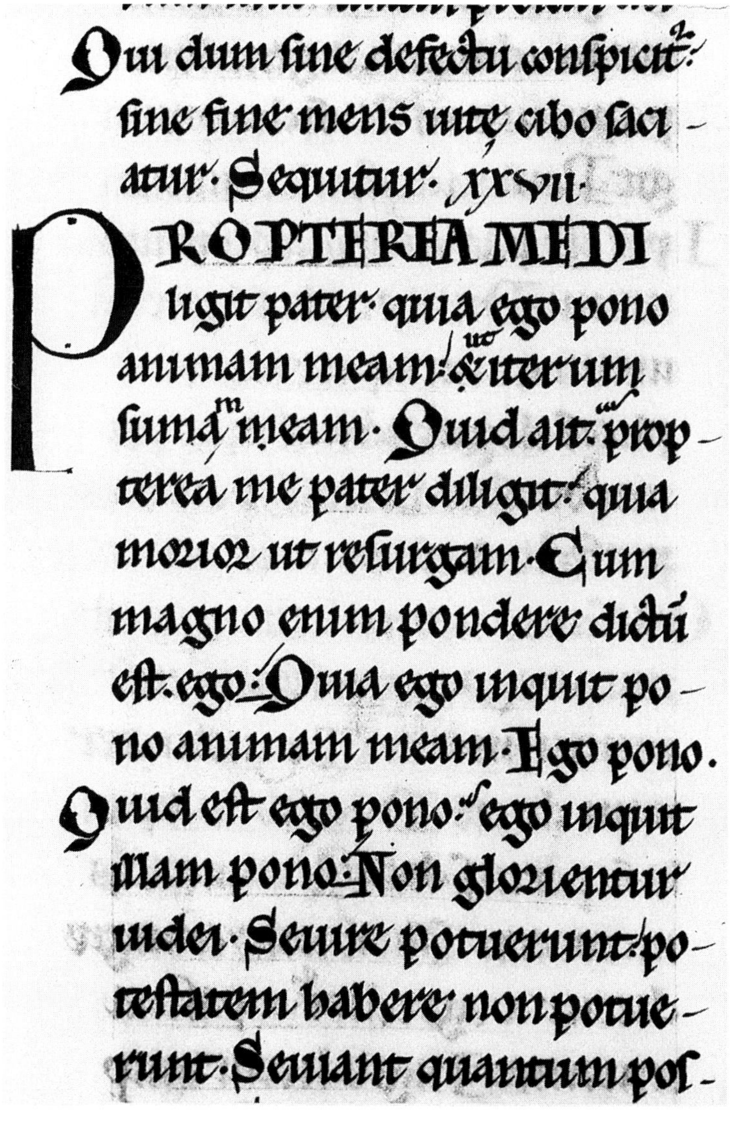

Qui dum sine defectu conspicit⸴
sine fine mens vitę cibo saci -
atur. Sequitur. xxvii·

P ROPTEREA MEDI
ligit pater· quia ego pono
animam meam/& iterum
sumᵐ meam. Quid ait· prop -
terea me pater diligit· quia
morior ut resurgam· Cum
magno enim pondere· dictú
eft. ego: Quia ego inquit po -
no animam meam· Ego pono.
Quid est ego pono· ego inquit
illam pono: Non glorientur
iudei. Seuire potuerunt· po -
testatem habere· non potue -
runt· Seuiant quantum pos -

Pl. 6. Alcuinus, *Commentum in Iohannem*, copied in the abbey of Clairvaux in the middle of
the twelfth century. Troyes, Bibl. mun., MS 441, f. 112v (*CMDF*, v, pl. 196): Qui dum sine
defectu conspicitur, / sine fine mens vitę cibo saci/atur. Sequitur. XXVII. / Propterea me
di/ligit Pater, quia ego pono / animam meam

In spite of the wide distance between the lines, an advanced specimen of Pregothic script,
bold, narrow and angular, with marked 'Gothic' treatment of the feet of ascenders and
minims. Note round **s** in final position ('mens', l. 2), **e** caudata, the conspicuous round **r**
('morior', l. 9), and the 'atrophied' **ct**-ligature ('defectu', l. 1). The punctuation consists of
punctus, *punctus elevatus* and *punctus interrogativus*. Correction is by expunction ('et', l. 6) and
superscript writing. The incipit is in Capitals.

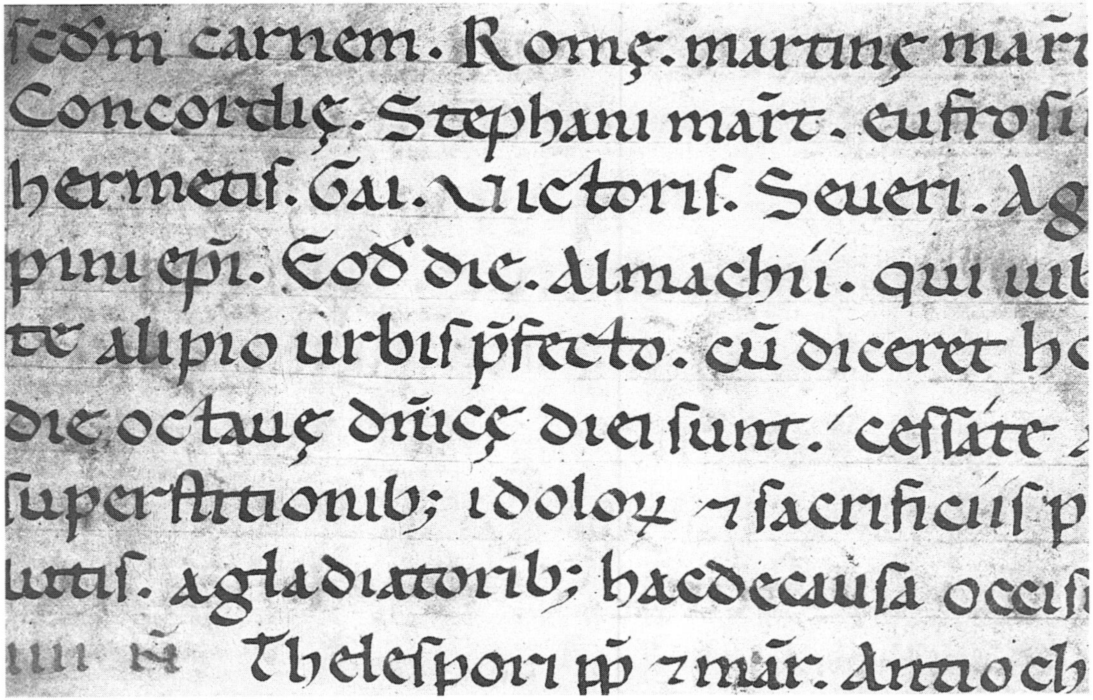

Pl. 7. *Martyrologium*, copied in the abbey of San Gregorio in Venice in 1157. Metz, Bibl. mun., MS 1154, f. 1v (*CMDF*, v, pl. 17): secundum carnem. Romę Martinę martyris, / Concordię Stephani martyris, Eufrosi[i], / Hermetis, Gai, Victoris, Severi Ag[rip]/pini episcopi. Eodem die Almachii, qui iub[en]/te Alipio Urbis prefecto, cum diceret

A large Praegothica still close to Carolingian script. Note the 8-shaped **g**, the **ct**-ligature, the **bus**-abbreviation, the 'Southern' form of the tironian sign, the accents ('cessáte', l. 6), the incomplete word separation ('hacdecausa', l. 8), the **pp** fusion ('papę', l. 9); straight **d** is still used in addition to Uncial **d**.

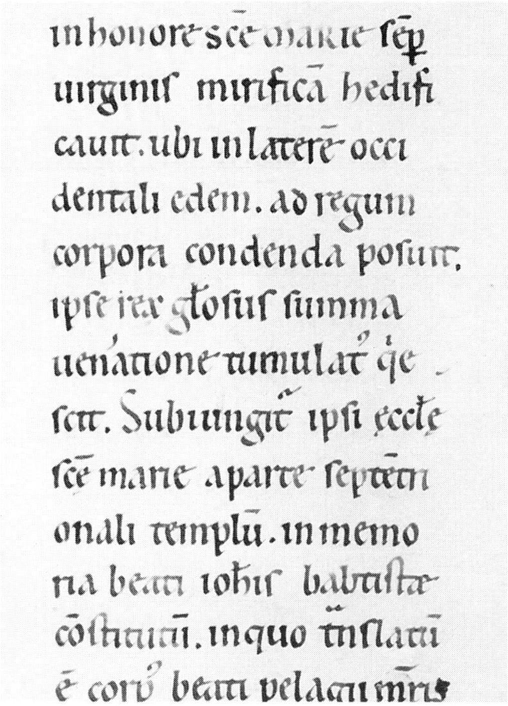

Pl. 8. *Excerptum ex Adefonsi regis Legionensis chronica*, Compostella, 1160. Madrid, Bibl. Nacional, MS 1358, f. 30rb (Canellas, *Exempla*, II, pl. 37): in honore sancte Marie semper / virginis mirificam hedifi/cavit, ubi in laterem occi/dentali edem ad regum / corpora condenda posuit

In this Spanish Praegothica ('Galician Carolina' according to Canellas) the following features are typical: **a**, the two forms of **d**, **f**, **g**, **x** ('rex', l. 6), **r** sometimes extending below the baseline, the **r**-abbreviation ('veneratione', l. 7), and the Iberian spellings 'hedificavit' and 'Babtistae' (l. 11, still with **ae**-ligature).

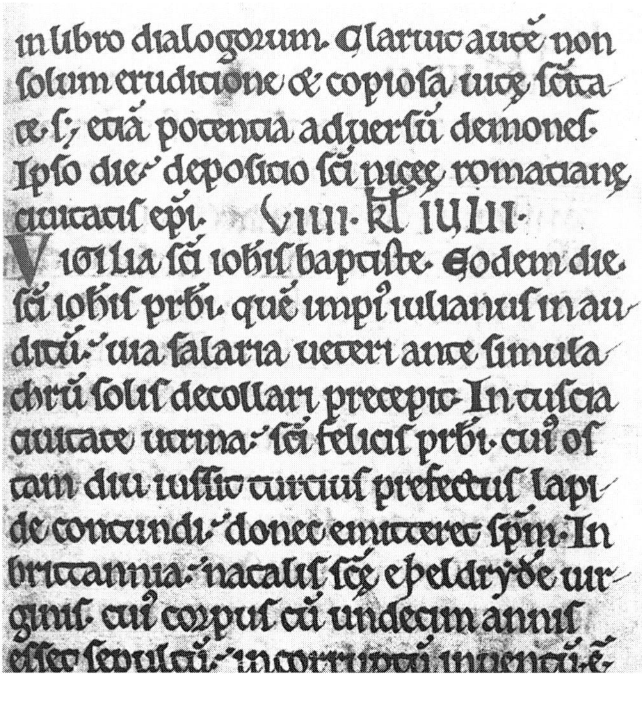

Pl. 9. *Calendarium*, copied in the priory of Wareham, *c.* 1173. Evreux, Bibl. mun., MS 17, f. 70r (*CMDF*, VII, pl. 48): in libro dialogorum. Claruit autem non / solum eruditione et copiosa vitę sanctita/te, sed etiam potentia adversum demones. / Ipso die depositio sancti Niceę Romatianę / civitatis episcopi. VIIII kal. Iulii. / Vigilia sancti Iohannis Baptiste

Praegothica. Note the bold round letter forms, the very short ascenders, straight **d**, straight **s** in final position; the ampersand; on l. 13 the two Anglo-Saxon letters thorn and eth ('Eþeldryðe').

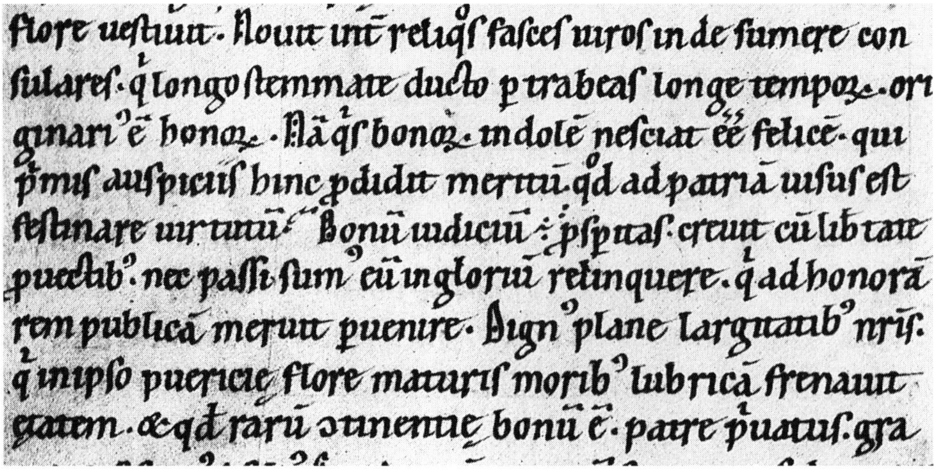

Pl. 10. Cassiodorus, *Variae*, etc., copied in the abbey of Fulda, 1176–7. Leiden, Univ. Libr., MS Vulc. 46, f. 32r (*CMDNL*, I, pl. 89): flore vestivit. Novit inter reliquos fasces viros inde sumere con/sulares, qui longo stemmate ducto per trabeas longe temporum ori/ginarius est honorum

Praegothica. Note in this somewhat irregular hand **f**, **r**, **s** slightly descending below the baseline, the stroked **ii** ('auspiciis', l. 4), the high **ct**-ligature, the **est**-abbreviation (l. 5) and the typical German **con**-abbreviation ('continentię', l. 9); round **r** is not used.

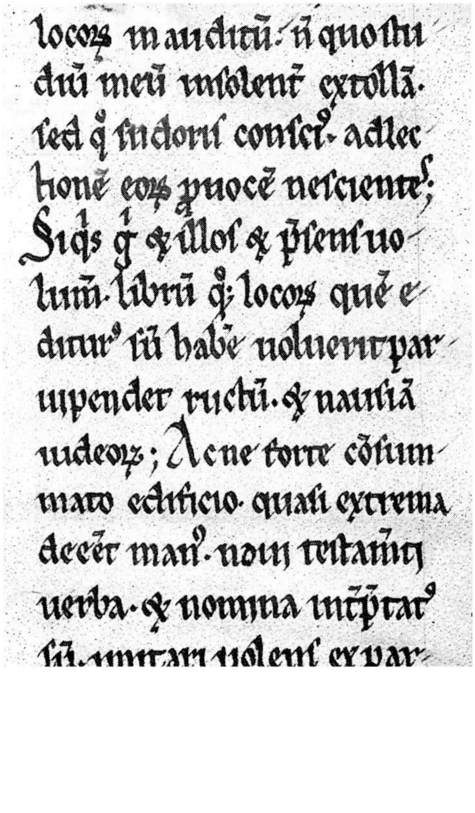

Pl. 11. Hieronymus, *De viris illustribus*, etc., copied in the abbey of Bonne-Espérance in Belgium, 1178–83. The Hague, Royal Libr., MS 76 E 15, f. 56rb (*CMDNL*, I, pl. 99): locorum inauditum, non quo stu/dium meum insolenter extollam, / sed quo sudoris conscius ad lec/tionem eorum provocem nesciente

A compressed Praegothica with relatively long ascenders and descenders. Note **i** longa ('par/vipendet', ll. 7–8), the unusual form of the ampersand, the two different **orum**-abbreviations ('locorum', l. 1, 'Iudeorum', l. 9), the **ct**-ligature maintained even when the two letters are separated ('lec/tionem', ll. 3–4), the superscript **s** at the end of the line (l. 4). The punctuation consists of *punctus* (at mid-height), *punctus elevatus* and *punctus versus*.

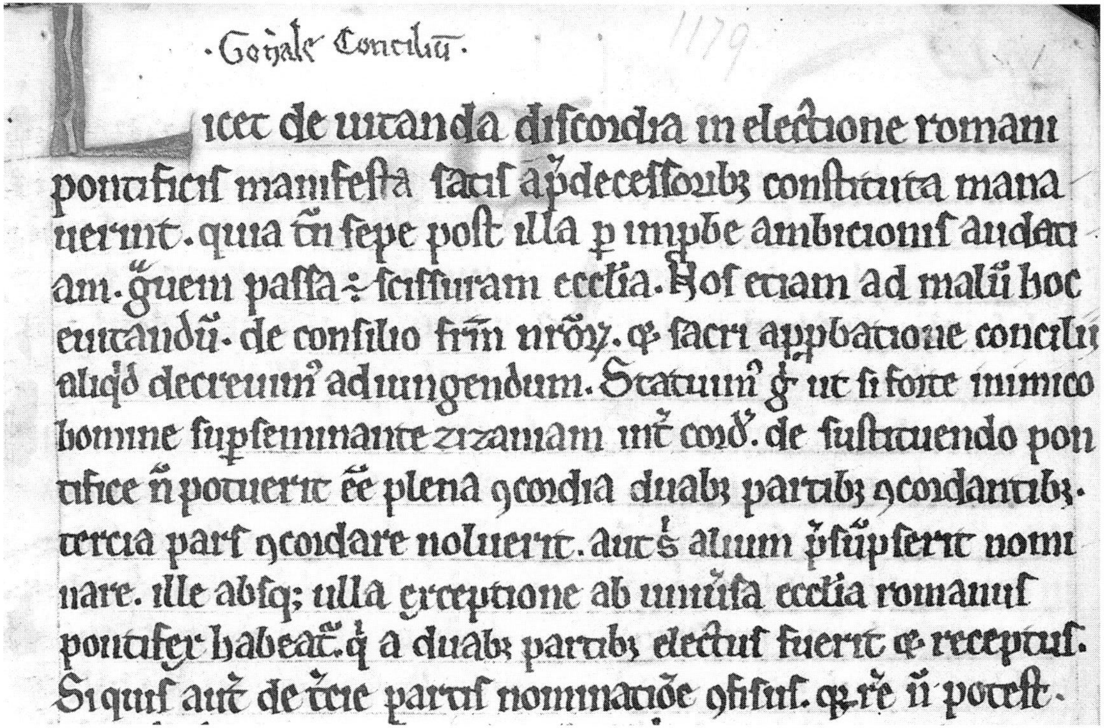

Pl. 12. *Concilium Lateranense*, England, after 1179. Cambridge, Fitzwilliam Mus., MS McClean 134. f. 1r (*CMDGBCam*, pl. 90): Licet de vitanda discordia in electione Romani / pontificis manifesta satis a predecessoribus constituta mana/verint, quia tamen sepe post illa per improbe ambicionis audati/am gravem passa est scissuram ecclesia

This Praegothica is Fere Textus Praescissus. It has straight **d**, rarely Uncial **d** ('evitandum', l. 5) and straight **s** (an exception: 'sibi', l. 9). Note the high **ct**-ligature (l. 1), the Insular **est**-abbreviation (l. 4) and the accent on 'á predecessoribus' (l. 2).

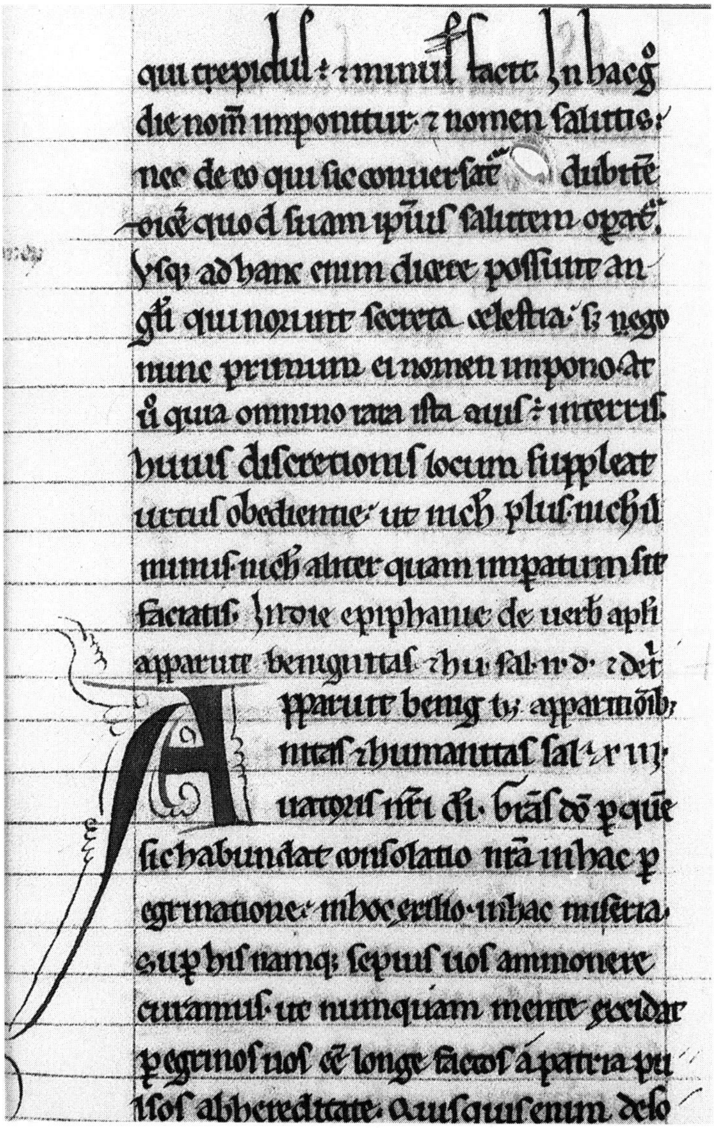

Pl. 13. Bernardus Claraevallensis, *Sermones*, copied in the abbey of Marmoutier near Tours in 1185. Tours, Bibl. mun., MS 344, f. 12rb (*CMDF*, VII, pl. 51): qui tepidus [trepidus *with expunged* r] est et minus facit. In hac ergo / die nomen imponitur et nomen salutis, / nec de eo qui sic conversatur dubitem / dicere quod suam ipsius salutem operatur. / Usque ad hanc enim dicere possunt an/geli

A slightly irregular Praegothica, marked by several advanced features: *litterae elongatae* on the top line, 'falling' **d** ('dicere', l. 4), hairlines at the bottom of round **r** ('norunt', l. 6) and at the top of straight **r** ('curamus', l. 3 from bottom). Note the two forms of **d** and of **s** in final position and the Insular abbreviation for **est** (ll. 1, 8), the **pp** fusion ('apparuit', l. 13), the absence of **ct**-ligature ('factos', l. 2 from bottom).

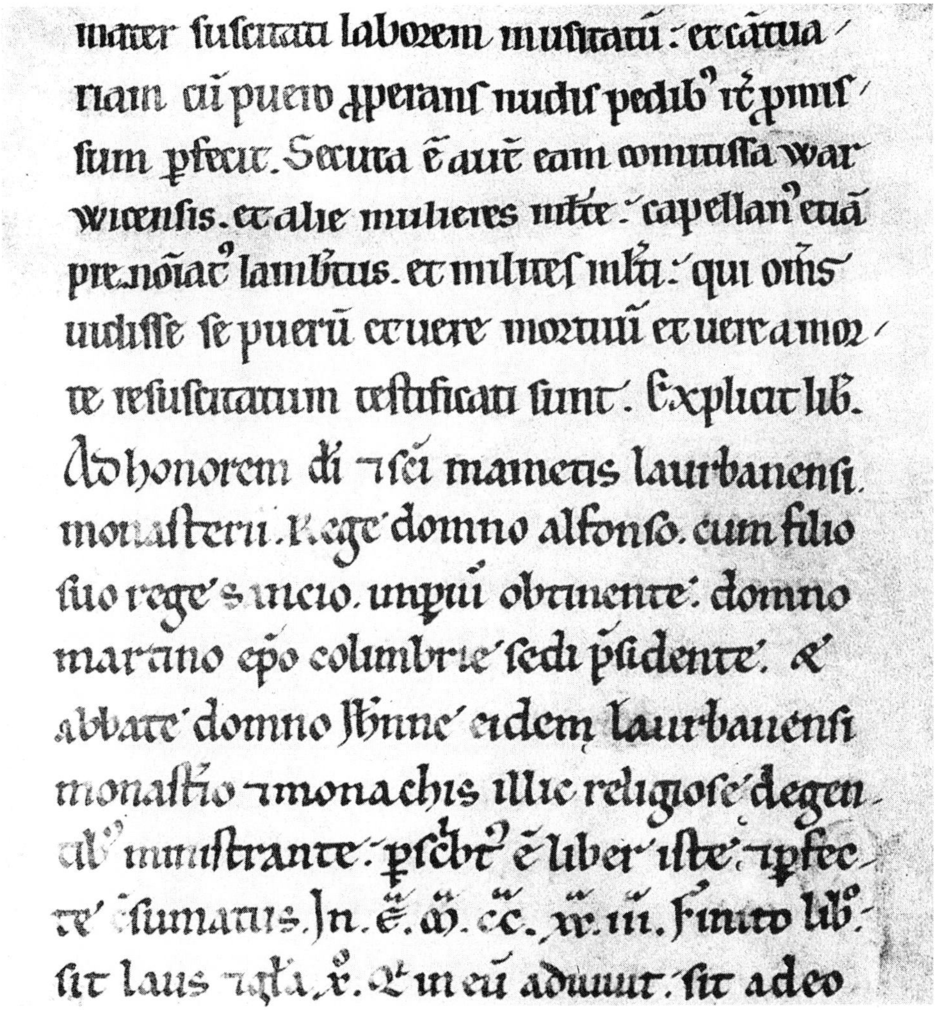

Pl. 14. *Passio et miracula S. Thomae Cantuariensis*, copied in the abbey of Lorvão (Portugal) in 1185. Lisbon, Bibl. Nacional, MS Alcob. 133, f. 139r (Burnam, *Palaeographia*, pl. 9; another page: Kirchner, *Scriptura Gothica*, pl. 5): mater suscitati laborem inusitatum, et Cantua/riam cum puero properans nudis pedibus iter promis/sum perfecit. Secuta est autem eam comitissa War/wicensis et alie mulieres multe, capellanus etiam

Iberian Praegothica. Note the typical **a**, the **pp** fusion ('properans', l. 2), the headstroke of final **t** ('et', l. 4), and, in a second hand writing the colophon (ll. 8 ff.), the tironian **et** in addition to the ampersand, the Iberian abbreviation for 'Iohanne' (l. 12) and the spelling 'perscribtus' (l. 14).

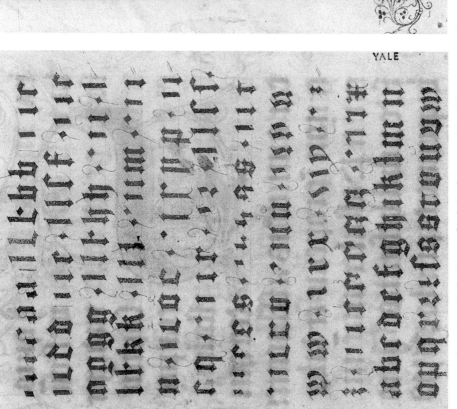

Pls. 15–16. Gregorius Bock, *Pattern book*, Swabia, 1510. New Haven, Yale Univ., Beinecke Libr., MS 439, ff. 1v–2r.

A rare contemporary demonstration of how the letters, signs, abbreviations and fusions in a Textus Quadratus type of Textualis Formata were traced stroke by stroke. In the letters (pl. 15) the sequence of the strokes for **o** was wrong and was corrected by numbering the four stages. Note the three forms of **r** and **u** (bottom l.).

Pl. 17. (reduced: 50 per cent of actual size): Johann vom Hagen, *Advertisement sheet*, Lower Saxony, early fifteenth century, upper section. Berlin, Staatsbibl. Preuss. Kulturbesitz, MS lat. fol. 384 v: Beatus vir qui non / abiit in consilio inpi/orum... Verba mea auribus / percipe Domine... Cum invocarem exaudivit me / Deus iusticie... Quare fremuerunt gentes et populi / meditati sunt

The four samples of Textualis Formata are labelled respectively 'textus quadratus', 'textus prescisus vel sine pedibus', 'semiquadratus' and 'textus rotundus'. The two intermediate samples show German texts in two forms of Cursiva, labelled 'nottula simplex' and 'notula acuta'.

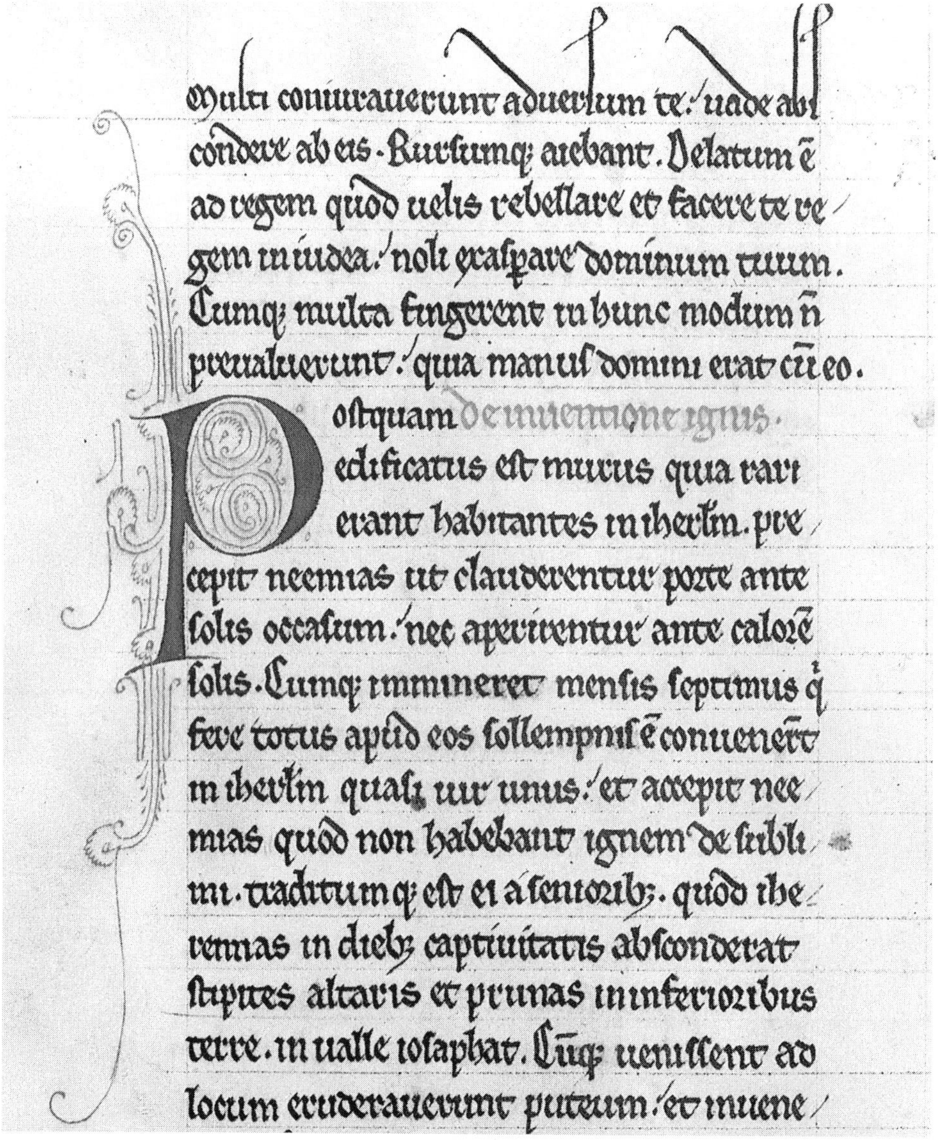

Pl. 18. Petrus Comestor, *Historia scholastica*, France, 1229. New Haven, Yale Univ., Beinecke Libr., MS 214, f. 133v: Multi coniuraverunt adversum te: vade abs/condere ab eis. Rursumque aiebant: Delatum est / ad regem quod velis rebellare et facere te re/gem in Iudea. Noli exasperare Dominum tuum. / Cumque multa fingerent in hunc modum, non / prevaluerunt, quia manus Domini erat cum eo

Textualis Libraria with heavy forking at the top of the ascenders and the minims and few fusions. Note the use of Half-Uncial and Uncial **d** (the Uncial one either with short shaft or as 'falling' **d**), the hook at the base of the descender of **p** and **q** and at the headstroke of final **t**, round **r** after **o**, final **s** mostly round, sometimes still straight, the extended and decorated ascenders at the top line.

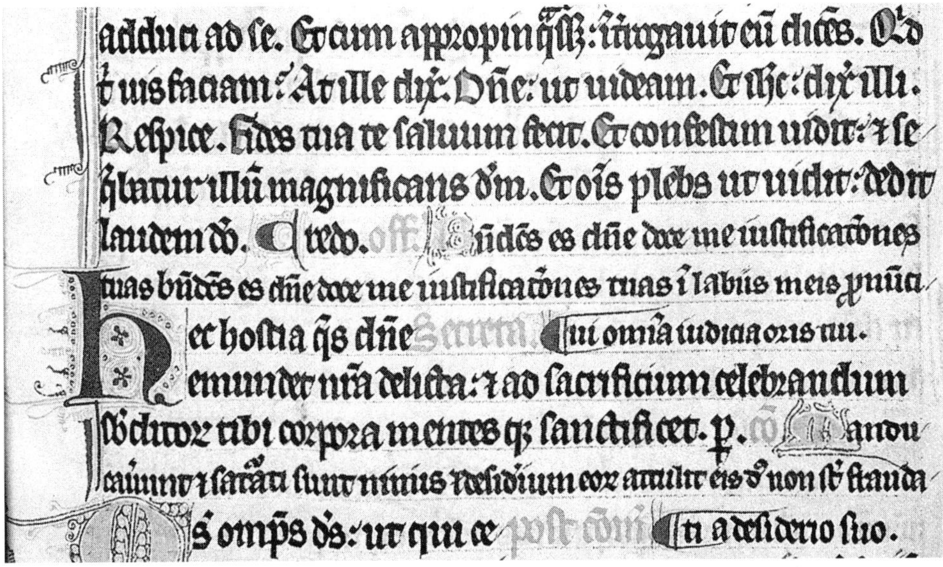

Pl. 19. *Missale*, copied in the abbey of St Pierre of Jumièges (Seine Maritime), before 1213. Rouen, Bibl. mun., MS 299, f. 31r (another page: *CMDF*, VII, pl. 54): adduci ad se. Et cum appropinquasset, interrogavit eum dicens: Quid / tibi vis faciam? At ille dixit: Domine, ut videam. Et Ihesus dixit illi

One of the earliest examples of Textualis Formata illustrating Variant VII in the Oeser system. Note the two forms of **d**, the broad round **s**, the vertical hairline on final **t**, the **ct**-ligature ('delicta', l. 8), the **orum**-abbreviation ('subditorum', l. 9), the numerous fusions, even with **a** as second letter ('sequebatur', ll. 3–4). The rubrics and the two sizes of script are typical of liturgical books.

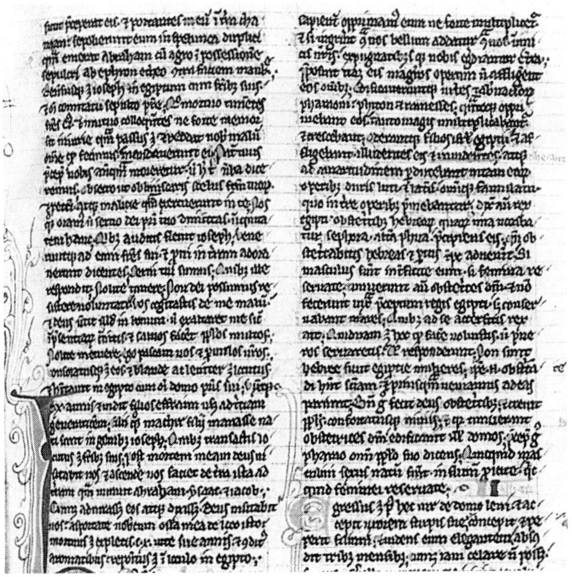

Pl. 20. *Biblia*, France (Paris?), 1234. Dole, Bibl. mun., MS 15, p. 41 (*CMDF*, V, pl. 23): [*col. a*] sicut preceperat eis; et portantes eum [*corr. from* in eum] in terra Cha/naan sepelierunt eum in spelunca duplici, / quam emerat Abraham cum agro in possessionem / sepulcri ab Ephron etheo contra faciem Manbre

A small Textualis ('pearl script') with many abbreviations, written with great care in a 'Parisian' pocket Bible. The ascenders and descenders are very short; the letters are simplified; due to the extremely small size Gothic features such as the pointed form of **e** and the bifurcation of the ascenders are exaggerated; round **s** does not occur. Note the high crossed tironian **et** and the **est**-abbreviation written as a vertical zigzag line (col. a, l. 5).

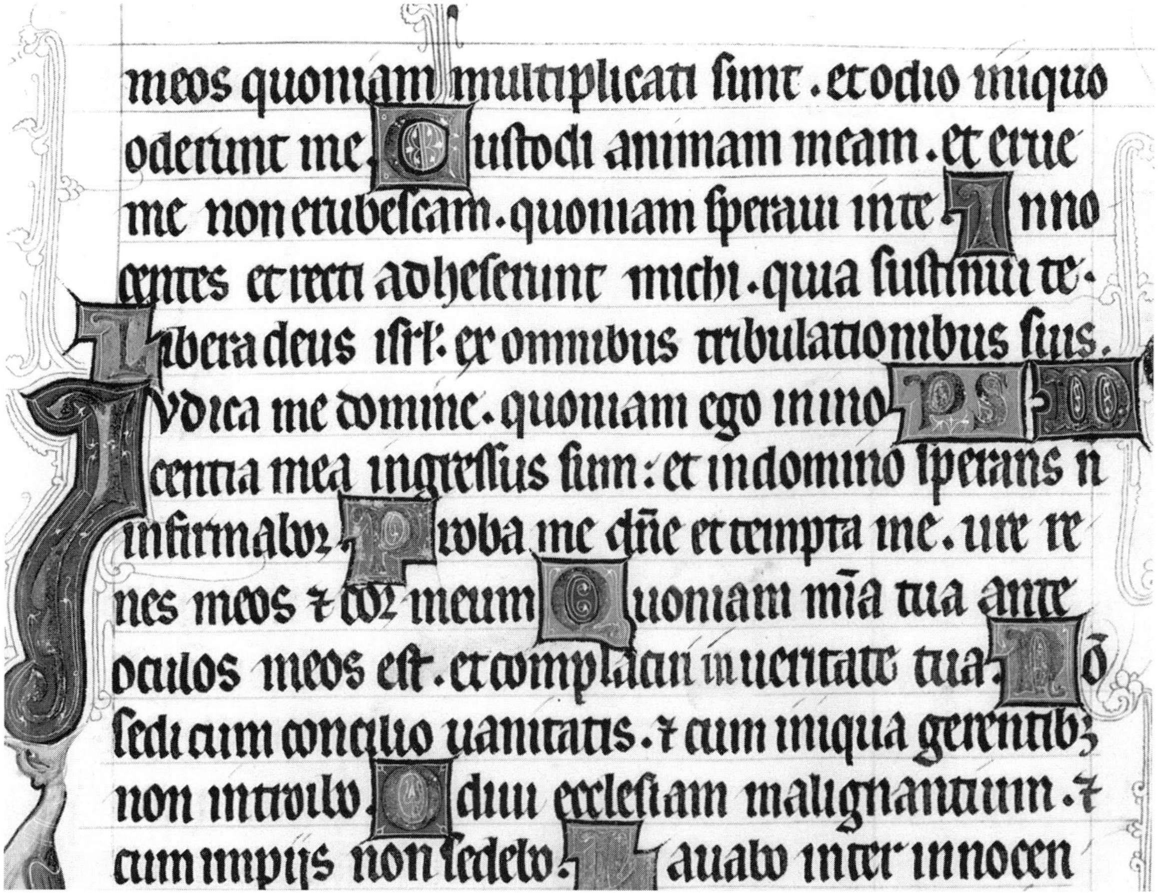

Pl. 21. *Psalterium*, Germany, 1255–67? Cambridge, Fitzwilliam Mus., MS 36–1950, f. 38r (*CMDGBCam*, pl. 113): meos quoniam multiplicati sunt, et odio iniquo / oderunt me. Custodi animam meam et erue / me, non erubescam, quoniam speravi in te. Inno/centes et recti adheserunt michi

A large Textualis Formata as used in an illuminated psalter. Note the two forms of **d**, the very short ascenders and descenders, the hairline at the top of some straight **r**s, the absence of **ct**-ligature and the extremely restricted use of fusions: only **bo** and **do** ('infirmabor', l. 8; 'Domine', l. 6, with Uncial **d**). A tendency towards Textus Praescissus is visible.

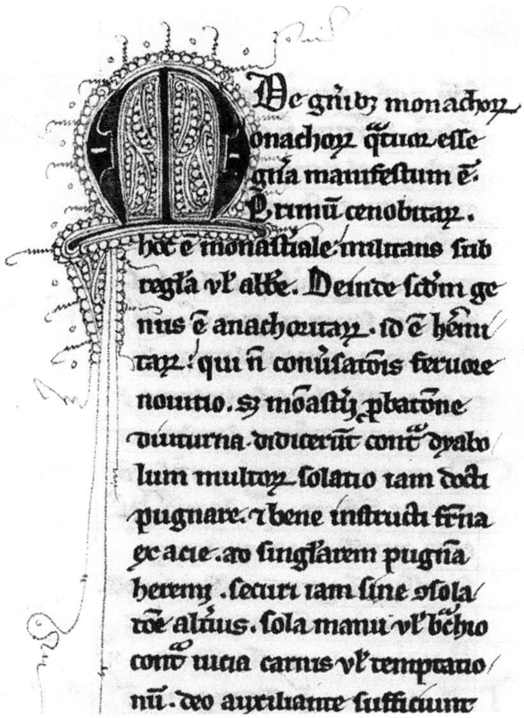

Pl. 22. *Regula S. Benedicti*, copied in the abbey of Sint-Truiden (Belgium)? in 1265. Brussels, Royal Libr., MS II.1031, f. 5r (*CMDB*, I, pl. 50a): De generibus monachorum. / Monachorum quatuor esse / genera manifestum est. / Primum cenobitarum, / hoc est monasteriale, militans sub / regula vel abbate. Deinde secundum ge/nus est anachoritarum, id est heremi/tarum

Textualis Libraria. Note the 'falling' **d** ('diuturna', l. 10), **i** longa in final position after **i** and **m** (ll. 9 and 14), the **ct**-ligature ('docti', l. 11), the **v** in 'vel' (ll. 6 and 15), the **con**-abbreviation ('consolatione', ll. 14–15).

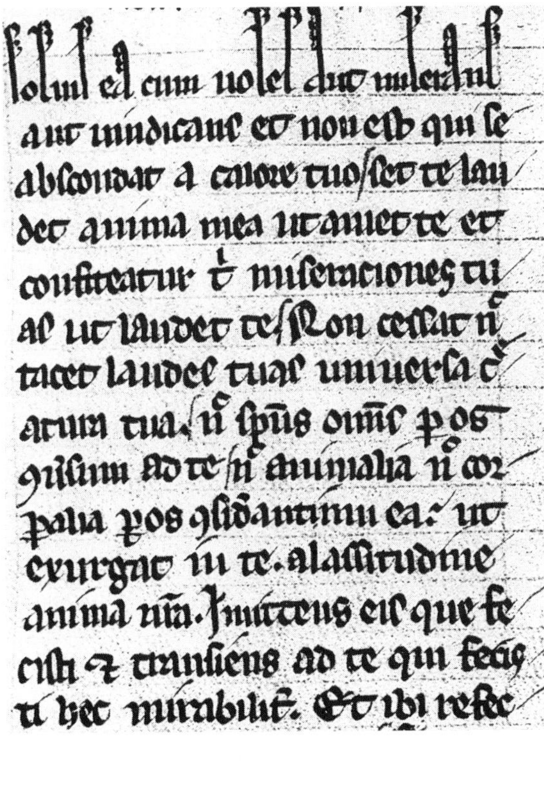

Pl. 23. Augustinus, *Confessiones*, copied in the abbey of Saint-Allyre in Clermont in 1265. Clermont-Ferrand, Bibl. mun., MS 102, f. 24ra (*CMDF*, VI, pl. 23): solvis ea cum voles aut miserans / aut vindicans, et non est qui se / abscondat a calore tuo, set te lau/det anima mea ut amet te et / confiteatur tibi miseraciones tu/as

A rather irregular Textualis Libraria with lengthened and decorated ascenders on the top line. Note the short ascenders, the varying shapes of **a**, the use of straight **s** and various forms of round **s** in final position (e.g. 'spiritus omnis per os', l. 8), the **con**-abbreviation ('conversum', l. 9), the long strokes on **i** and the long hyphens.

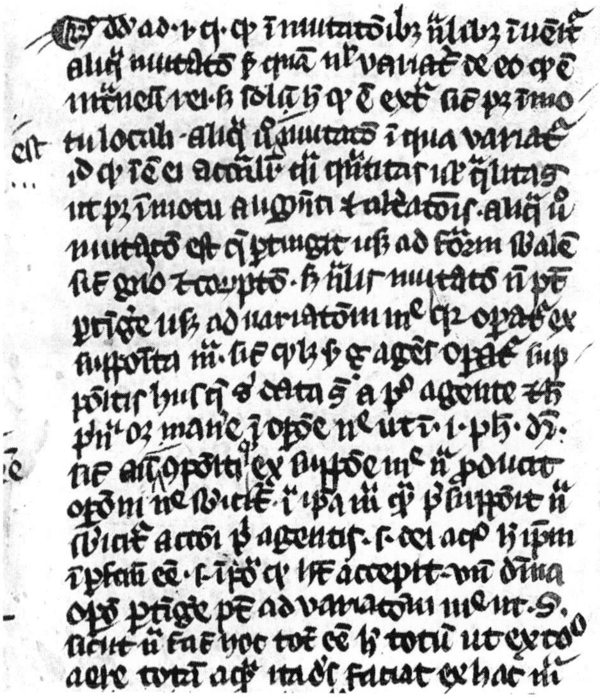

Pl. 24. Thomas Aquinas, *In quartum librum sententiarum*, Paris, between 1290 and 1305. Ghent, Univ. Libr., MS 117, p. 161a (another page: Destrez, *La pecia*, pl. 13): Responsio. Dicendum ad I. questionem quod in mutationibus naturalibus invenitur / aliqua mutatio, secundum quam nichil variatur de eo quod est / intraneum rei, sed solum hoc quod est extra

Textualis Currens (Littera Parisiensis) in a *pecia* manuscript. Note the irregularity, compression and boldness, the numerous abbreviations, the alternation of small single-compartment and high two-compartment **a**, the typical hook-shaped straight **s** used in all positions, and the general disintegration of the letters due to the rapid writing. Corrections are placed in the margin.

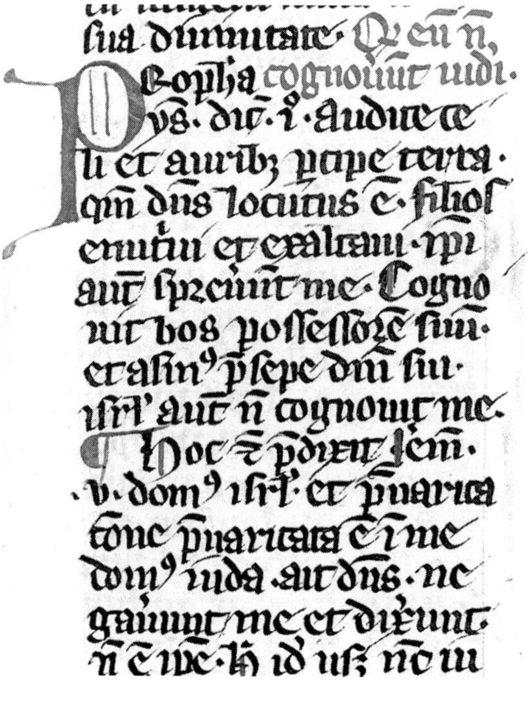

Pl. 25. Guillelmus de Sancto Amore, *Libellus de pseudoapostolis*, etc., Germany, 1303. Cambridge, Fitzwilliam Mus., MS McClean 122, f. 40ra (*CMDGBCam*, pl. 132): Quod eum non / cognoverunt Iudei. / Propheta Ysaias dicit I°: Audite, ce/li, et auribus percipe, terra, / quoniam Dominus locutus est. Filios / enutrivi et exaltavi

Textualis Libraria. Note the bold two-compartment **a**, the long horizontal serif at the left of the top of the ascenders, round **r** after **o** and **p**, crossed **x** and undotted **y**, the absence of fusions, the abbreviation for **etiam** (l. 11).

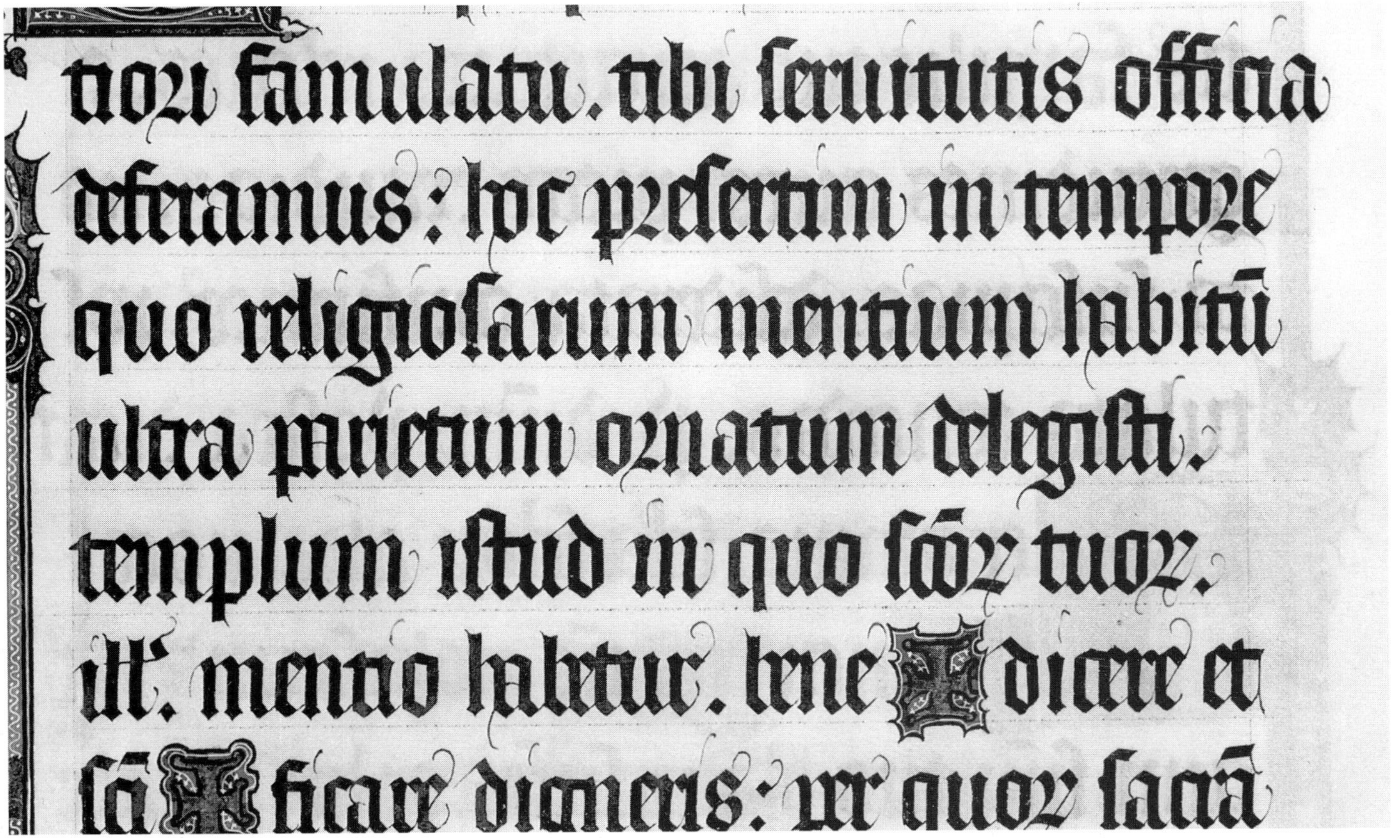

Pl. 26. *Pontificale*, France, 1302–16. Cambridge, Fitzwilliam Mus., MS 298, f. 34v (*CMDGBCam*, pl. 131): [atten]/tiori famulatu, tibi servituitis officia / deferamus; hoc presertim in tempore, / quo religiosarum mentium habitum / ultra parietum ornatum delegisti templum istud in quo sacr[or]um sacr[or]um / in manu habetur. bene dicere et / [sa]nctificare dignemus; ut quod sacra[tum] the religiosarum mentium habitum / ultra parietum ornatum delegisti templum istud in quo sacr[or]um sacr[or]um / in manu habetur. The Textualis Formata (Textus Quadratus) of the highest level. The large size and the wide distance between the lines are normal for the copying of the Preface of the Mass. The fusions include **be, de, ha, ho, pa,** but not **oc** ('hoc', l. 2). Decorative hairlines are found at the baseline at **h,** final **m** and round **r,** at the shaft of **d,** and at the top of final **c, e, r, s, t.** Elision is visible in many places.

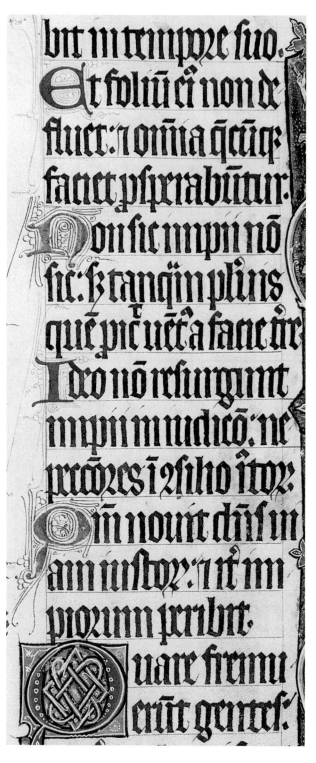

Pl. 27. *Psalterium*, England, between 1304 and 1321. Cambridge, Corpus Christi College, MS 53, f. 19rb (*CMDGBCam*, pl. 133b): [da]/bit in tempore suo. / Et folium eius non de/fluet, et omnia quecumque / faciet prosperabuntur. / Non sic, impii, non / sic; sed tanquam pulvis / quem proicit ventus a facie terre. / Ideo non resurgunt / impii in iudicio

Textualis Formata (Textus Praescissus). Extremely narrow and high letter bodies and short ascenders and descenders. The following letters and signs are 'Praescissus': **a**, **f**, **h**, **i**, **m**, **n**, **r**, straight **s**, **u** (second minim) and tironian **et**. Note the two forms of **d**, the form of **g** (l. 8), the 'cursive' **r** abbreviation ('iter', l. 12; see also 'pulvis', l. 6), the **con**-abbreviation ('consilio', l. 10), the long hairline on tironian **et**.

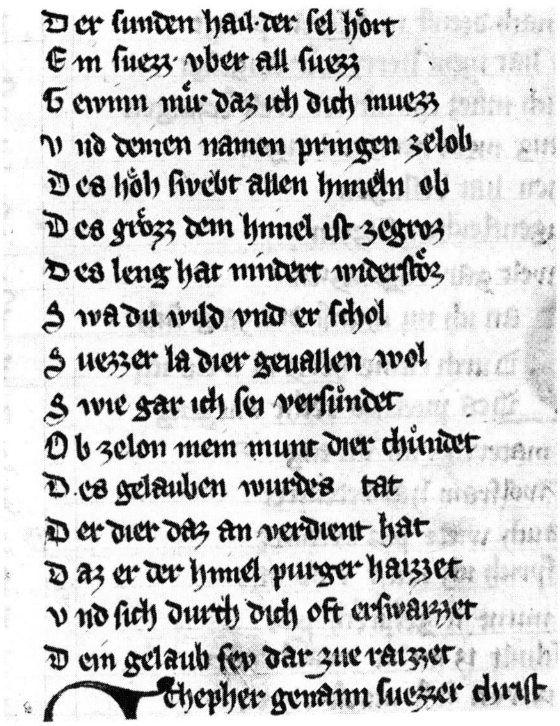

D er sunden hail·der sel hort
E m suezz vber all suezz
G ewinn mir daz ich dich muezz
V nd deinen namen pringen zelob
D es höh sivebt allen himeln ob
D es grözz dem himel ist zegroz
D es leng hat nindert widerstöz
S wa du wild vnd er schol
S uezzer la dier geuallen wol
S wie gar ich sei versünder
O b zelon mein munt dier chündet
D·es gelauben wurdes tat
D er dier das an verdient hat
D az er der himel purger haizzet
V nd sich durch dich oft erswaizzet
D ein gelaub sey dar zue raizzet
Thepher genant suezzer christ

Pl. 28. Ulrich von dem Türlin, *Arabel*, Southern Germany? 1320. Vienna, Österreichische Nationalbibl., MS 2670, f. 1rb (*CMDA*, I, pl. 82): Der sunden hail, der sel hört, / Ein suezz uber all suezz. / Gewinn nür, daz ich dich muezz / Und deinen namen pringen ze lob

A small Textualis Libraria. Note the high **a**, **v** in initial position, **w**, **z**, the little hairline at the top of the ascenders, the absence of abbreviations and the rarity of fusions (only **de** is used).

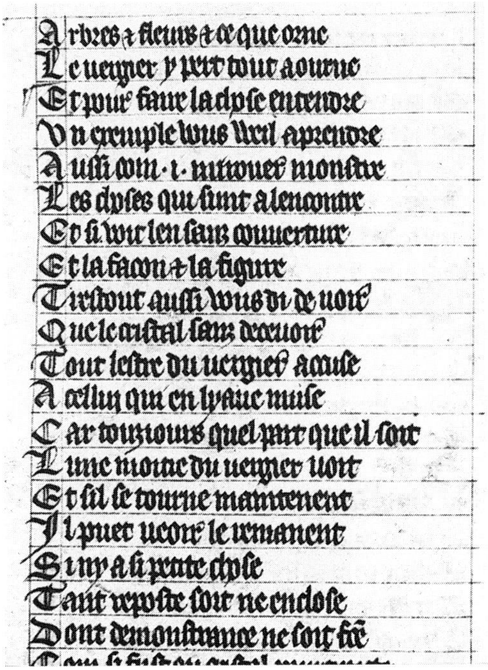

A rbres et fleurs et ce que orne
L e uergier y pert tout aourne
E t pour faire la chose entendre
V n exemple vous vueil aprendre
A ussi com·i· nitrouez monstre
L es choses qui sunt alencontre
E o si wir len sans conuerture
E t la facon et la figure
T irldout aussi vous di de uoir
Q ue le cristal sans decouoir
T out lestre du uergier accuse
A cellui qui en lyaue muise
C ar toux iours quel part que il soit
L une moitie du uergier uoit
E t sil se tourne maintenent
I l pueet ueorr le remanent
S i ny a si petite chose
T ant repostee soit ne enclose
D ont demonstrance ne soit faie

Pl. 29. *Roman de la rose*, Paris, 1355–62. Dijon, Bibl. mun., MS 525, f. 11ra (*CMDF*, VI, pl. 58): Arbres et fleurs et ce que orne / Le vergier y pert tout aourne / Et pour faire la chose entendre / Un exemple vous vueil aprendre

A small and compressed Textualis Formata, Variant II in the Oeser system. Note the occasional long **i** after **u** ('cellui', l. 12), the frequent use of round **r** (after **b**, **d**, etc.), the high **v** and **w**, the latter also used instead of **vu** ('vueil', l. 4), the hairlines on crossed tironian **et** and on straight **r** in final position, the frequent fusions.

Pl. 30. *Horae* ('Hours of Philip the Bold'), Paris, 1376–8. Cambridge, Fitzwilliam Mus., MS 3–1954, f. 57r (*CMDGBCam*, pl. 161): vigere presta, quesumus, ut eorum quoque perpe/tuo aggregentur consorcio. Alia oratio. / Fidelium Deus omnium conditor et redemp/tor, animabus famulorum famularum/que tuarum remissionem cunctorum tribue pec/catorum

Textualis Formata (Textus Quadratus) in an illuminated Book of Hours. Note the typical **g** and **x**, the rarity of abbreviations and the numerous fusions, including such unusual forms as **da**, **ha**, **oq**.

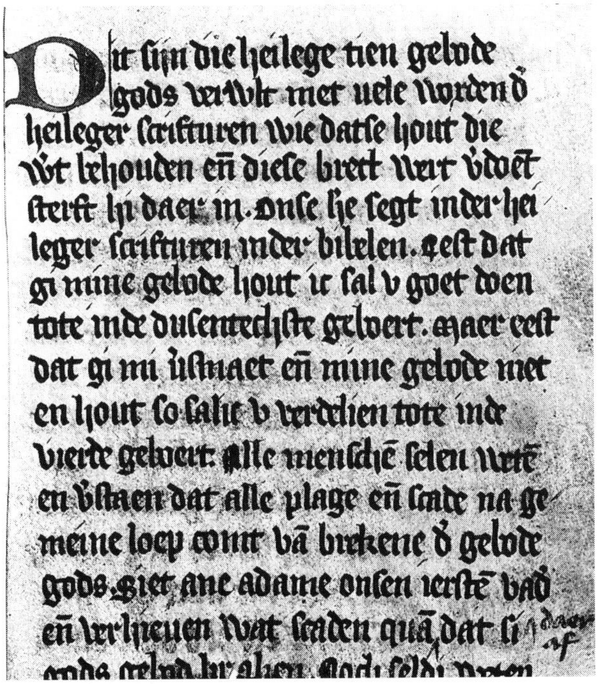

Pl. 31. *Treatise on the Ten Commandments* in Middle Dutch, Southern Low Countries, 1361. Brussels, Royal Libr., MS 3067–73, f. 94r (*CMDB*, I, pl. 157b): Dit sijn die heilege tien gebode / Gods vervult met vele worden der / heileger scrifturen. Wie dat se hout die / wert behouden ende die se brect wert verdoemt

Textualis Libraria with relatively long ascenders. Note the high **v** and **w**, the latter used also instead of **vu** ('vervult', l. 2), and the **t** with ascender in the **ct**-ligature ('brect', l. 4). Fusions of **e** and **o** were made with preceding **b**, **d**, **v**, **w**. The round **r** in 'worden' (l. 2) was originally a straight **r**.

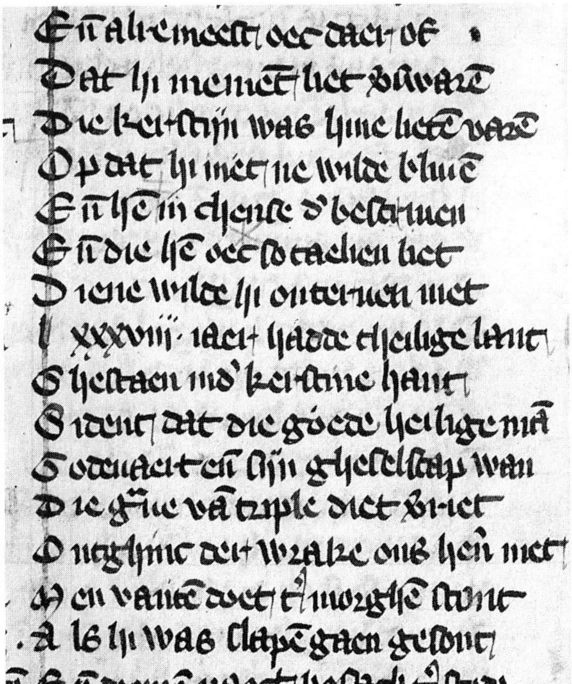

Pl. 32. Melis Stoke, *Rijmkroniek* (in Middle Dutch), copied in Naaldwijk (South-Holland) in 1390. The Hague, Royal Libr., MS 128 E 5, f. 16vb (another page: *CMDNL*, II, pl. 504): Ende alremeest oec daerof, / Dat hi niement liet verswaren / Die kerstijn was, hine lieten varen, / Opdat hi niet ne wilde bliven / Ende hem in chense daer bescriven. / Ende die hem oec so taelien liet, / Diene wilde hi onterven niet

A rapid Textualis (Textus Rotundus). Note the high **a** and 'cursive' round **s**, the simplified forms of **e** and **h**, the frequent use of round **r**, the 'open' **v** and **w**, the conspicuous vertical hairline on **r** and final **t**.

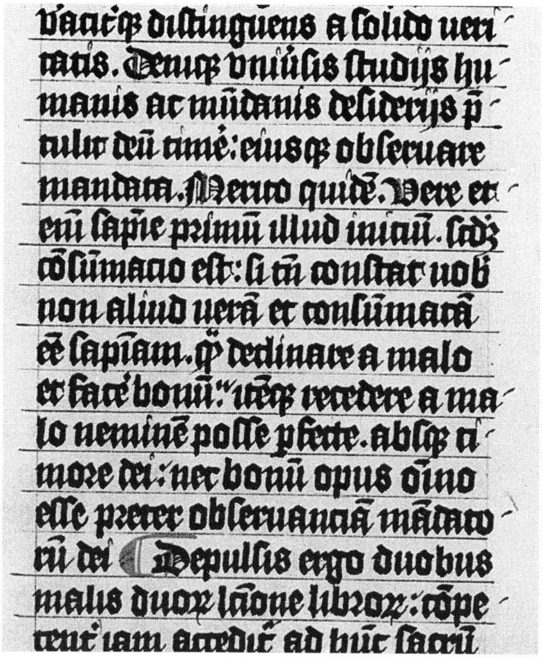

Pl. 33. Bernardus Claraevallensis, *Sermones in Cantica Canticorum*, Utrecht, 1402. Utrecht, Univ. Libr., MS 155, f. 1rb (*CMDNL*, II, pl. 514): veraciterque distinguens a solido veri/tatis. Denique universis studiis hu/manis ac mundanis desideriis pre/tulit Deum timere eiusque observare / mandata. Merito quidem

Textualis Libraria/Formata (Textus Rotundus). Note the flourish on **i**, the restricted use of fusions (limited to **da**, **de**, **do**), the **ct**-ligature ('perfecte', l. 11), the small open **v** in initial position (in addition to **u**: 'universis', l. 2), and the majuscules. The punctuation consists of *punctus, punctus elevatus* and *punctus flexus.*

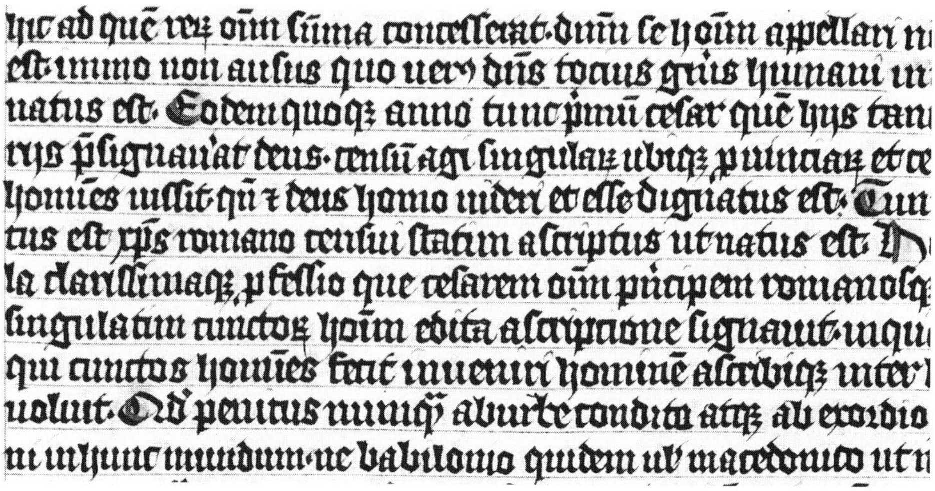

Pl. 34. Orosius, *Historiae adversus paganos*, Vienna, 1402. Vienna, Österreichische Nationalbibl., MS 381, f. 72v (another page: *CMDA*, II, pl. 13): hic ad quem rerum omnium summa concesserat dominum se hominem appellari n[on passus] / est, immo non ausus, quo verus dominus tocius generis humani in[ter homines] / natus est. Eodem quoque anno tunc primum Cesar, quem hiis tan[tis]

A compressed Textualis Formata (Textus Rotundus). The bold and angular shapes, the heavy triangular serifs on the short ascenders, and the abbreviations for **que, arum, erum, orum** are typical of Central European Textualis. Note also **g** and the Cursiva form of **t**.

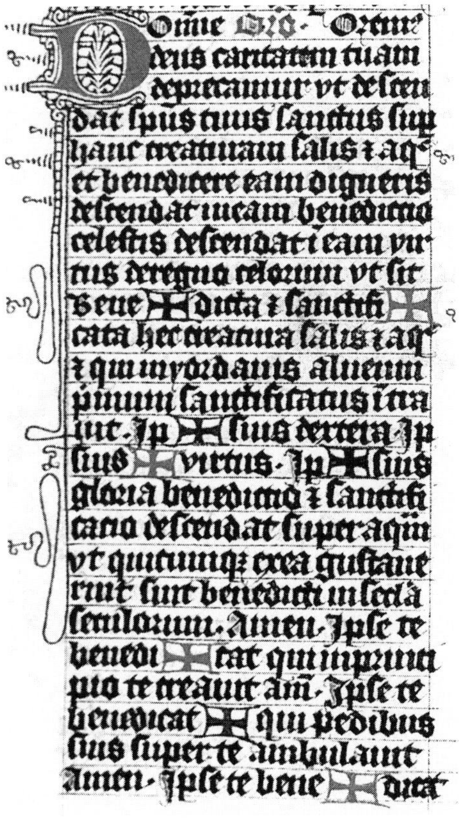

Pl. 35. *Missale*, Prague, 1409. Vienna, Österreichische Nationalbibl., MS 1844, f. 330va (*CMDA*, II, pl. 62): Oratio. Oremus / Domine / Deus, caritatem tuam / deprecamur, ut descen/dat Spiritus tuus Sanctus super / hanc creaturam salis et aque / et benedicere eam digneris; / descendat in eam benedictio / celestis

Script of the same type as the preceding example, even more spiky but with the same characteristics except for **t**. Note **t** written as an ascender in the **ct**-ligature ('sanctus', l. 4); the sharp **v** in initial position. **y** ('Yordanis', l. 12) is undotted.

Pl. 36. *Collectarium*, Angers, 1410. Angers, Bibl. mun., MS 106, f. 63r (another page: *CMDF*, VII, pl. 98): Primo quilibet prior seu administrator cuiuslibet prio/ratus seu administracionis vel officii ad dictum monas/terium pertinentis seu a dicto monasterio dependentis in prima / sui instituc<i>one seu commissione

Textualis Libraria/Formata (Variant III in the Oeser system). Note the bifurcated ascenders and descenders, the numerous fusions, including **ho** ('honorem', l. 5), the stylized Cursiva round **s** ('administracionis', l. 2), the **tt**-ligature ('promittet', l. 5).

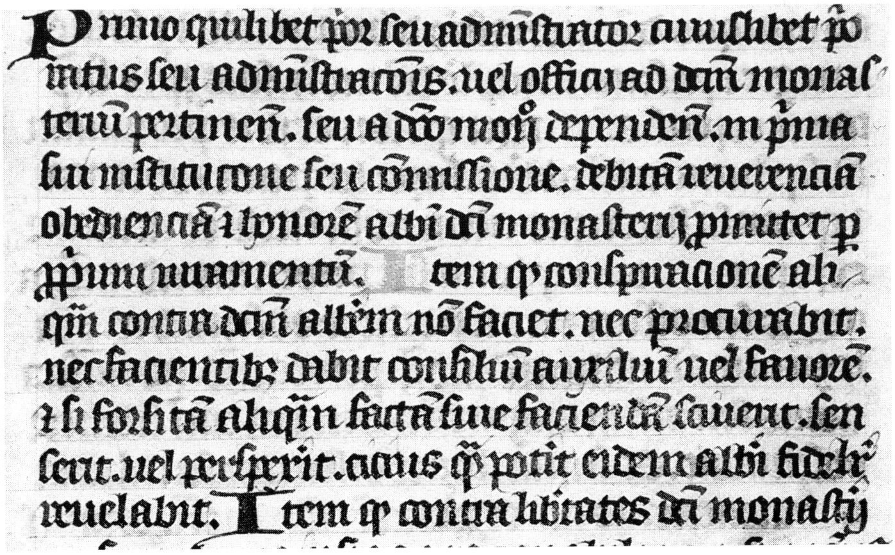

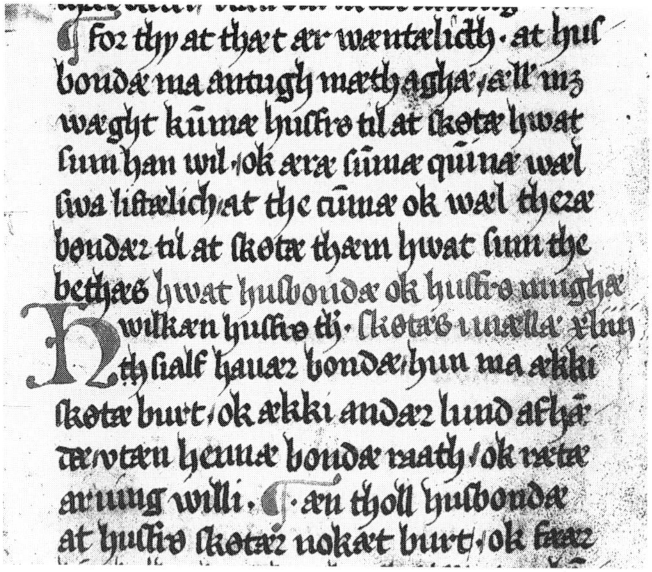

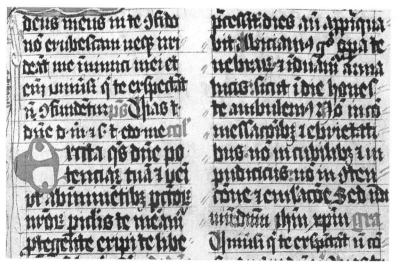

Pl. 37. *Law of Jutland* (in Danish), Denmark, 1457. Lund, Univ. Libr., MS Mh 25, f. 101r (*CMDS*, II, pl. 62): ¶ For thy at thæt ær wæntælicth at hus/bondæ ma antugh mæthaghæ æller met / wæght kummæ husfrø til at skøtæ hwat / sum han wil ok æræ summæ quinnæ wæl / swa listælich at the cummæ ok wæl theræ / bøndær til at skøtæ thæm hwat sum the / bethæs

Textualis Libraria with very conspicuous hairline forking at the top of the ascenders and an occasional vertical hairline on straight **r**. Round **s** is of the Cursiva type. Note the Scandinavian forms: crossed **o** and the **ae**-ligature.

Pl. 38. *Missale*, Stockholm, 1460. Stockholm, Royal Libr., MS A 50 a, f. 11r (*CMDS*, II, pl. 75): [*col. b*] [Nox] / precessit, dies autem appropinqua/bit. Abiciamus ergo opera te/nebrarum et induamur arma / lucis, sicut in die hones/te ambulemus

A slightly backward-sloping Textualis Formata (Textus Quadratus), bold, angular and spiky. Note the typical abbreviations: **bus** ('commessacionibus', b, ll. 5–6, in addition to the normal form: 'cubilibus', b, l. 7), final **m** in the same shape and equally with hairline ('potenciam', a, ll. 7–8), **orum** ('peccatorum', a, l. 9), **con** ('confido', a, l. 1). The top of **t** is often treated as an ascender. Tironian **et** is double-crossed. Double hyphens are found at both sides of the text column.

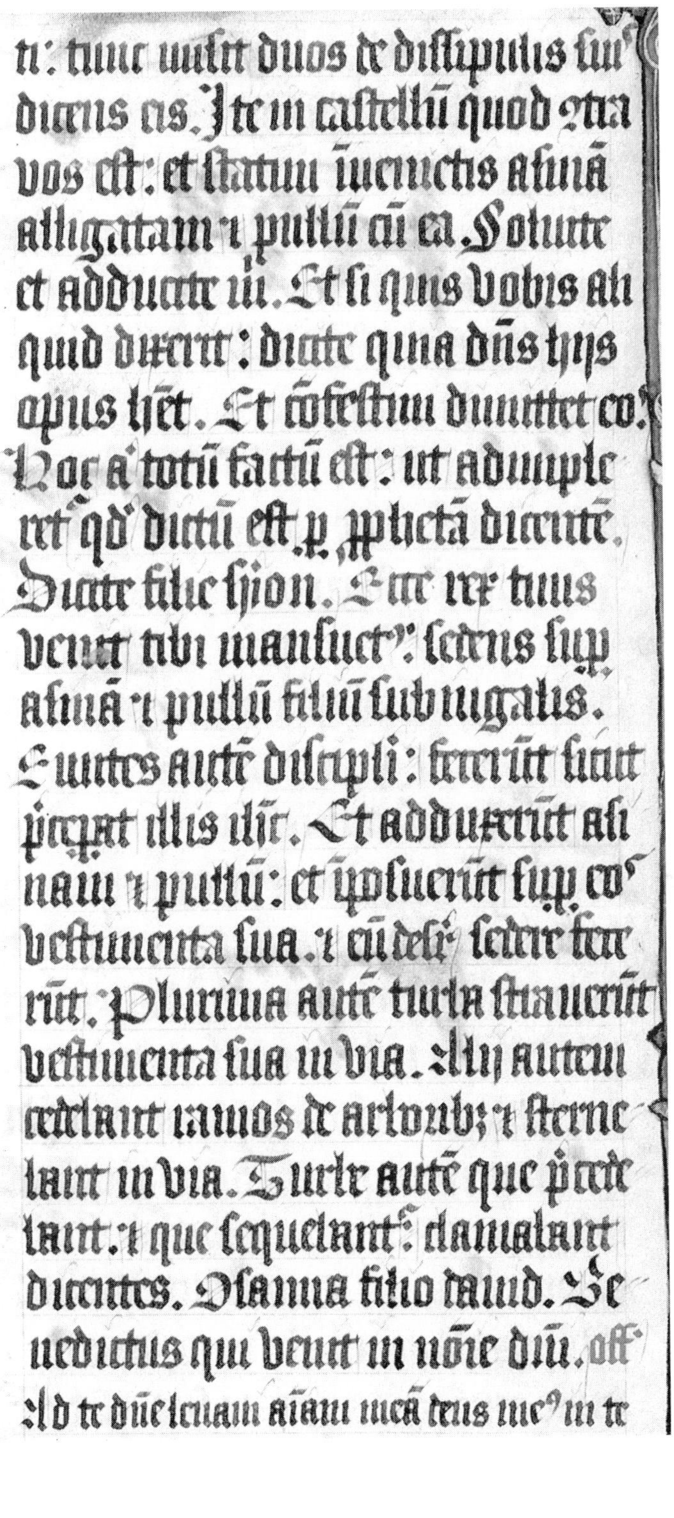

ti: tunc misit duos de dissipulis suis dicens eis. Ite in castellum quod contra vos est: et statim invenietis asinam alligatam et pullum cum ea. Solvite et adducite michi. Et si quis vobis aliquid dixerit: dicite quia dominus hiis opus habet. Et confestim dimittet eos. Hoc autem totum factum est: ut adimpleretur quod dictum est, per prophetam dicentem. Dicite filie syion. Ecce rex tuus venit tibi mansuetus: sedens super asinam et pullum filium subiugalis. Euntes autem discipuli: fecerunt sicut precepit illis ihesus. Et adduxerunt asinam et pullum: et imposuerunt super eos vestimenta sua. et eum desuper sedere fecerunt. Plurima autem turba straverunt vestimenta sua in via. Alii autem cedebant ramos de arboribus: et sternebant in via. Turbe autem que precedebant: et que sequebantur: clamabant dicentes. Osanna filio dauid. Benedictus qui venit in nomine domini. off:

... d te domine levavi animam meam deus meus in te

Pl. 39. *Missale* ('Fitzwilliam Missal'), England, 1465–79. Cambridge, Fitzwilliam Mus., MS 34, p. 21b (*CMDGBCam*, pl. 293): [Olive]/ti, tunc misit duos de dissipulis suis / dicens eis: Ite in castellum quod contra / vos est, et statim invenietis asinam / alligatam et pullum cum ea. Solvite / et adducite michi. Et si quis vobis ali/quid dixerit

A narrow Textualis Formata (Variant IV in the Oeser system) with long ascenders and descenders and wide interlinear space. Note the systematic use of the two forms of **a**, the high open **v**, crossed **x**, double-crossed tironian **et**, spurs on all ascenders (except where there is elision), abundant decorative hairlines, the typical **con**- and **per**-abbreviations ('contra', l. 2, 'per', l. 9). Fusions occur only after **b, d, p**.

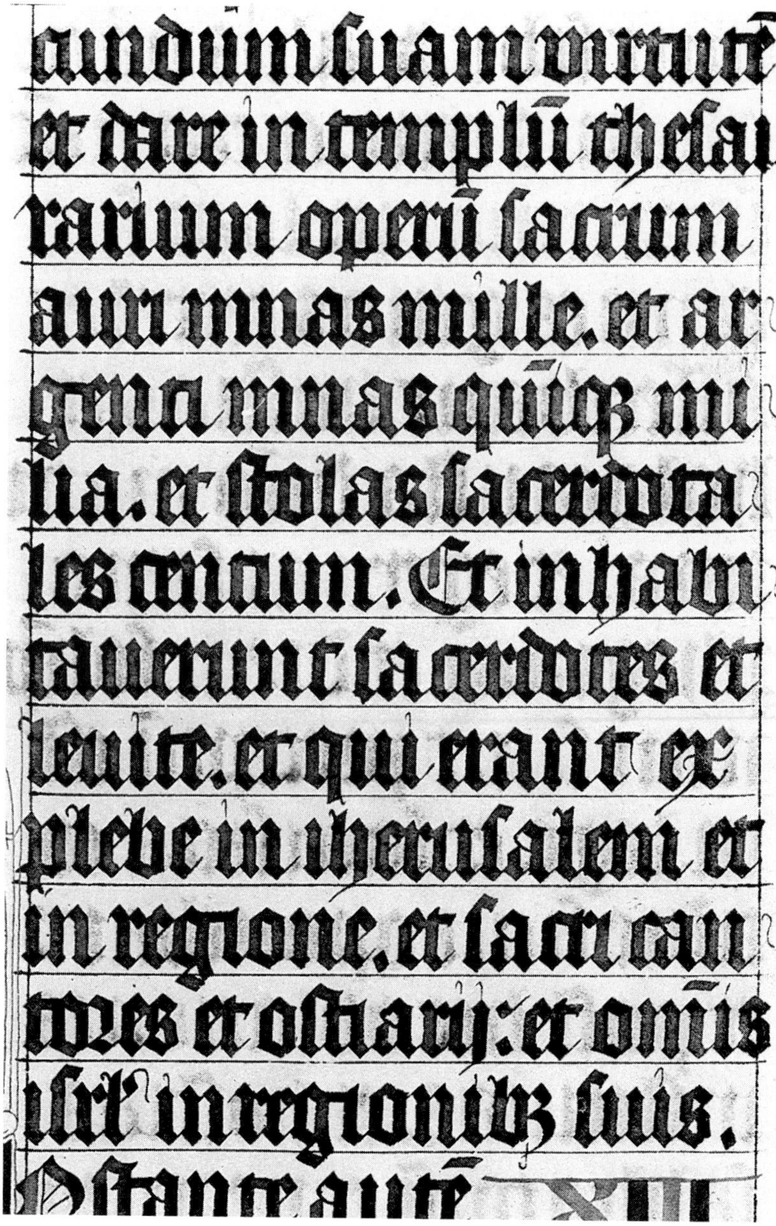

Pl. 40. *Biblia* in 6 vols., copied in the House of the Brethren of Common Life in Zwolle (The Netherlands), 1467 (this vol.). Utrecht, Univ. Libr., MS 31 II, f. 269rb (another page: *CMDNL*, II, pl. 578): [se]/cundum suam virtutem, / et dare in templum thesau/rarium operum sacrum / auri mnas mille et ar/genti mnas quinque mi/lia et stolas sacerdota/les centum. Et inhabi/taverunt sacerdotes et

A large angular Textualis Formata (Textus Quadratus) of the highest level and perfect execution. Note the tiny spurs on the ascenders and the many instances of elision (e.g. **tu** in 'virtutem', l. 1, **ri** in 'auri', l. 4, **ti** in 'argenti', ll. 4–5, **gi** in 'regionibus', l. 13). Fusions occur only after the letter **d**. The hyphens are hairline flourishes.

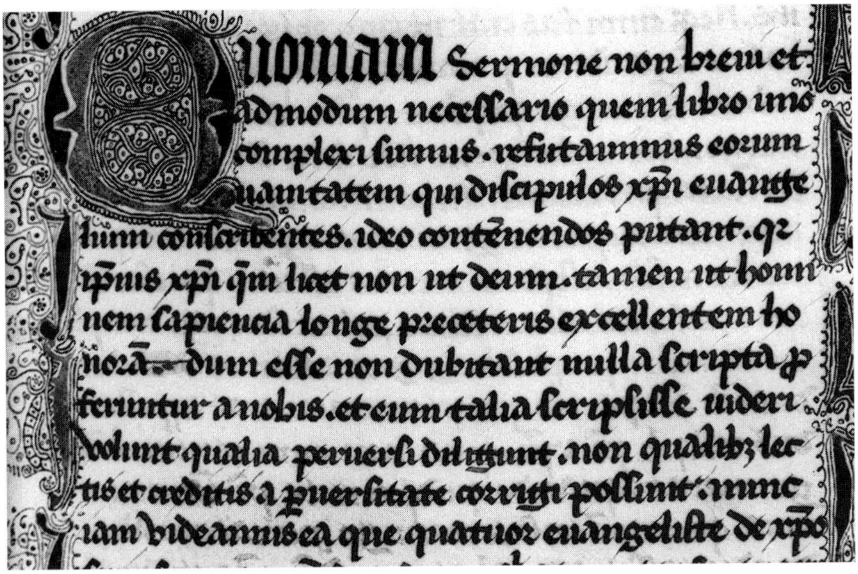

Pl. 41. Augustinus, *De consensu evangelistarum*, Lisieux (Calvados), 1464. Caen, Bibl. mun., MS 26, f. 21r (another page: *CMDF*, VII, pl. 133): Quoniam sermone non brevi et / admodum necessario, quem libro uno / complexi sumus, refutavimus eorum / vanitatem qui discipulos Christi evange/lium conscribentes

Apart from the first word, in Textualis Formata, the script is an unusual broad Textualis Libraria with long ascenders (provided with spurs) and descenders, no doubt under Humanistic influence. **a** has a conspicuous open upper compartment, and the scribe alternates between Textualis and Cursiva **g** ('longe', l. 7, 'evangelium', ll. 4–5).

Pl. 42. Mechthildis de Hackeborn, *Liber specialis gratiae*, London, 1492. Cambridge, Univ. Libr., MS Ff.I.19, f. 18r (*CMDGBCam*, pl. 338): De pu/rificacione beate Marie et Anna matre eius. XXIIII^{tum}. / In sancta / nocte purificacionis beate Marie vidit ipsam gloriosam / virginem et matrem in ulnis suis baiulantem regalem / puerum Ihesum

A narrow Textualis Libraria under cursive (Anglicana) influence. Note the curious high **a**, the almost vertical **d**, the high **v** and the ascenders occasionally provided with loops; the vertical hairline on final **t** and tironian **et**; the crown above the majuscule of 'Maria'.

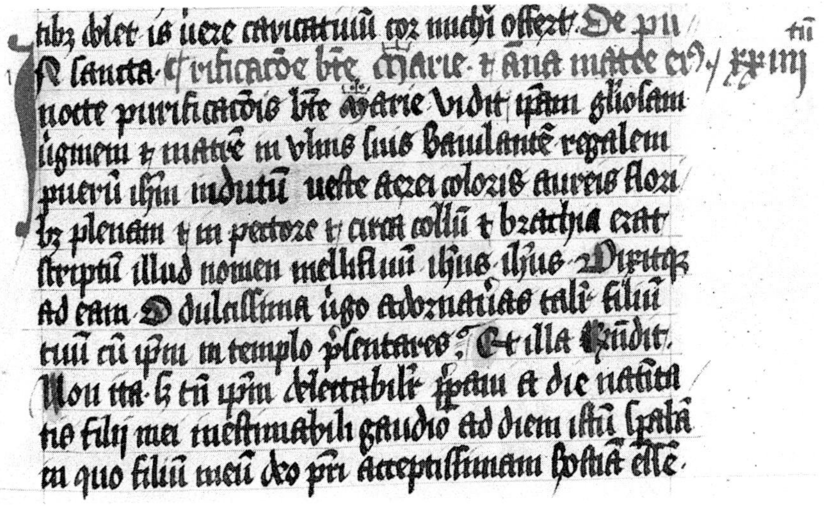

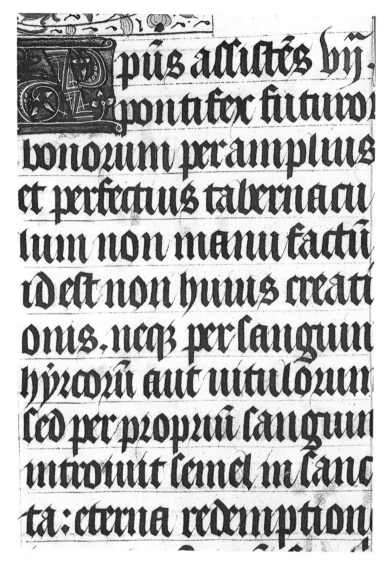

Pl. 43. *Antiphonarium,* Chaumont (Haute-Marne), 1488. Chaumont, Bibl. mun., MS 273, f. 34v (*CMDF*, v, pl. 171): VII[a]. Christus assistens / pontifex futuro[rum] / bonorum per amplius / et perfectius tabernacu/lum non manu factum, / id est non huius creati/onis, neque per sanguin[em]

A large, slightly rounded late Textualis Formata (Variant IV in the Oeser system), showing clearly the quadrangles and spikes of Textus Quadratus, all the hairlines running in the same upward diagonal direction, and the overlapping imperfect fusions ('pontifex', l. 2, 'bonorum', 'per', l. 3, 'redemptione', l. 11). Note the convex shaft of **d**.

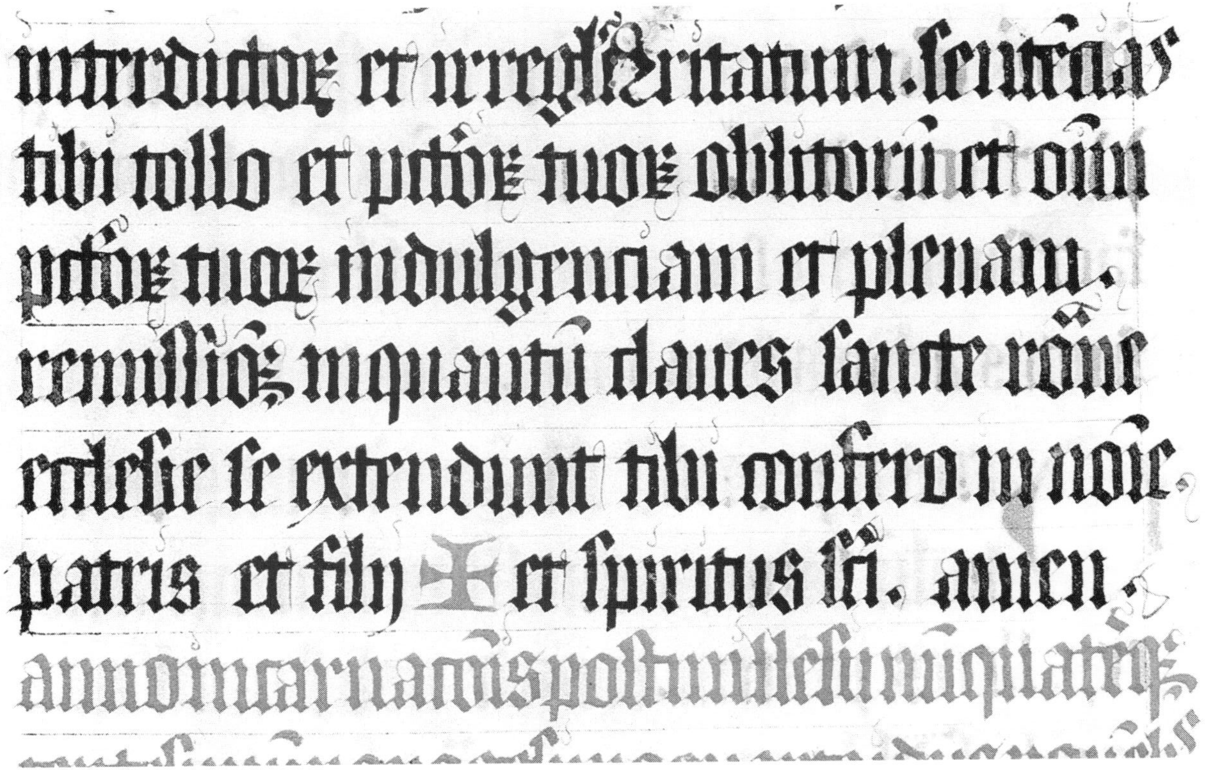

Pl. 44. *Missale speciale*, Austria, 1494. Vienna, Österreichische Nationalbibl., MS 1811, f. 30v (*CMDA*, III, pl. 587): interdictorum et irregularitatum sentencias / tibi tollo et peccatorum tuorum oblitorum et omnium / peccatorum tuorum indulgenciam et plenam / remissionem in quantum claves sancte Romane / ecclesie se extendunt tibi confero

An extra large, angular, narrow and somewhat irregular Textualis Formata (Textus Quadratus). Note the uneven height of the ascenders, the typical **orum**-abbreviation in two forms, the final **m** ('remissionem', l. 4), the typical narrow and high round **s** (superscript 's' at the end of the line), the **x**, the ascenders with spurs (except where there is elision: 'claves', l. 4) and triangular forked top, the fanciful decorative hairlines. A possible defect in the middle of l. 1 may explain why the word 'irregularitatum' has been partly rewritten.

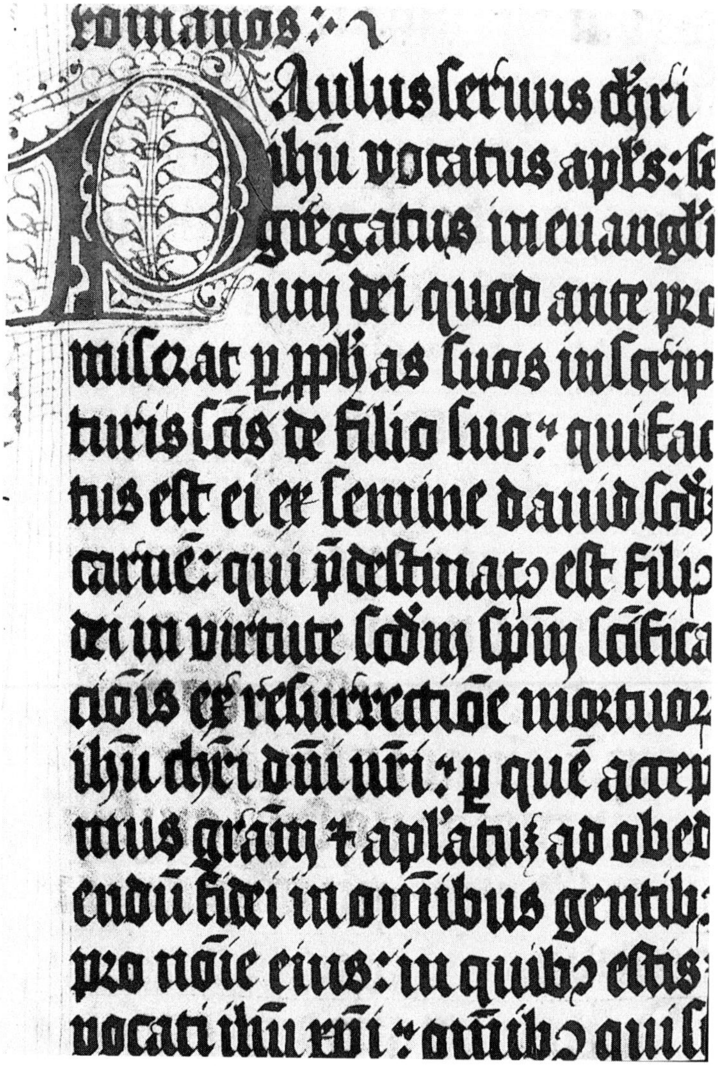

Pl. 45. S. Paulus, *Epistolae*, copied in the Charterhouse of Portemont in Switzerland in 1520. Grenoble, Bibl. mun., MS 113, f. 56r (another page: *CMDF*, VI, pl. 157): Romanos. / Paulus servus Christi / Ihesu vocatus apostolus, se/gregatus in evangeli/um Dei quod ante pro/miserat per prophetas suos in scrip/turis sanctis de filio suo

Like the preceding example, this late Textualis Formata (Textus Quadratus) is rather irregular, has relatively long ascenders and descenders and contains fusions only after **d**. Note the 'German' final **m** ('apostolatum', l. 13), the **v**, the hairline at the top of straight **r**, the unusual abbreviation for 'Christi' (l. 2). The sinuous alternative straight **r** in 'Romanos' (l. 1) and 'resurrectione' (l. 11) is no doubt due to Fractura influence; the lengthened last minim of final **m** (e.g. 'spiritum', l. 10) is derived from cursive script, and the 'Italian' **us**- and **bus**-abbreviation ('predestinatus', l. 9; 'quibus', l. 15) is also seen in Southern Germany and Austria. Punctuation: *punctus, punctus elevatus* and *punctus flexus*.

Pl. 46. *Collectarium*, England, 1523. Cambridge, Fitzwilliam Mus., MS 3–1967, f. 7r (*CMDGBCam*, pl. 362): Modus [**d** *and* **o** *are inverted*] / inchoan/di horas. / Converte nos, Deus / salutaris noster. Responsum. Et averte iram / tuam a nobis. Domine, labia / mea aperies. Responsum. Et os meum an/nunciabit laudem tuam

Textualis Formata (Variant III in the Oeser system). Note the hairlines at the top of the ascenders (**t** is treated as an ascender), on straight **r** and on final **s** and **t**. Final **s** has the Cursiva, not the Textualis form. Note the 'shaky' round **r** in the rubric ('horas').

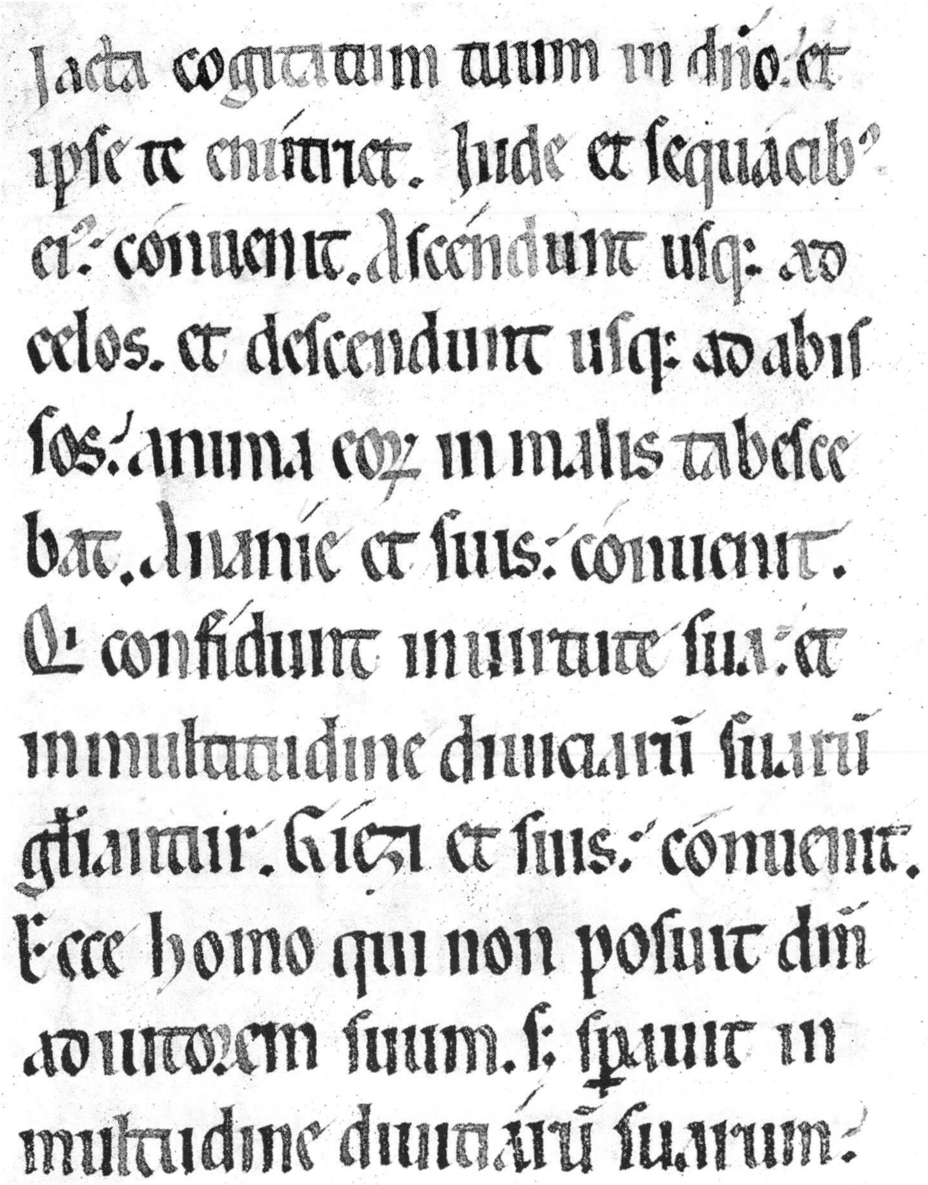

Iacta cogitatum tuum in dño. et
ipse te enutriet. Iude et sequacib
et conuenit. Ascendunt usq; ad
celos. et descendunt usq; ad abis
sos. anima eoy in malis tabesce
bat. Ananie et suis: conuenit.
Et confidunt inuirtute sua. et
inmultitudine diuiciarū suarū
gliantur. Giezi et suis: conuenit.
Ecce homo qui non posuit dñm
adiutorem suum. s; sperauit in
multitudine diuiciarū suarum.

Pl. 47. *Regula S. Augustini*, Toledo? 1208. Madrid, Bibl. Nacional, MS 10100, f. 107v
(Kirchner, *Scriptura Gothica*, pl. 9a; another page: Thomson, *Bookhands*, pl. 114): Iacta
cogitatum tuum in Domino, et / ipse te enutriet. Iude et sequacibus / eius convenit:
Ascendunt usque ad / celos et descendunt usque ad abis/sos; anima eorum in malis
tabesce/bat. Ananie et suis convenit

A large, angular, narrow and bold Southern Textualis with marked Textus Praescissus
character. Note the typical Iberian **a** and the ligature **ta**, the Rotunda **g**, the very limited use
of Uncial **d** with horizontal shaft, the looped **f** and unlooped straight **s**, diamond-shaped **o**,
round **s** in final position, the typical **z** ('Giezi', l. 9) and the high **ct**-ligature ('Iacta', l. 1). The
text is accented.

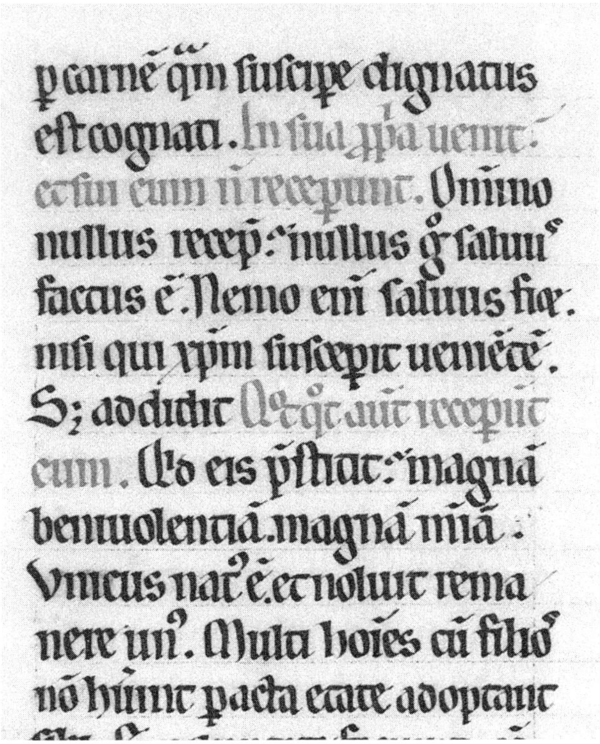

Pl. 48. Augustinus, *Tractatus in evangelium Iohannis*, Portugal, monastery of S. Salvador de Grijó, 1223. Porto, Bibl. Pública Municipal, MS 39 (Santa Cruz 13), f. [ ] ra: per carnem quam suscipere dignatus / est cognati. In sua propria venit / et sui eum non receperunt. Omnino / nullus recepit? Nullus ergo salvus / factus est

An early rounded Southern Textualis, with typical Iberian **a**, two forms of **d** ('addidit', l. 7), broad round **s**, no **ct**-ligature ('factus', l. 5). Note superscript **s** at the end of the line ('salvus', l. 4) and the use of the ampersand in 'fiet' (l. 5). The Gospel quotations are in red.

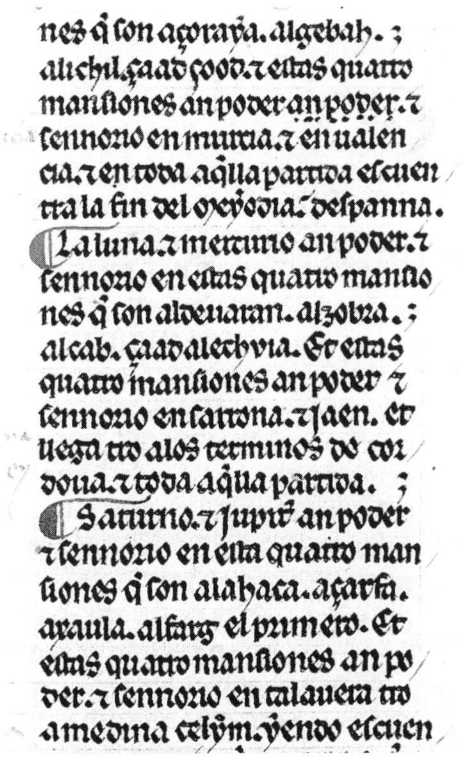

Pl. 49. *Libro de las Cruces*, Spain, 1259. Madrid, Bibl. Nacional, MS 9294, f. 196rb (Millares Carlo, *Tratado*, pl. 196): [mansio]/nes que son Açoraya, Algebah, / Alichil, Çaad, Çood, et estas quatro / mansiones an poder [*expunged:* an poder] et / sennorio en Murcia et en Valen/cia et en toda aquella partida

In this small and compressed Southern Textualis Libraria the short ascenders and descenders and the Textus Praescissus character of many letters are conspicuous. Note the form of **a**, the pointed **e** and **o**, the small straight **s**, the Iberian **z** ('Alzobra', l. 9), the **ç** and the line-fillers (ll. 1, 9, 14).

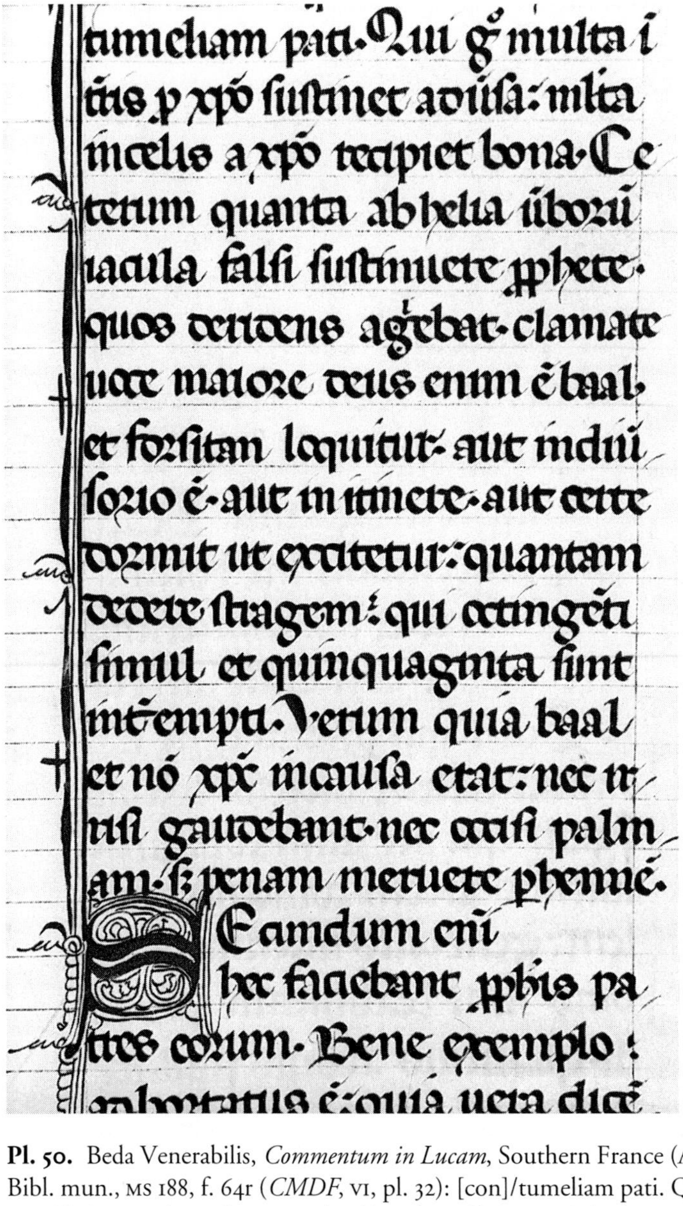

Pl. 50. Beda Venerabilis, *Commentum in Lucam*, Southern France (Albi?), 1298. Toulouse, Bibl. mun., MS 188, f. 64r (*CMDF*, VI, pl. 32): [con]/tumeliam pati. Qui ergo multa in / terris pro Christo sustinet adversa, multa / in celis a Christo recipiet bona. Ce/terum quanta ab Helia verborum / iacula falsi sustinuere prophete

    Southern Textualis Formata close to Italian Rotunda, with many fusions. Note, however, the form of **g** ('ergo', l. 1) and the hairline extensions at **h** and round **r** below the baseline. A line-filler occurs after 'exemplo' on the second last line.

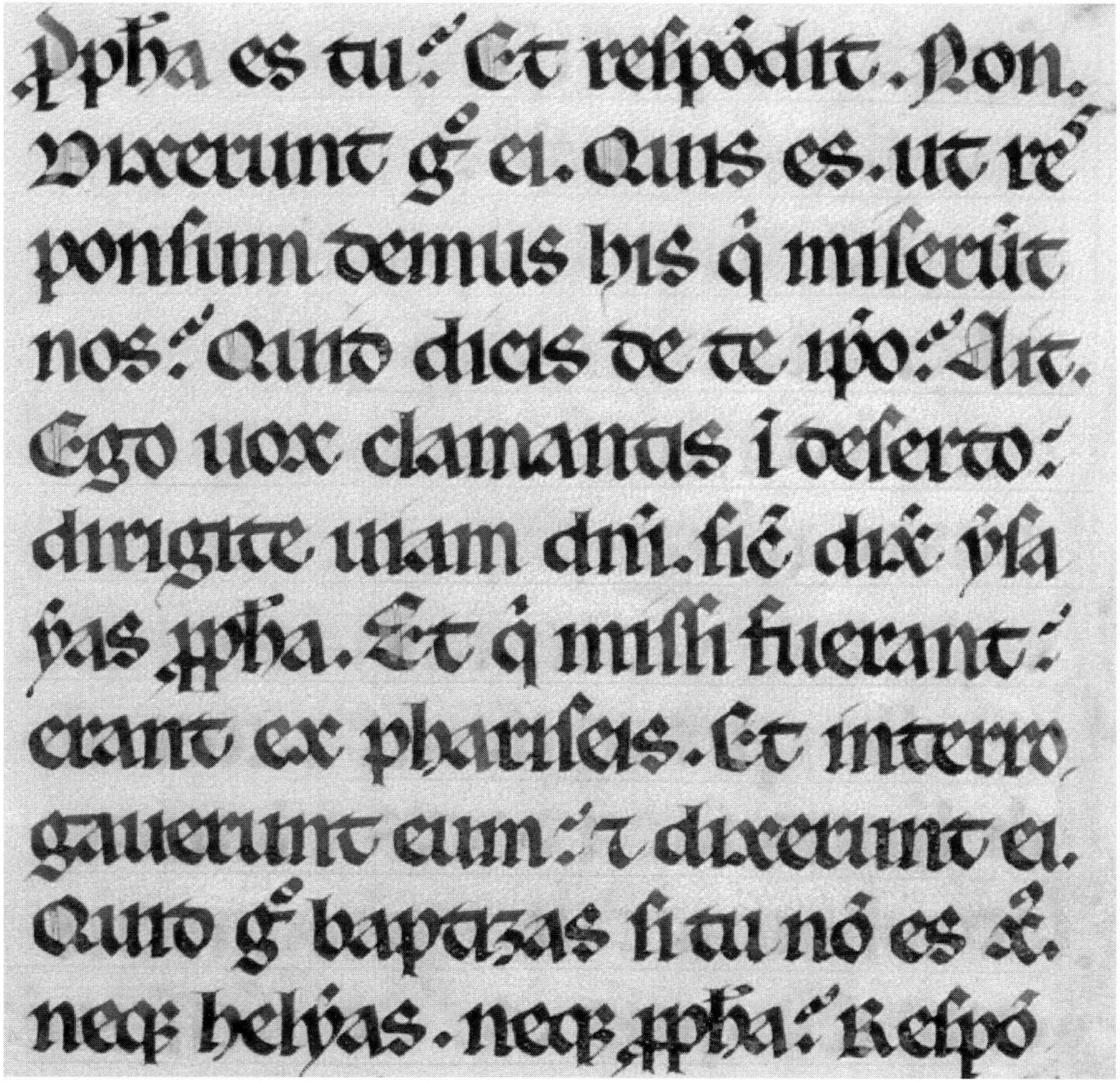

Pl. 51. *Missale*, Avignon, 1305–14. Cambridge, Fitzwilliam Mus., MS McClean 51, f. 8rv (another page: *CMDGBCam*, pl. 134):

Propheta es tu? Et respondit: Non. / Dixerunt ergo ei: Quis es, ut res/ponsum demus his qui miserunt / nos? Quid dicis de teipso? Ait: / Ego vox clamantis in deserto

A large Southern Textualis Formata, bold and quite angular. Note the treatment of the feet of the ascenders and minims, the form of **a**, the use of the two forms of **d** in order to produce the frequent fusions, the diamond-shaped **o**, rounded **t**, and typical **x** and **z**.

Pl. 52. *Missale*, Southern France, probably Grasse (Alpes Maritimes), 1316–34. Grasse, Bibl. mun., MS 3, f. 11rb (another page: *CMDF*, VI, pl. 42): [omni]/bus, pro redemptione animarum / suarum, pro spe salutis et inco/lumitatis sue, tibique red/dunt vota sua eterno Deo, / vivo et vero. / Communicantes et memo/riam venerantes, in / primis gloriose semperque vir/ginis Marie, genitricis / Dei et Domini nostri Ihesu Christi

Southern Textualis with many Northern elements, such as 'box'-**a** in addition to Rotunda **a**, the forking of the top of the ascenders, the absence of Textus Praescissus feet (see, for example, **m** and **n** in Textus Rotundus style) and the crossed tironian **et**. A line-filler occurs on l. 13.

Pl. 53. Bernardus Guidonis, *Speculum sanctorale*, Toulouse? 1329–31. Toulouse, Bibl. mun., MS 480, f. 1ra (*CMDF*, VI, pl. 46): Sanctissimo in Christo pa/tri domino Iohanni, divina / providente clementia / sancte Romane ac uni/versalis ecclesie summo / pontifici, frater B. Gui/donis [*this name on erasure*], Dei ac eius apostolice sanctitatis gratia

Southern Textualis Libraria close in general appearance to Italian Rotunda. Note, however, the form of **g**, the long decorative hairline extension of round **r**, the use of **v** in initial position ('universalis', ll. 4–5) and the conspicuous number of majuscules at the beginning of proper names and other important words.

[Manuscript text in Southern Textualis Formata (Rotunda) script]

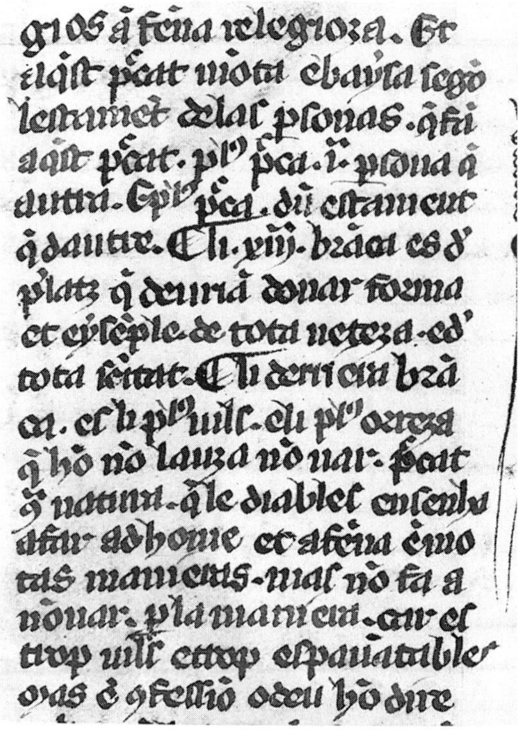

Pl. 55. Frère Laurent, *Libri de vicis e de vertutz* (in Provençal), Southern France, 1336. Avignon, Bibl. mun., MS 313, f. 24va (*CMDF*, VI, pl. 50): [...]/gios an fenna relegioza. Et / aquest peccat monta e baysa segon / l'estament de las personas que fan / aquest peccat. Plus pecca una persona que / autra

Southern Semitextualis Libraria, but sometimes including two-compartment **a**, especially in initial position, and using straight or round **s** in final position. There are almost no Textus Praescissus letters, and the ascenders display marked forking. The abbreviation strokes, however, are typically Rotunda.

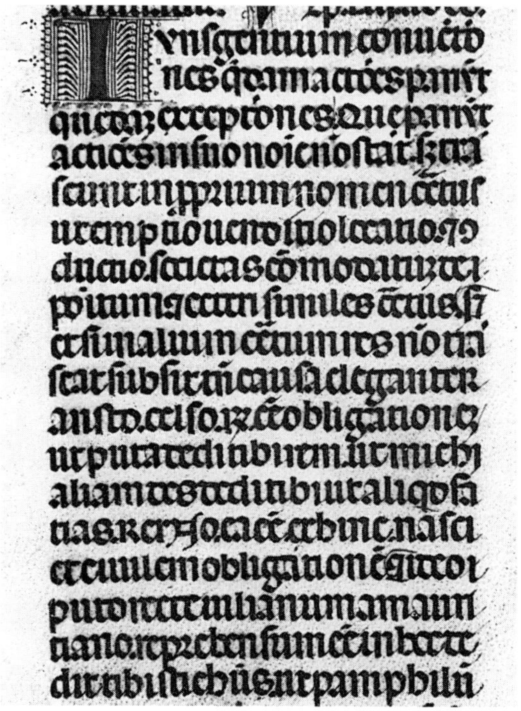

Pl. 56. *Digestum vetus cum glosa Accursii*, Bologna, 1340. Roermond, City Mus., MS 1, f. 32ra (another page: *CMDNL*, I, pl. 390): Iuris gentium conventio/nes quedam actiones pariunt, / quedam exceptiones. Que pariunt / actiones, in suo nomine non stant, sed tran/seunt in proprium nomen

Southern Textualis Libraria (Littera Bononiensis), extremely compact, barely separating words and presenting countless fusions and other characteristics of Rotunda. Note, for example, the abbreviations for **et** and **con** in l. 6. In order to maintain the same length of lines **v** was sometimes used instead of **u**, straight **s** instead of round **s** and **R** instead of **r** at the end of the line (ll. 2, 3, 5, 10).

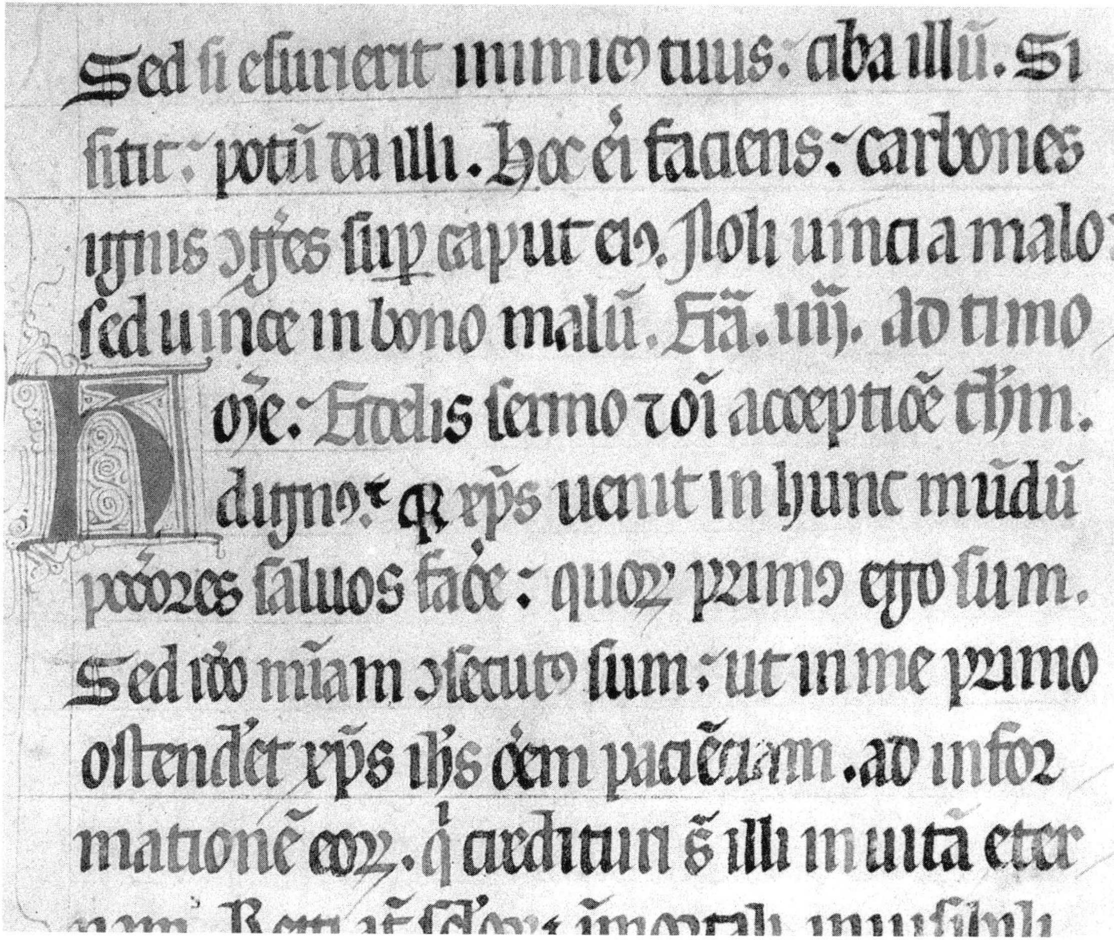

Pl. 57. *Epistolarium,*
Portugal, abbey of Santa
Cruz, 1351, Porto, Bibl.
Pública Municipal, ms 46
(Santa Cruz 39), f. 1xr: Sed
si esurierit inimicus tuus, ciba
illum. Si / sitit, potum da illi.
Hoc enim faciens carbones /
ignis congeres super caput
eius. Noli vinci a malo, / sed
vince in bono malum. Feria
IIII[a]. Ad Timo/theum. /
Karissime, fidelis sermo et
omni acceptione / dignus,
quod Christus venit in hunc
mundum / peccatores salvos
facere

A large but narrow
rounded Iberian Textualis
Formata. Note the fusions,
the treatment of the top of
the ascenders, the form of **a**,
the two forms of **d**, the
'Cursiva' **g**, the form of **x**,
tironian **et** (l. 5), the
abbreviations for **enim** (l. 2),
orum ('quorum', l. 7), **con**
and **us** ('consecutus', l. 8).
Punctuation: *punctus, punctus
elevatus* and *punctus flexus.*

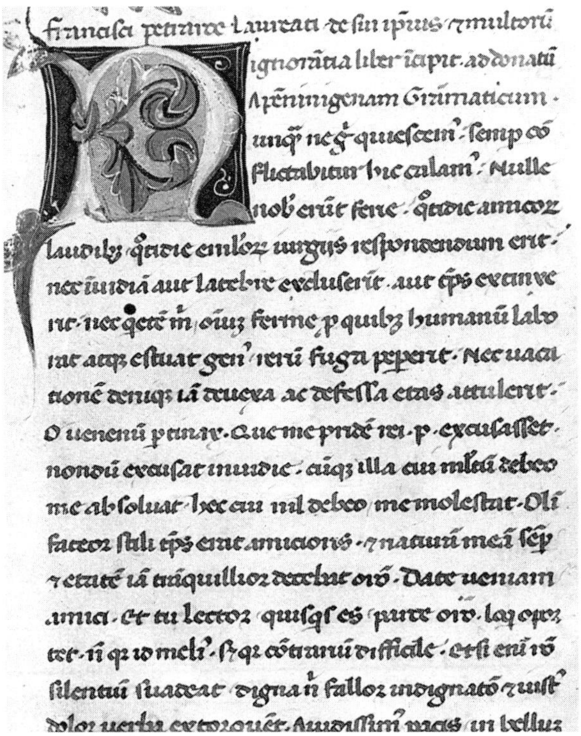

Pl. 58. Francesco Petrarca, *De sui ipsius et multorum ignorantia*, autograph, 1368. Berlin, Staatsbibl. Preuss. Kulturbesitz, MS Ham. 493, f. 3r (Crous and Kirchner, *Schriftarten*, fig. 17; Ehrle and Liebaert, *Specimina*, pl. 45): Francisci Petrarce laureati de sui ipsius et multorum / ignorantia liber incipit ad Donatum / Apenninigenam grammaticum. / Nunquamne igitur quiescemus, semper con/flictabitur hic calamus? Nulle / nobis erunt ferie

A small, broad Semitextualis Libraria in Petrarch's hand. Apart from the form of **a** and in spite of the large distance between the lines, this script is basically a Rotunda. Note, however, the use of round **r** exclusively after **o**; **f** and straight **s** tending to extend slightly below the baseline; the occasional use of straight **s** in final position ('quisquis', l. 17) and especially the Capitalis **A** and **N**. Note also the abbreviation for **sed** (= **set**, l. 18).

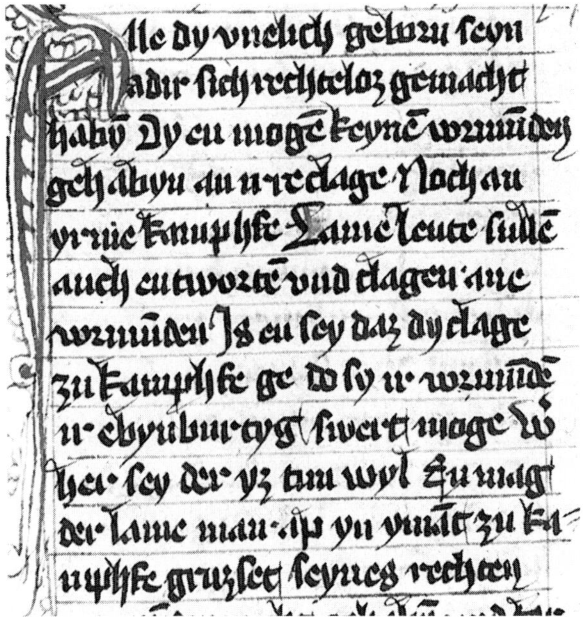

Pl. 59. *Sachsenspiegel*, Germany, 1382. Strasbourg, Bibl. nat. et univ., MS 2117, f. 12v (*CMDF*, v, pl. 63): Alle dy unelich geborn seyn / adir sich rechteloz gemacht / habyn, dy en mogen keynen vormunden / gehabyn an irre clage noch an / yrme kamphfe. Lame leute sullen / auch entworten und clagen ane / vormunden, is en sey, daz dy clage / zu kamphfe ge

A rare example of Northern Semitextualis Libraria. Note the hairlines (mostly flourishes) at the top of the ascenders and the vertical hairlines on final **g**, **t** etc.; the form of **k** and round **s**; **v** in initial position; undotted **y**; the sequence **zs** in 'gruzset' (l. 12); the double hyphen and remarkable word division of 'ka/mphfe' (ll. 11–12).

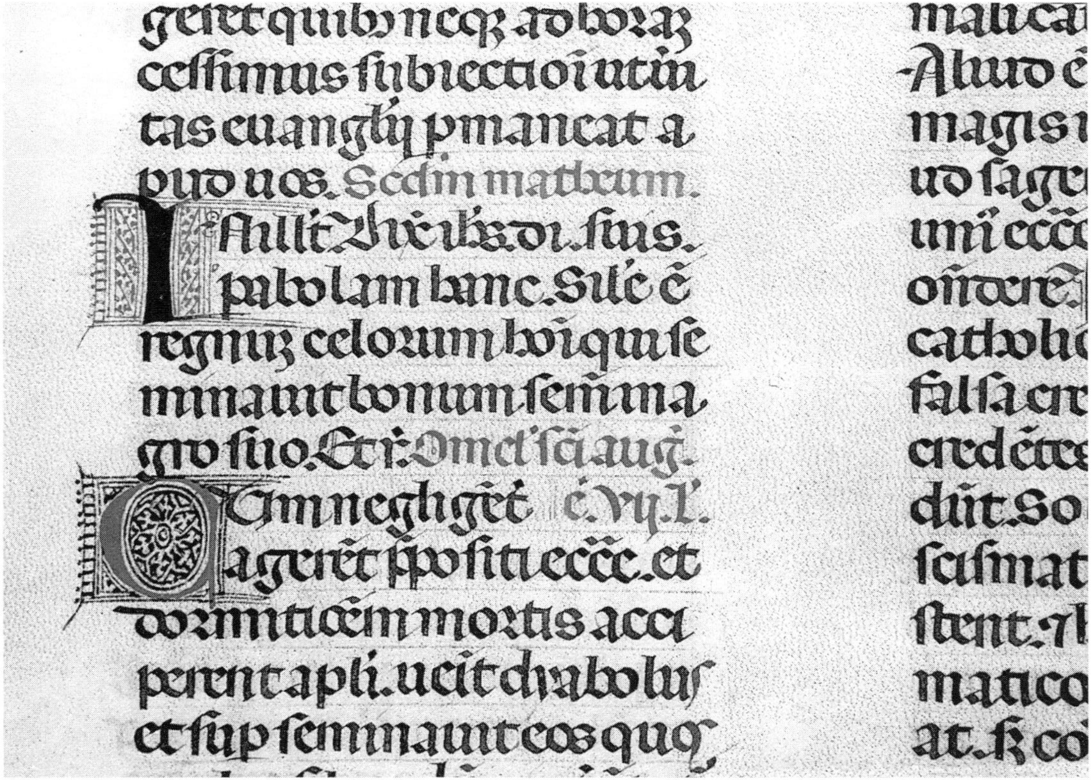

Pl. 60. *Lectionarium*, Bologna, 1377. Bourges, Bibl. mun., MS 19, f. 45r (*CMDF*, VII, pl. 86): [*col. a*] [...]/geret quibus neque ad horam / cessimus subiectioni ut veri/tas evangelii permaneat a/pud vos. Secundum Matheum. / In illo tempore dixit Ihesus discipulis suis / parabolam hanc: Simile est / regnum celorum homini qui se/minavit bonum semen in a/gro suo. Et reliqua. Omelia sancti Augustini / est VII. lectio. / Cum negligenter / agerent prepositi ecclesie et / dormitionem mortis acci/perent

A large Southern Textualis Formata, showing clearly all the characteristics of Rotunda but retaining a marked angularity. Note especially the numerous fusions (including **ha**, **hs**, **os** in two shapes, 'eos quos', a, l. 14), the form of **g**, trailing **s** (ll. 13, 14), tironian **et** (b, l. 12).

insup et antecede omnibus nobis ad
ipsum sancte scalle uirtutem sursum
currens. et uinctus karitati. Ka
ritas autem est deus. consumato
ri bonorum. Deo gratias amen.

Explicit commendatio sancti
johannis climaci edita a Johne
abbate montis rayzbu. 2—2
Benedictus sit dominus thesus
xpistus nini dei filius et beatissi
ma uirgo maria cum tota celesti
curia amen

eritas tua domine ihesu xp
ste maneat semper in cor
dibus nostris. et omnis inimici
falsitas destruatur qui pro nobis
passus fuisti mer uce. custodi cur
sum et exitum uite nostre. Qui
uiuis et regnas in secula seculo

   A large, somewhat irregular Iberian Textualis Formata (Rotunda) with short ascenders and descenders. Note the strong Praescissus character, the typical **a**, the two forms of **d**, the form of **x** and **y**, the long hairline on final **t**, the line-fillers in the shape of figure 2 (ll. 8 and 14). The text is accented.

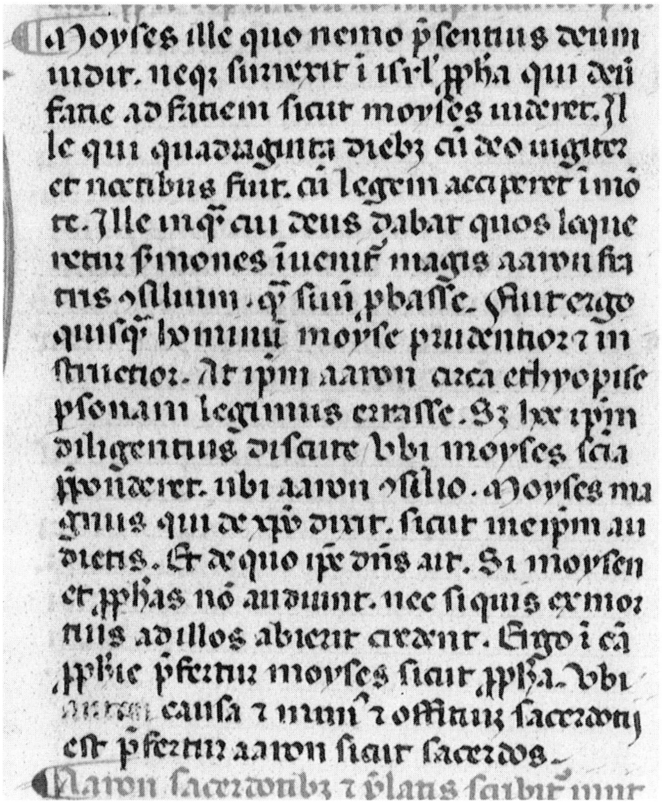

Pl. 62. Bartholomaeus Simeon Carusio, *Ambrosianum*, Somma Lombardo (diocese of Milan), 1408. Cambridge, Fitzwilliam Mus., MS CFM 9, f. 7va (*CMDGBCam*, pl. 196): ¶ Moyses ille quo nemo presentius Deum / vidit neque surrexit in Israel propheta qui Deum / fatie ad fatiem sicut Moyses videret. Il/le qui quadraginta diebus

A broad Southern Textualis Libraria (Rotunda). Note the few abbreviations, the frequent use of round **r** (see also the succession **rr** in 'surrexit', l. 2), undotted **y**, the absence of **v** as a minuscule, the form of the **con**-abbreviation ('consilium', l. 8), and the spellings 'fatiem' (for 'faciem', l. 3) and 'Ethyopise' (for 'Ethyophisse', l. 10).

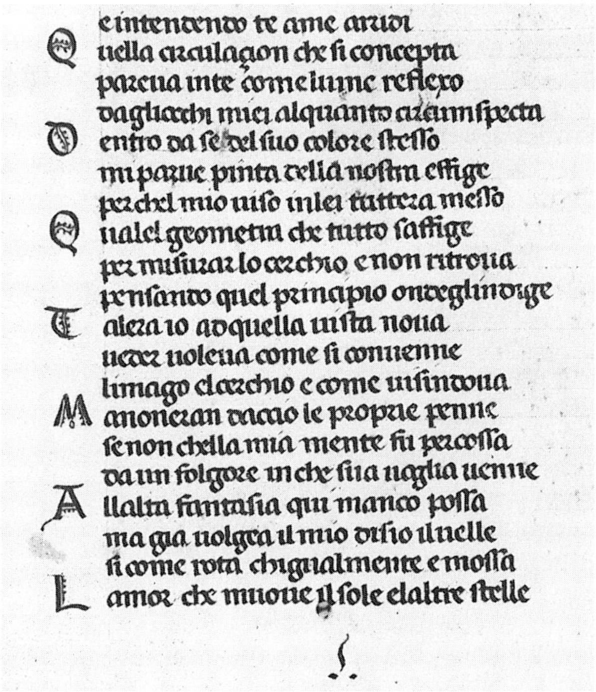

Pl. 63. Dante, *Divina commedia*, Padua? 1411. Paris, Bibl. nat. de France, MS ital. 530, f. 143r: e intendendo te am e arridi. / Quella circulaçion che si concepta / pareva in te come lume reflexo / dagli occhi miei alquanto circumspecta. / Dentro da sé, del suo colore stesso / mi parve pinta della nostra effige / per che'l mio viso in lei tutt'era messo. / Qual è'l geometra che tutto s'affige / per misurar lo cerchio e non ritrova, / pensando, quel principio ond' egl'indige

Semitextualis Formata, identical to Italian Rotunda except for **a**. Note the abundant use of round **r** (and the succession **rr** in 'arridi', l. 1), the absence of abbreviations and the curious majuscules.

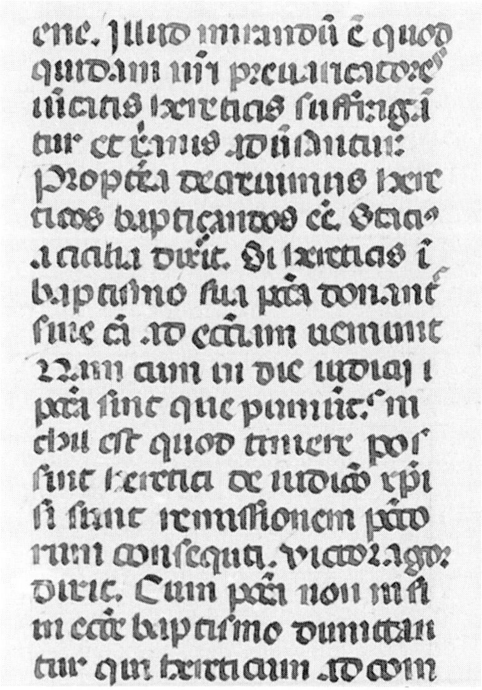

Pl. 64. Cyprianus, *Sententiae episcoporum LXXXVII de haereticis baptizandis*, Seville, 1416. Madrid, Bibl. Nacional, MS 5569, f. 93ra (Canellas, *Exempla*, II, pl. 51): [ali]/ene. Illud mirandum est quod / quidam nostri prevaricatores / veritatis hereticis suffragan/tur et Christianis adversantur. / Propterea decrevimus here/ticos baptiçandos esse. Stacius / a Cicilia dixit

Southern Textualis Libraria (Rotunda; 'Libraria caligráfica redonda' according to Canellas) with short ascenders and descenders. Note **c** caudata for **z**, the peculiar form of **x** ('Christianis', l. 4) and the line-filler on l. 10.

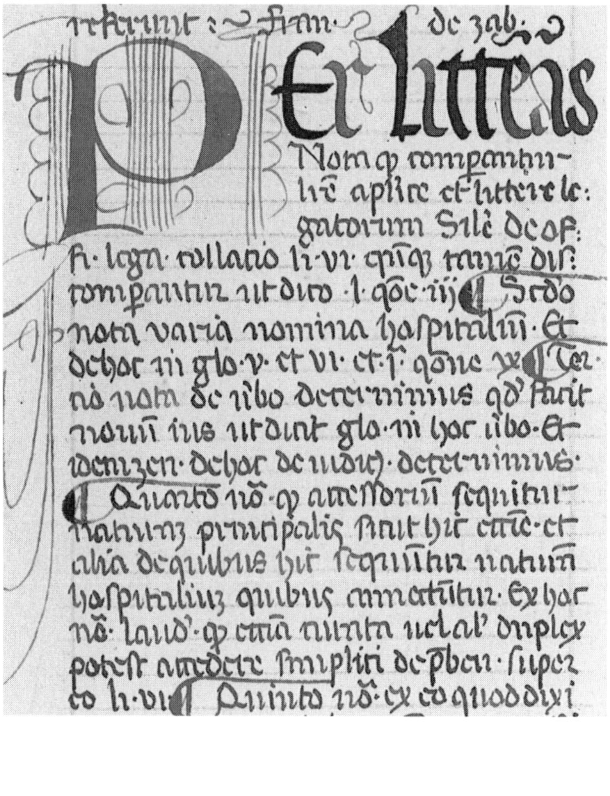

Pl. 65. Franciscus de Zabarella, *Lectura super Clementinis*, North-eastern Italy, 1437. New Haven, Yale Univ., Beinecke Libr., MS 343, f. 179v: Per litteras. / Nota quod comparantur / littere apostolice et littere le/gatorum. Simile de of/ficio legatorum collacio libro VI. Quandoque tamen dis/comparantur ut dico I. questione III. ¶ Secundo / nota varia nomina hospitalium

The lemma is in a large Rotunda Formata, the text in a rapid simplified Semitextualis Libraria without any shading. Note the hyphen in the form of a colon. The manuscript is written on paper, rake-ruled, and the writing sits on the lines, not above them.

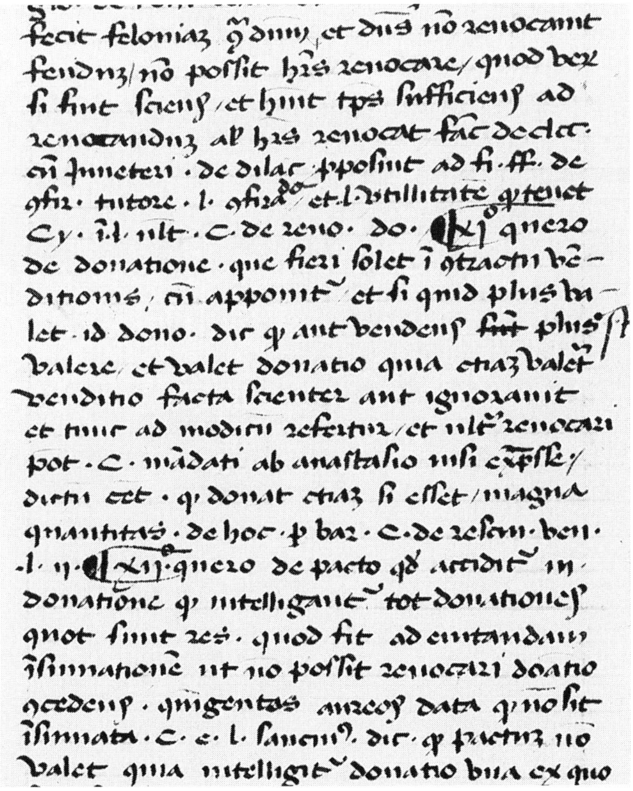

Pl. 66. Franciscus de Zabarella, *Lectura in librum III decretalium*, Pavia, 1445. Grenoble, Bibl. mun., MS 494, vol. I, f. 176v (another page: *CMDF*, VI, pl. 96): fecit feloniam contra dominum et dominus non revocavit / feudum, non possit heres revocare; quod verum, / si fuit sciens et habuit tempus sufficiens ad / revocandum alias heres revocat

A small Southern Semitextualis Libraria/Currens, broad and without fusions. Note the form of **g** and the **ur**-abbreviation in 'intelligantur' (l. 18), the exclusive use of round **r**, the trailing **s** in addition to the normal round **s**, the high **v**, the frequent use of final 3-shaped **m**. There are many juridical abbreviations.

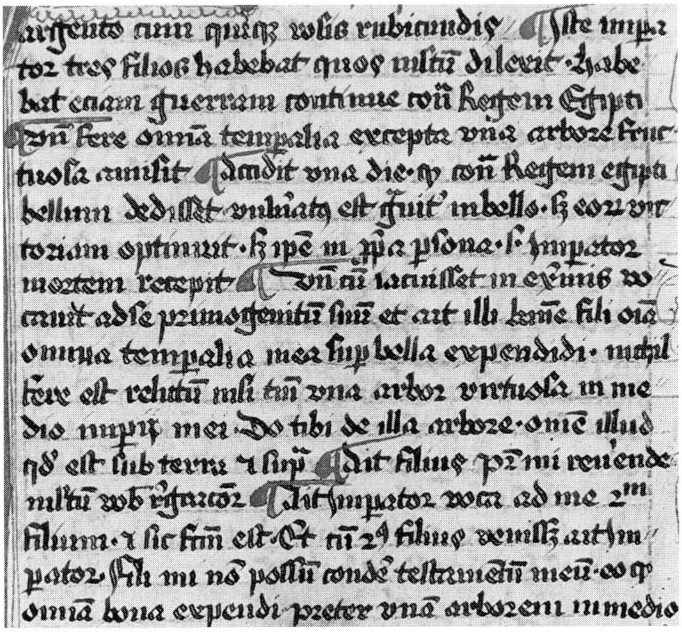

Pl. 67. *Gesta Romanorum*, copied in Oxford by a German scribe in 1449. Cambridge, Univ. Libr., MS Ii.6.1, f. 8v (*CMDGBCam*, pl. 250): argento cum quinque rosis rubicundis. ¶ Iste impera/tor tres filios habebat, quos multum dilexit. Habe/bat eciam guerram continue contra regem Egipti. / ¶ Unde fere omnia temporalia excepta una arbore fruc/tuosa amisit

A curious example of Northern Semitextualis, with 'German' boldness and angularity. Note the peculiar form of **a** (which is Cursiva), **o**, **v**, **x**, the long shaft of **d**, final **s** either as Cursiva or as angular trailing **s** ('rosis rubicundis', l. 1). Cursiva influence is also visible in **g** and in the use of majuscules ('Regem Egipti', l. 3).

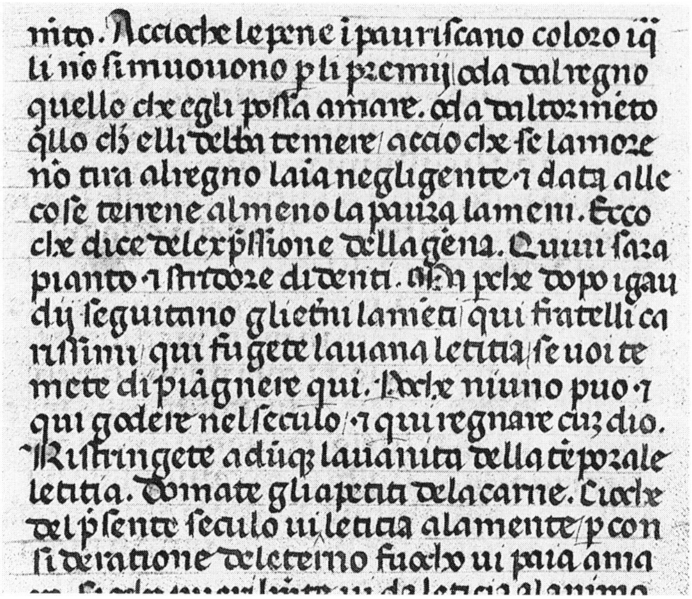

Pl. 68. Gregorius Magnus, *Homiliae* (in Italian), Italy, 1454. Berlin, Staatsbibl. Preuss. Kulturbesitz, MS Ham. 284, f. 235v (Crous and Kirchner, *Schriftarten*, fig. 25): [...]/mento. Accioché le pene impauriscano coloro i qua/li non si muovono per li premii o da tal regno / quello che egli possa amare, o da tal tormento / quello ch'elli debba temere, accioché se l'amore / non tira al regno l'anima negligente e data alle / cose terrene

Semitextualis Libraria very close to Rotunda, as is clear, for example, from the two forms of **a** used by the scribe. Note also the two forms of **d**, the **g** without a connecting stroke. The short pauses in the sentences are marked with a vertical hairline (*virgula suspensiva*).

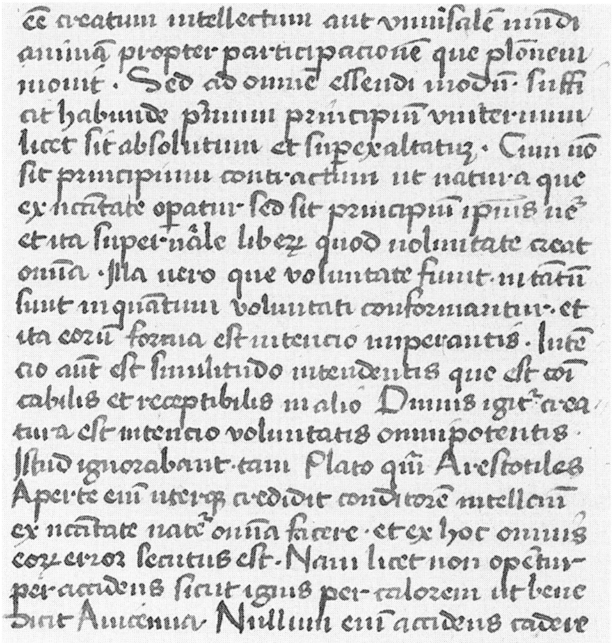

Pl. 69. Nicolaus Cusanus, *De beryllo*, copied in Italy (Rome?) for the author, 1459. New Haven, Yale Univ., Beinecke Libr., MS 334, f. 11v: esse creatum intellectum aut universalem mundi / animam propter participacionem que Platonem / movit. Sed ad omnem essendi modum suffi/cit habunde primum principium uniternum, / licet sit absolutum et superexaltatum

A small Semitextualis Libraria under Humanistic influence, evident from the long ascenders and descenders, the broad letters, the rarity of fusions and the Roman Capitals. Note the **d**, the **g** ('ignorabant', l. 15), the **rs** in 'error' (l. 18) and the round **s**.

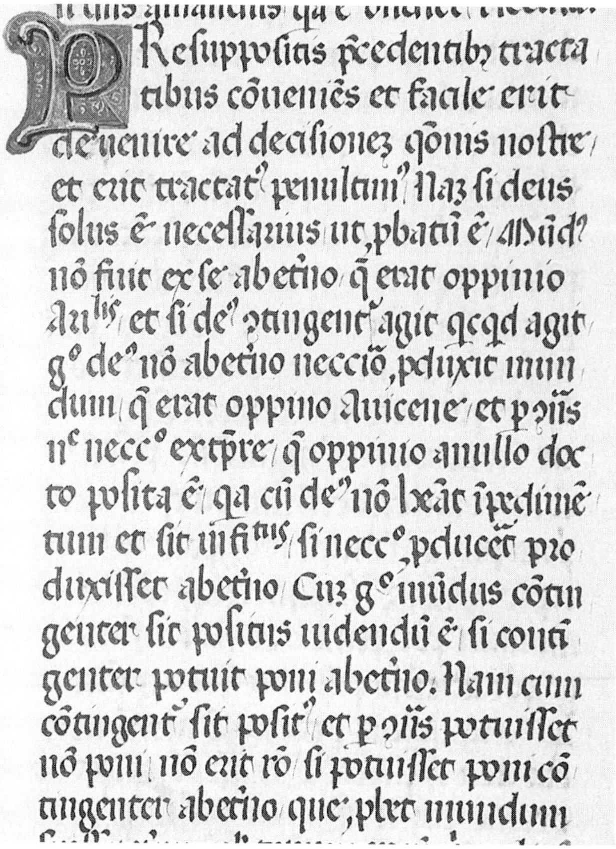

Pl. 72. Leonardus Nogarolus, *Liber de mundi aeternitate*, Vicenza, 1485. Rouen, Bibl. mun., MS 596, f. 117r (*CMDF*, VII, pl. 149): Presuppositis precedentibus tracta/tibus conveniens et facile erit / devenire ad decisionem questionis nostre; / et erit tractatus penultimus

Italian Textualis Libraria (Rotunda) under Humanistic influence, evident from the long ascenders and descenders and exclusive use of straight **d**. Note, however, the fusions (but not **pp**: 'oppinio', l. 6), the frequent use of round **r**, etc. The hairlines on straight **r** and final **t** are conspicuous.

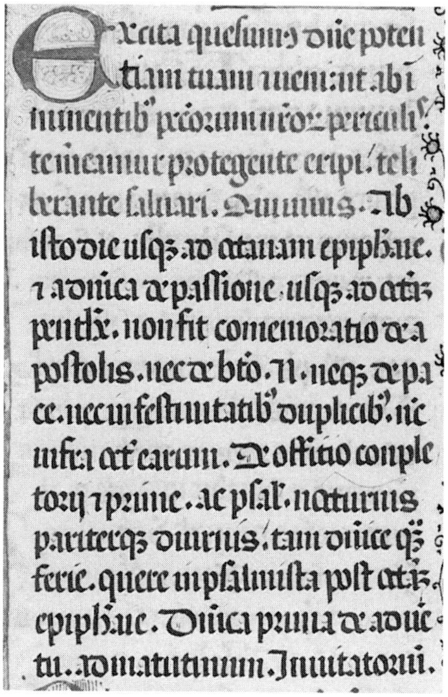

Pl. 73. *Breviarium Romanum*, Horta, The Azores, 1489. Cambridge, Univ. Libr., MS MM.5.21, f. 75rb (*CMDGBCam*, pl. 333): Excita, quesumus, Domine, poten/tiam tuam et veni, ut ab im/minentibus peccatorum nostrorum periculis / te mereamur protegente eripi, te li/berante salvari. Qui vivis. Ab / isto die usque ad octavam Epiphanie / et a dominica de Passione usque ad octavam / Penthecosten non fit comemoratio de a/postolis

Southern Textualis Formata (Rotunda) with relatively long ascenders and descenders. The scribe had difficulty in maintaining the height of the minuscules, especially in the **oc** fusion.

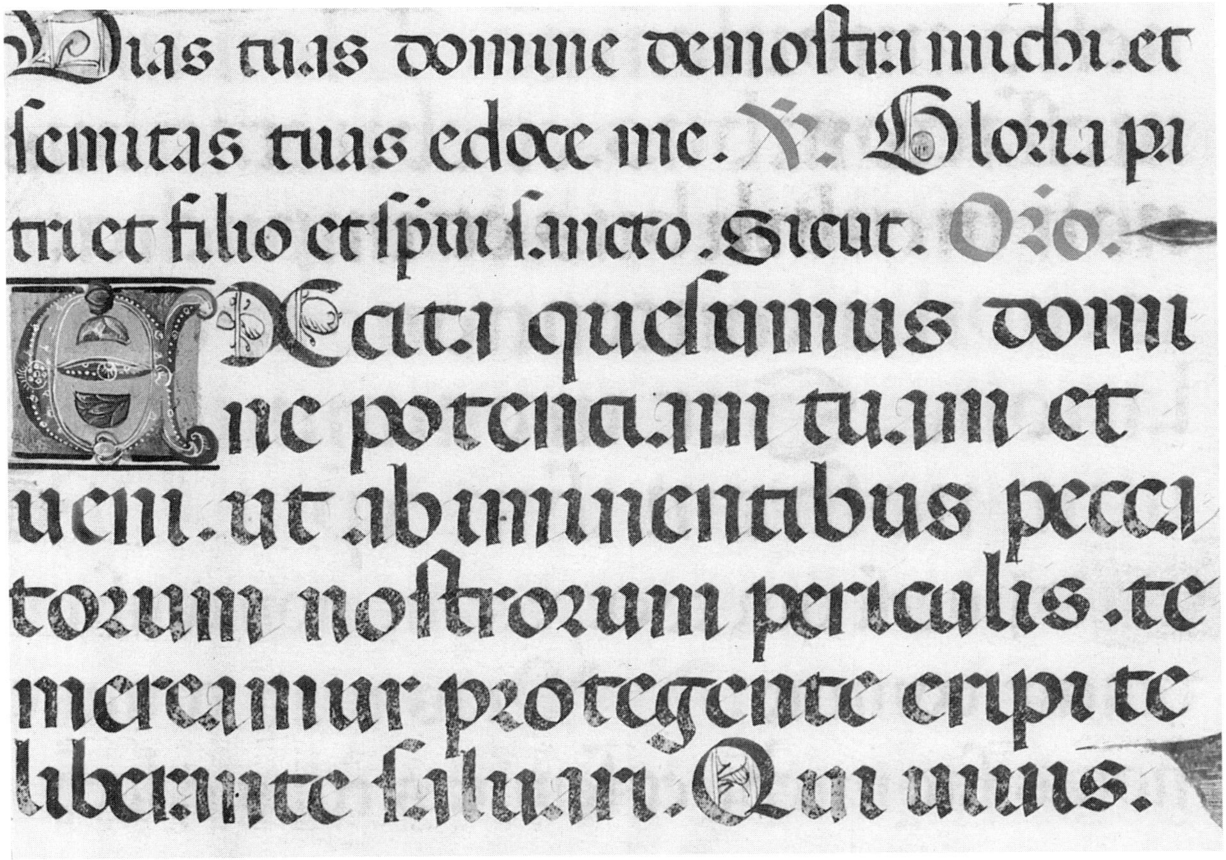

Pl. 74. *Missale* ('Missal of cardinal Oliviero Carafa'), Italy, 1488. Cambridge, Fitzwilliam Mus., MS Marlay 10, f. 5r (*CMDGBCam*, pl. 331): *Vias tuas, Domine, demostra michi, et / semitas tuas edoce me. Versus. Gloria Pa/tri et Filio et Spiritui Sancto. Sicut. Oratio. / Excita, quesumus, Domi/ne, potenciam tuam et / veni, ut ab iminentibus pecca/torum nostrorum periculis*

A late Southern Textualis Formata (Rotunda) of exceptional size and calligraphy, as used in a luxurious illuminated Missal. Note the two forms of **d** and the Italian spelling 'demostra'. As the entire text is written on the same ruling, the lines of smaller script look widely spaced, but in the large script the long ascenders and descenders interfere with each other.

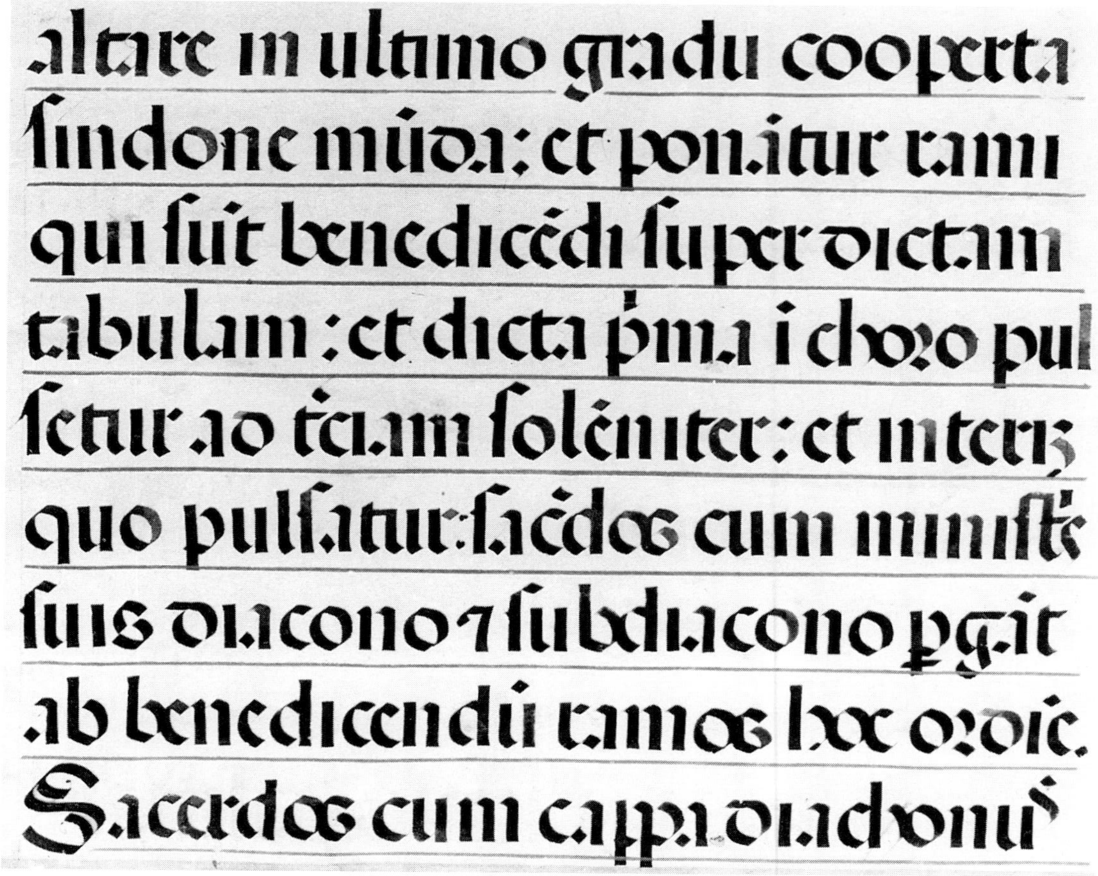

Pl. 75. (reduced: 65 per cent of actual size). *Missale*, Toledo, about 1510. Madrid, Bibl. Nacional, MS 1543, f. 1r (Canellas, *Exempla*, II, pl. 48): altare in ultimo gradu cooperta / sindone munda, et ponantur rami / qui sunt benedicendi super dictam / tabulam; et dicta prima in choro

Canellas calls this calligraphic script of immense size 'Libraria caligráfica fracturada'. In fact, although it is more 'drawn' than actually written, it presents all the characteristics of Iberian Textualis Formata (Rotunda). Note especially the full Textus Praescissus character of **m** and **n**, in addition to **a**, straight **d**, **f**, **h**, **i**; straight **s**, second minim of **u**. Note the occasional use of Cursiva round **s** ('Sacerdos', bottom l.).

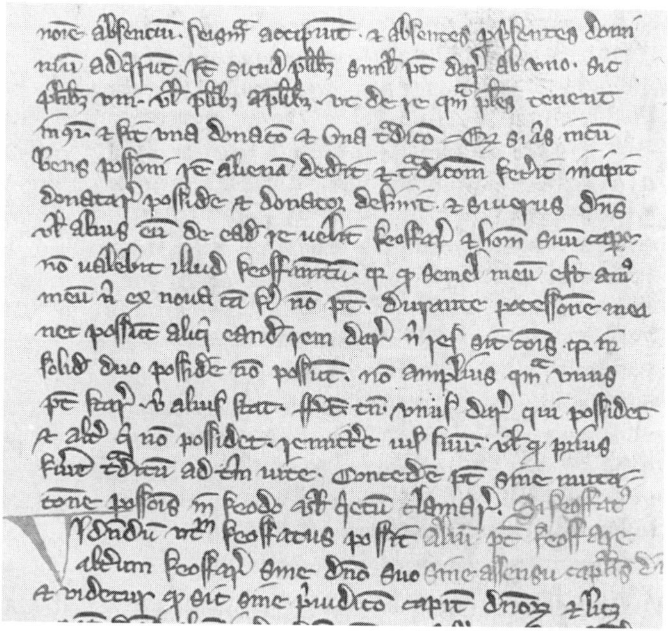

Pl. 77. Ranulphus de Glanvilla?, *De legibus et consuetudinibus regni Angliae* ('Book of Luffield'), Luffield (England), 1280–89. Cambridge, Univ. Libr., MS Ee.I.1, f. 60rb (*CMDGBCam*, pl. 123): nomine absentium seignoriam accipiunt et absentes per presentes domi/nium adquirunt. Item sicud pluribus simul potest dari ab uno, sic / pluribus uni vel pluribus a pluribus, ut de re quam plures tenent

A small irregular Cursiva Antiquior

Libraria/Currens (Anglicana), sloping to the left. Note the two forms of **a** ('nova causa', l. 9) and of **v** ('una', 'una', l. 4) and the bold curved abbreviation strokes.

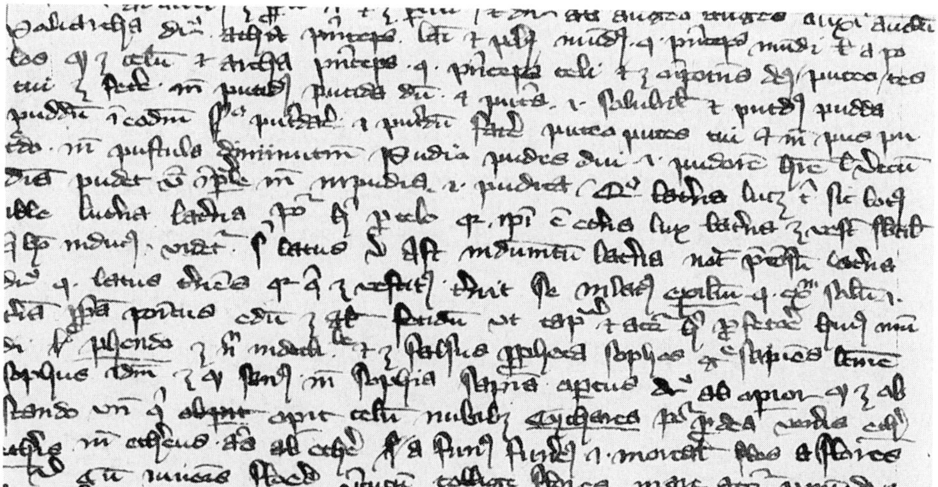

Pl. 78. *Varia latina*, Freising, 1346. Vienna, Österreichische Nationalbibl., MS 15071, f. 53r (other pages: *CMDA*, I, pls. 122–3): Poliarcha dicitur a cha princeps lai et polus mundus, quasi princeps mundi; vel a po/los, quod est celum, et archa princeps, quasi princeps celi, et est omnipotens Deus. Puteo, tes

A small Cursiva Antiquior Currens, sloping to the left and highly abbreviated. Due to the rapid writing and the ligatures, the letters in this grammatical treatise are uneven in size and often poorly formed. Note the shape of **f** and straight **s**.

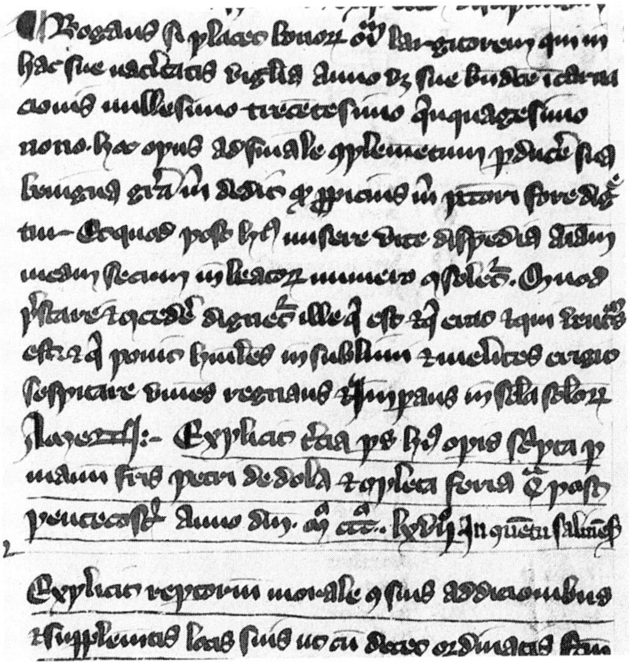

Pl. 79. Petrus Berchorius, *Repertorium morale*, copied in the convent of the Observantines of Salins (Jura) in 1367. Besançon, Bibl. mun., MS 217, f. 369r (*CMDF*, V, pl. 60): ¶ Rogans si placet bonorum omnium largitorem, qui in / hac sue nativitatis vig<i>lia, anno videlicet sue benedicte incarna/cionis millesimo trecentesimo quinquagesimo / nono, hoc opus ad finale complementum perducere sua

A small, bold Cursiva Antiquior Libraria/Currens. Note the two forms of **a** ('nativitatis', l. 2), the short **g**, the endstrokes of **h** ('hoc', l. 4) and of final **m** and **n**, the form of **t** ('placet', l. 1), and the fusions (made despite the rapid writing: 'peccatori', l. 5).

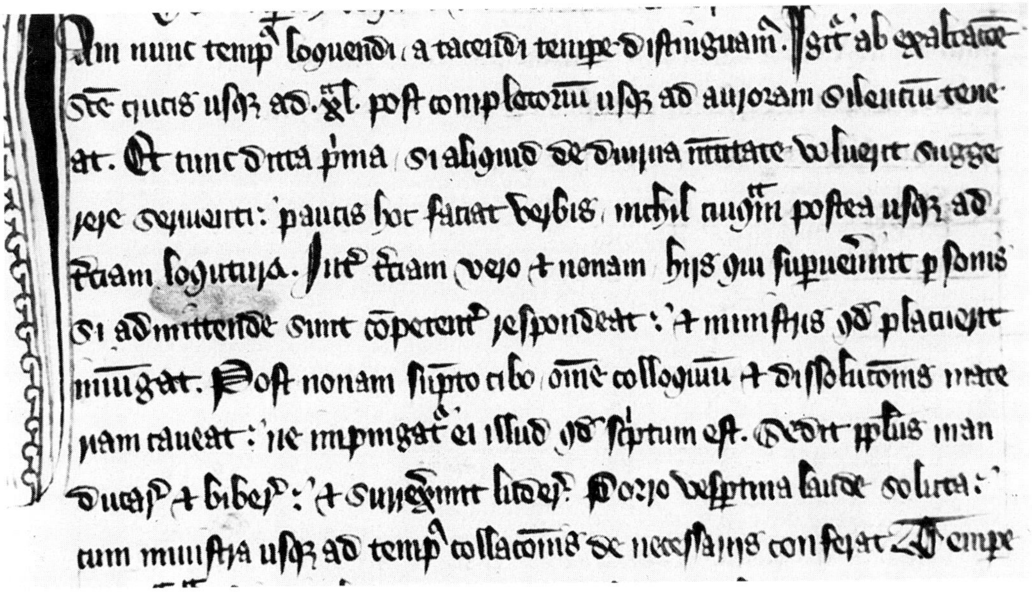

Pl. 80. *Varia latina*, copied in the abbey of Whalley (England) in 1373. Paris, Bibl. univ., MS 790, f. 4v (*CMDF*, I, pl. 54): Iam nunc tempus loquendi a tacendi tempore distinguamus. Igitur ab exaltacione / sancte Crucis usque ad Quadragesimam post completorium usque ad auroram silentium tene/at. Et tunc dicta prima

Cursiva Antiquior Libraria (Anglicana). Note the relatively low height of **a**, the peculiar form of **q**, the two forms of initial **v** ('voluerit', l. 3, 'vero', l. 5), the approach stroke of tironian **et**.

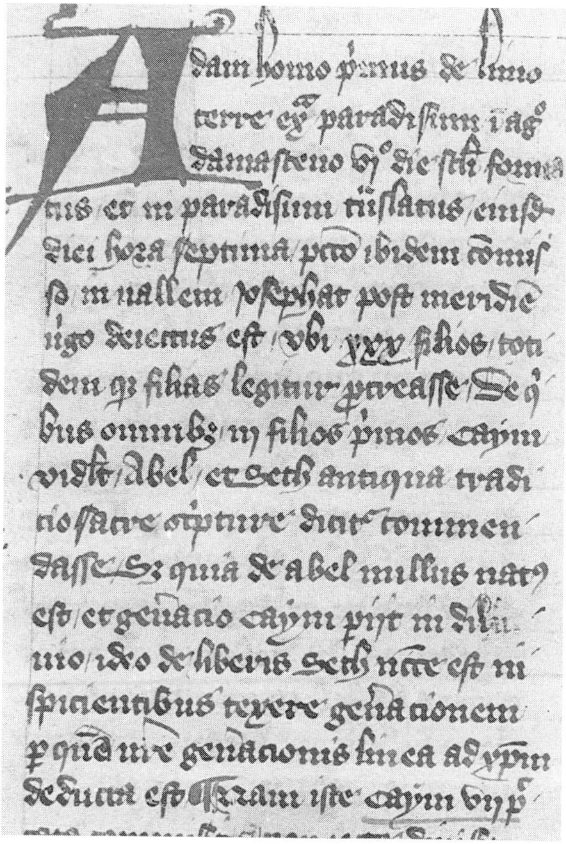

Pl. 81. *Thomae Sprotti Chronica,* Canterbury? 1377–96. Cambridge, Univ. Libr., MS Add. 3578, p. 33a (*CMDGBCam,* pl. 163): Adam homo primus de limo / terre extra paradisum in agro / Damasceno VI° die seculi forma/tus et in paradisum translatus eiusdem / diei hora septima peccato ibidem commis/so in vallem Iosephat post meridiem

A bold Cursiva Antiquior Libraria/Formata (Anglicana); the level is Formata according to the criteria formulated by Parkes. The quadrangles at the headline and the baseline in **m** and **n** remind us of Textus Quadratus. Note also the 'cursive' tracing of straight **s** ('septima', l. 5) and the **sc**-ligatures ('Damasceno', l. 3; 'scripture', l. 11).

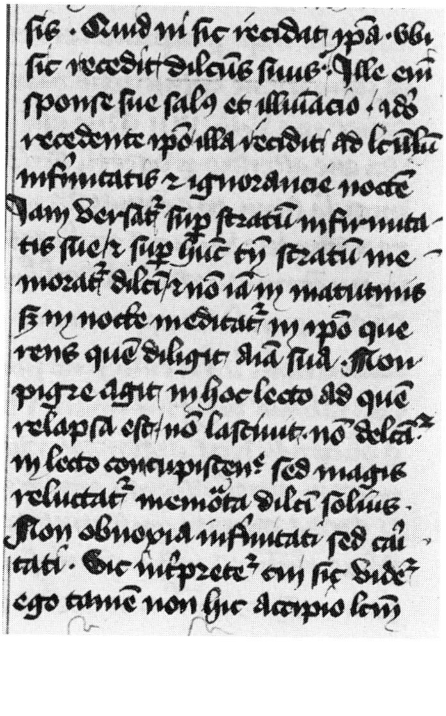

Pl. 82. Gilbertus de Hoylandia, *Sermones in Cantica Canticorum,* Utrecht? 1405. Utrecht, Univ. Libr., MS 207, f. 1vb (*CMDNL,* II, pl. 634): [lumino]/sis. Quidni sic recidat ipsa, ubi / sic recedit dilectus suus? Ille enim / sponse sue salus et illuminacio; ideo / recedente ipso illa recidit ad lectulum / infirmitatis et ignorancie noctem

Cursiva Antiquior/Cursiva Recentior Libraria. The general appearance and letters such as final **s** and **x** are proper to Cursiva Recentior, but one-compartment and two-compartment **a** alternate. Note the endstroke on final **m** and **n** (bottom l.), the looped or unlooped **ct**-ligature ('nocte', l. 9; 'lecto', l. 11), the vertical hairline on final **t**.

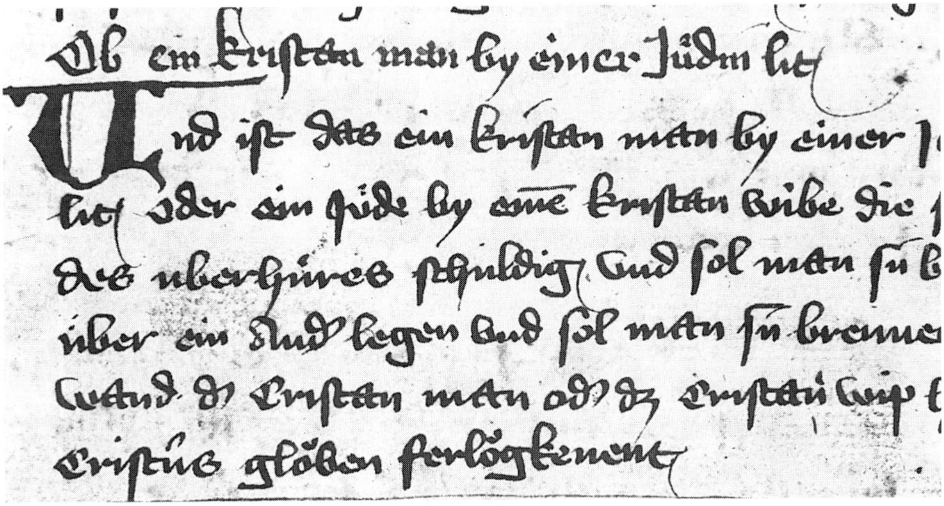

Pl. 83. *Schwabenspiegel*, Germany, 1422. Colmar, Bibl. mun., MS 80, f. 163v (another page: *CMDF*, V, pl. 86): Ob ein kristan man by einer Judin lit. / Und ist, das ein kristan man by einer J[udin] / lit oder ein Jude by einem kristan wibe, die [sint] / des uberhures schuldig, und sol man sii b[ede] / über einander legen und sol man sii brenne[n]

    A late example of continental Cursiva Antiquior Currens. Note the numerous ligatures; **i** dotted or with a hairline (**ii** has one hairline); the form of **w** ('wand', l. 6); the umlaut on diphthong **o** and **u**; the excessive hairline decoration on final **t**.

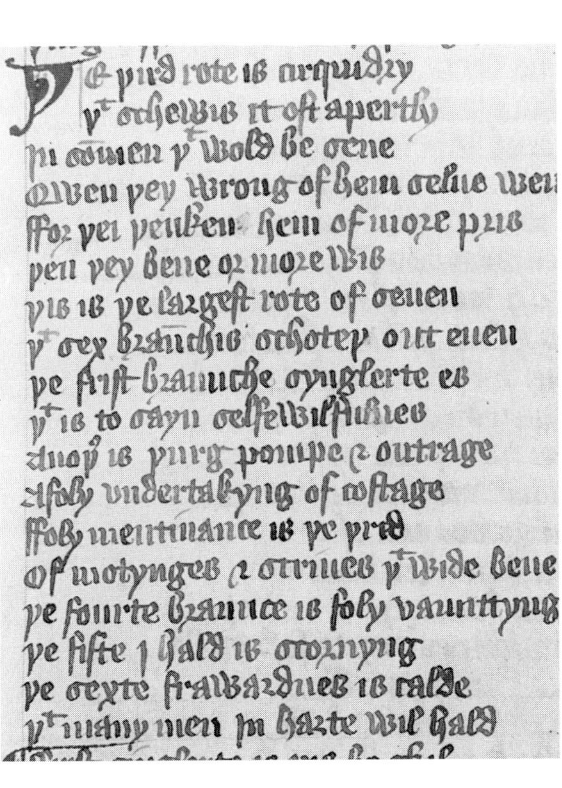

Pl. 84. Guillelmus de Nassington, *Speculum vitae* (in English), England, 1423. Cambridge, Univ. Libr., MS ii.1.36, f. 53r (*CMDGBCam*, pl. 206): Þe þird rote is cirquidry / Þat schewis it oft apertly / In somen þat wold be sene / Qwen þey wrong of hem selve we[ne]. / For þei þenken hem of more pris / Þen þey bene or more wis

    Cursiva Antiquior Libraria (Anglicana), using Cursiva (Secretary) final round **s**. Note double **f** used as a majuscule, the conspicuous approach stroke to tironian **et** (l. 11), and long hairline on round **r**, the form of thorn (þ), which is clearly different from **y**.

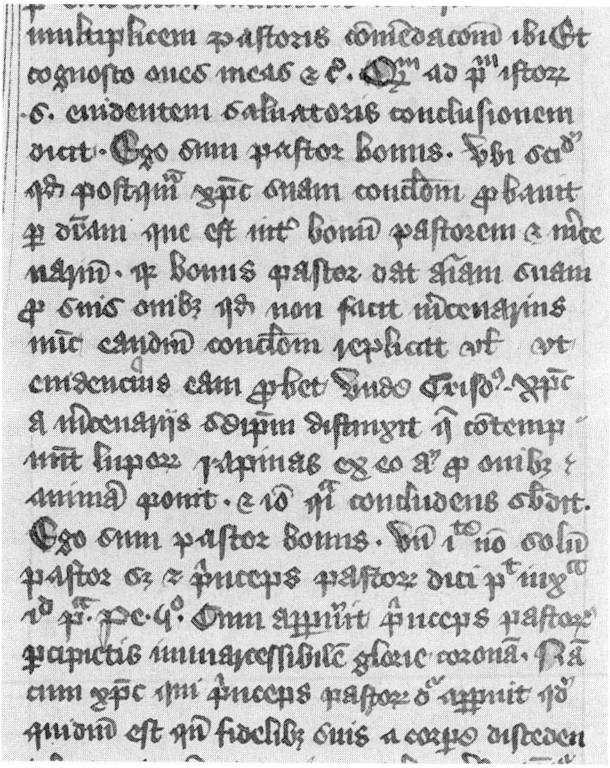

Pl. 85. Philippus de Monte Calerio, *Sermones Dominicales*, Lincoln, 1425. Cambridge, Univ. Libr., MS Gg.4.19, f. 29va (*CMDGBCam*, pl. 212): multiplicem pastoris commendacionem ibi. Et / cognosco oves meas, etc. Quoniam ad primum istorum, / scilicet evidentem Salvatoris conclusionem, / dicit: Ego sum pastor bonus. Ubi sciendum / quod postquam Christus suam conclusionem probavit

An angular Cursiva Antiquior/Cursiva Recentior Libraria/Formata (Anglicana). Note the two forms of **a**, of **d** (looped and loopless), of **e** ('probet unde', l. 10), the four forms of **r** ('differentiam', 'pastorem', l. 6; 'mercenarius', l. 8; 'rapinas', l. 12) and of **s** (the Cursiva form of the latter in 'concludens', l. 13).

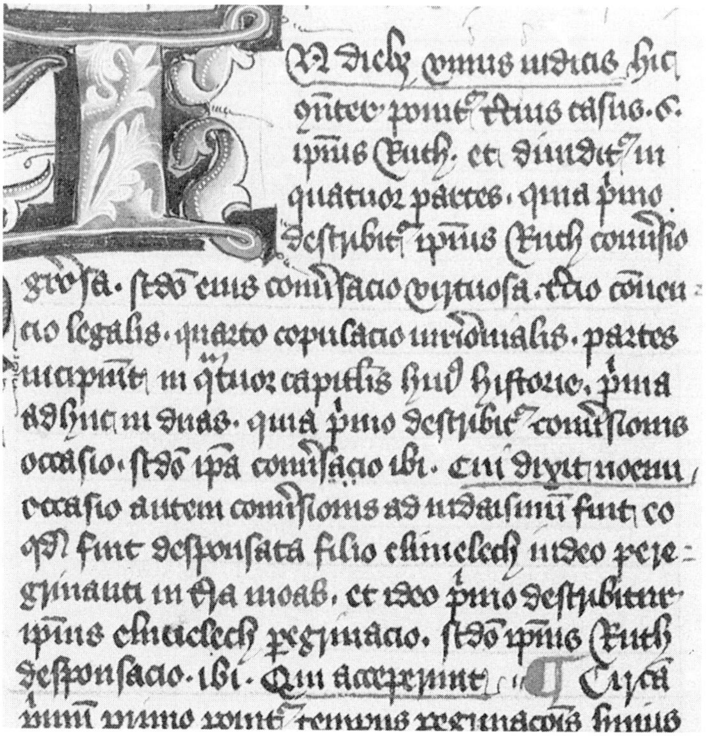

Pl. 86. Nicolaus de Lyra, *Postillae in Bibliam*, England, c. 1453–7? Cambridge, Univ. Libr., MS Dd.7.7, f. 191rb (*CMDGBCam*, pl. 265): In diebus unius iudicis. Hic / communiter ponitur tercius casus, scilicet / ipsius Ruth, et dividitur in / quatuor partes, quia primo / describitur ipsius Ruth conversio

A bold and angular Cursiva Antiquior Libraria/Formata (Anglicana). Anglicana round **s** in initial position is here generally replaced by straight **s**; final **s** is sometimes Cursiva ('partes', l. 4). Note the long approach strokes to initial **v** ('unius', l. 1) and majuscule **R** ('Ruth', l. 3).

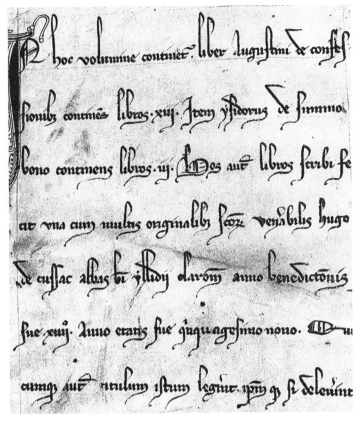

Pl. 87. (reduced: 65 per cent of actual size). Augustinus, *Confessiones*; Isidorus Hispalensis, *De summo bono*, Clermont, abbey of St Allyre, 1265. Clermont-Ferrand, Bibl. mun., MS 102, f. AV (another page: *CMDF*, VI, pl. 23): In hoc volumine continetur liber Augustini de confes/sionibus continens libros XIII. Item Ysidorus de summo / bono continens libros III

For the table of contents, ownership-mark and note on the making of this codex, a large and solemn documentary cursive script was used. Note the long looped ascenders; the curved descenders and endstrokes of **f**, **p**, **q**, straight **s**, and of **m** and round **s** in final position; the abbreviation signs.

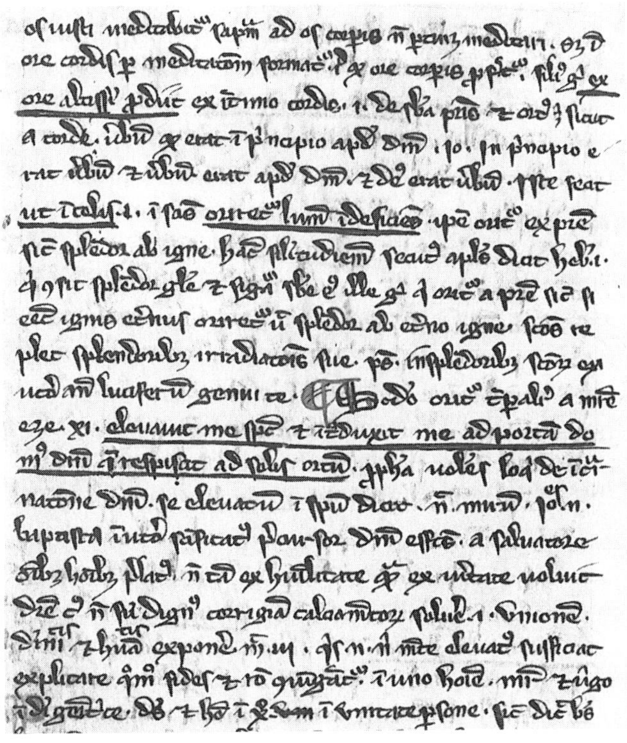

Pl. 88. *Summa sermonum*; *Themata sermonum*, copied in the abbey of Clairvaux in 1298. Troyes, Bibl. mun., MS 1999, f. 118v (another page: *CMDF*, V, pl. 35): Os iusti meditabitur sapienciam. Ad os corporis non pertinet meditari, sed in / ore cordis per meditacionem formatur id quod ore corporis profertur. Filius igitur ex / ore Altissimi prodiit ex intimo cordis, id est de substancia Patris

A small early Cursiva Currens, close to early Cursiva Antiquior Currens as is evident from the occasional use of two-compartment **a** and the bold diagonal strokes. The script is irregular, sloping to the left and highly abbreviated.

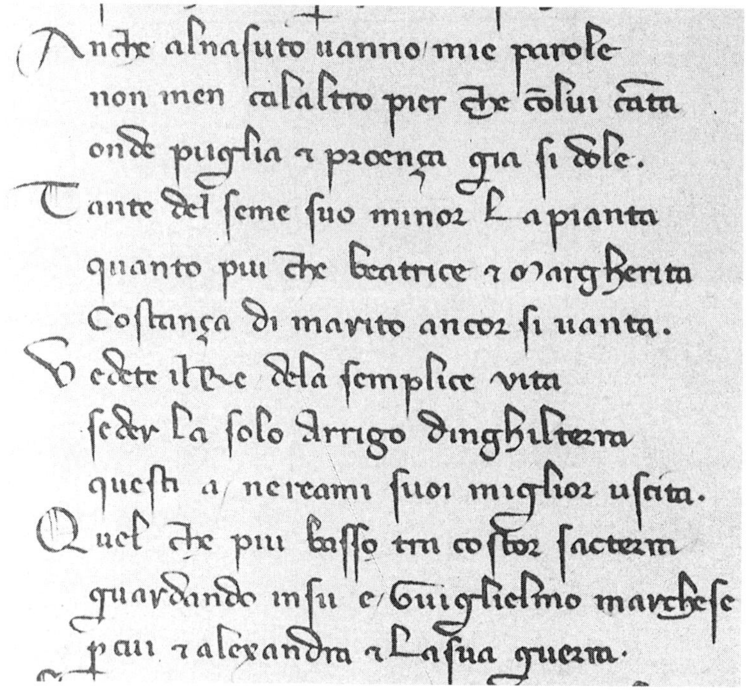

Pl. 89. Dante, *Divina commedia*, Florence, 1347. Florence, Bibl. Medicea Laurenziana, MS Gaddi 90, f. 75ra (*Archivio Paleografico Italiano*, x, fasc. 69 [*Codici Danteschi*], pl. 16): Anche al nasuto vanno mie parole / non men ca l'altro pier che con lui canta, / onde puglia et proença gia si dole. / Tante del seme suo minor la pianta

Cursiva Formata (Cancelleresca). Due to the occasional appearance of loopless ascenders ('che', ll. 2, 5) the hand tends to Semihybrida. Note the three forms of **r** and the Southern form of tironian **et**.

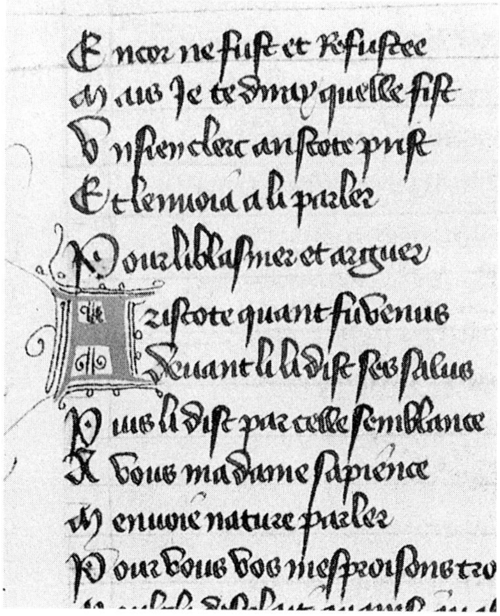

Pl. 90. Guillaume de Digulleville, *Le pèlerinage de vie humaine*, France, 1385–90. Reims, Bibl. mun., MS 1276, f. 18r (*CMDF*, v, pl. 65): Encor ne fust et refustee, / Mais je te diray qu'elle fist: / Un sien clerc Aristote prist / Et l'envoia a li parler / Pour li blasmer et arguer

An early example of rather angular Cursiva Libraria tending towards Bastarda. Note the three forms of **r** (ll. 1–2, although round **r** is dominant), the use of long **i** in 'je' and the typical **st**-ligature (l. 1).

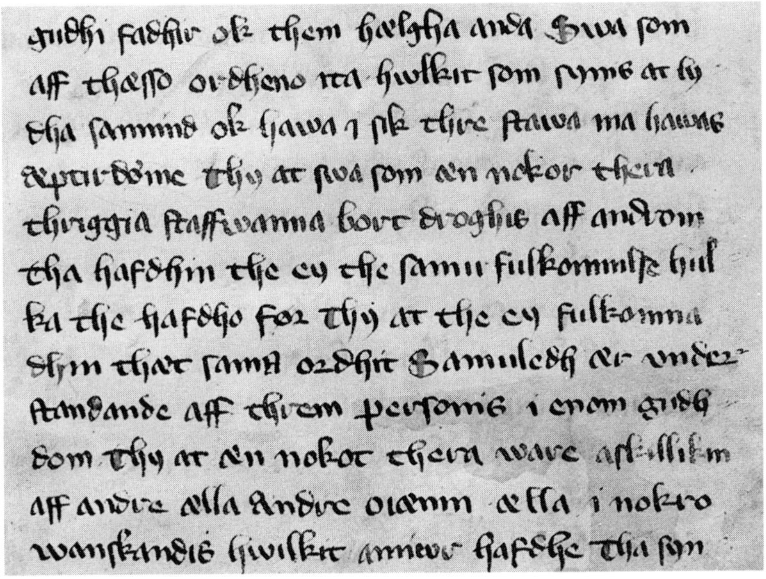

Pl. 91. *Codex Oxenstiernianus* (S. Birgitta, *Sermo angelicus*, in Swedish), Sweden, 1385. Stockholm, Royal Libr., MS A 110, f. 2r (*CMDS*, II, pl. 13): gudhi fadhir ok them hælgha anda swa som / aff thæsso ordheno ita hwlkit som synis at ly/dha sannind ok hawa i sik thre stawa ma hawas / æptirdøme

A largely disconnected Cursiva Libraria. Note as special signs the **ae**-ligature and crossed **o**, and the form of **g**. The direction of the ascenders is not constant, but is variously forward-sloping, backward-sloping or vertical.

Pl. 92. Petrus de Vineis, *Opera*, Padua, 1386. Vatican Libr., MS Ott. lat. 1738, f. 37v (*CMDVat*, I, pl. 18): Pre omnibus tamen infelix Mediolanum ingemescat et doleat et am[are] / prorumpat in lacrimas pro tantis occisorum catervis militum et civi[um] / occisorum vel captivorum et amodo obedire domino asuescat

Italian Cursiva Libraria/Currens, the letter forms of which remind us of Cancelleresca. Note **d** and **x**, majuscule **B** ('Brixiensis', l. 7), the curious long curving hairline abbreviation marks, the Italian **et**- and **bus**-abbreviations ('Mediolanensibus', l. 8), the long endstrokes of various letters, etc. The greasy appearance is typical of many Italian paper manuscripts of the period (cf. pls. 118 and 133).

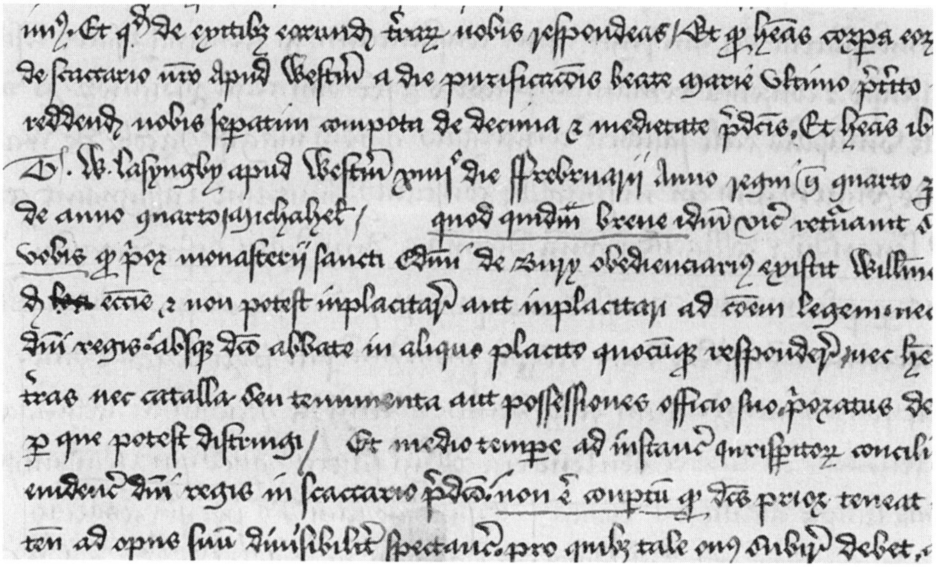

Pl. 93. *Registrum vestiarii monasterii S. Edmundi*, Bury St Edmunds, *c.* 1401–17? Cambridge, Univ. Libr., MS Ff.2.29, f. 80v (*CMDGBCam*, pl. 189): [preceper]/imus et quod de exitibus earundem terrarum nobis respondeas, et quod habeas corpora eorum [coram baronibus] / de scaccario nostro apud Westmonasterium a die Purificacionis beate Marie ultimo preterito [in XV dies ad] / reddendum nobis

An angular Cursiva Libraria (Secretary). Apart from most **a**s, which are single-compartment, this example is still very close to Anglicana, i.e. Cursiva Antiquior, as is evident from the letter forms and from the general aspect of the page.

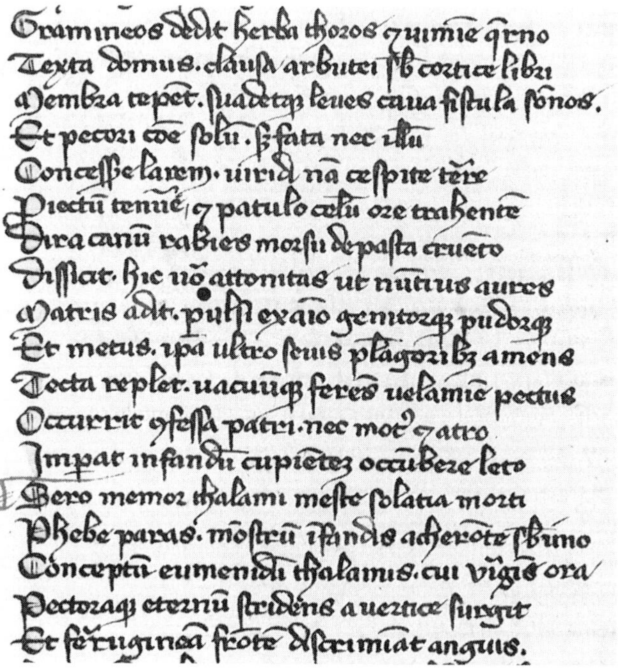

Pl. 94. Statius, *Thebais*, Italy, 1406. New Haven, Yale Univ., Beinecke Libr., MS Marston 42, f. 8r: Gramineos dedit herba thoros et vimine querno / Texta domus, clausa arbutei sub cortice libri / Membra tepent, suadetque leves cava fistula somnos, / Et pecori commune solum, sed fata nec illum

Cursiva Libraria (Cancelleresca) used for copying a classical Latin text. Note the form of straight **r** ('Occurrit', l. 12) and of tironian **et**, and the long endstrokes of **h** and final **m**. Minuscule **v** is not used.

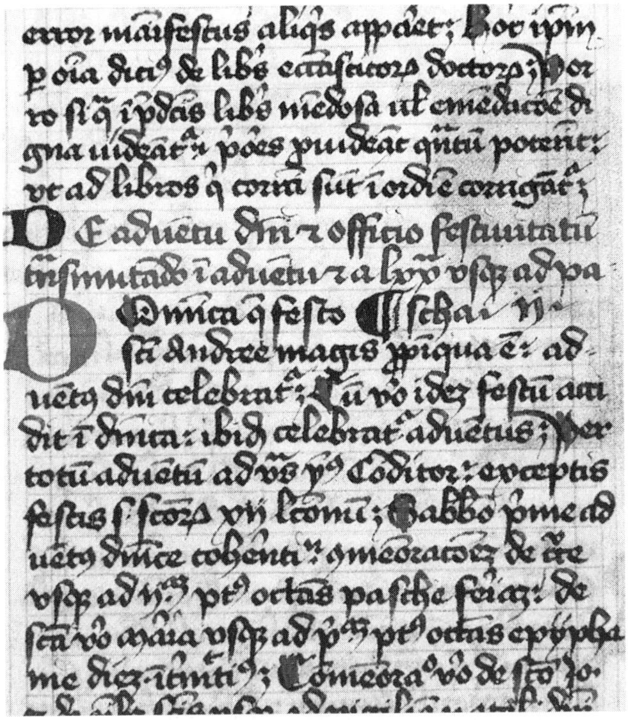

Pl. 95. *Statuta Ordinis Carthusiensis*, Prague, 1414. Vienna, Österreichische Nationalbibl., MS 1670, f. 3v (Mazal, *Buchkunst der Gotik*, pl. 36; another page: *CMDA*, II, pl. 107): error manifestus aliquis apparet. Hoc ipsum / per omnia dicimus de libris ecclesiasticorum doctorum. Por/ro si qua in predictis libris mendosa vel emendacione di/gna videantur, priores provideant quantum poterint

A bold Cursiva Libraria/Formata ('Böhmische Bastarda' according to Mazal). Note the typical form of **d**, straight **r**, double-stroked **y** ('Epyphanie', ll. 16–17), the **ct**-ligature ('octavas', l. 16), the **r**-, **con**- and **ru**-abbreviations ('coherenti commemoracionem de Cruce', l. 14). Punctuation: *punctus elevatus, punctus flexus* and *punctus versus*.

Pl. 96. Cicero, *Opuscula*, Constance, 1417. Reims, Bibl. mun., MS 1110, f. 32v (*CMDF*, V, pl. 82): Multa michi necessario, iudices, pre/termittenda sunt, ut possim aliquo modo / aliquando de his rebus que fidei commisse [*correction*] / sunt dicere. Recepi enim causam Sicilie

Incipit in Textualis Formata, the text in Cursiva Libraria. Note the shortness of the ascenders, the angular form of **a**, **o** and other letters, the occasional use of trailing **s** ('iuribus', l. 12), the **tt**-ligature ('pretermittenda', ll. 1–2), but especially the loopless **d**; approach strokes at initial **v** and tironian **et**. The manuscript was written for a French participant in the Council of Constance.

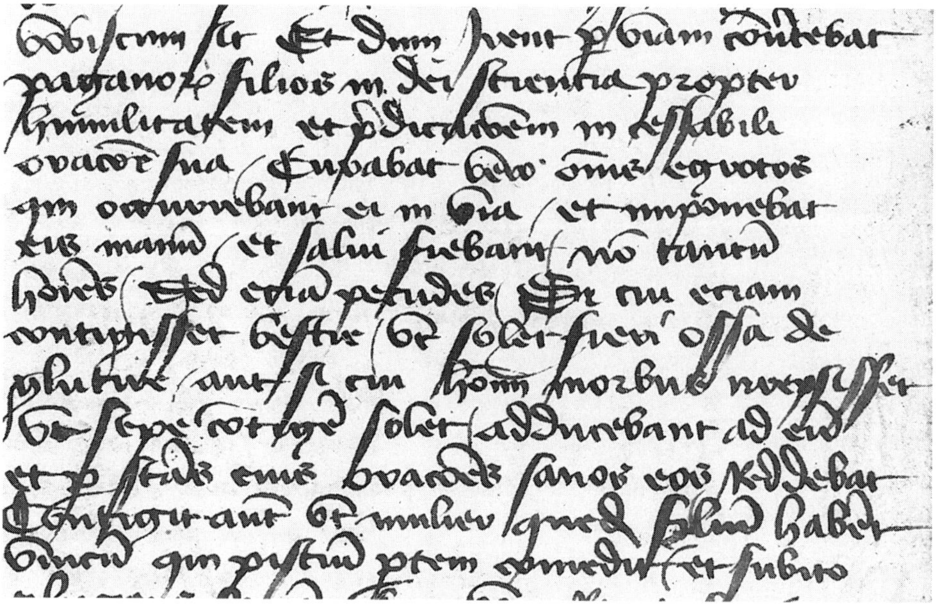

Pl. 97. *Lectionarium,* Tours, 1418. Tours, Bibl. mun., MS 157, f. 34r (another page: *CMDF,* VII, pl. 103): vobiscum sit. Et dum irent per viam convertebat / paganorum filios in Dei sciencia propter / humilitatem et predicacionem incessabili / oracione sua. Curabat vero omnes egrotos / qui occurrebant ei in via et imponebat

Cursiva Currens displaying numerous ligatures (e.g. **sc, so**). Note the long and steeply sloping **f** and straight **s** (their construction is visible in the poorly formed **ss** of 'ossa', l. 8), the form of **e** ('et', l. 3), the structure of **g** ('contigisset', l. 8), the use of majuscule **i** in initial position ('irent', l. 1).

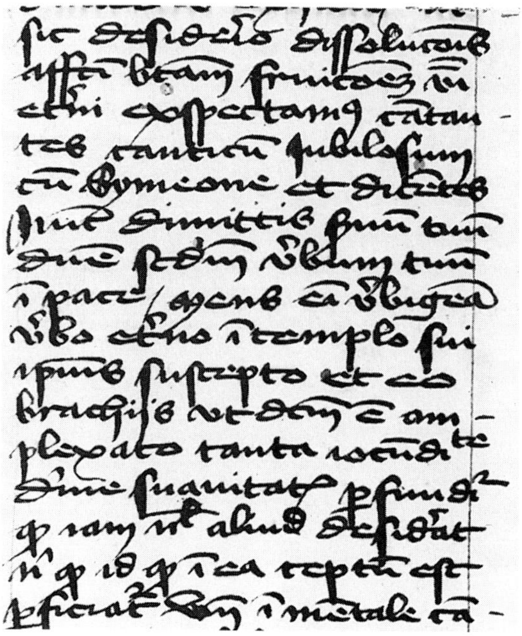

Pl. 98. Iordanus de Quedlinburg, *Sermones,* Sélestat? 1433. Sélestat, Bibl. mun., MS 19, f. 271ra (*CMDF,* v, pl. 92): Sic desiderio dissolucionis / affecti beatam fruicionem verbi / eterni exspectamus, cantan/tes canticum iubilosum / cum Symeone et dicentes: / Nunc dimittis servum tuum

Cursiva Currens written in Western Germany by a scribe from Erfurt. Note the highly dislocated and broad character of this rapid hand (e.g. 'et eo', l. 10), the exclusive use of straight **r**, the double abbreviation stroke on 'verbi' (l. 2). The vertical direction of **f** and straight **s** and the dotted **is** are typical of German Cursiva.

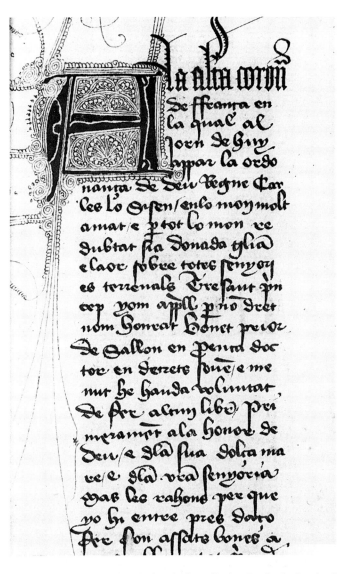

Pl. 99. Honoré Bonet, *L'arbre des batailles* (in Catalan), Catalonia, 1429. Paris, Bibl. nat. de France, MS esp. 206, f. 5r (another page: *CMDF*, IV, 1, pl. 58): A la alta corona / de Ffrança, en / la qual al / jorn de huy / appar la ordo/nança de Deu regne Car/les lo sisen, en lo mon molt / amat e per tot lo mon re/dubtat, sia donada gloria / e laor sobre totes senyori/es terrenals

Incipit in Textualis Formata, the rest in bold Cursiva Libraria, with an occasional loopless ascender ('lo', l. 7). Note in this Iberian hand the long vertical **f**, **p**, **q** and straight **s**, the form of **ç**, **h**, straight **r** and **y**. Typical are the occasional Iberian use of long **i** ('senyories', ll. 10–11), the **pri**-abbreviation ('princep', ll. 11–12), and the dagger-like horizontal abbreviation marks.

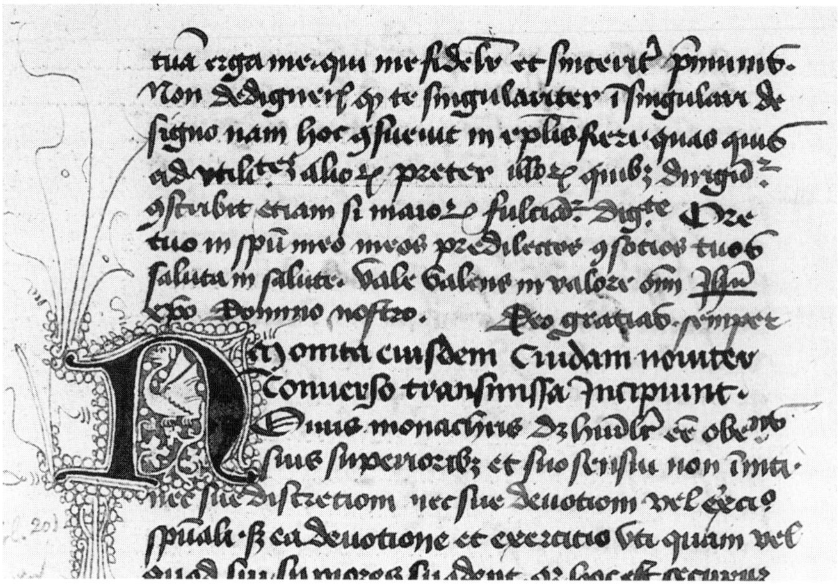

Pl. 100. *Regula S. Basilii*, Southern Low Countries? 1439. The Hague, Royal Libr., MS 78 J 55:1, f. 16v (*CMDNL*, I, pl. 186): tuam erga me, qui me fideliter et sinceriter premunis. / Non dedigneris quod te singulariter in singulari de/signo, nam hoc consuevit in epistolis fieri, quas quis / ad utilitatem aliorum preter illorum quibus diriguntur

Cursiva Libraria (Formata according to Lieftinck). Note the 'majuscule' form of **d** in initial position, the alternative form of cursive round **s** at the end of the lines and the tendency for spiky forms to be made at the headline ('quas', l. 3, 'quibus', l. 4).

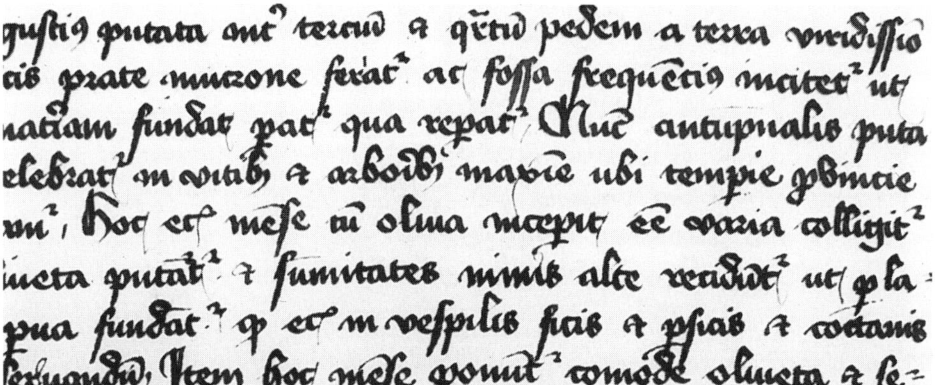

Pl. 101. Petrus de Crescentiis, *Liber ruralium commodorum*, Southern Germany (Nuremberg?), *c.* 1439. Deventer, Stadsarchief en Athenaeumbibl., MS 107, f. 257v (another page: *CMDNL*, I, pl. 312): [et an]gustius putata intus tercium et quartum pedem a terra viridissimo / [corti]cis prate mucrone feriatur [*corrected from* feratur] ac fossa frequencius incitetur, ut / [ibi m]ateriam fundat paratur qua reparatur. Nunc autumpnalis puta/[tio]

Cursiva Libraria (Formata according to Lieftinck), with rather thin, sloping **f** and straight **s**. Note the form of **d**, the triangular loops on the ascenders, the use of **v** in initial and even in medial position ('provincie', l. 4), the vertical hairline on final **c** and **t** and the flourish on straight **r** ('servandum', l. 8), the double hyphens. The Italian **bus**-abbreviation ('arboribus', l. 4) occurs frequently in Southern German manuscripts.

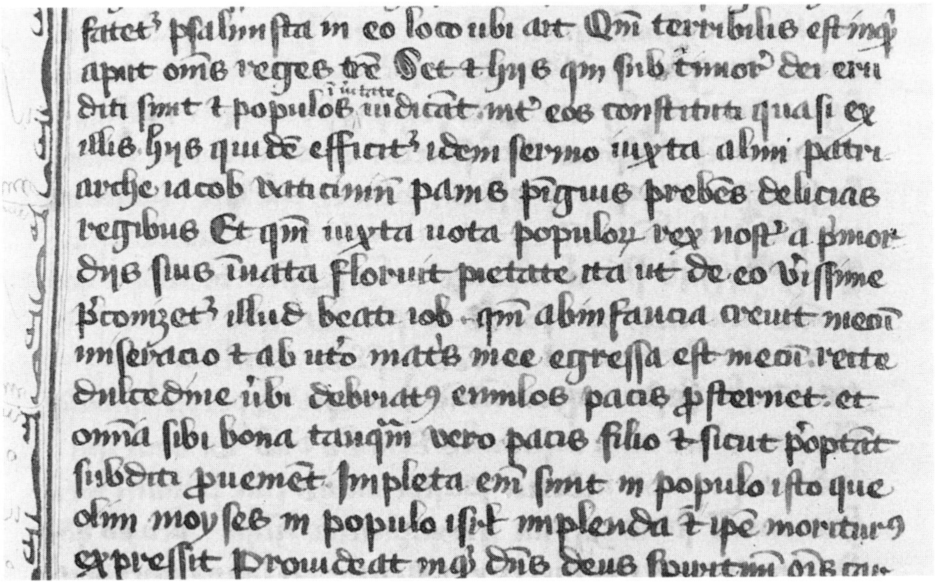

Pl. 102. Iohannes Capgrave, *De illustribus Henricis*, King's Lynn, *c.* 1440–7. Cambridge, Corpus Christi Coll., MS 408, p. 1 (*CMDGBCam*, pl. 236): fatetur psalmista in eo loco ubi ait: Quam terribilis est, inquit, / aput omnes reges terre. Set et hiis qui sub timore Dei eru/diti sunt et populos in veritate [*these two words added above the l.*] iudicant inter eos constituti quasi ex

Cursiva Libraria (Secretary) of unusual round aspect. The occasional two-compartment **a** ('aput', l. 2) and the **x** ('ex', l. 3) are the sole remnants of Anglicana. Note the long shaft of **p**, the hairline loops on the ascenders, the exclusive use of straight **r**. The abbreviation by suspension for 'timore' (l. 2) would be most uncommon on the Continent.

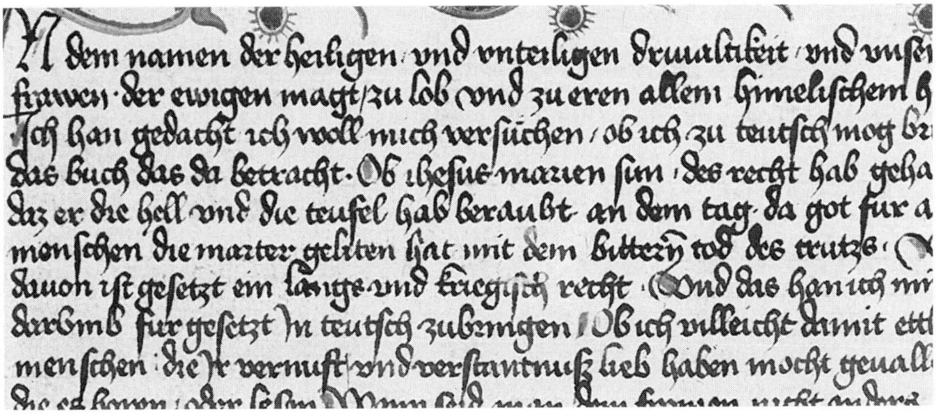

Pl. 103. Iacobus de Theramo, *Belial* (in German), Germany, 1445. Berlin, Staatsbibl. Preuss. Kulturbesitz, MS germ. fol. 657, f. 1r (Crous and Kirchner, *Schriftarten*, fig. 44): [I]n dem namen der heiligen und unteiligen Drivaltikeit und unse[r] / Frawen der ewigen Magt zu lob und zu eren allem himelischem h[eer], / ich han gedacht, ich woll mich versuchen ob ich zu teutsch mog br[ingen] / das buch das da betracht

Cursiva Libraria ('Fränkische Bastarda' according to Kirchner, i.e. a script supposed to be typical of Central Germany). Note the boldness of the hand, the form of **a**, of **c** ('crutzs', l. 6), of straight **r** ('eren', l. 2) the narrow high **d**, the unusual form of **v** when used in medial position ('darumb', l. 8).

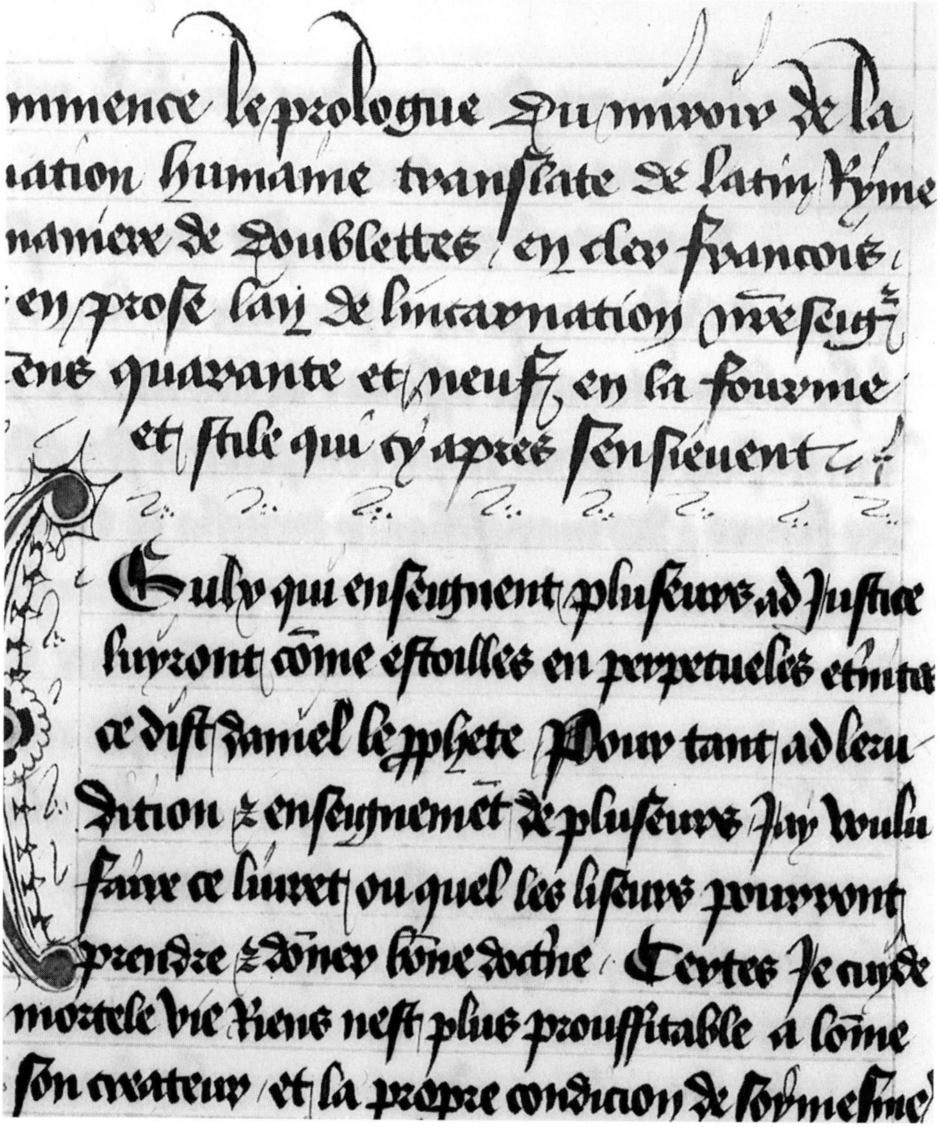

Pl. 104. *Speculum humanae salvationis* (in French), Flanders, 1449. Brussels, Royal Libr., MS 9249–50, f. 101r (*CMDB*, III, pl. 530): [*from l.* 7] [C]eulx qui enseignent pluseurs ad justice / luyront comme estoilles en perpetueles eternité[s]. / Ce dist Daniel le prophete. Pour tant ad l'eru/dition et enseignement de pluseurs j'ay voulu / faire ce livret ouquel les liseurs pourront / prendre et donner bonne doctrine

Cursiva Formata (Bastarda) in an illuminated manuscript produced by the scribe Jean Miélot. The text in this bold Burgundian Bastarda is much more compressed than the rubric. Note the mixture of roundness and angularity, the abundant decorative hairlines and the flourishes on **i**, the use of looped (mostly in initial position) and loopless **d**, of round **r**, angular cursive **r** ('pourront', l. 11) and majuscule **r** in initial position ('riens', l. 13).

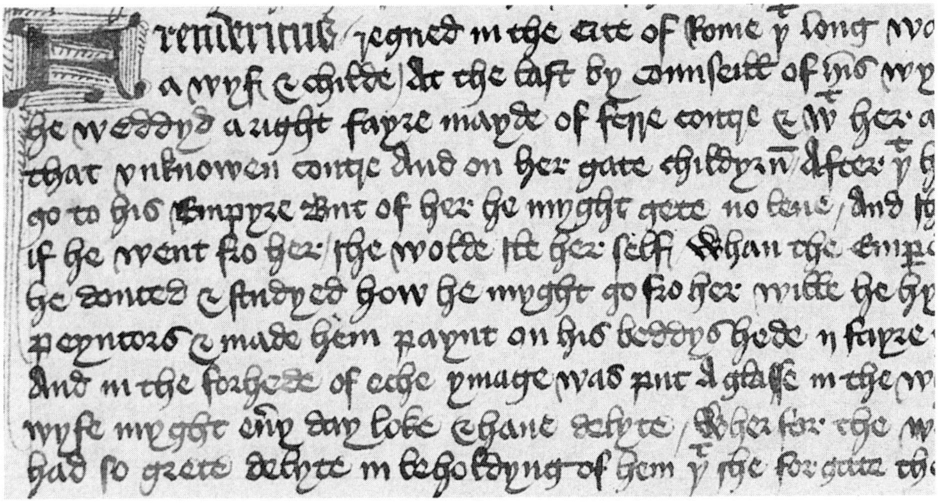

Pl. 105. *Various English texts*, St Albans (England), 1449–54. Cambridge, Univ. Libr., MS
KK.1.6, f. 229r (*CMDGBCam*, pl. 252b): Frendericus regned in the cite of Rome þat long
w[as without] / a wyf and childe. At the last by counseill of his wy[se men] / he weddyd a
right fayre mayde of ferre contre and with her a[bode in] / that unknowen contre

Cursiva Libraria (Secretary) with many Anglicana features: see the occasional appearance
of two-compartment **a**, of Anglicana **e** ('weddyd', l. 3) and the use of Anglicana **r** (next to two
other forms) and round **s**. Note the formation of horizontal strokes at the headline, for
example in **dd** and **ll**, and possible otiose strokes in 'wyf' and 'self' (ll. 2, 6).

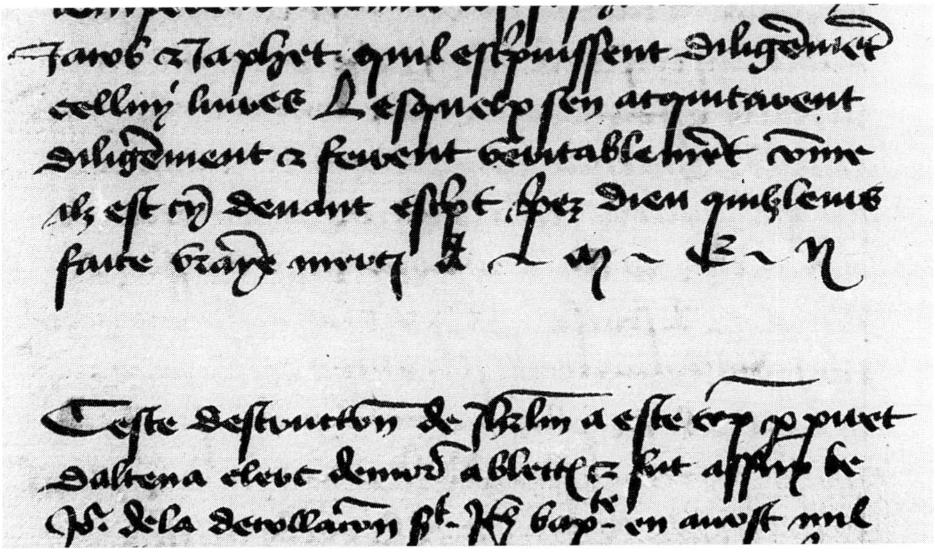

Pl. 106. *Vengeance de Jésus-Christ*, Bletterans (Jura), 1450. Lyons, Bibl. mun., MS 864, f. 180v
(*CMDF*, VI, pl. 102): Jacob et Japhet qu'il escripvissent diligemment / celluy livres. Lesquelx
s'en acquitarent / diligemment et feirent veritablement comme / ilz est cy devant escript

Cursiva Currens. Among the many ligatures see **het** in 'Japhet', **co** in 'comme', **ci** in
'merci' (l. 5). Note the cursive form of **c, e, m, n, u, v**; the dot on **y** made as if it were an
abbreviation mark; the word 'Amen' written in majuscules (l. 5).

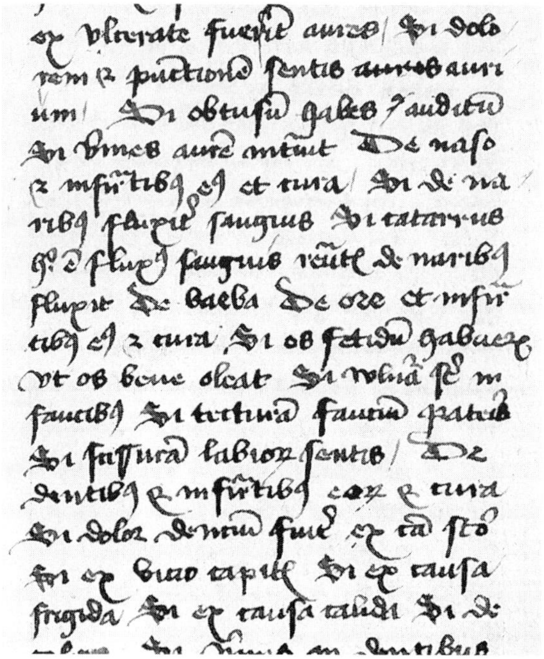

Pl. 107. Thomas Cantimpratensis, *De naturis rerum*, Utrecht, 1460. The Hague, Royal Libr., MS 78 D 29, f. 3r (another page: *CMDNL*, II, pl. 666): exulcerate fuerint aures. Si dolo/rem et putritionem sentis [aures *deleted*] auri/um. Si obtusum habes auditum. / Si vermes aurem intravit. De naso / et infirmitatibus eius et cura. Si de na/ribus fluxerit sanguis

A small irregular Cursiva Currens/Libraria. Note the simplified **a**, the 'open' **d** in initial position, the **g** without horns, the **h** with exaggerated limb, the high round Cursiva **s** in final position, the long endstroke of **x** and the long approach stroke of tironian **et**.

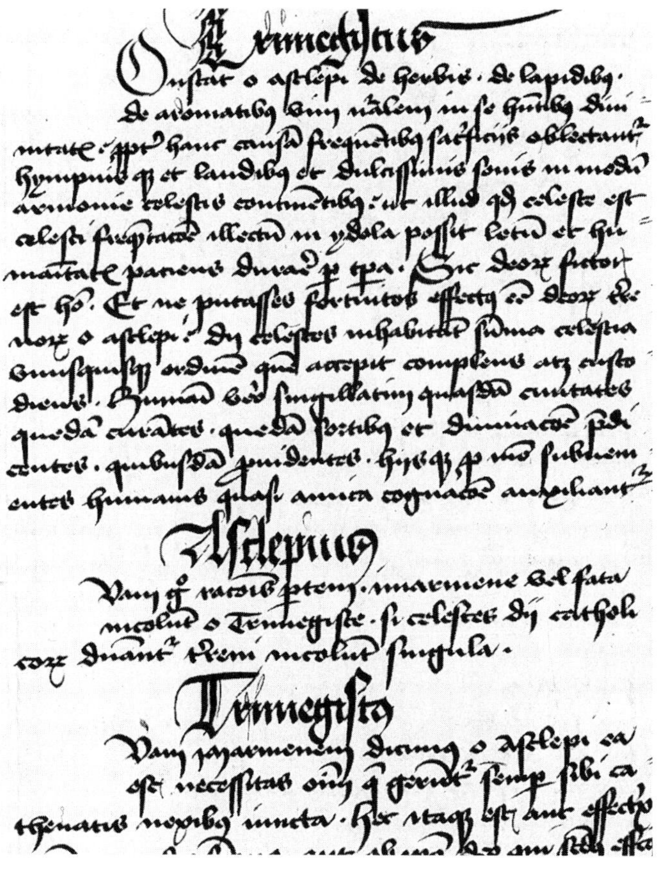

Pl. 108. Ps.-Apuleius, *Asclepius*, copied in the abbey of Altenberg near Wetzlar in 1461. Troyes, Bibl. mun., MS 1948, f. 62v (*CMDF*, V, pl. 133): Trimegistus. / [C]onstat, o Asclepi, de herbis, de lapidibus, / de aromatibus vim naturalem in se habentibus divi/nitatis, propter hanc causam frequentibus sacrificiis oblectantur

A very small and broad Cursiva Currens/Libraria in a manuscript of Humanistic content. Note the effect of rapid writing on the minims in 'divinacione' (l. 13), the difference between initial and medial **d**, the looped **g** ('singillatim', l. 12), the cursive **r** with hairline decoration ('fictor', l. 8), the special **orum**-abbreviation ('deorum', l. 8), the double hyphens.

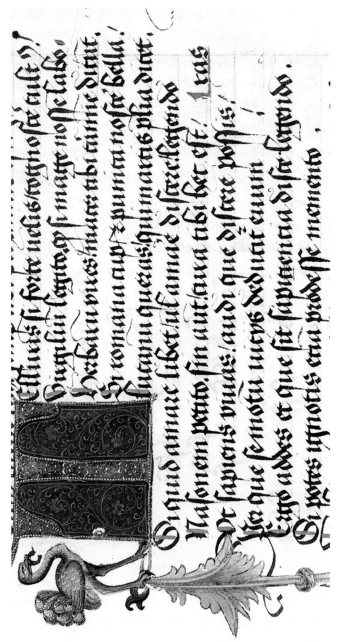

Pl. III. *Schoolbook for Maximilian I* (in Latin), Vienna or Wiener-Neustadt, 1466–7. Vienna, Österreichische Nationalbibl., MS Ser. n. 2617, f. 10r (another page: Kirchner, *Scriptura Gothica*, pl. 63; *CMDA*, III, pl. 284): Telluris si forte velis cognoscere cultus, / Virgilium legito, quod si mage nosse laboras / Herbarum vires, Macer tibi carmine dicent. / Si Romana cupis et Punica noscere bella, / Lucanum queras, qui Martis prelia dicet. / Si quid amare libet vel amare discere legendo, / Nasonem petito. Sin autem cura tibi hec est / Ut sapiens vivas, audi que discere possis

Cursiva Formata (Fractura) written by Wolfgang Spitzweg in a schoolbook for the future Emperor Maximilian, highly calligraphic but fanciful and not of the highest quality. Some ascenders have no loops ('bella', l. 4) or small loops ('libet', l. 6). Note the many quadrangles, spikes or horns at the headline, the spurs on the ascenders, the lozenge form of unlooped **d** and of **o** ('legendo', l. 6), the pointed **p** and **q**, the form of straight **r** ('vires', l. 3), the forms of final **s**, the small **v** ('vivas', l. 8), **y** used for **ii** ('viciis', l. 9).

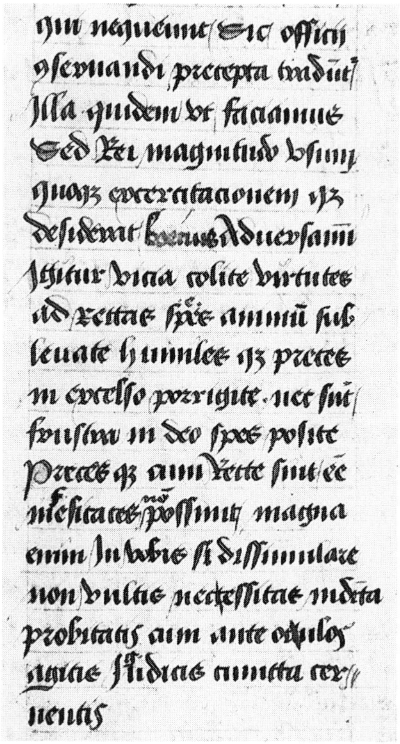

Pl. 112. Guillelmus de Conchis, *Moralium dogma philosophorum*, Western France? 1475. Nantes, Bibl. mun., MS 82, f. 69rb (*CMDF*, VII, pl. 144): [conse]/qui nequeunt. Sic officii / conservandi precepta traduntur, / illa quidem ut faciamus. / Sed rei magnitudo usum / quoque excercitacionem que / desiderat Boecius [*on erasure*]: / Adversamini / igitur vicia, colite virtutes, / ad rectas spes animum sub/levate humilesque preces / in excelso porrigite

A small Cursiva Libraria with relatively long ascenders and descenders but short **f** and straight **s**. Note the fusions; the angular or spiky form of **b**, **c**, **e**, **g**, round **s**, **v**, etc.; the form of **d**; the four different forms of **r**; the occasional appearance of trailing **s** ('oculos', l. 16). The superscript letters are reference-marks to the marginal gloss.

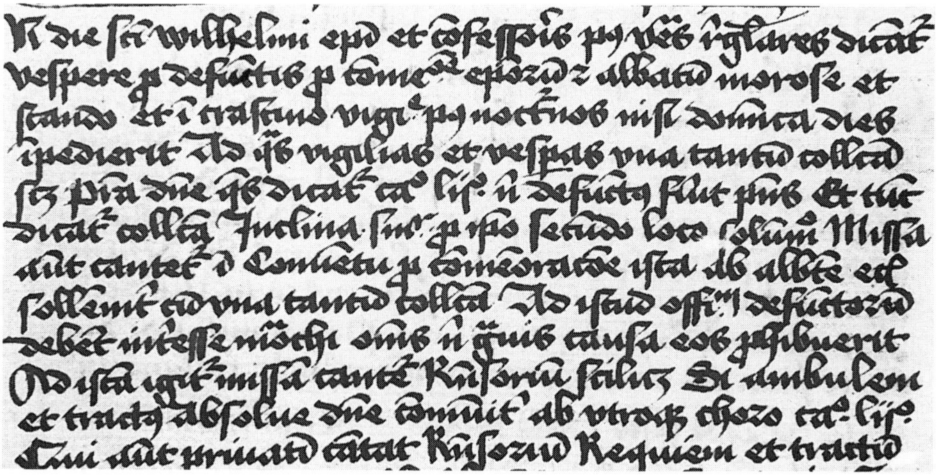

Pl. 113. *Ordinarium*, Strasbourg, abbey of St Bernard, 1481. Colmar, Bibl. mun., MS 101, f. 25r (*CMDF*, V, pl. 169): [I]n die sancti Wilhelmi episcopi et confessoris post vesperas regulares dicantur / vespere pro defunctis pro commemoracione episcoporum et abbatum morose et / stando et in crastino vigilie post nocturnos, nisi Dominica dies

A bold and angular Cursiva Libraria. Note unlooped **d**; **g** without horns; vertical and un-pointed **f**, **p**, **q** and straight **s**; the three forms of **r** (majuscule in 'responsorium', l. 10); the high round **s**; **v** and **w**; the ligature **bb** ('abbatum', l. 2); the bold curved abbreviation strokes.

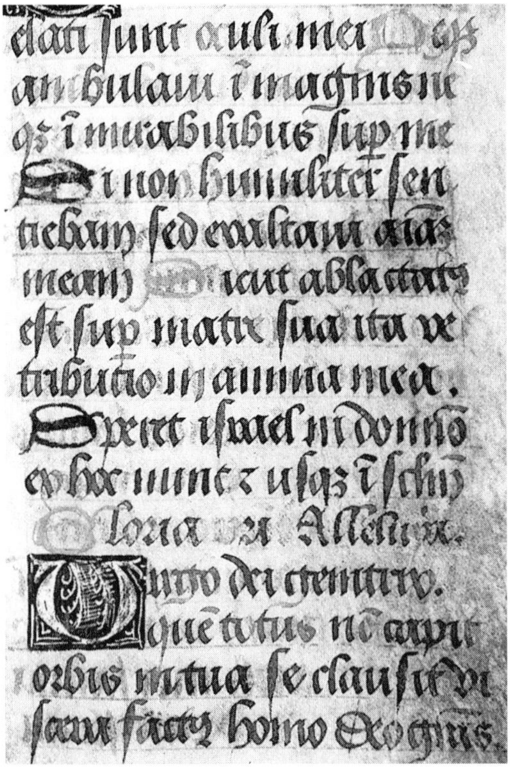

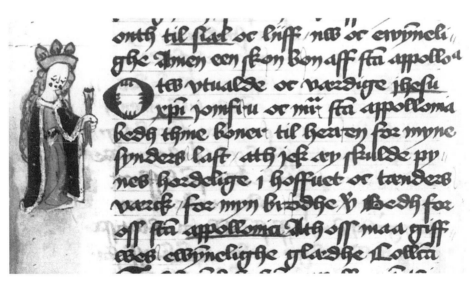

Pl. 114. *Horae*, France, 1486. Angers, Bibl. mun., MS 131, f. 86r (*CMDF*, VII, pl. 150): elati sunt oculi mei, neque / ambulavi in magnis ne/que in mirabilibus super me. / Si non humiliter sen/tiebam sed exaltavi animam / meam. Sicut ablactatus / est super matre sua

Cursiva Formata (Bastarda) with narrow letter forms and many fusions, including **ra** ('Israel', l. 9) and **xa** ('exaltavi', l. 5). Note the thorny form of **a**, **b**, **e**, **g** etc.; the unlooped **d**; the forms of initial and final **m** in 'meam' (l. 6); the rarity of abbreviations.

Pl. 115. *Prayer Book* (in Danish), Maribo (Denmark), 1497. Copenhagen, Royal Libr., MS Thott 553 4°, f. 189v : onth til siæl oc liiff nw oc ewynneli/ghe. Amen. Een skøn bøn aff sancta Appollonia. / O tw utualde oc værdige Ihesu / Christi jomfru oc martir

A large and bold Cursiva Libraria. Note the Danish **ae**-ligature and crossed **o**, **j** instead of **i** in initial position ('iek', l. 6), **k** going under the baseline, the two forms of **r** ('herren', l. 5) and of **w** ('ewynnelighe', ll. 1–2 and 10), the double hyphens.

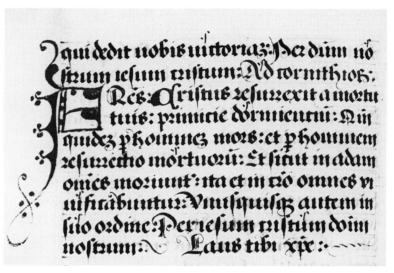

Pl. 116. *Epistolarium*, Cracow, 1500. Cracow, Archiwum i Biblioteka Kapituły Metropolitalnej, MS 22, unfoliated: qui dedit nobis victoriam. Per Dominum no/strum Iesum Cristum. Ad Corinthios. / Fratres, Cristus resurrexit a mortu/tuis, primicie dormientium. Quoniam / quidem per hominem mors

Cursiva Formata (Fractura) close to Textualis Formata (Textus Quadratus). Note the small loops and the spurs on the ascenders, unlooped **d**, final **m** in 'victoriam' (l. 1), the unorthodox use of both forms of **r**, the form of final **s** and of **x**, the uncommon abbreviation for 'Cristo' (l. 7).

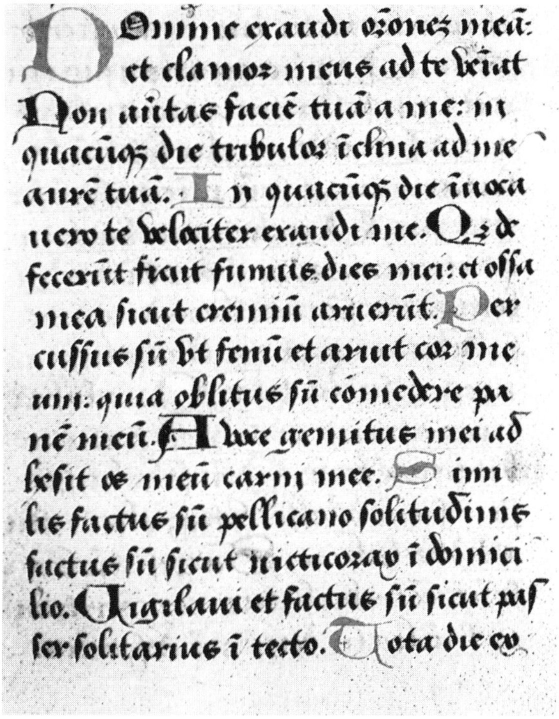

Pl. 117. *Horae* for the use of the abbey of St Florent in Saumur (Maine-et-Loire), c. 1519. Angers, Bibl. mun., MS 137, f. 73v (*CMDF*, VII, pl. 169): Domine exaudi oracionem meam, / et clamor meus ad te veniat. / Non avertas faciem tuam a me: in / quacumque die tribulor inclina ad me / aurem tuam

Cursiva Formata of medium quality. Note the spurs on the ascenders, unlooped **d** (although its shaft is more developed in 'ad', l. 11), short **f** and straight **s**, the form of **q**, of **r** in 'aurem' (l. 5), the high **v**.

Pl. 118. *Gloss on Dante's Inferno* (in Italian), Italy, 1383. Vatican Libr., MS Barb. lat. 4049, f. 1r (*CMDVat*, I, pl. 17): Ad vengnia che lla inve/stigabile prudenzia de/l celestiale emcreato / principe abbia beatifi/cati di prudenza e di vi/rtute molti huomini. Neente meno / Dante Alighieri cittadino di Firenze, hu/omo di nobile e profonda sapienzia

Semihybrida Currens (Mercantesca). Note some loopless ascenders, the short **g**, the curving endstrokes of **h** and **z**, long **i** after **l**, **n**, **u** in final position, the ligature **ll** ('ellautore', l. 10), the cursive loops on **f**, **p**, straight **s**. The non-syllabic division of words is an Italian feature.

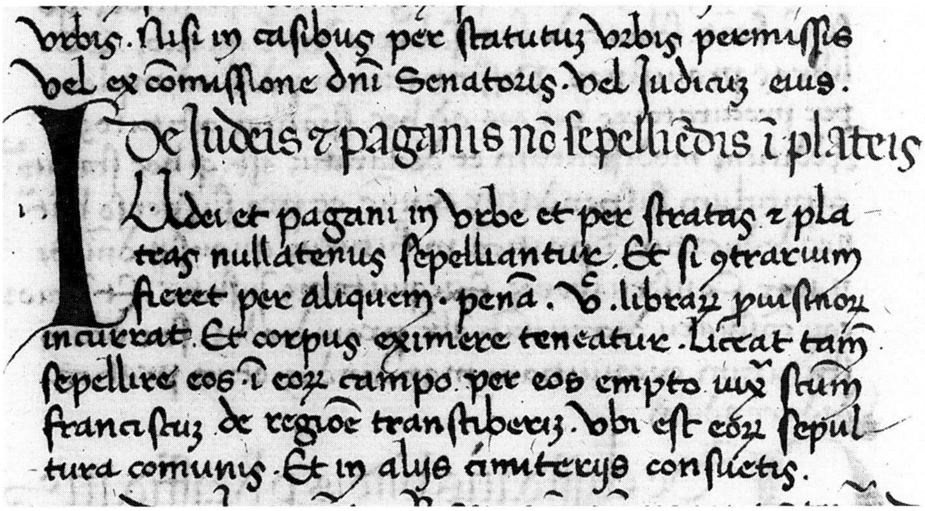

Pl. 119. *Statuta Romae*, Rome? 1413. Vatican Libr., MS Ott. lat. 741, f. 65r (*CMDVat*, I, pl. 25): urbis, nisi in casibus per statutum urbis permissis / vel ex commissione domini senatoris vel iudicum eius. / De Iudeis et paganis non sepelliendis in plateis. / Iudei et pagani in urbe et per stratas et pla/teas

Slightly backward-sloping Hybrida Libraria (rubric in Textualis Rotunda Libraria). Note the loopless **d** with long shaft, the tops of the ascenders with or without serifs, the form of **g**, the sign replacing **m** at the end of some words ('Franciscum', l. 9), the very typical straight **r**, final cursive **s** alternating with Textualis **s** and trailing **s**, and the high open **v**.

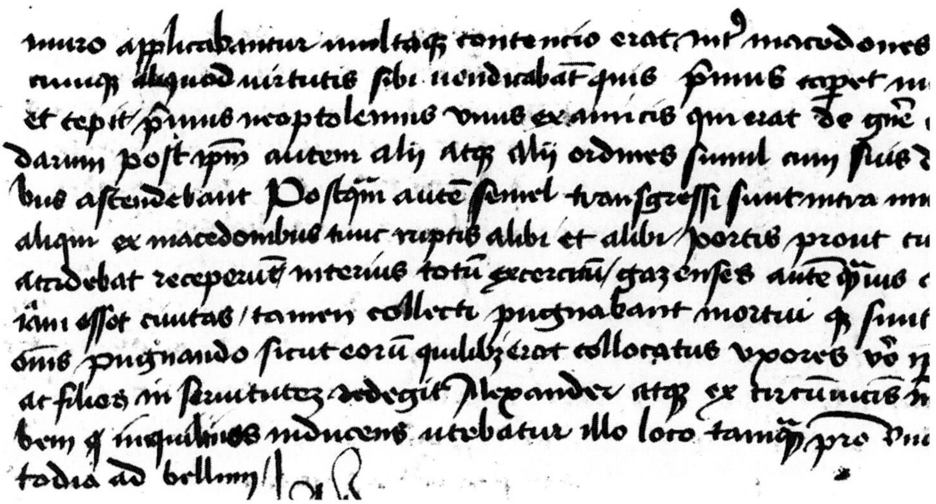

Pl. 120. Gualterus Burley, *De vita et moribus philosophorum*, Constance, 1417. Brussels, Royal Libr., MS 9893–94, f. 32v (another page: *CMDB*, II, pl. 261): muro applicabantur multaque [*corrected from* multoque] contencio erat inter Macedones [qui]/cumque aliquod virtutis sibi vendicabant, quis primus caperet m[urum]; / et cepit primus Neoptolemus, unus ex amicis qui erat de genere

An early example of Northern Hybrida (here Libraria/Currens), copied during the Council of Constance. Note the form of **c** ('cepit', l. 3), the link between an ascender and the preceding letter ('collocatus', l. 9), the two forms of straight **s** ('suis', l. 4, 'sicut', l. 9) and of **x** ('excercitum', l. 7, 'uxores', l. 9), the uncertainty in writing **u** or **v** in initial position.

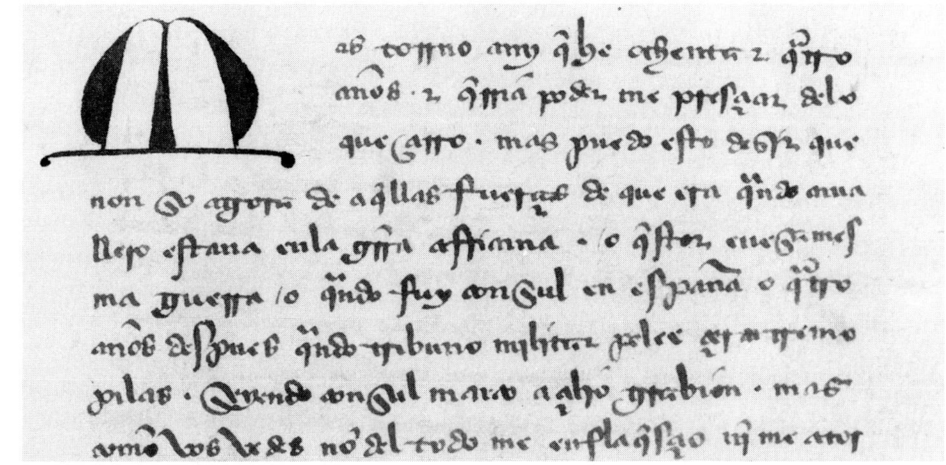

Pl. 121. Cicero, *De senectute* (in Spanish), Montemayor (Spain), 1422. Madrid, Bibl. Nacional, MS 7815, f. 14v (Canellas, *Exempla*, II, pl. 61): Mas torrno a mi que he ochenta et quatro / annos et querria poderme presçiar de lo / que sarro, mas puedo esto desir que / non so agora de aquellas fuerças de que era quando cava/llero estava en la guerra Africana

An idiosyncratic example of Spanish Hybrida Libraria/Currens ('cursiva textual' according to Canellas), with long, slightly backsloping club-shaped ascenders. Note the various forms of **a**, sometimes altered beyond recognition, **ç** with detached cedilla, short looped **d**, Iberian long **i** and **r** ('tribuno militar', l. 7), looped **p**, a third form of **s** ('consul', l. 6), the long sloping **v** ('vos vedes', l. 9).

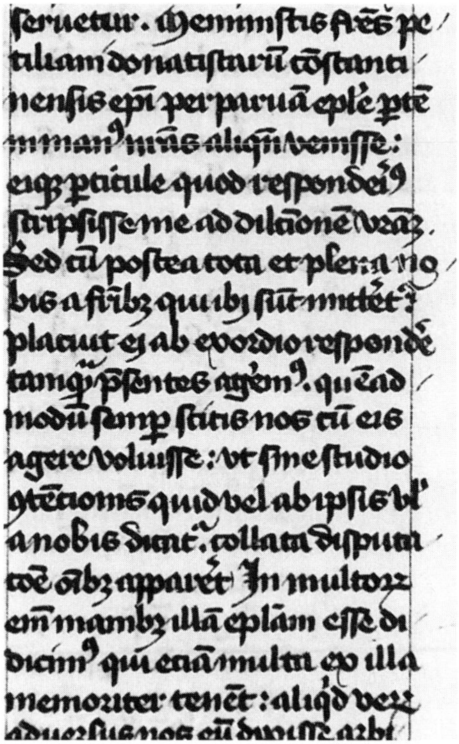

Pl. 122. Augustinus, *Opuscula*, copied in the Windesheim priory of Frenswegen (Niedersachsen), 1425. Leiden, Univ. Libr., MS Voss. lat. 4° 14, f. 67ra (*CMDNL*, II, pl. 935): servetur. Meministis, fratres, Pe/tiliani Donatistarum Constanti/nensis episcopi perparvam epistole partem / in manus nostras aliquando venisse, / eique particule quod responderimus / scripsisse me ad dilectionem vestram

Netherlandish Semihybrida Libraria. Note looped and unlooped **d** and ascenders, cursive **x**, the ligature **tt** ('mitteretur', l. 8). The long **i** in final or almost final position ('ibi', l. 8) is an uncommon feature in this type of script.

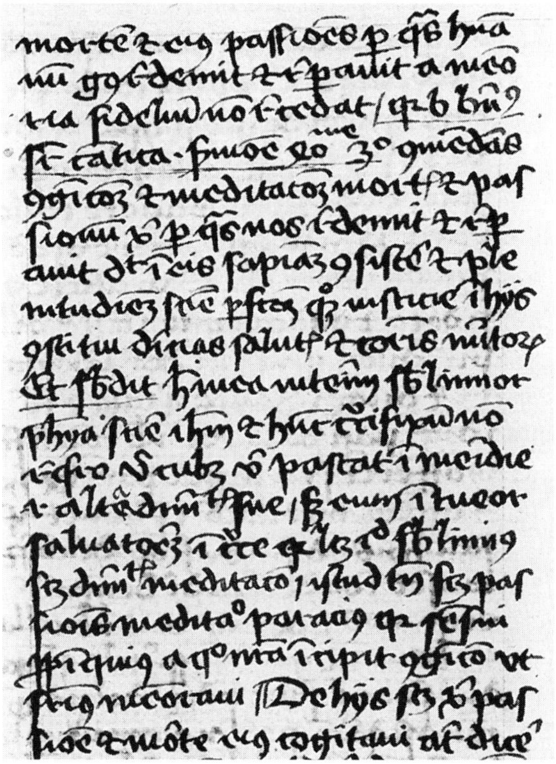

Pl. 123. Nicolaus de Dinckelsbühl, *Sermones*, Bohemia, 1433. Brussels, Royal Libr., MS IV.248, f. 160rb (*CMDB*, II, pl. 348; for the correct origin, see the note pasted in the copy of *CMDB* in the Manuscript Department of the Royal Libr.): mortem et eius passiones, per quas huma/num genus redemit et reparavit, a memo/ria fidelium non recedat. Quod beatus Bernardus / super Cantica sermone 43° commendans / cognicionem et meditacionem mortis

Although this is Hybrida Currens, the tops of the ascenders often display bifurcation. Note **y** with two dots used for **ii** in the German manner ('hiis', l. 8), the double abbreviation stroke ('sciencie', l. 8) and the numerous, often uncommon abbreviations ('genus', 'redemit', l. 2).

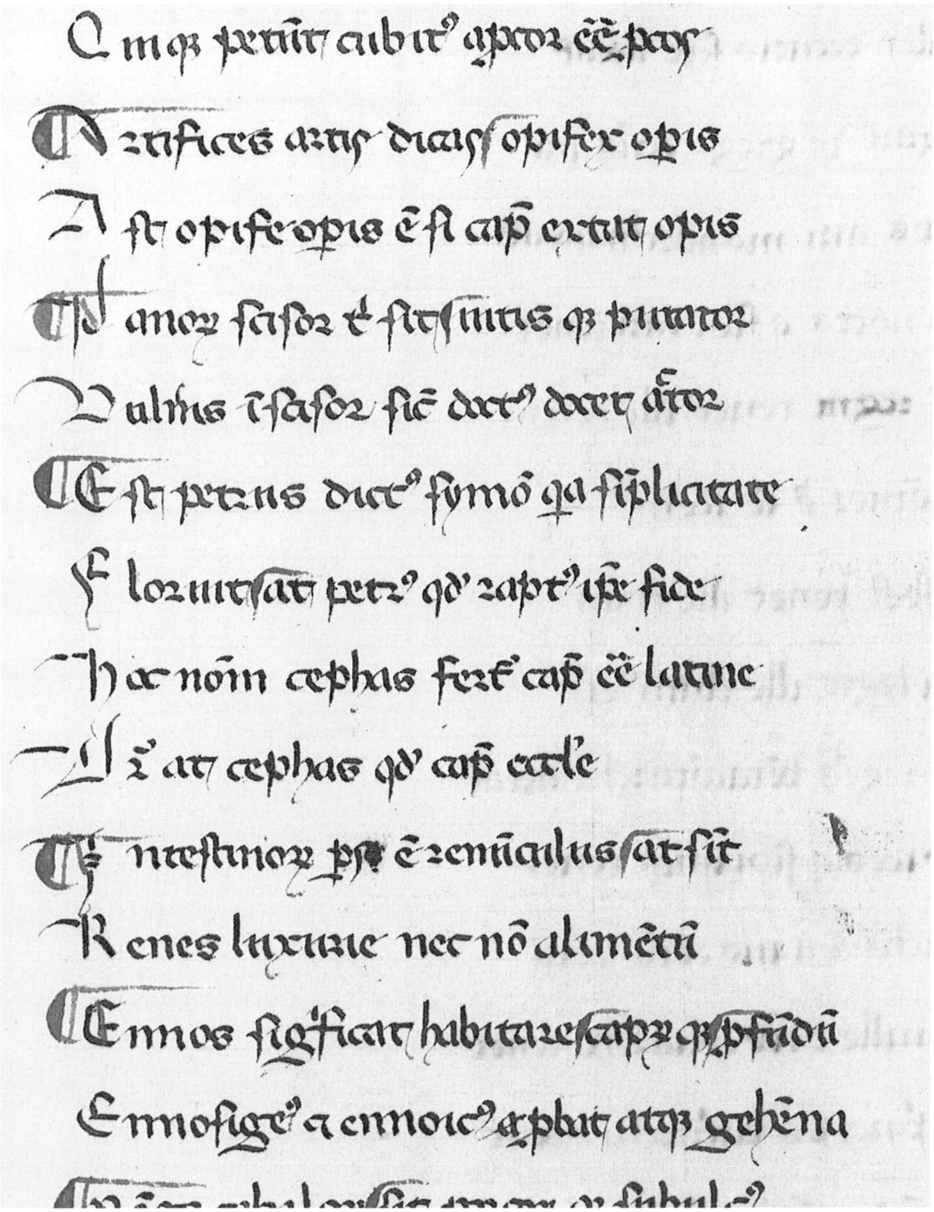

Pl. 124. Eberhardus Bethuniensis, *Graecismus*, Northern Italy, 1426. New Haven, Yale Univ., Beinecke Libr., ms Marston 46, f. 28r: Quique petunt cubitus a procor esse procos. / ¶ Artifices artis dicas, opifex operis. / Ast opife operis est si caput extat opis. / ¶ Panorum scisor tibi sit vitisque putator, / Vulneris inscisor sicut doctus docet actor. / ¶ Est Petrus dictus Symon quia simplicitate / Floruit, at Petrus quod raptus ipse fide

A large, rather angular Hybrida Libraria, written in such a way as to provide ample space for marginal and interlinear glosses. Numerous fusions occur. The scribe uses round **r** as the only form in all positions; final **s** is either Textualis or trailing **s**. Note the marked spurs on straight **s**, the curving endstrokes of **h**, **x**, **y** below the baseline, and the vertical hairline on final **t**. The **qui**-abbreviation ('quia', l. 6) and the tironian **et** (l. 13) are typically Italian.

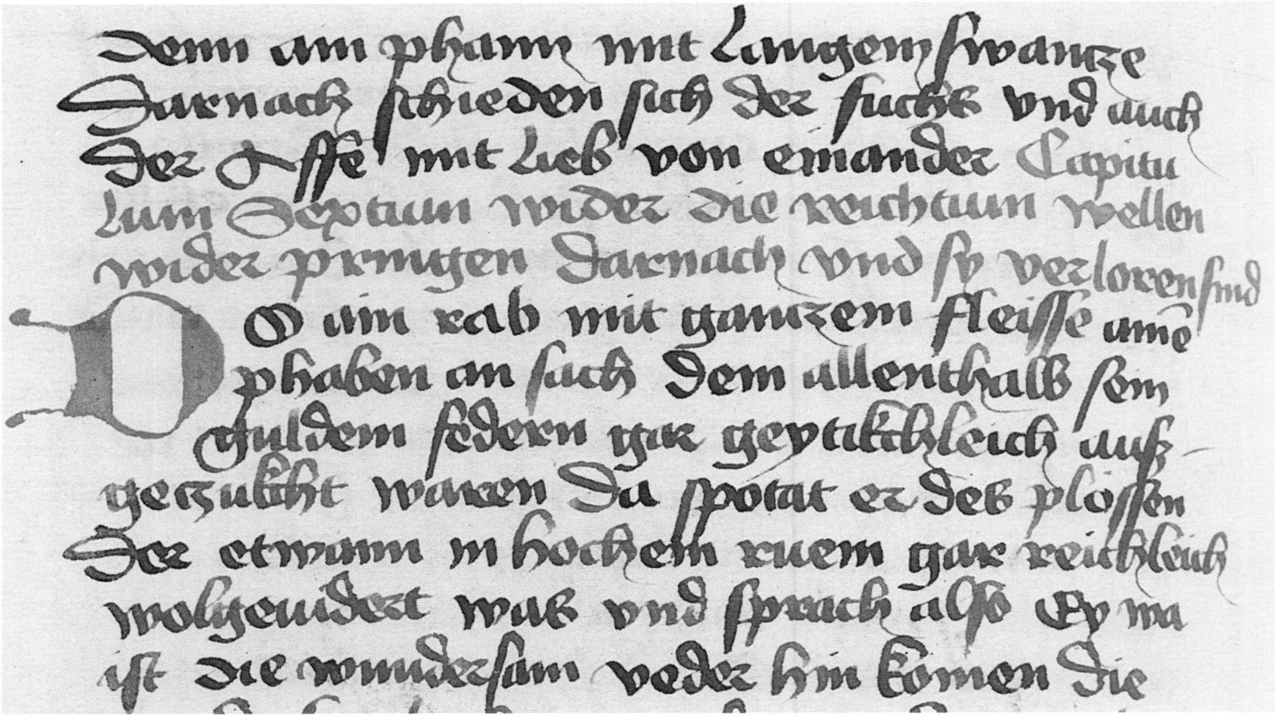

Pl. 125. Ulrich von Pottenstein, *Fabulae Cyrilli* (in German), Western Upper Bavaria? 1432. Berlin, Staatsbibl. Preuss. Kulturbesitz, ms germ. fol. 459, f. 162v (Crous and Kirchner, *Schriftarten*, fig. 38): denn ain phann mit langem swancze. / Darnach schieden sich der fuchs und auch / der affe mit lieb von einander. Capitu/lum sextum. Wider die reichtum wellen / wider pringen darnach und sy verloren sind. / Do ain rab mit ganczem fleisse ainen / phaben an sach dem allenthalb sein / guldein federn gar geytikchleich ausz/geczukcht waren

A large and bold Semihybrida Libraria/Currens ('Übergangstypus' according to Kirchner, i.e. a script not showing the supposed distinctive features of the area). Note looped and unlooped **d**, looped **g** ('guldein', l. 8), the concave ascender of **l** when unlooped in initial position, the typical form of straight **r** ('rab', l. 6).

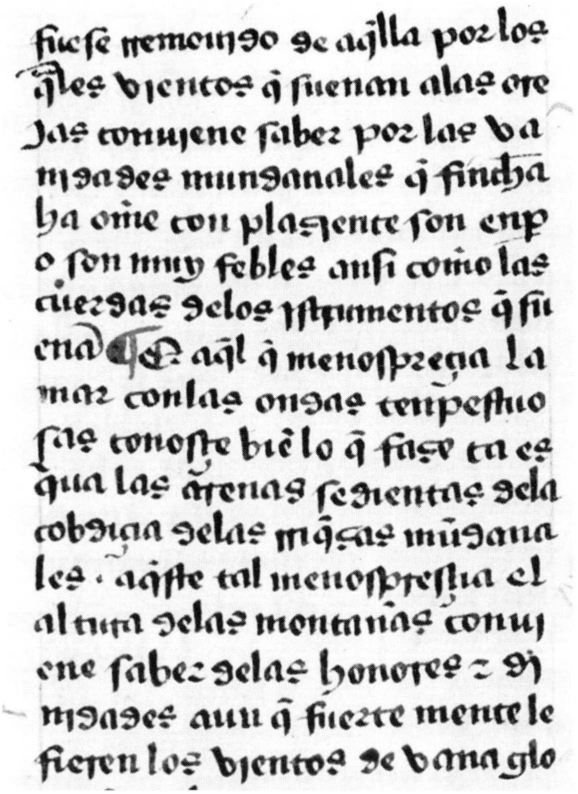

Pl. 126. Boethius, *De consolatione philosophiae* (in Spanish), Alcañiz (Spain), 1436. Madrid, Bibl. Nacional, MS 10193, f. 28ra (Canellas, *Exempla*, II, pl. 64): fuese rremovido de aquella por los / quales vientos que suenan a las ore/jas conviene saber por las va/nidades mundanales que finchan / ha omme con plaziente son

A Spanish Hybrida Libraria ('cursiva formada' according to Canellas) with club-shaped, somewhat backwards-sloping ascenders. Note ç with detached cedilla ('menospreçia', l. 8), the very short looped **d**, the curving limb of **h**, the three forms of **i** (**i**, **j** and **I**, the latter used when the letter is a consonant), the long straight **r**, the sloping **v** and the typical **z** ('plaziente', l. 5).

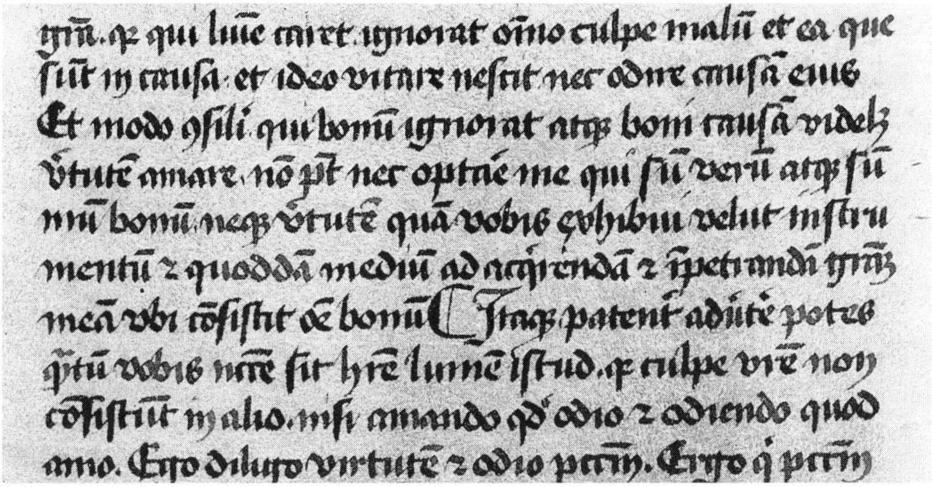

Pl. 127. Catharina de Senis, *Liber divinae doctrinae*, Utrecht, 1438. Utrecht, Univ. Libr., MS 180, f. 103v (*CMDNL*, II, pl. 693): gracia, quia qui lumine caret, ignorat omnino culpe malum et ea que / sunt in causa, et ideo vitare nescit nec odire causam eius. / Et modo consimili qui bonum ignorat atque boni causam, videlicet

A Netherlandish Hybrida Libraria. Note the sloping hairline approach stroke at the top of the ascenders, angular **c**, loopless **d**, 3-shaped **m** at the end of lines ('graciam', l. 6), the sole use of straight **r**, cursive round **s** and **x**, the low, angular **v**.

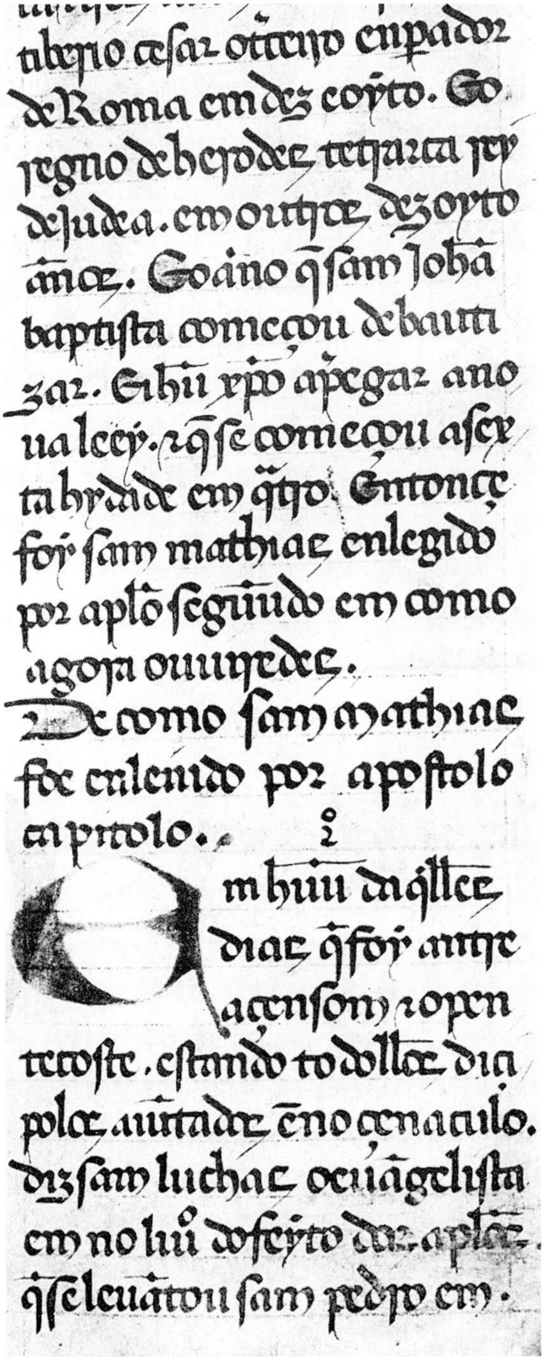

Pl. 128. *Vitae apostolorum et evangelistarum* (in Portuguese), Alcobaça, 1442–3. Lisbon, Bibl. Nacional, MS Alcob. 280, f. 11ra (Burnam, *Palaeographia*, pl. 56): Tiberio Cesar o terceiro enperador / de Roma em dez e oyto. Eo / regno de Herodes tetrarca rey / de Judea em outros dezoyto / annos. Eo anno que sam Joham / Baptista começou de bauti/zar e Jhesu Christo a pregar

A large Portuguese Hybrida Formata with round letter forms. Note the forking of the top of the ascenders, ç with detached cedilla, **d** with long sloping shaft, the form of **g**, and the typical Portuguese forms: long straight **r**, round **s** in final position, **z**, and the dotted abbreviation stroke.

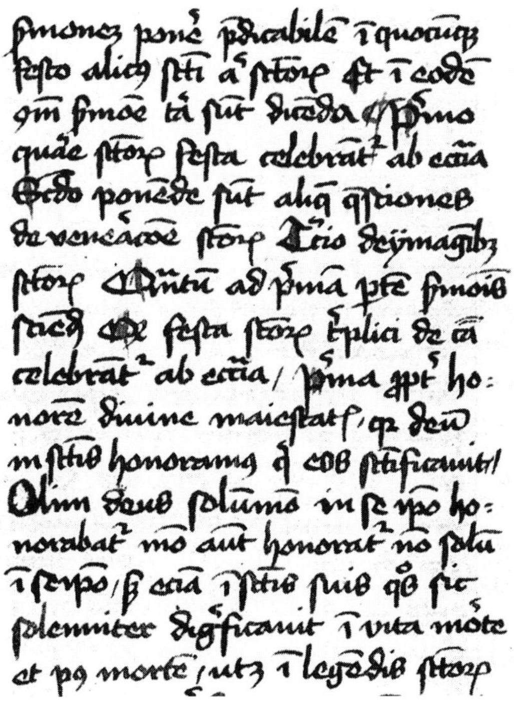

Pl. 129. Iohannes Herolt, *Sermones Discipuli de sanctis*, Neustift near Freising, 1442. Amsterdam, Univ. Libr., MS XII E 24, f. 15rb (*CMDNL*, II, pl. 938c): sermonem ponere predicabilem in quocumque / festo alicuius sancti aut sanctorum. Et in eodem / communi sermone tria sunt dicenda. Primo / quare sanctorum festa celebrantur ab ecclesia

A rapid Hybrida Libraria with many abbreviations. Note the narrow **d**, pointed at the left especially in initial position, **g** without horns and **y** surmounted with two dots sometimes used for **i** ('ymaginibus', l. 6), **r** only in its straight form, the **sc**-ligature ('sanctorum', l. 2), the double abbreviation mark on 'causa' (l. 8) and the double hyphens.

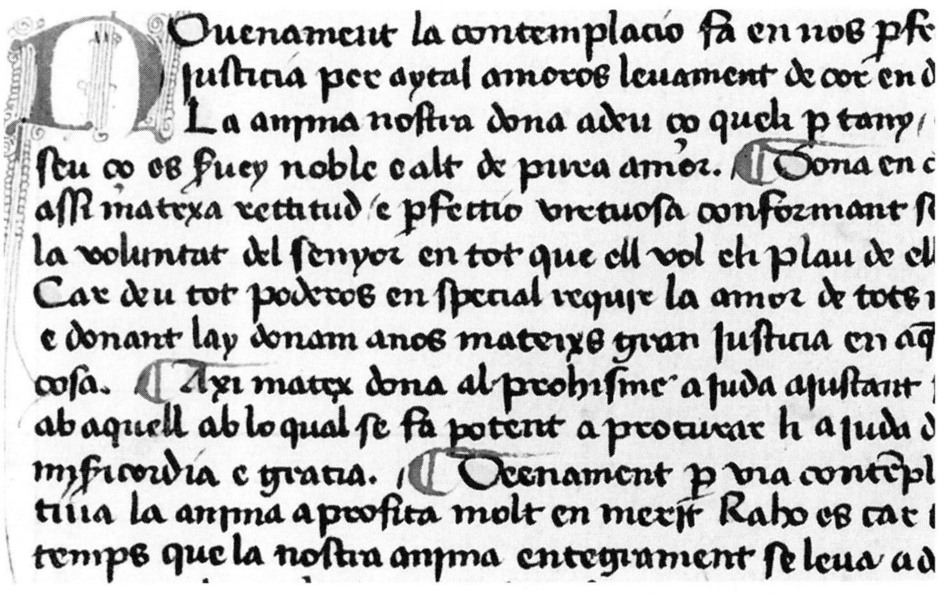

Pl. 130. Eximenis, *Scala Dei* (in Catalan), Barcelona? 1444. Madrid, Bibl. Nacional, MS 92, f. 87r (Canellas, *Exempla*, II, pl. 78): Novenament la contemplacio fa en nos perfe[ta] / justicia per aytal amoros levament de cor en D[eu]. / La anima nostra dona a Deu ço que li pertany

A vertical and round Spanish Hybrida Libraria. Note the **ç** with detached cedilla, the narrow **d**. Long **i** is frequent (majuscule **I** is used for the consonant: 'justicia', l. 2), but long **r** does not occur. Note the form of straight **r**, for example in 'pura' (l. 4), and the **per**-abbreviation ('perfeta', l. 1). Final **s** is cursive, but **x** is Textualis.

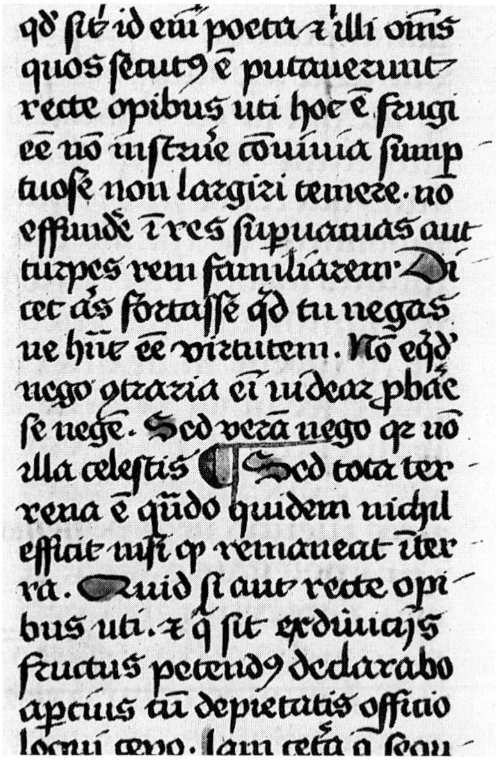

Pl. 131. Lactantius, *Divinae institutiones*, Strasbourg, 1451. Colmar, Bibl. mun., MS 8, f. 128va (*CMDF*, V, pl. 112): quid sit, id enim poeta et illi omnes / quos secutus est putaverunt / recte opibus uti, hoc est frugi / esse, non instruere convivia sump/tuose, non largiri temere, non / effundere in res supervacuas aut / turpes rem familiarem. Di/cet aliquis fortasse quod tu negas

An angular Hybrida Formata. Note especially the form of **a** and **v**, the Textus Rotundus shaping of **m** and **n**, the Bastarda form of **f** and straight **s**, contrasting with the Textualis form of round **s** and **x**. Note also the frequent use of round **r** and the **con**-abbreviation in 'contraria' (l. 10), the **r**-abbreviation in 'probare' (l. 10).

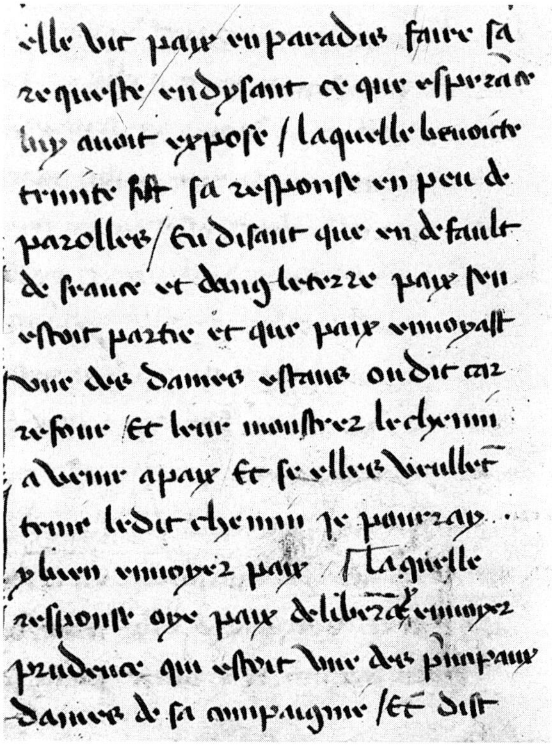

Pl. 132. *Discours sur le Traité d'Arras*, Nîmes, 1451. Troyes, Bibl. mun., MS 2380, f. 30v (*CMDF*, V, pl. 113): elle vit Paix en paradis faire sa / requeste en dysant ce que Esperance / luy avoit exposé. Laquelle benoicte / Trinité fist sa response en peu de / parolles, en disant que en default / de France et d'Angleterre Paix s'en / estoit partie

A rare example of Southern French Hybrida Libraria/Currens, the letters almost entirely unconnected. Note the high sloping **d** and **v**, the simplified forms of **e**, **m**, **n**, **p**, **u** etc., the absence of boldness in **f** and straight **s**, the use of Textualis **x**, the curious use of straight and round **r** ('Angleterre', l. 6, 'pourray', l. 11).

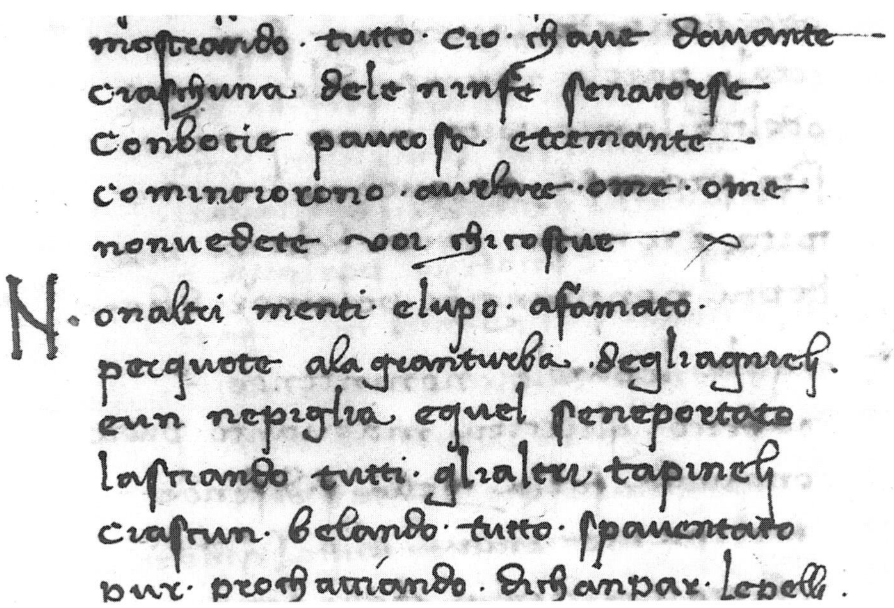

Pl. 133. Boccaccio, *Ninfale Fiesolano*, Italy, 1454. Vatican Libr., MS Capp. 243, f. 40r (*CMDVat*, I, pl. 64): mostrando tutto ciò ch'ave davante / ciaschuna de le ninfe se n'acorse / con bocie paurosa e tremante / cominciorono a urlare: 'Omè, omè, / non vedete voi chi costu'è?'

Semihybrida Libraria/Currens (Mercantesca), with cursive tracing and many ligatures. Note the unusually thin loops on many ascenders and the button at the top of unlooped **l**, the **li**-ligature in final position ('tapineli', l. 9), the long endstroke of **h**, and the generally 'modern' appearance of the script.

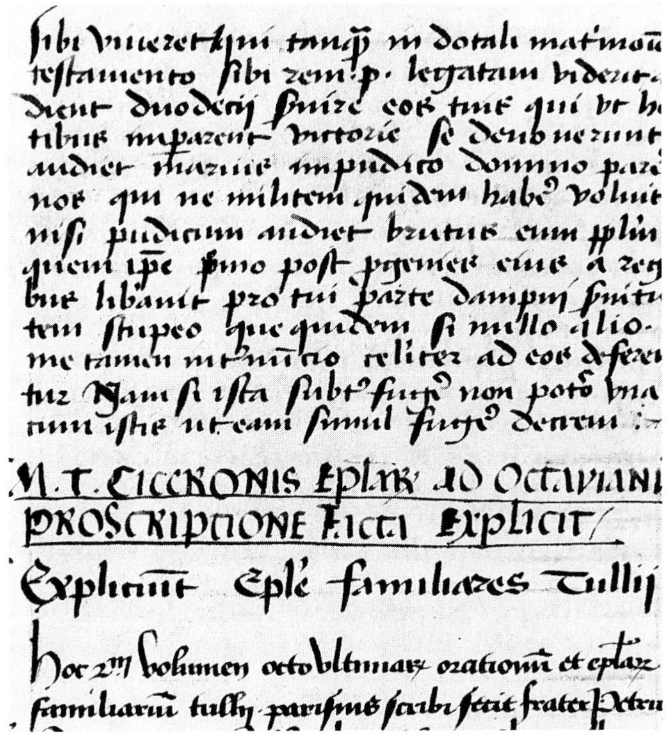

Pl. 134. Cicero, *Orationes et epistolae*, Paris, 1456? Montpellier, Bibl. de la Fac. de Médecine, MS 359, II, f. 299v (*CMDF*, VI, pl. 109): sibi viveret. Qui tanquam in dotali matrimon[io] / testamento sibi rem publicam legatam viderit, [au]/dient duo Decii servire eos tuis qui ut h[os]/tibus imperarent victorie se devoverunt, / audiet Marius impudico domino pare[re] / nos, qui ne militem quidem habere voluit

A small rapid Hybrida Libraria, unconnected but with Cursiva features such as horned **g**, round **s**, fat sloping **f** and straight **s**, the **r**-abbreviation, the high **v**. Note loopless **d** with long sloping shaft, the pointed bow of **b**, angular **c** ('cum', l. 13), and especially the explicit in a defective imitation of Humanistic Capitals.

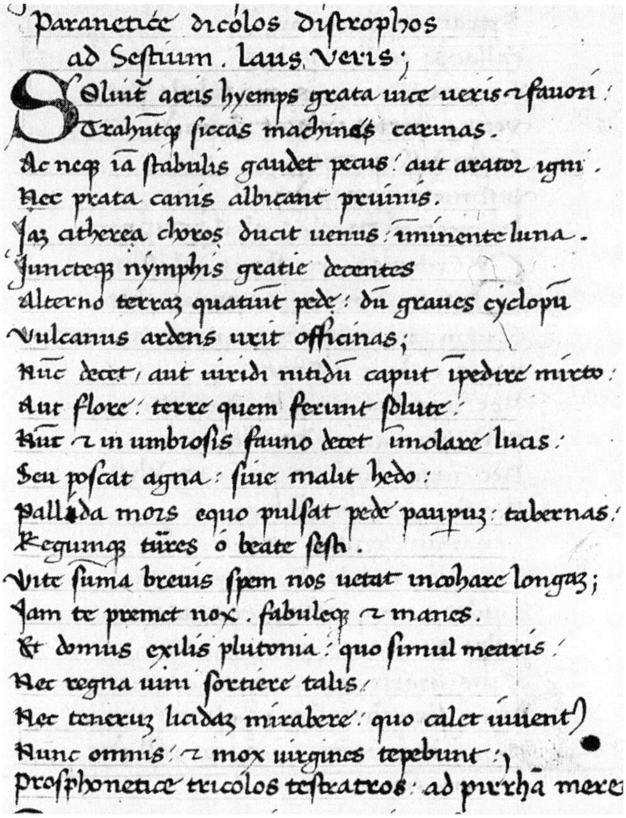

> ·paranetice dicolos distrophos
> ad Sestium. Laus veris;
> Soluit acris hyemps grata uice ueris ⁊ fauoni
> Trahuntcʒ siccas machinas carinas.
> Ac necʒ ia stabulis gaudet pecus, aut arator igni.
> Nec prata canis albicant pruinis.
> Jaʒ ætherea choros ducit uenus, iminente luna.
> Junctecʒ nymphis gratie decentes
> Alterno terraʒ quatiut pede: dū graues cyclopu
> Vulcanus ardens urit officinas;
> Nuc decet, aut uiridi nitidu caput ipedire mirto.
> Aut flore: terre quem ferunt solute.
> Nuc ⁊ in umbrosis fauno decet imolare lucas:
> Seu poscat agna: siue malit hedo:
> Pallida mors equo pulsat pede paupuʒ tabernas.
> Regumcʒ tures o beate sesti.
> Vite suma breuis spem nos uetat incohare longaʒ;
> Jam te premet nox: fabulecʒ ⁊ manes.
> Et domus exilis plutonia: quo simul mearis.
> Nec regna uini sortiere talis.
> Nec teneruʒ liadaʒ mirabere: quo calet iuuent⁊
> Nunc omnis ⁊ mox uirgines tepebunt:
> prosphonetice tricolos tetratros: ad purrhā mere

Pl. 135. Horatius, *Odae*, Pesaro, 1457. Clermont-Ferrand, Bibl. mun., MS 242, f. 3r (*CMDF*, VI, pl. III): Paranetice dicolos distrophos / ad Sestium. Laus veris. / Solvitur acris hyemps grata vice veris et favori, / Trahuntque siccas machine [*corr. from* machinas] carinas, / Ac neque iam stabulis gaudet pecus aut arator igni

A small Hybrida Libraria. Note the approach stroke at the top of the ascenders, the long ascenders and descenders, the fusions, the long loopless **d**, the looped **f**, the sign replacing **m** in final position, the typical straight **r** and the final **s**, the absence of **v** as a minuscule, the **ur**-abbreviation ('Solvitur', l. 3) and Italian tironian **et**. The script is close to Humanistica.

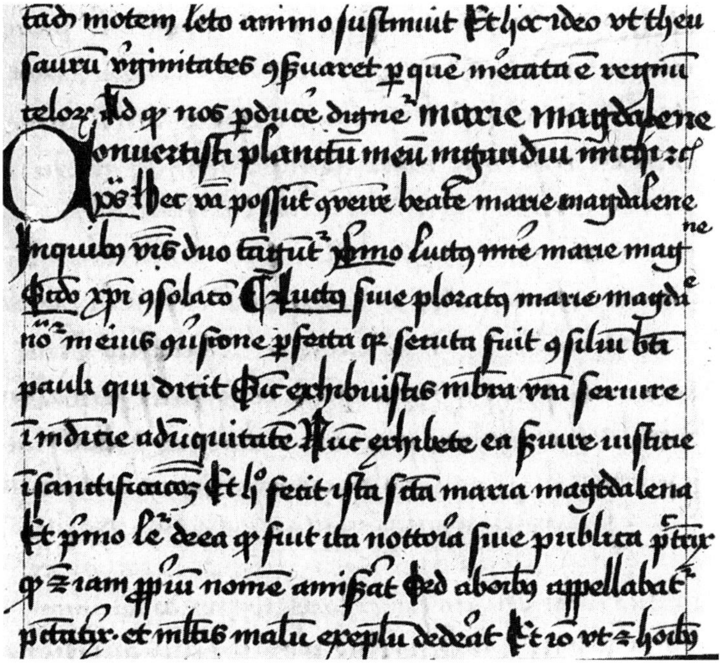

Pl. 136. *Miscellanea pia*, Saint-Nabor (Bas-Rhin), 1461. Colmar, Bibl. mun., MS 251, f. 76r (*CMDF*, V, pl. 131): [*starting l. 6*] In quibus verbis duo tanguntur: Primo luctus [*letters cancelled*] Marie Magdalene, / secundo Christi consolacio. ¶ Luctus sive ploratus Marie Magdalene / notatur in eius conversione perfecta, quia secuta fuit consilium beati / Pauli

Semihybrida Libraria. Note the angularity, the long ascenders and descenders, the dotted **i**, the bold pointed **f** and straight **s**, the **x** extending far under the baseline, the abbreviations for **etiam** (l. 13) and **r**

('dederat', l. 14), the double abbreviation stroke ('verbis', l. 6) and the lack of distinction between the **cc**-, **ct**- and **tt**-ligatures ('sanctificacionem', l. 11; 'peccatrix', l. 14; 'nottoria', l. 12).

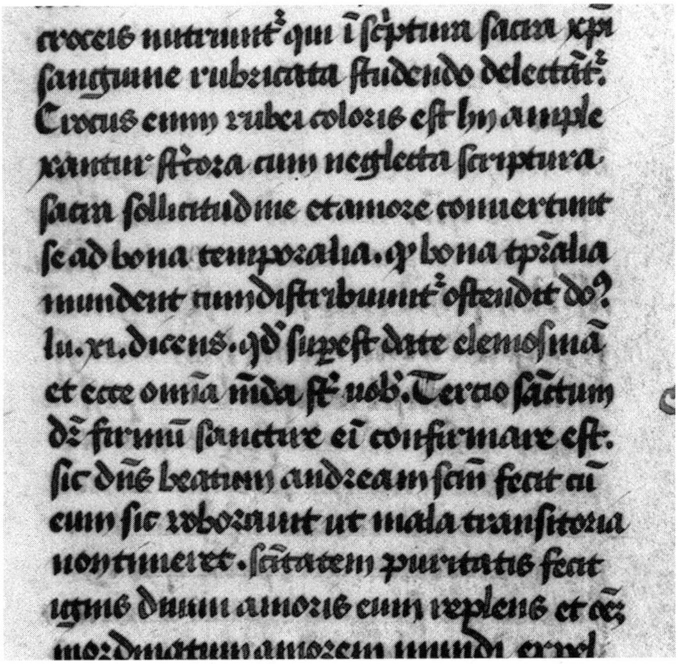

Pl. 137. Guillelmus Peraldus, *Sermones*, Lisieux, 1461–2. Caen, Bibl. mun., MS 38, f. 1r (another page: *CMDF*, VII, pl. 130): croceis nutriuntur, qui in scriptura sacra Christi / sanguine rubricata studendo delectantur. / Crocus enim rubei coloris est. Hii ample/xantur stercora, cum neglecta scriptura / sacra sollicitudine et amore convertunt / se ad bona temporalia. Quod bona temporalia / mundent cum distribuuntur ostendit Dominus

Hybrida Libraria. Note the loopless **d**, the fusions **be**, **bo**, **da**, **de**, **do**, **pe**, **po**; the uniform treatment of the minims ('divini', l. 14); the 3-shaped **m** at the end of the line ('omnem', l. 14); the frequent use of round **r**; the form of straight **r** in initial position ('roboravit', l. 12).

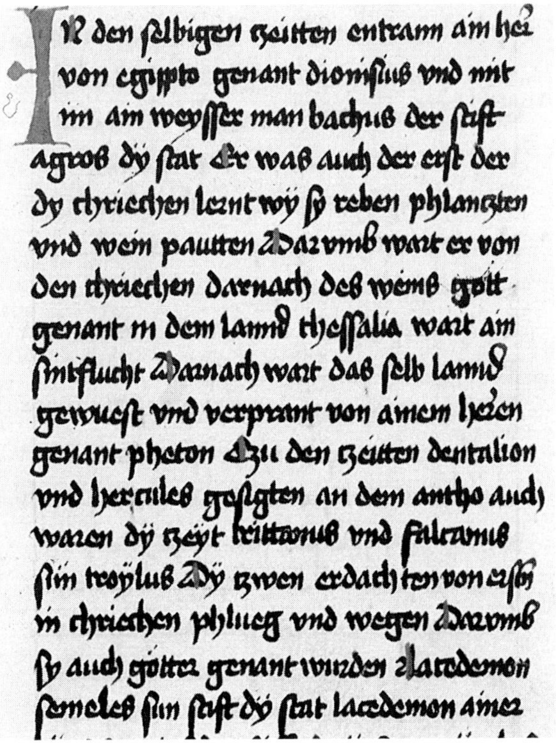

Pl. 138. *Biblia historiata* (in German), Eberau (Styria), 1464. Berlin, Staatsbibl. Preuss. Kulturbesitz, MS germ. fol. 567a, f. 52rb (Crous and Kirchner, *Schriftarten*, fig. 40): In den selbigen czeitten entrann ain herr / von Egippto genant Dionisius und mit / im ain weysser man Bachus, der stift / Agros dy stat. Er was auch der erst der

A small Semihybrida Libraria ('Bayrisch-Österreichische Bastarda' according to Kirchner). Note the alternation of 'counterclockwise' looped and unlooped **d**, the simplified **e**, the form of **c** ('Deucalion', l. 11), the German use of **y** with two dots and the **r**-abbreviation ('herr', l. 1; 'herren', l. 10).

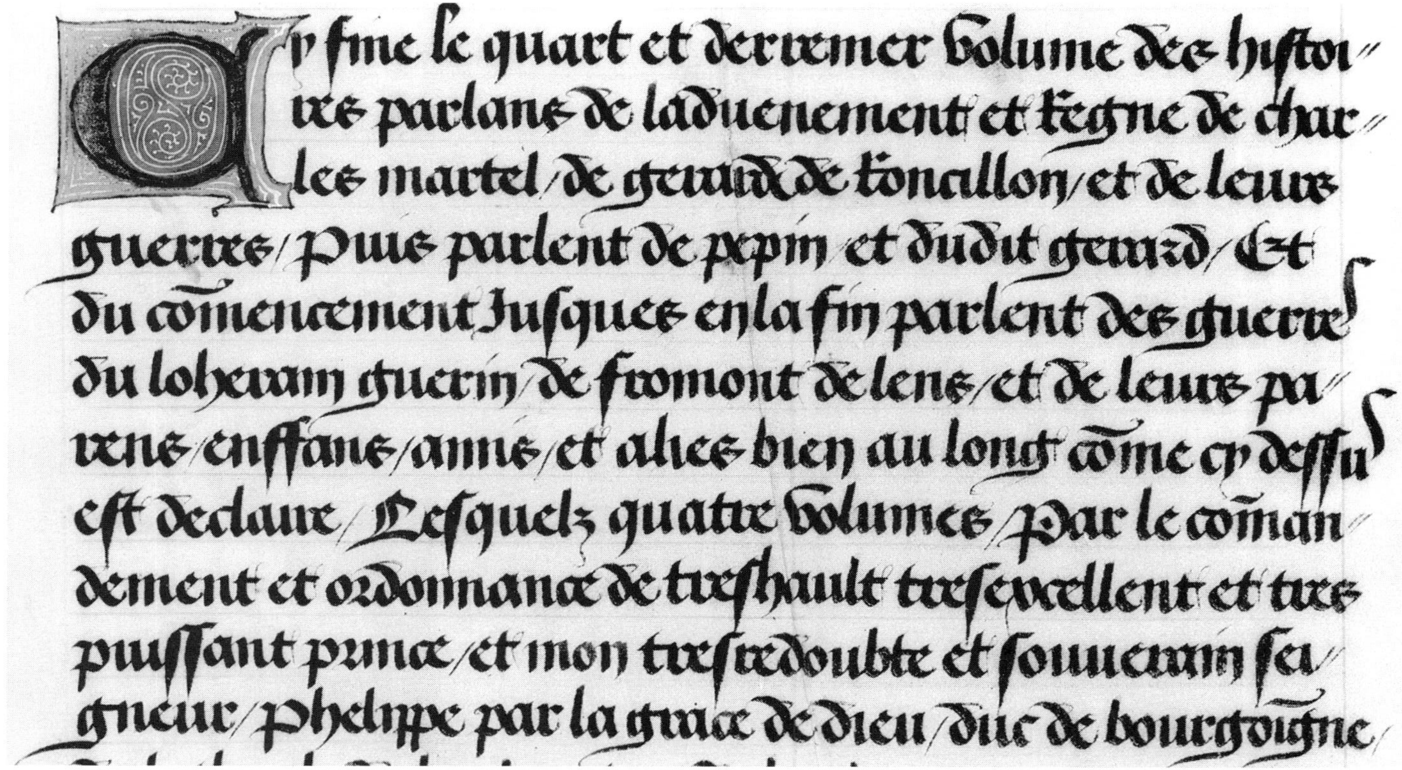

Pl. 139. *Histoire de Charles Martel*, Brussels, 1463–5, copied by David Aubert. Brussels, Royal Libr., MS 9, f. 559r (*CMDB*, IV, pl. 726): Cy fine le quart et derrenier volume des histoi/res parlans de l'advenement et regne de Char/les Martel, de Gerard de Roncillon et de leurs / guerres. Puis parlent de Pepin et dudit Gerard et

A large and bold Hybrida Formata (Bastarda) in an illuminated manuscript made for Philip the Good, Duke of Burgundy. Note the spiky forms of **a**, **e**, final **s** etc., the typical forms of **d**, **f**, **g**, straight **s**, **v**; the preponderant use of straight **r** as compared with round **r** and majuscule **r** ('regne', l. 2); the hairline at final **t**, the sloping hairlines (*virgulae suspensivae*) used as punctuation and the double hyphens.

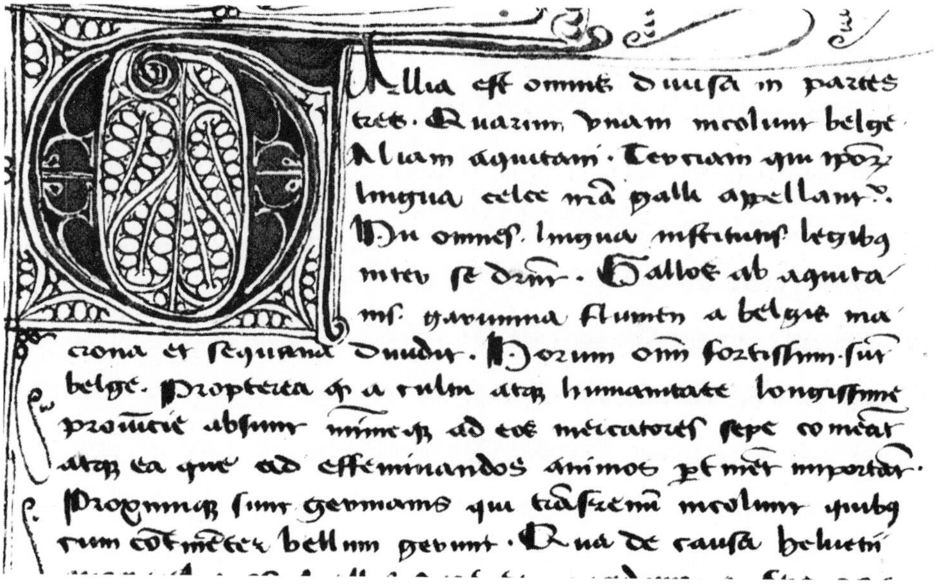

Pl. 141. Caesar, *De bello Gallico*, Southern Low Countries? 1464. Leiden, Univ. Libr., MS BPL 38 E, f. 1r (*CMDNL*, I, pl. 205): Gallia est omnis divisa in partes / tres. Quarum unam incolunt Belge, / aliam Aquitani, terciam qui ipsorum / lingua Celte, nostra Galli appellantur

Hybrida Currens under Humanistic influence. Note the occasional intrusion of two-compartment **a** ('Sequana', l. 8), cursive **e**, the rapid small **g**, the sharp **v** and cursive **x**. Note especially final **s**, which is either cursive in one of two forms, or Textualis or straight ('eos mercatores', l. 10; 'effeminandos animos', l. 11).

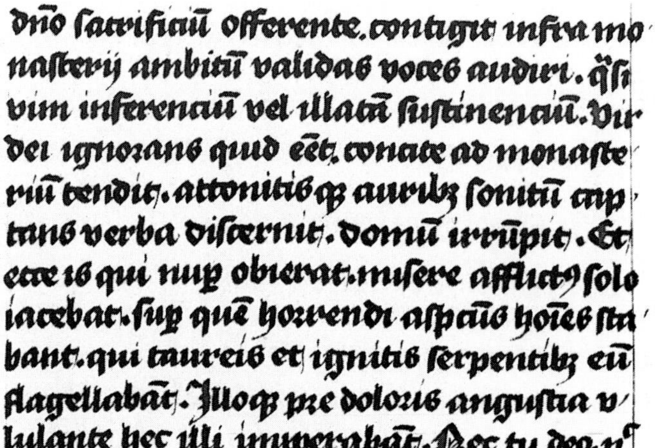

Pl. 142. Vincentius Bellovacensis, *Speculum historiale*, Northern Low Countries (Deventer?), 1472. Utrecht, Univ. Libr., MS 738, vol. IV, f. 38rb (another page: *MDNL*, II, pl. 748): Domino sacrificium offerente, contigit infra mo/nasterii ambitum validas voces audiri, quasi / vim inferencium vel illatam sustinencium

Netherlandish Hybrida Libraria of high quality, with short ascenders that have a subtle hairline forking at their top. Note the form of **g** and **h**, the very short **f** and straight **s** without shading or pointed ending, the correct use of straight and round **r**, the vertical hairline on final **t**, the absence of fusions.

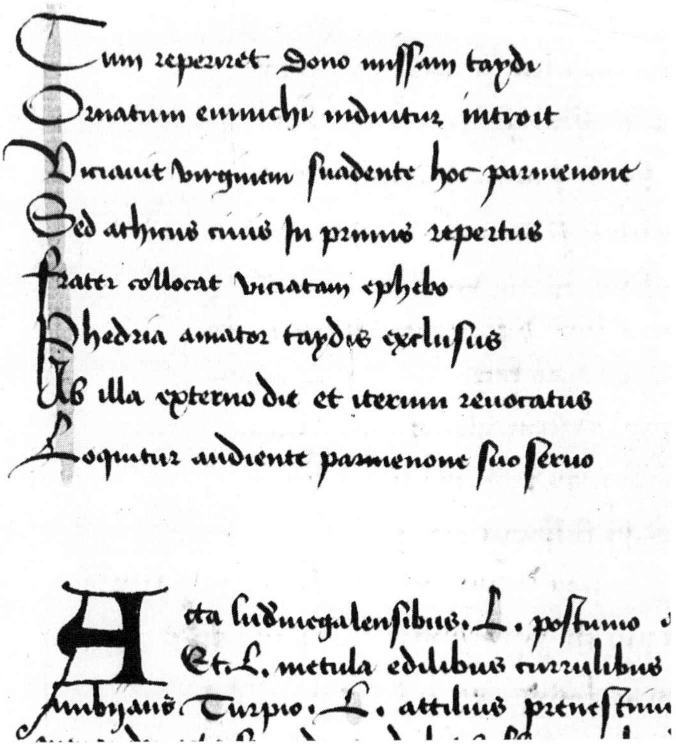

Pl. 143. Terentius, *Comoediae*, Cleves? 1467, by a Flemish scribe. Groningen, Univ. Libr., MS 157, f. 26v (*CMDNL*, I, pl. 350): Cum reperiret dono missam Taydi / Ornatum eunuchi induitur, introit, / Viciavit virginem suadente hoc Parmenone. / Sed Athicus civis in primis repertus

A small Hybrida Currens used in a schoolbook, the distance between the lines permitting the addition of interlinear notes. Note the two forms of **d** (the looped 'majuscule' one only in initial position), the use of round **r** in the majority of cases, the ligatures of straight **s** with the subsequent letter ('suo servo', l. 8).

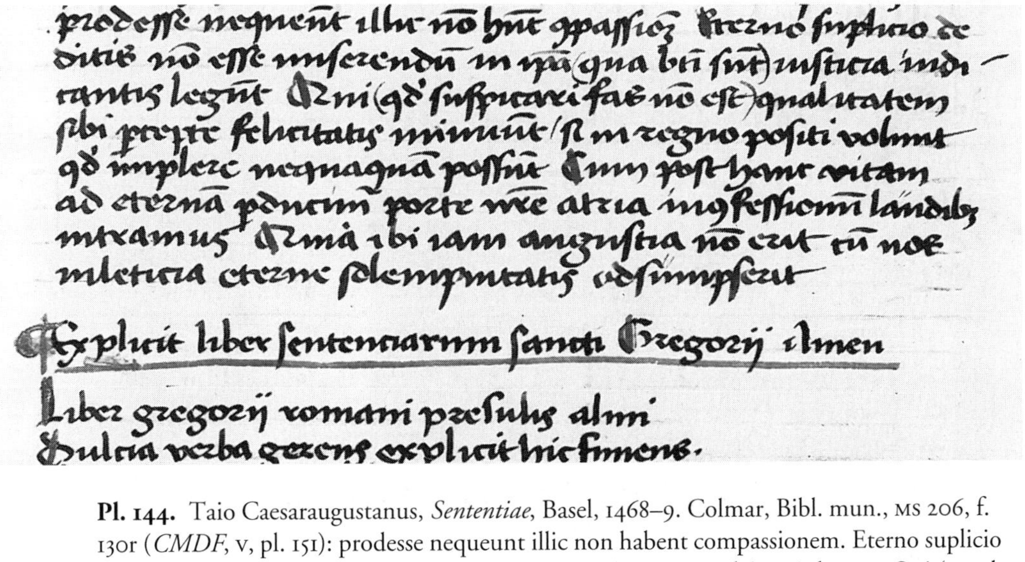

Pl. 144. Taio Caesaraugustanus, *Sententiae*, Basel, 1468–9. Colmar, Bibl. mun., MS 206, f. 130r (*CMDF*, V, pl. 151): prodesse nequeunt illic non habent compassionem. Eterno suplicio de/ditis non esse miserendum in ipsa (qua beati sunt) iusticia iudi/cantis legunt. Qui (quod suspicari fas non est) qualitatem

Hybrida Libraria/Currens. Note the looped **f**, the Humanistic **g** ('legunt', l. 3), the **q** with rounded descender, the various forms of **r** (e.g. 'regno', l. 4), trailing **s** as well as Cursiva **s** in final position, the many ligatures, such as **so** ('solempnitatis', l. 8), the parentheses. The verses after the explicit, by the same hand, tend towards Semitextualis.

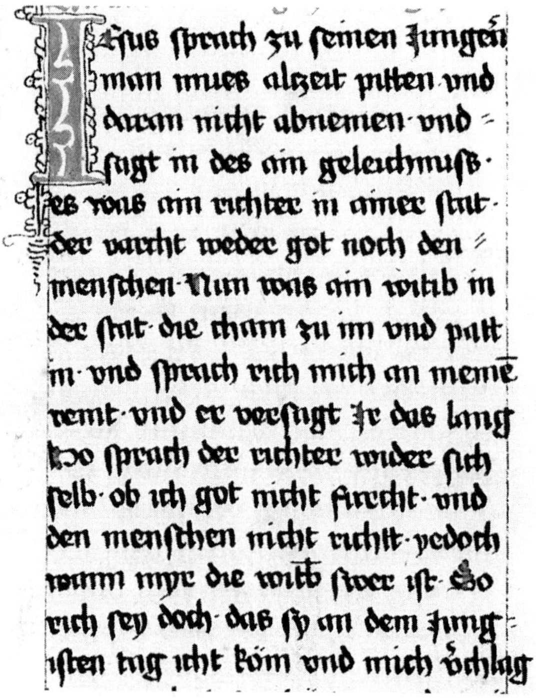

Pl. 145. *Postillae super epistolas* (in German), copied in the convent Porta Caeli in Vienna, 1468. Stockholm, Royal Libr., MS A 194, f. 360r (*CMDS*, II, pl. 91): Iesus sprach zu seinen jungern: / man mues alczeit pitten und / daran nicht abnemen; und / sagt in des ain geleichnuss: / es was ain richter in ainer stat

A careful and even Hybrida Libraria. Note the form of loopless **d**, of **r**, of double **s** in final position (the origin of the German **sz**), and the slight backwards slope of the script.

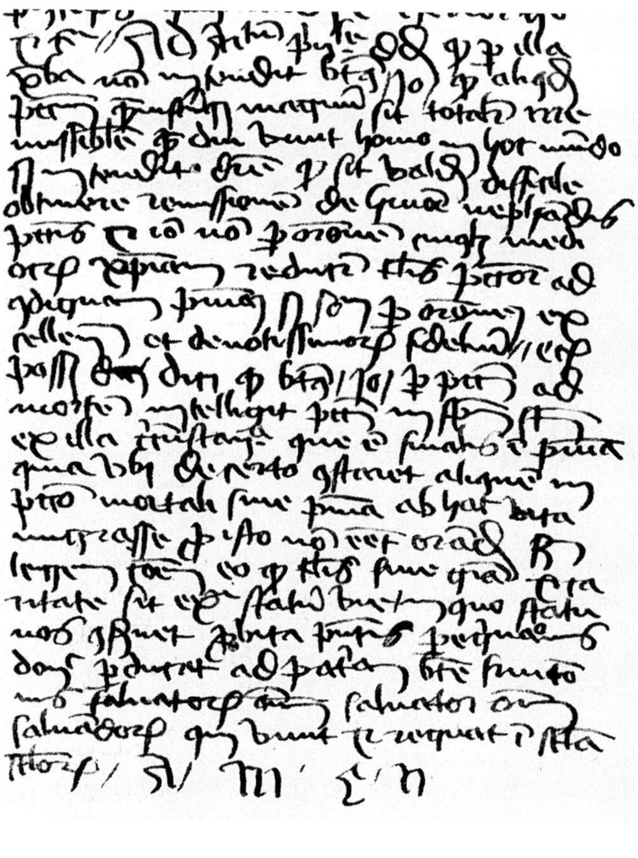

Pl. 146. Thomas de Argentina, *Commentum in secundo libro sententiarum*, Paris, 1471. Bordeaux, Bibl. mun., MS 129, f. 122r (*CMDF*, VI, pl. 135): Ad argumentum principale dicendum quod per illa / verba non intendit beatus Iohannes, quod aliquod / peccatum quantumviscumque magnum sit totaliter irre/missibile quamdiu vivit homo in hoc mundo

An extremely rapid and irregular Semihybrida Currens, highly abbreviated. Note, for example, the looped or unlooped **d**, the dislocated **e**, the cursive tendency to make **m** or **n** as an undulating line.

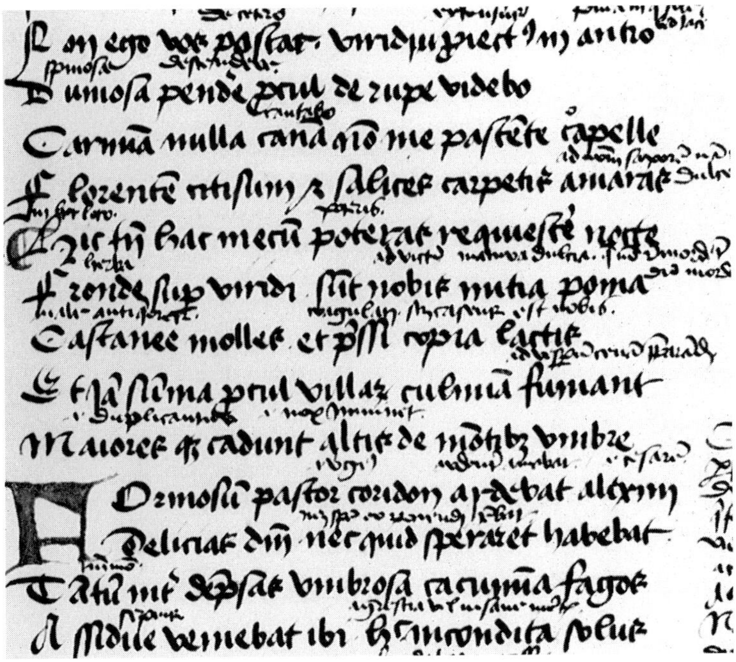

Pl. 147. Vergilius, *Bucolica, cum commento.* France, *c.* 1472. Auxerre, Bibl. mun., MS 84, f. 116r (*CMDF*, VI, pl. 138): Non ego vos postac viridui proiectus in antro / Dumosa pendere procul de rupe videbo. / Carmina nulla canam, non me pascente, capelle, / Florentem citisum et salices carpetis amaras

Semihybrida Currens. Note the slight backwards slope of the ascenders when they are unlooped, the tendency to use long **i** in initial position, the angular and pointed Cursiva **s**, the many ligatures, for example **sa**, **sc**, **si**, **st**, **co** ('copia', l. 7), etc.

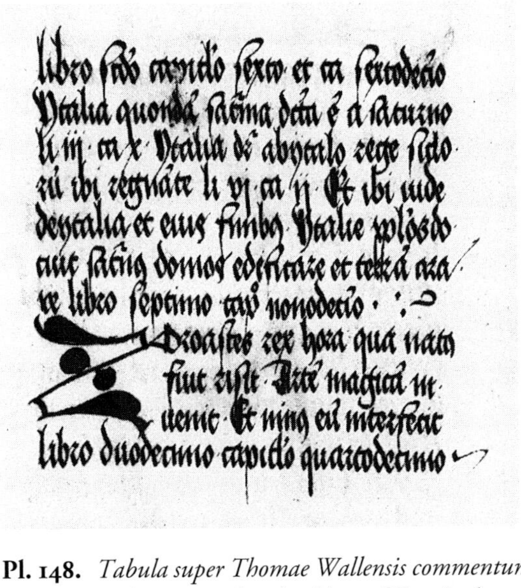

Pl. 148. *Tabula super Thomae Wallensis commentum in libros S. Augustini de civitate Dei,* Heilsbronn (near Nürnberg), abbey of Our Lady, 1473. Dijon, Bibl. mun., MS 161, f. 156v (*CMDF*, VI, pl. 139): libro secundo capitulo sexto et capitulo sextodecimo. / Ytalia quondam Saturnia dicta est a Saturno, / libro III capitulo X. Ytalia dicitur ab Ytalo rege

Hybrida Libraria/Formata (Fractura), narrow and compressed. Note the typical forms of **d** and **o**, the points appearing at the headline in many letters (**a**, **g**, **m**, **n**, **y** etc.), the irregular application of quadrangles at the top of the minims, the forking of the tops of the remarkably long ascenders, the developed loops of **f** and straight **s**, the occasional use of trailing **s** ('eius', l. 5).

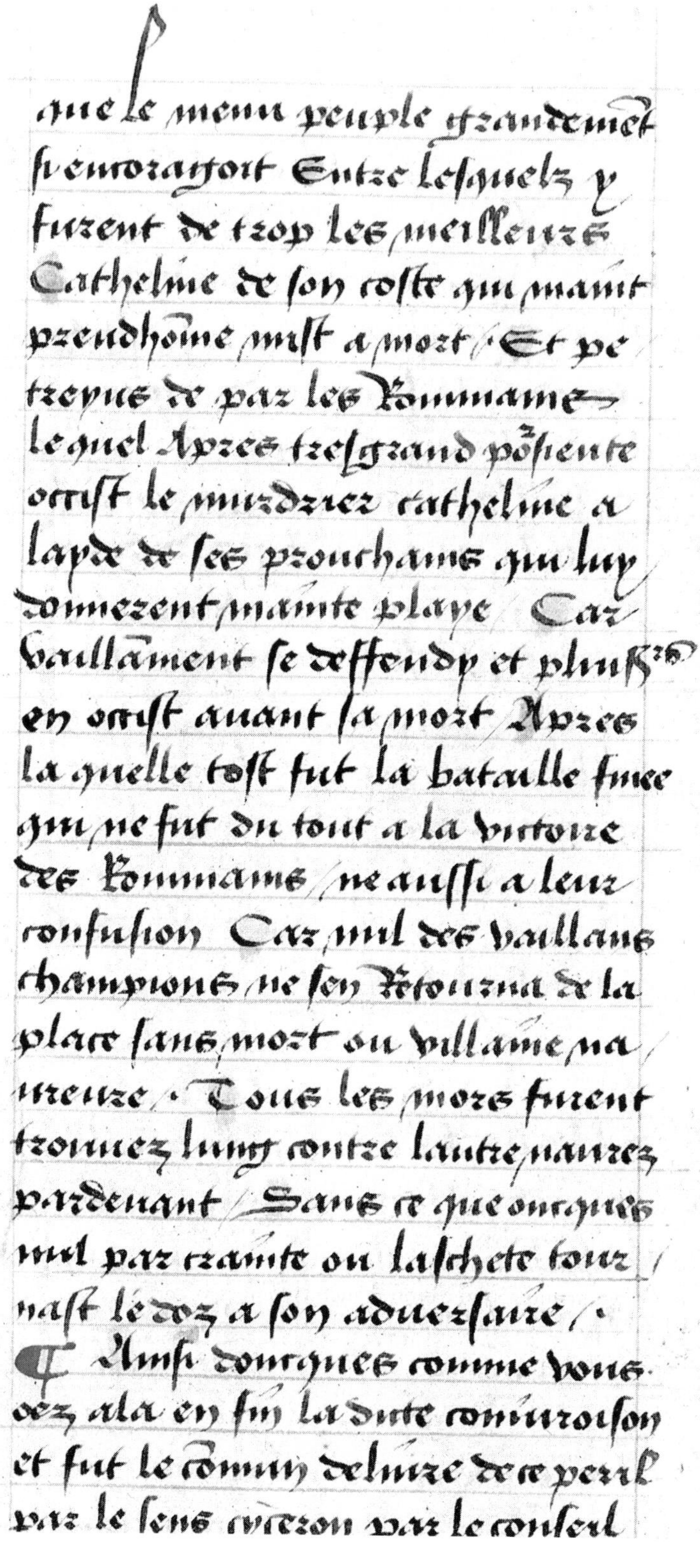

que le menu peuple grandemet
si encorayoit Entre lesquelz y
furent de trop les meilleurs
Cathelme de son coste qui maint
preudhoume mist a mort Et pe
treyus de par les Rommams
lequel Apres tresgrand posieute
occist le murdrier catheline a
layde de ses prouchams qui luy
donmerent mainte playe Car
vaillamment se deffendy et plus
en occist auant sa mort Apres
la quelle tost fut la bataille fmee
qui ne fut du tout a la victoire
des Rommams ne auffi a leur
confufion Car mul des vaillans
champions ne sen Retourna de la
place sans mort ou villame na
ureuze Tous les mors furent
trouuez lumg contre lautre naurez
pardenant Sans ce que oncques
mul par crainte ou lascheté tour
naft le dos a son aduersaire
Amfi doncques comme vous
oez ala en fm la dute conmuroifon
et fut le commu delmure dece peril
var le sens oureron var le confeil

Pl. 149. Caesar, *Commentarii de bello Gallico* (in French), Flanders, 1476. New Haven, Yale Univ., Beinecke Libr., MS 226, f. 51rb: que le menu peuple grandement / si encoragoit. Entre lesquelz y / furent de trop les meilleurs. / Catheline de son costé, qui maint / preudhomme mist a mort, et Pe/treyus de par les Rommains, / lequel apres tres grand poursieute / occist le murdrier Catheline a / l'ayde de ses prouchains, qui luy / donnerent mainte playe

Semihybrida Formata (Bastarda) in a luxury illuminated manuscript written on paper. Note the pointed **a**, the **d** with concave shaft (sometimes looped), the spiky forms of the ascenders at the baseline, the typical form of **g**, the exclusive use of round **r** (except in initial position, where majuscule **r** is used), the slight development of the descenders of **p** and **q**, the approach strokes to initial **m** and **n**, the one-stroke **y** and the form of **z**.

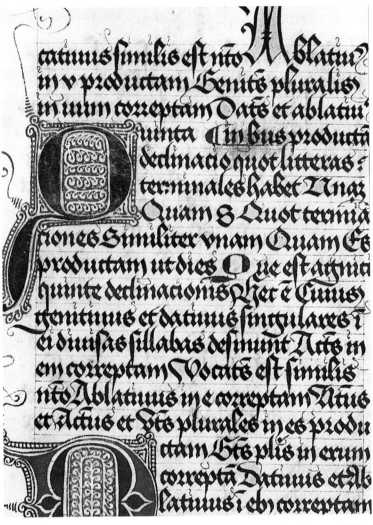

Pl. 150. Donatus, *Ars minor*, Western Germany, 1490. Strasbourg, Bibl. nat. et univ., MS 310, f. 7r (*CMDF*, v, pl. 174): [Vo]/cativus similis est nominativo. Ablativus / in -u productam. Genitivus pluralis / in -uum correptam. Dativus et ablativus / in -bus productam. Quinta / declinacio quot litteras / terminales habet? Unam

Semihybrida Formata (Fractura) with many and unusual abbreviations. The bold, narrow and spiky forms and the Textus Quadratus character are conspicuous. Note especially **a, d, o**; the tops of the ascenders, with triangular loops or loopless, are curved to the right. All ascenders have spurs. The use of straight and round **r** is often inconsistent (see 'correptam', ll. 3 and 13; 'productam', ll. 4 and 9). The form of round final **s** is especially fanciful: Textualis, Cursiva, or the fancy form proper to Fractura ('pluralis', l. 2). Note also the Southern **bus**-abbreviation ('ebus', bottom l.) and the absence of question-marks.

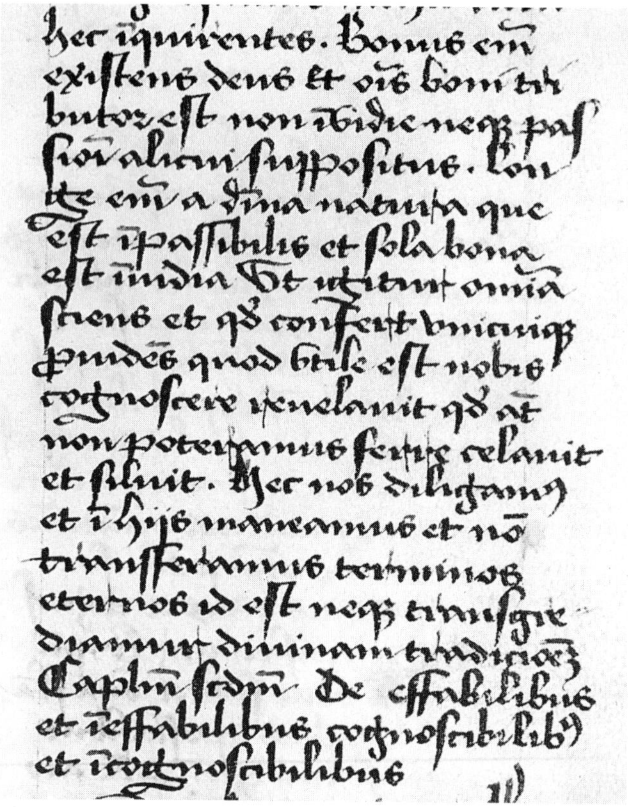

Pl. 151. Iohannes Damascenus, *Opuscula*, Utrecht, Charterhouse, 1489. Utrecht, Univ. Libr., MS 117, f. 3rb (*CMDNL*, II, pl. 677): hec inquirentes. Bonus enim / existens Deus et omnis boni tri/butor est non invidie neque pas/sioni alicui suppositus; lon/ge enim a divina natura que

Semihybrida Libraria. Note looped and unlooped **d**, the developed **g**, the three-strokes **p**, straight **r** always provided with a decorative hairline ('ferre', l. 11), the two forms of **v** ('unicuique', l. 8, 'utile', l. 9), the use of **v** in medial position ('invidie', l. 3), Textualis **x**.

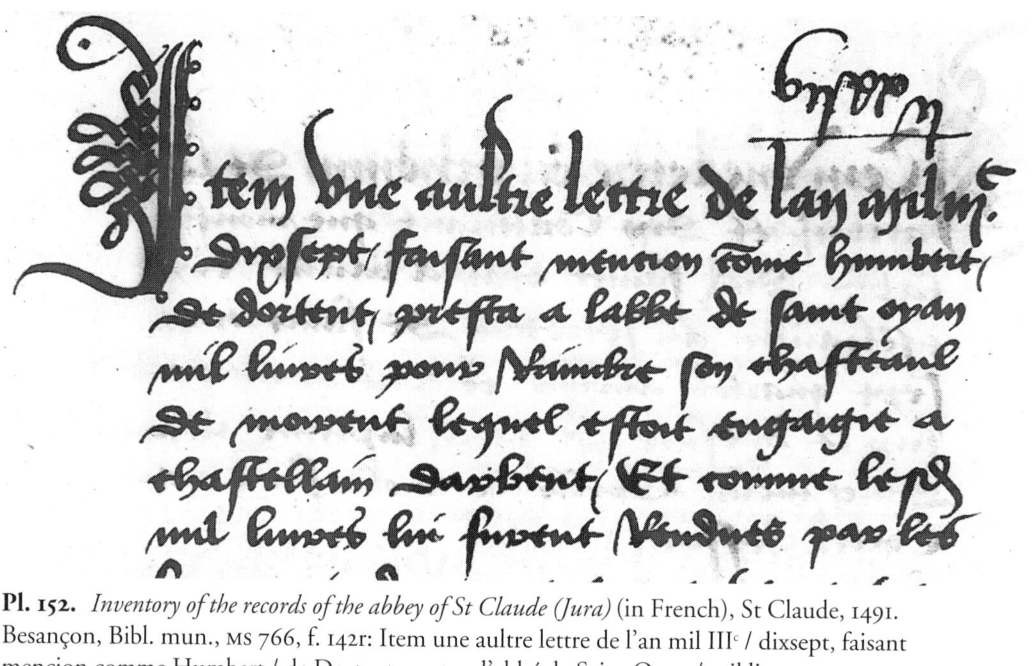

Pl. 152. *Inventory of the records of the abbey of St Claude (Jura)* (in French), St Claude, 1491. Besançon, Bibl. mun., MS 766, f. 142r: Item une aultre lettre de l'an mil IIIᶜ / dixsept, faisant mencion comme Humbert / de Dortent presta a l'abbé de Saint Oyan / mil livres pour raimbre son chasteaul

Semihybrida Currens used here for a document. Note the typical forms of **c**, **e**, **m**, **n**, **u**, final **s** ('livres', l. 4, 'rendues', l. 7), the pointed form of **b** and cursive **r** at the baseline; the two forms of initial **d** ('de Dortent', l. 3), majuscule **r** in initial position.

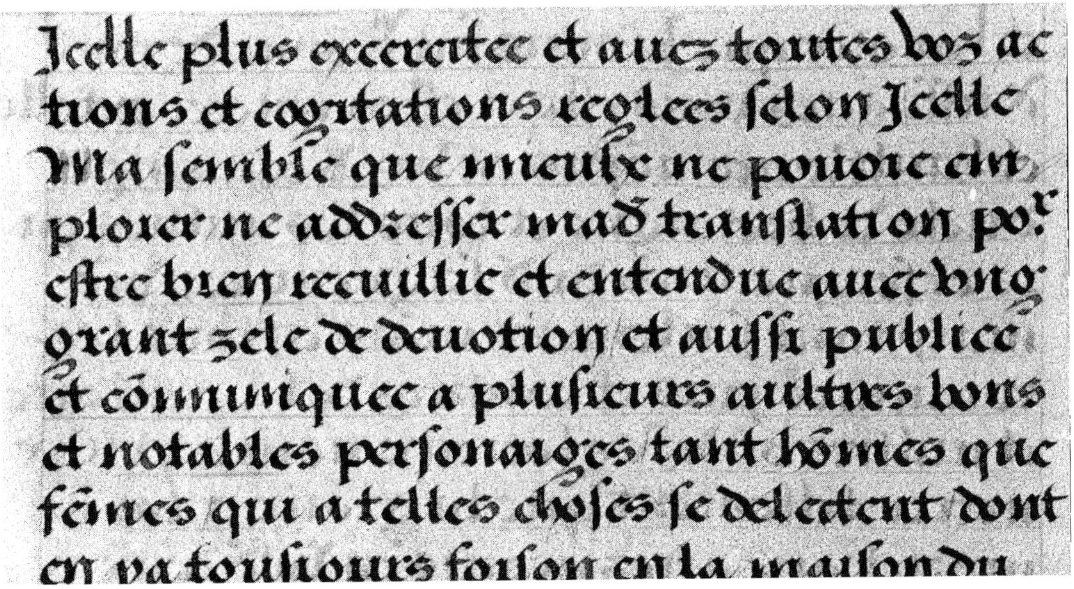

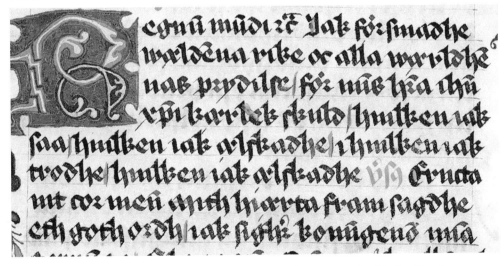

Pl. 153. Eusebius Caesariensis, *Historia ecclesiastica* (in French). France, 1509–14, written for Queen Anne de Bretagne. Versailles, Bibl. mun., MS 1 bis, f. 1vv (another page: *CMDF*, VII, pl. 161): icelle plus excercitee et avez toutes voz ac/tions et cogitations reglees selon icelle. / M'a semblé que mieulx ne povoie em/ploier ne addresser madite translation pour

A late Hybrida Formata under Humanistic influence, apparent from the form of **g**, **p**, final **s**, **f** and straight **s**, **x**. Note the spurs on the ascenders and the clear distinction between **c** and **t**.

Pl. 154. *Rituale of the Vadstena convent* (in Swedish), Vadstena, 1510. Stockholm, Royal Libr., MS A 12, f. 130r (*CMDS*, II, pl. 132): Regnum mundi, etc. Iak førsmadhe / wældenna rike oc alla wærldhen / nas prydilse før mins Herra Ihesu / Christi kærlek skuld huilken iak

An extremely bold Hybrida Libraria. Note the heavy forking at the top of the ascenders, the Textus Rotundus form of **m**, **n**, **u**, and the special Swedish graphs: the stroked **o** and the **ae**-ligature.

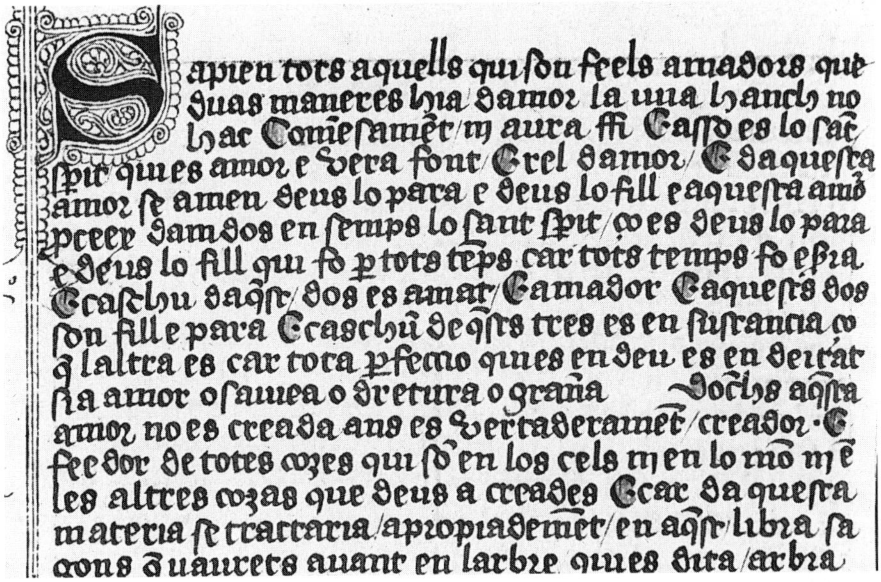

Pl. 157. Matfré Ermengaud, *Breviari d'amor* (in Catalan), Catalonia, 1400. Paris, Bibl. nat. de France, MS esp. 205, f. 3v (*CMDF*, IV, I, pl. 52): Sapien tots aquells qui son feels amadors que / duas maneres hi a d'amor: la una hanch no / hac comensament ni aura ffi. E asso es lo Sant / Spirit qui es amor e vera font e rel d'amor

An example of the Spanish 'hors système' script close to Hybrida but with two-compartment **a**. Note especially the form of **a**, the small looped **d**, the **h** with wide limb, the occasional use of round **s** in medial position ('caschun', l. 9), the form of **v**.

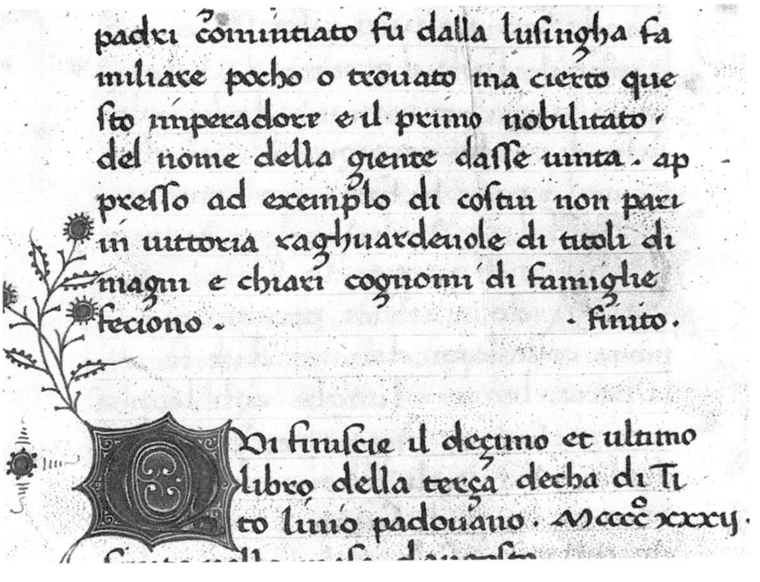

Pl. 158. Livius, *Ab Urbe condita* (in Italian), Italy, 1432. Paris, Bibl. nat. de France, MS ital. 118, f. 191vb: padri cominciato fu dalla lusingha fa/miliare. Pocho o trovato ma cierto que/sto imperadore è il primo nobilitato / del nome della giente dasse vinta. Ap/presso ad exemplo di costui non pari / in vittoria

raghuardevole di titoli di / magni e chiari cognomi di famiglie / feciono. Finito.

Gothico-Antiqua close to Humanistic script in its proportions, the long ascenders and descenders, the Capitals, the Half-Uncial **d**, the **g**. The **a**, however, is Semitextualis, and the angularity of **e**, the use of **ç** ('deçimo', l. 9) and the form of **r** point to Gothic influence.

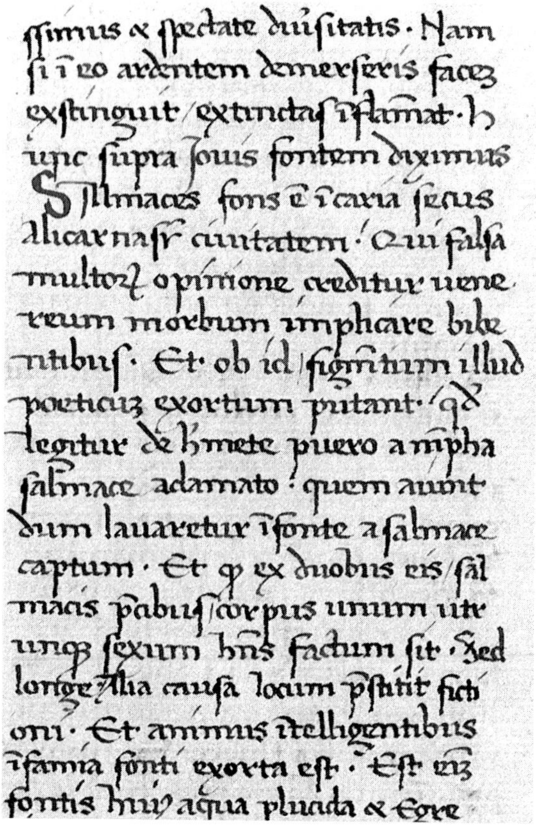

Pl. 159. Boccaccio, *De montibus, silvis, fontibus...*, Roccacontrada (now Arcevia), 1434. New Haven, Yale Univ., Beinecke Libr., MS Marston 17, f. 26rb: [frigidi]/ssimus et spectate diversitatis. Nam / si in eo ardentem demerseris facem, / extinguit, extinctas inflammat. H/unc supra Iovis fontem diximus

Gothico-Antiqua. The widely spaced unconnected script, the majuscules, the long ascenders and descenders and several letter forms are Humanistic, for example **g** and the ampersand (l. 1). But Half-Uncial **d** and straight **s** in final position are rarely used ('id', l. 9, 'extinctas', l. 3), 3-shaped **m** occurs often, **i** is stroked, **f** and straight **s** extend far below the baseline, and there are many fusions. Note also the non-syllabic division of words.

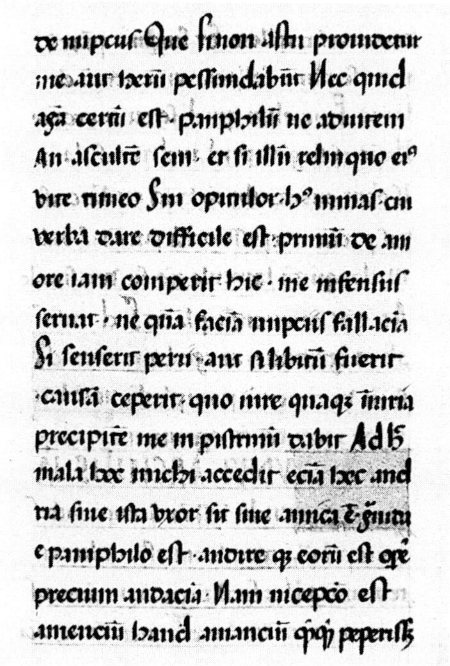

Pl. 160. Terentius, *Comoediae*, Paris, 1465. Toulouse, Bibl. mun., MS 803, f. 10r (*CMDF*, VI, pl. 122): de nupciis, que si non astu providetur / me aut herum pessundabunt. Nec quid / agam certum est: Panphilumne adiutem / an ascultem seni. Et si illum relinquo eius / vite timeo, sin opitulor huius minas, cui

A small Gothico-Antiqua in many respects distant from Humanistic conventions. **d** is either Gothic Rotunda or Humanistic; letters such as **h**, the many fusions and the short abbreviation strokes are proper to Rotunda. But **g** and straight **s** consistently used in final position point to the scribe's aspiration to write Humanistic script. The initials are mediocre imitations of Roman Capitals (especially **N**).